W9-DHG-555

GAYSPEAK

Gay Male & Lesbian Communication

GAYSPEAK

Gay Male & Lesbian Communication

edited by
James W. Chesebro

The Pilgrim Press
New York

This publishing project was initiated by the Caucus on Gay Male and Lesbian Concerns of the Speech Communication Association.

Library of Congress Cataloging in Publication Data
Main entry under title:

Gayspeak: gay male & lesbian communication.

Includes bibliographical references.
1. Homosexuality—United States—Addresses, essays, lectures. 2. Homosexuality—United States—Public opinion—Addresses, essays, lectures. 3. Public opinion—United States—Addresses, essays, lectures. 4. Symbolism in communication. 5. Deviant behavior—Labeling theory—Addresses, essays, lectures. I. Chesebro, James W. II. Speech Communication Association. Caucus on Gay Male and Lesbian Concerns.
HQ72.U53G39 306.7′6 81–11960

ISBN 0–8298–0472–2 AACR2
ISBN 0–8298–0456–0 (pbk.)

Acknowledgments of the use of copyrighted materials appear in Acknowledgments and in Notes.

The Pilgrim Press, 132 West 31 Street, New York, NY 10001

Contents

Acknowledgments

I am indebted to a number of individuals and organizations who were instrumental in the publication of this collection of essays. The late Prof. Joseph J. Hayes' massive annotated bibliographies of gay male and lesbian "languages" supplied important guidelines in the initial literature searches. In addition, Prof. Joseph A. DeVito, of Queens College, City University of New York, and Dr. Fred E. Jandt, of the Human Productivity Institute, Inc., functioned as associate editors, and their critical responses to submitted essays provided invaluable assistance in the final selection of the essays to be included. Further, José (Gahye) Angel Hernández and Michael Koenig furnished a good deal of the motivation and stimulation for my personal involvement in this project. Finally, Ms. Marion M. Meyer, senior editor of The Pilgrim Press, must be recognized as the driving force who organized, streamlined, adapted, and transformed a manuscript into a book.

I also wish to express appreciation for permission to reprint the following essays: Chapter 1, "Homosexual Labeling and the Male Role" by Rodney G. Karr, is reprinted with permission from *The Journal of Social Issues,* Vol. 34, No. 3 (1978), pp. 73–83. Chapter 4, "Gayspeak" by Joseph J. Hayes, is reprinted with permission of the Speech Communication Association from *The Quarterly Journal of Speech,* Vol. 62 (October 1976), pp. 256–66. Chapter 10, "Male Homophobia" by Stephen F. Morin and Ellen M. Garfinkle, is reprinted with permission from *The Journal of Social Issues,* Vol. 34, No. 1 (1978), pp. 29–44. Chapter 15, "Views of Homosexuality Among Social Scientists" by James W. Chesebro, originally appeared as "Paradoxical Views of 'Homosexuality' in the Rhetoric of Social Scientists: A Fantasy Theme Analysis," and is reprinted with permission of the Speech Communication Association from *The Quarterly Journal of Speech,* Vol. 66 (1980), pp. 127–39. Chapter 18, "Consciousness-raising Among Gay Males" by James W. Chesebro, John F. Cragan, and Patricia McCullough, originally appeared as "The Small Group Technique of the Radical Revolutionary: A Synthetic Study of Consciousness-Raising," and is reprinted with permission of the Speech Communication Association from *Speech Monologues,* Vol. 40 (June 1973), pp. 136–46. Chapter 22,

"Gay Civil Rights and the Roots of Oppression" by Sally Miller Gearhart, is reprinted with permission of the Speech Communication Association from the *Association for Communication Administration Bulletin,* April 1976, issue #16. Chapter 24, "Ideologies in Two Gay Rights Controversies" by Barry Brummett, originally appeared as "A Pentadic Analysis of Ideologies in Two Gay Rights Controversies," and is reprinted with permission from *Central States Speech Journal,* Vol. 30 (Fall 1979), pp. 250–61. Chapter 25, "Religious Fundamentalism and the Democratic Process" by Ronald Fischli, originally appeared as "Anita Bryant's Stand Against 'Militant Homosexuality': Religious Fundamentalism and the Democratic Process," and is reprinted with permission from *Central States Speech Journal,* Vol. 30 (Fall 1979), pp. 262–71.

James W. Chesebro

Introduction

Homosexuality is both an enigma and a dilemma for Americans today. In the popular arena only two options—equally unsatisfactory—seem to exist for dealing with homosexuality.

Two Unsuccessful Attempts

Option one entails the belief that homosexuality will somehow disappear. Americans clearly reject homosexuality and would seek to eliminate the behavior. In a 1978 poll, for example, 70 percent of Americans believed that homosexual acts are always wrong, even if the individuals involved are in love.[1] Moreover, when specifically asked, of UCLA's entering freshmen in 1979, 39 percent of the females and 56 percent of the males stated that "homosexual relations should be prohibited."[2] Typically, Americans feel that homosexuality can be eliminated by concerted social action, and in a 1977 Gallup poll 56 percent of a random sample were of the opinion that "homosexuality is due to upbringing and environment."[3] However, after 200 years of social rejection, religious condemnation, legal prosecution, and more recently, intensive psychotherapeutic conversion programs, homosexuality has not disappeared. These rejection strategies have failed to produce any identifiable effect on homosexuality. While people today may be more conscious of homosexuality, "it is impossible to establish" that homosexuality has "actually increased or decreased," even under the harshest of condemnations.[4] Homosexuality has existed in every culture and in every era. There is no reason to believe that attempts to deny, conceal, alter, or institutionalize homosexuals can function as a meaningful social policy. Furthermore, these policies have been overtly challenged as inhumane by gay males and lesbians who have demanded to be recognized as human beings, citizens, and taxpayers, with the same rights as heterosexuals. We seem to be left with the conclusion that homosexuality will not go away.

Option two entails a wider range of efforts to integrate the homosexual into the mainstream of American society by creating a universe of understanding regarding homosexuality. Accordingly, social scientists and academics have sought to identify and describe homosexuality in behavioral terms, the diverse elevated and decadent roles homosexuals have occupied in various religious systems, the legal myths and realities of homosexuality, and the psychic problems of those homosexuals seeking therapy. Yet, this wealth of information has characteristically failed to help homosexuals or the parents and friends of homosexuals, or to relieve the public's general concern about homosexuality. While we certainly need to know what homosexuality is behaviorally, morally, legally, and psychologically, these research efforts have not—if we are to believe public opinion polls—contributed to the solace of the typical American. If anything, such studies may have generated anxiety and confusion. For many Americans uncertain or worried about homosexuality, a host of new issues have emerged. It is no longer clear, for example, if a distinction now exists between homosexuals and heterosexuals, if anyone can be humanistic and also reject a particular mode of self-actualization selected by a prosecuted minority, if moral injunctions can ever be made of any relationship involving human love, or if the legal system can ever intervene morally in the private, consenting relationships of adults. Certainly, when Washington State University students rank homosexuality as one of the most serious national threats, second only to murder,[5] people are left with the impression that efforts to understand homosexual behavior have thus far failed to produce an appreciation of the homosexual as a segment of the American life-style.

A New Approach

This book posits a new approach for dealing with homosexuality as a social issue. Previous approaches have focused on homosexuality as behavior; the emphasis has been grossly incomplete and actually misleading, for other equally important approaches have been overshadowed as a result. As I argue in an essay included in this book:

> the word homosexual draws attention primarily to an overt biological and sexual release that gains its specificity because the release occurs between two members of the same sex. With this release as a central definitional base for research, the consequential social behaviors and responses to those behaviors are examined predominantly as extended by-products of the sexual and biological release. The word homosexual thus places its focus on an explicit sexual act and then on its coincidental behavior [see p. 186].[6]

Homosexuality is, after all, a biological term which specifies only that a physical sexual release can occur between members of the same sex. The word homosexual is a rather meaningless word as a social concept. It cannot tell us how, under what conditions, when, or why a homosexual acts; nor does the word specify a type of person or what the reactions to homosexual behavior will be. Social customs, norms, and the rules governing homosexual behavior are as varied as the number of persons engaged in such behavior. Alan P. Bell and Martin S. Weinberg identify five different types of homosexuality in San Francisco alone.[7] A unifying presumption of this book is that homosexual behavior itself, especially as a unitary concept, can no longer be the only subject of inquiry.

Homosexuality—A Communication Perspective

Social reactions to homosexuality constitute an equally important issue to be examined. A central premise of this book is that homosexuality is a social issue because of the social reality people have created about homosexuality. In this view, there is nothing intrinsically good or evil, healthy or dangerous, and disturbing or consoling about homosexuality. However, human attitudes and reactions have made homosexuality a social issue. Indeed, a good deal of evidence now exists which suggests that the social response to homosexuality is the issue, not the behavior itself. The obvious is perhaps the best point of departure: virtually all homosexual acts are carried out in the privacy of the bedroom; the homosexual act itself is not in the public domain. Moreover, as members of the public sector, homosexuals are now an active and productive element of society. As the Task Force on Homosexuality of the National Institute of Mental Health concluded, "society at large inevitably loses in a number of ways—loss of manpower, economic costs, human costs, etc." whenever "homosexuality is considered maladaptive and approbrious."[8] In addition, homosexuals permeate all dimensions of society as males and females, blacks and whites, poor and rich, rural and urban. They are, in fact, randomly distributed across all social classes, maintain the same diversity and range of opinions as other Americans, and endorse the complete gambit of political policies.[9] Yet, as the Sex Information and Education Council of the U.S. reports, 85 percent of homosexuals are not recognized as homosexuals in daily interactions.[10] Furthermore, insofar as some homosexuals are associated with some forms of opposite-sex characteristics, it is more difficult to employ stereotypes with any confidence today, for some 35 percent of the American population are now classified as androgynous.[11] Other studies have suggested that the label *homosexual* has more impact than the actual existence of a homosexual person. In experimental studies, for example, groups of subjects were given inconsequential tasks to accomplish. With some of these experimental groups, a heterosexual research confederate in the group was incidentally identified as homosexual, but with other groups no reference was made to the confederate's sexual preference. Regardless of the confederate's actual heterosexual preference, the label homosexual generated overtly negative behavioral and attitudinal responses to the confederate.[12]

These data are based on the reactions of Americans; Americans are not typical of people of other cultures. The word homosexual does not universally produce negative responses. In cultures other than that of the United States—the majority, as a matter of fact—homosexuality is not considered a problematic behavior. Of 193 world cultures, 28 percent accepted male homosexuality, 14 percent rejected it, and in the remaining 58 percent there was partial acceptance or some equivocation involved.[13] Of these comparative cultural findings, Wardell B. Pomeroy, coauthor of the famous Kinsey studies, has observed that "our own culture is plainly in the minority, not only in rejecting homosexuality but also in rejecting male homosexuality more forcibly than female homosexuality. Among the religions of the world, the Judeo-Christian system gives one of the harshest condemnations of homosexuality."[14] These observations and interpretations suggest that homosexual behavior itself is not universally an issue, and that insofar as homosexuality is an issue, the issue is created by how people respond to homosexuality, not by the behavior itself.

Overall, as we sum up such research findings it becomes clear that there is no uniform way of dealing with homosexuality. Our response to homosexuality is, theoretically, a choice-item. As a society, we can respond to homosexuality as we wish. The issue of homosexuality ultimately turns on how we do or do not respond to the behavior. The facts suggest that homosexual acts are private; that homosexuals are an integral, productive, and diverse dimension of society; that the label homosexual has more power than the reality of a person's actual sexual preference; and that the response of Americans to homosexuality constitutes a minority, if not unreasoned, approach.

The Human Response as the Subject of Inquiry

If we are to unravel the responses that cast homosexuality as an issue, we need to focus directly on these responses as the subject of inquiry. A communication perspective is particularly designed to deal with an inquiry into the use of human responses and counterresponses. Accordingly, the substance of this book is the language, nonverbal acts, and symbols of gay males and lesbians. As Arno Karlen has aptly put it, "there has been very little thought given to homosexual behavior as a communication system, and careful study in this direction would probably lead to a better understanding of various homosexual roles and the 'scripts' for those roles."[15] However, the substance of this book is also the symbols employed by heterosexuals to conceive of and to respond to homosexual behavior. Finally, the symbols of gay males, lesbians, and heterosexuals are examined in the context of communication principles established by a host of previous researchers. Thus, the content and context of this book is grounded in the belief that the issue of homosexuality is predominantly a communication problem, and that a humane understanding and resolution of this issue is to be found in established frameworks, methods, principles, and perspectives of the discipline of communication.

Homosexuality and the Professional Communicologist

Yet, a communication perspective of homosexuality has been extremely slow to emerge. Certainly, the national association of communication scholars has been hesitant to deal with homosexuality and sexual preference as communication phenomena. From the time the Speech Communication Association (SCA) began publishing academic essays, in 1915, until the beginning of 1980, only two essays explored the way in which homosexuality could be conceived in communication terms and as a communication system.[16] As is true of the disciplines of law,[17] health science,[18] psychology,[19] and anthropology,[20] the speech-communication discipline has only recently assessed its neglect of this research area and established a mechanism to encourage and to examine homosexuality and sexual preference as communication phenomena. As a result of the leadership of Sally Gearhart, at its 1978 annual convention, SCA first considered and approved the formation of a temporary unit to consider homosexuality as a communication phenomenon. At the first session of this action caucus, in November 1978, those present petitioned SCA's Legislative Council to become a permanent unit of SCA and to be known as the Caucus on Gay Male and Lesbian Concerns of SCA. During its first year as a permanent unit of SCA, the caucus sought to stimulate research in the area of gay and lesbian communication. This book is one of the products of the caucus' endeavors.

The Objectives of This Book

This book is intended to satisfy four objectives:

To initiate a new research approach to an old topic. The essays are designed to stimulate interest in the study of the symbols that define homosexuality as a social issue and, accordingly, are not meant to be definitive but only exploratory or heuristic in aim. While these essays suggest a new approach is possible—of that I am confident—they also generate a major question: "What theories, methods, and applied symbol-using patterns account for homosexuality as a social issue?" If this question is to be meaningfully answered, others will want to contribute to the probes provided here. We hope that this book does produce such contributions.

To provide a framework and substantive research findings for viewing homosexuality as a communication phenomenon and as a communication system. Six questions control the six-part framework or structure of this book:

1. *What are the social meanings of the key words—homosexual, gay, and lesbian—that divide and unify people into different social groups and thereby create distinct communication systems?* This question presumes that human interactions are created and regulated by verbal and nonverbal symbols. Symbol-using and symbol-management are thus treated as acts that determine what, how, why, when, and under what conditions human beings function socially. Symbol-using is viewed as the determinant of social action. Moreover, symbol-using is perceived here as a phenomenon composed of different sets, patterns, or forms of systematic behaviors that unify and divide humans into different kinds of communication systems. What people say and how they say it verbally and nonverbally become the criteria for determining which communication and social system people belong to. Concomitantly, those communicating in the same way are socially unified but are also separated or divided from other human groups who employ alternative terminologies, concepts, and strategies. Thus, each of these diverse communication systems is a dramatic or social construction of the members of each system. These dramatic constructions involve a mutual decision to endorse, reject, or ignore certain kinds of situations, roles, modes of interaction, behavior, values, beliefs, attitudes, and objectives or purposes. Nonetheless, each communication system can potentially affect every other communication system, for these systems are unified by mass media such as television, the printed word, everyday communication, the English language, and other commonly shared channels of communication. Part I of this book deals with this first question and is therefore appropriately entitled "The Social Meanings of the Words Homosexual, Gay, and Lesbian."

2. *What constitutes the intersubjective reality of those who label themselves gay or lesbian?* An intersubjective reality is presumed here to be a linguistic-thought community characterized by common patterns of interaction. However, it is appropriate to note that multiple subgroups exist within the linguistic-thought community of those conceiving of themselves as gay male or lesbian. As the essays within this book demonstrate, there are multiple ways of identifying these subgroups; critical, experimental, experiential, and ethnographic methods are employed. This diversity in method generates issues, and these issues are overtly argued in some of the essays. Moreover, multiple topics are necessarily involved when raising this question. The topics considered in Part II of this book include, as a result, private language uses, social language uses, radical language uses,

the recognition of lesbians as a communicative act, attitudes and modes of interactions of lesbian couples, gay masculinity in the gay disco, and gay fantasies. While the list is extensive, it is by no means complete.

3. What constellation of symbols constitutes the major response to the intersubjective reality of gay males and lesbians? Part III, "Homophobia," constitutes the answer to this question. As the essays in this section indicate, definitions of homophobia can be problematic. Briefly, homophobia is a fear or rejection of homosexuals. The essays in this section explore several questions related to homophobia: What is homophobia? How does homophobia affect the personal lives of gay males and lesbians? What is the origin of homophobia? This section concludes with an analysis of the relationships among androgyny, sex role rigidity, and homophobia, and finally considers the degree to which homophobia permeates television.

4. What institutional forces shape the public's image of gay males and lesbians, and account for the existence of homophobia? Only four such institutional forces are explored in Part IV of this book—the image of gays and lesbians as presented in drama, by social scientists, in the media, and in the educational system. A host of other institutional forces could be and need to be explored, such as the institution of marriage, the entire legal system, the family, and the church, to name a few.

5. How have gay males and lesbians sought to alter the institutional forces that affect them, and what have been the counterstatements to the efforts of gay males and lesbians? Part V includes essays that deal with gay and lesbian liberation as a rhetorical movement. While one essay identifies the small-group process that leads to the rhetoric of confrontation which characterizes the rhetorical movement, other essays deal directly with various efforts to change the "system" from the outside. Although particular attention is paid to the evolution of the homophile movement in the United States, and to the established Christian church as an agent earmarked for change, this section also deals with the emergence of the new lesbian-feminist movement. The conceptions that bring a rhetorical movement into existence and the strategies used by these movements receive special attention.

6. How have gay males and lesbians worked within the system for change, and how have those changes been resisted and in some cases reversed? In Part VI the civil rights approach is initially assessed in general, but the campaign efforts of pro- and antigay forces are considered as they operated in Miami and St. Paul as extended examples, concluding with a more general consideration of major philosophic issues related to such controversies.

To provide a research resource for scholarly use. A new research area generates a host of questions from diverse scholarly perspectives. The essays in this book are intended to provide some of the answers to these questions. In this regard, the method controlling each essay is explicit, for an assertion of "what is" depends on how it was obtained and the theoretical perspective governing a researcher's method of procedure. Because there are multiple ways of knowing, there are multiple methods and multiple theories, and multiple vocabularies to express these different methods and theories. The experimental scholars therefore focus on "hypotheses," manipulate "variables," and generate "data" and "conclusions," thereby employing a very different language than, for example, the experiential critic who seeks to specify where he or she was at the time of the study, the mood affecting the critic, and the influence of such biases. Clearly, then, the essays in this collection are pluralistic in theoretical approach, method, application, and in language. It is hoped that this pluralism is eclectic in the sense that the best is drawn together from various methods, doctrines, and styles.

To function as a supplementary textbook for sexual communication and interpersonal communication courses. Currently, standard textbooks employed in both sexual and interpersonal communication courses slight, if not ignore, the entire issue of homosexuality, even though 4 percent to 37 percent of the population is homosexual (depending on definitions and methods of measurement). These essays provide a wide range of topics and methods of presentation that allow a classroom instructor to assign those essays which are most appropriate to their students' abilities, interests, and level of sophistication. While less directly obvious, it is possible that this collection might also be useful to those who are concerned with contemporary issues in communication, or who wish to deal with gay and lesbian liberation and elections as rhetorical movements and campaigns in a political communication course, or who believe that the substantive issue of this book and its diverse set of methods might provide an intriguing approach to the study of communication and rhetorical methods and criticism.

Ultimately, then, I hope this collection generates new research, provides a framework and substantive base for dealing with homosexuality as a communication system, and constitutes a useful research resource as well as functioning as an important supplement in classrooms.

James W. Chesebro
Philadelphia, 1981

Part I

The Social Meanings of the Words Homosexual, Gay, and Lesbian

Chapter 1

Homosexual Labeling and the Male Role

Rodney G. Karr

For homosexuals, a major problem is that of living creatively in a culture where homosexuality has historically been perceived as pathological, immoral, and criminal. Often homosexuals are accused of being paranoid, with reassurances that labels don't really matter. Obviously, how one is viewed does have an impact on one's life. This study attempted to isolate and examine the effects of the label "homosexual" when applied to males by exploring how a man is perceived and reacted to by other men when he either is or is not labeled homosexual. In addition, this study looked at the extent to which men react with increased social distance when they believe they are interacting with a homosexual man and the extent to which group and individual problem-solving performance is adversely affected by the presence of a perceived homosexual.

Attribution theory suggests that the perception and evaluation of an individual are in part a function of the personality of the perceiver and the social situation in which the perception takes place.[1] Thus, the effects of applying the label homosexual to men in an experimental situation can be used to study some of the meaning and function of this label.

Fear of the label homosexual, with its connotation of sex-role violation, appears to function to keep men within their traditionally defined roles. G. K. Lehne has pointed out the effectiveness of accusations of being a "fag," "sissy," or "queer" in controlling males' behavior, beginning in childhood.[2] Several studies have found that the need to preserve the double standard between men and women is a more pervasive characteristic of negative attitudes toward homosexuality than is sexual conservatism.[3] Since the male role is perceived to be a healthier, more ideal role than the female role,[4] the pressure to maintain the male role may be greater than the pressure to maintain the female role.

Previous research on the effects of the label homosexual has sought to assess the extent to which men behave differently if they believe they have been labeled homosexual. A. Farina found that when men were labeled homosexual their behavior changed in the opposite direction from the stereotype associated with homosexual men, i.e., they became increasingly more stereotypically masculine.[5] Fear of the label homosexual appears to keep men acting in accordance with the traditional expectations of the male sex role.

This study examined the following hypotheses:

1. Men will sit significantly further from a man labeled as homosexual than when the same man is not so labeled.
2. Men will engage in less total communication regarding a specific problem-solving task requiring group cooperation with a man labeled homosexual than with the same man when not so labeled.
3. Group problem-solving efficiency will be significantly lower in those groups which believe that a homosexual man is present than in groups which are not led to believe a homosexual is present.
4. A man labeled homosexual will be rated differently on a semantic differential measure than the same man when not so labeled.
5. A man labeled homosexual will receive significantly lower preference rankings than the same man when not labeled homosexual.
6. Men who score high on a measure of homophobia will respond in greater degree to each of the above predictions than men who score low on the homophobia measure.

Method

Within the context of an experiment on group cooperation, communication, and perception, participants were deceived by two experimental confederates, posing as fellow participants. In one half of the eighteen groups, the *primary labeler* and the *secondary labeler* led the other participants to believe that a third experimental confederate, the *labelee,* was homosexual. In the Control Condition, the third experimental confederate was not labeled homosexual. Each group contained five authentic participants.

The participants were ninety male college students from the University of Washington, recruited from a subject pool of students in introductory psychology courses. They ranged in age from 18 to 27 (M = 20.8 years) and were 84 percent Anglo.

Dependent Measures

Dependent measures included (a) participants' seating distance from the labelee, (b) group and individual communication patterns, (c) group and individual problem-solving performance, (d) semantic differential ratings of the labelee and the primary labeler, and (e) preference rankings of the labelee and the primary labeler.

Seating position. After each participant was interviewed, he was shown to the experimental room. The labelee, always the first person to arrive, sat in a coded position, which provided a standard point to measure from for participants' subsequent choices of seating position. Participants had a choice of sitting anywhere from one to four positions to the right or left of the labelee. The dependent measure of seating distance was influenced by the variable of participants' order of entrance into the room: thus, seating options ranged from eight (for the first participant to enter the room) to four (for the last). The primary labeler always entered the room last, and chose the furthest position remaining to the left of the labelee. Two extra box positions were included in order to increase the seating options of later participants. Comparisons were made between participants' choice of seating distance from the labelee in the experimental versus control conditions, taking order of room entrance into consideration.

Group cooperation and communication. For the experimental communication task a card was given each of the seven members of the group (five authentic participants, the primary labeler, and the labelee). On each card there appeared a set of seven (out of eight possible) symbols, such that in any set of seven cards there was only one symbol in common. The problem was for every member to find the common symbol. To accomplish this, each member was allowed to communicate, by means of written messages only, with all other members of the group. No verbal communication was allowed after the beginning of the experiment. Comparisons were made between quantity, type, and order of written communications received by the labelee, primary labeler, and all other participants in the experimental versus the control groups.

Semantic differential. After the completion of the task, participants rated one another along a continuum in terms of thirty-two different semantic differential adjective pairs. Comparisons were made between how participants perceived the labelee and the primary labeler in the experimental versus the control condition for each adjective pair.

Preference rankings. Participants ranked the other participants, including the labelee and primary labeler, from 1 (most preferred) to 6 (least preferred) in terms of wanting to be in another experiment with them. Comparisons were made between participants' preference rankings of the labelee and the primary labeler in the experimental versus the control conditions.

Homophobia scale. A nine-item homophobia scale adapted from K.T. Smith was administered postexperimentally.[6]

Experimental Assistants

Three teams, each composed of four male undergraduate assistants, were selected on the basis of their being both heterosexual and unremarkable in behavior and appearance. Each team consisted of an experimenter, who recruited participants and conducted the research; a confederate (labelee), who was either labeled homosexual or not so labeled; a primary labeler, who did the actual labeling of the labelee as a homosexual; and a secondary labeler, who assisted in the labeling process. Each team participated in three experimental and three control conditions.

The assistants were not informed of the hypotheses, purposes, or groupings of this study, but instead were falsely informed that they were involved in an investigation of the effects of three stigma labels: homosexual, ex-mental patient, and ex-convict. They expected to be labeled (or to label another) as being a homosexual, ex-convict, or ex-mental patient in random order in half their groups.

The labelee was kept ignorant of the condition and label being used in any particular instance. Labeling occurred while he was absent from the room, ostensibly being interviewed by the experimenter. He was unaware of whether or not he had been labeled and with which label.

Comparisons were made between how the same labelee and primary labeler were perceived and reacted to by authentic participants. Thus, individual personality characteristics of individual labelers and labelees were controlled for and isolated from the effects of the label homosexual.

Experimental Procedure

Participants were met by the experimenter, shown to a waiting room, asked to wait "until enough subjects have arrived for the experiment to begin," and told that "because some subjects are undependable, and this experiment requires seven subjects, more of you have been called than are necessary. Therefore, you may be an extra subject and not participate." When there were a minimum of five authentic participants seated in the waiting room with the three confederates, who had been escorted to the room intermittently with authentic participants, the experimenter returned and said, "There are enough subjects for us to begin. I need to set up some equipment but will return shortly. When I return, I will begin individually interviewing you and will ask you each to sign a statement of voluntary participation in this study." He then left the room.

At that point the primary labeler, who had already been purposefully talkative with other participants, appeared to recognize the labelee and said to him, "You sure seem familiar to me. Didn't you come and speak on a panel in Sociology 101 last quarter?" To which the labelee responded, "Yes, I did." This conversation was terminated by the return of the experimenter, who called the labelee from the waiting room to be interviewed.

In the experimental condition the secondary labeler then asked the primary labeler, "What did that guy talk on the panel about?" To this, the primary labeler responded, "He came and talked about being a homosexual." The secondary labeler asked, "Do you mean that guy is a homosexual?" And the primary labeler responded, "Yes, he is." Authentic subjects sometimes entered the conversation at this point. Restating and clarifying that the labelee was a homosexual was included in order to increase the likelihood that participants heard and understood the labeling. The labeling procedure was designed to be matter of fact and not deprecatory or hostile. The procedure in the control condition was the same except that the primary labeler's response to "What did that guy talk about?", was, "He and some other students in the class presented a panel discussion about American subcultures."

Individual interviews. Subsequent to the labeling procedure, the five authentic participants were individually called from the waiting room to be interviewed by the experimenter. The primary labeler was called last and the secondary labeler was left out of the experiment as an "extra subject." In addition to allowing for the labelee's temporary absence from the waiting room, the individual interview served several purposes: (a) participants were asked to read and sign (if they agreed) a statement of voluntary participation in this study; (b) demographic data were gathered; (c) seven authoritarian personality scale items were administered preexperimentally; and (d) participants were given and asked to read a written explanation of the group task in which they were about to participate.

Individual postexperimental interview. Participants in the control condition were asked to fill out a survey concerning their attitudes toward homosexuals. Participants in the experimental condition were interviewed by the investigator or another advanced clinical graduate student and given an opportunity to discuss any problems created for them by the nature of this experiment.

Results

For all dependent measures there were no significant differences found between the three teams of experimental assistants. Therefore, the data were collapsed across teams and analyzed in terms of experimental versus control conditions.

Authoritarianism and Homophobia

Separate t-tests performed on each item revealed no significant differences between the experimental and the control groups on any of the seven authoritarian personality items or on any of the nine homophobia items.

Participants' homophobia and authoritarian personality scores were significantly correlated, $r = .43$, $p < .001$. A significant but low correlation was also found between homophobia and educational level, with less educated persons being more homophobic, $r = .10$, $p < .04$. Composite homophobia scores ranged from a low of 10 to a high of 65 ($M = 33.40$, $SD = 16.84$). For subsequent analyses, the experimental and the control groups were subdivided into high and low homophobia participants (*N*s of 20 to 25 per subgroup).

Seating Distance

No statistically significant difference was found in chosen seating distance from labelee between the experimental and the control condition. However, in the experimental condition, high homophobia participants sat significantly further from the labelee than did low homophobia participants, $t(43) = 2.15$, $p < .01$. In the control condition, no significant difference was found.

Task Communication Patterns

Data on communication patterns were separated into communications received by all participants, labelers, and labelees, and then compared in terms of three different types of communications (questions, answers, and statements) received from each of the nine different seating positions. No significant differences were found in the number of communications received by the labelee or the labeler between the experimental and the control conditions.

Group Problem-solving Efficiency

Group problem-solving efficiency was measured as the ratio of each participant's number of communication cards received by the time he took to solve the problem. A significant difference was found, with the experimental condition being less efficient, i.e., having larger ratios, $t(87) = 1.86$, $p < .03$.

On this same measure, in the experimental condition the high homophobia group had significantly larger ratios of card numbers to time than did the low homophobia group members, $t(43) = 2.55$, $p < .01$.

Semantic Differential

Significant differences were found between the experimental and the control conditions in terms of semantic differential ratings of the labelee and the primary labeler. In the experimental condition the labelee was rated as being less clean, softer, more womanly, more tense, more yielding, more impulsive, less rugged, more passive, and quieter (all $p < .05$). In the experimental condition the primary labeler was rated as being taller, larger, less honest, stronger, more handsome, more powerful, more violent, more impulsive, more rugged, more active, more friendly, less sad, faster, and less quiet (all $p < .05$).

These data were factor analyzed. An orthogonal rotation of principle-axes factors revealed three clear factors: an Evaluative factor, a Masculinity factor, and a Sociability factor.

On the Masculinity factor the labelee was significantly less masculine in the experimental than in the control condition ($p < .05$), but the primary labeler was perceived as being significantly more masculine ($p < .01$). On the Sociability factor no significant difference was found between the experimental and the control conditions on mean ratings of the labelee. However, the primary labeler was perceived as being significantly more sociable in the experimental than in the control condition ($p < .01$).

When the high and the low homophobia groups were compared on the three factors of the semantic differential, results were consistent with other findings. Comparisons of high and low homophobia groups on the Evaluative factor failed to find any significant differences between the experimental and the control conditions with regard to ratings of either the labelee or the primary labeler; however, the high homophobia group perceived all other participants as being significantly less valued in the experimental than in the control condition ($p < .05$). On the Masculinity factor the labelee was perceived as being significantly less masculine by the high homophobia group in the experimental than in the control condition ($p < .025$); the labelee was not significantly differentiated by the low homophobia group. The primary labeler was perceived as being significantly more masculine on the Masculinity factor by the high and the low homophobia groups in the experimental than in the control condition ($p < .025$).

On the Sociability factor no differences were found between the high and the low homophobia groups in their ratings of the labelee. However, the primary labeler was perceived as being more sociable by the high and the low homophobia groups in the experimental than in the control condition ($p < .025$).

Preference Rankings

The labelees were generally liked (i.e., ranked by participants in the three preferred rankings) when they were unlabeled, but they were usually placed in the three least preferred rankings when they were labeled homosexual ($p < .01$).

The preference rankings of the three primary labelers demonstrates a change in perception in an opposite direction from that of the labelees. Primary labelers were ranked in the three most preferred rankings to a significantly greater degree when they labeled the homosexual than when they did not ($p < .05$).

No significant differences were found between the high and the low homophobia groups in their preference rankings for either the labelee or the primary labeler.

Discussion

To summarize, this study found that high homophobia participants sat farther away from the individual labeled homosexual and described him as being less masculine than did low homophobia participants. While the presence of an identified homosexual did not affect group communication patterns, high homophobia subjects in particular were significantly less efficient at group problem-solving under these conditions. The ratings of the labelees shifted from "most preferred" to "least preferred" when the label homosexual was applied. Participants perceived the primary labelers as more masculine and more sociable, and gave them higher preference ratings when they labeled the homosexual than when they did not.

Thus, in the present study the interactions of groups of men were significantly altered when the group believed a homosexual man to be present. The same man was perceived as having a number of significantly different characteristics, depending on whether or not he was labeled homosexual. This finding is consistent with attribution theory in predicting that the values and expectations of the perceivers greatly influence the personality characteristics they assess in others. Also consistent with attribution theory is the finding that those who held more negative attitudes on a pretest measure of attitudes toward homosexuality demonstrated more exaggerated reactions to the presence of a homosexually labeled man in the group than did those who held less negative attitudes. In general, these results support the belief that perceptions of others may not represent a consensual reality, but rather are a function of already existing dispositions on the part of the observer to attribute certain characteristics to another based on the label homosexual being applied.

Apparently, the impact the homosexual label has is intertwined with expectations inherent in the male role. If an individual is perceived as homosexual, there is a general move to devalue him and to maintain social distance—perhaps an avoidance of guilt by association. The experimental results reflect a difference in attribution made by the perceivers, not any change in behavior on the part of the labelee. The labelee did not know which label had been applied to him in each condition. In fact, the three labelees reported afterward that they could not tell which condition and/or label had been in effect in any particular group, although they were curious. They were not aware during the study that only the label homosexual had been used.

That groups of men function less efficiently when they believe a homosexual man to be present speaks to the power that the label homosexual has for men. During the first two trials of an experimentally defined group problem-solving task, groups that believed a homosexual man was present functioned less efficiently. This effect might well have decreased if further trials were attempted as participants became used to interacting with a homosexual man. In any case, initial group efforts which flounder because of the presence of homosexuals and highly homophobic individuals are vulnerable to the dynamic of "blaming the victim": Decreased efficiency could be attributed inappropriately to the homosexuals, rather than to the homophobic group members.

This brings us to the importance of homophobia, or the irrational fear of homosexuality, as an intervening variable. Not only are homophobic individuals more negative in attitude toward homosexuals and toward the concept of nontraditional sex roles,[7] but behaviorally these individuals avoid labeled homosexuals and view them as less stereotypically masculine. Since the labelees were viewed as "appropriately masculine" in the control condition, the attribution of "femininity" to these same labelees by homophobic participants is clearly a function of their own fears.

Perhaps the most intriguing result was the finding that the man who performed the actual labeling was perceived by the other men in the group as both significantly more masculine and significantly more sociable than when the same man did not apply the homosexual label. Thus, it would appear that men are reinforced for publicly identifying homosexual men. Presumably the primary labeler is viewed more positively both because he is assertive enough to publicly label a societal deviant and because he helps group members conform to societal expectations by that act.

A. Bandura[8] and F.H. Kanfer,[9] among others, have demonstrated that imitative responsiveness is reduced by direct or vicarious punishment. Men who might be inclined to engage in homosexual behavior may refrain in order to avoid the punishment and pain they have observed inflicted on homosexual men. The majority of homosexual men likewise learn to conceal their sexual orientation from others and often live uncomfortable double lives in order to avoid punishment. Present findings do not bode well for homosexuals not wishing to conceal or downplay their sexual orientation, especially given the repressive political movement to revoke civil liberties from labeled homosexuals.

The results of the study are consistent in indicating that conformity to male role expectations is a powerful motivator and that the label homosexual can be an important factor in whether or not one is perceived as being masculine. The findings of this study support the belief that the fear of being labeled homosexual can operate to keep men acting in accordance with the expectations of the male role. Those interested in changing pejorative attitudes toward homosexual men would do well to pay increased attention to changing the more basic dynamics of the male role.

Chapter 2

Coming Out as a Communicative Process

Fred E. Jandt and James Darsey

This essay has been difficult for us to write. Not only have we been beset with the normal problems of two authors living in different parts of the United States, but our individual perspectives have caused repeated reassessment of our data. The result of this collaborative confrontation is a political statement; it is criticism in the tradition of Edmund Wilson and Lionel Trilling in its focus. We are not dispassionate explainers of a phenomenon—we have experienced coming out. We feel that the process is not strictly personal; we feel coming out is influenced by a heritage of reidentification within the gay community,[1] and we feel that this process can be evaluated and prescriptions made for its improvement based on a conception of what it should do for human beings.

There are those who make a sharp distinction between politics and scholarship, and who will find the inclusion of this essay in a scholarly collection inappropriate. Max Black, in a foreword to a collection of essays on the morality of scholarship, answers the charge: "Only an exceptionally self-satisfied scholar could stand pat, nowadays, on the traditional virtues of detachment, fidelity to the truth, and a lofty indifference to consequences."[2] In the same collection of essays Northrop Frye suggests that our criteria for scholarship have helped to assure its irrelevance and maintain its ivory-tower pallor. He writes: "The disinterested pursuit of knowledge acquires, for its very virtues, the reputation of being unrelated to social realities."[3] However, we make no claim to disinterestedness and, rather than finding it an impediment to valuable and disciplined inquiry, find involvement to be the only ethical perspective from which criticism can take place.

With this focus, this essay examines the problem of "spoiled identity" among gay men and lesbians; how coming out serves as a process of reidentification; how a sample of members of the Caucus on Gay and Lesbian Concerns, of the Speech Communication Association, has experienced this process; and a concluding statement on the values that are and the values that should be inculcated within the gay male and lesbian community as part of its heritage.

The Problem of "Spoiled Identity"

> My parents, my friends, my teachers told me that I was a victim, a loser. I must lose in a world where only the winner is a Man, a human being. I was not a real Man. I was a queer, a half-Man, a pseudo-Man, like a woman. I could never aspire to the dignity accorded only to the conqueror, the Man on top. Men fought and won, they fought other Men for the ownership of the rest of creation, lesser peoples, the losers, women, the Third World, as well as the natural environment. I could never be a real Man. I didn't want to own women. I didn't want to fight other men. I wanted to love them, and I can only stand in awe before the material world, not own it. This made me obscene in this society, a dirty joke, contemptuous, the worst thing a Man can be, a loser, a victim.[4]

The above excerpt illustrates the view of what Erving Goffman has termed "spoiled identity."[5] Lesbians and gay men are among those whose "moral careers" are such that they have usually assimilated society's view of their stigma before they identify themselves as so stigmatized. A young boy, for example, may grow up hearing or even telling censorious jokes about faggots and queers before he realizes that it is he at whom they have been laughing. Unlike the congenitally deformed or others stigmatized from early years—those who have grown up having to define themselves outside of society's norms—the gay man or lesbian is faced with the problem of reidentifying self with what one has learned is pitiful, sick, laughable, a loser. It is this pattern, according to Goffman, that is most likely to develop a disapproval of self. Peter Fisher sums up the problem:

> The person who thinks that he might be homosexual is not likely to embrace the idea with much joy at first. He knows that society strongly disapproves of homosexuals, he may have guilt feelings himself, and he can assume that life is likely to be more difficult as a homosexual than as a heterosexual. Even if he has an overwhelming preference for homosexual relations and has had extensive homosexual experience, he may hold back from the final admission that he is a homosexual. He may view his behavior as part of a phase that will someday come to an end, or he may feel that with a great deal of self-determination and control he can develop the heterosexual interests that he presently lacks. Many homosexuals go through an enormous inner struggle before finally accepting a homosexual identity and life-style.[6]

Martha Shelley reinforces the picture of struggle:

> Understand this—that the worst part of being a homosexual is having to keep it secret. Not the occasional murders by police or teenage queer-beaters, not the loss of jobs or expulsion from schools or dishonorable discharges—but the daily knowledge that what you are is so awful that it cannot be revealed.[7]

And in a typically understated passage suggesting the magnitude of his struggle to come to terms with himself, Merle Miller notes: "It took me almost fifty years to come out of the closet, to stop pretending to be something I was not, most of the time fooling nobody."[8]

The very real nature of the stigma that these people perceive as being attached to homosexuality is demonstrated by some statistics compiled on public views of homosexuality. Data collected by the Institute for Sex Research indicate that most (84 percent) respondents believed that "homosexuality is a social corruption that can cause the downfall of a civilization."[9] Research suggests that lesbians and gay men are either equally intensely disapproved of by the general public,[10] or that the former are somewhat more disapproved of by the general public.[11] Gay men and lesbians do learn these negative appraisals of homosexuals and homosexuality from a heterosexually biased society. In the media, in everyday conversations, through jokes, put-downs, and on public restroom walls, homosexuals are depicted as mentally ill, contemptible, and pitiable.

Lesbians and gay males can talk about secrets and closets, because they are part of what Goffman calls the discreditable rather than the discredited; they do not wear their stigma on the surface, where it is immediately obvious to all who care to look. The problem for the discreditable is one of information management; they may reap the rewards of being normal by "passing." This ability to pass is a mixed blessing; in opposition to the rewards it provides, it creates the constant anxiety of one who lives under a fragile construction of lies. (Goffman dismisses this with an unsupported assertion.[12]) Passing increases alienation from self as one continues to participate in society's view of one's stigma; it requires constant attention to elements in the social situation that others may take for granted.[13] This Janus-faced nature of passing has caused one gay writer to speculate how much easier things would be if all gays were colored lavender.[14] What is most important about passing is the degree to which it entails alienation from self. Passing, in the first place, requires that one assimilate the role of the normal well enough to play it convincingly. Second, this role of normal may specifically necessitate the depreciation of what one knows oneself to be, e.g., gay men who laugh at or tell "queer" jokes. The alternative to passing is coming out.

Coming Out as Reidentification Through Communication

The term coming out for girls in certain African tribes literally means to come out from the shelters or little huts where they had been confined until they had reached the age when they could come out to be married. The debutante eagerly looks forward to her coming out party. At one time coming out for a lesbian or gay man meant a debut, where an individual, for the first time, publicly identified herself or himself as a homosexual by an action, such as going to a gay bar.[15]

A second definition refers to defining of the self as gay.[16] Clearly, these two events need not be simultaneous. Goffman, for example, discusses the identification with a stigmatized group as a socialization process characterized by ambivalence and "affiliation cycles."[17] W. Simon and J.A. Gagnon define coming out as both a behavioral and a self-definitional event.[18] More recently coming out has referred to a developmental process. Assuming a covert-overt model in which private experiences occur before public experiences, the process has been ordered into three stages: signification or self-identification; coming out, including involvement in the gay community as well as telling heterosexual friends and co-workers; and going public by being identified as gay in the media.[19]

What all these definitions have in common is the redefinition of self from one of "us" to one of "them." "We" and "they" switch reference groups, and along with this change in reference groups is the rejection of one set of values and the adoption of another. "To come out," suggests D. Altman, "means bucking the most basic and deep-seated norms of a society that sees itself as based exclusively on the heterosexual family structure."[20]

The key to coming out, as suggested by Goffman's description of patterns of moral careers, is the reconstrual of a phenomenon in terms of the values that have been internalized for it; the fact of homosexuality remains the same, but its meaning changes.

G.A. Kelly's Personal Construct Theory (PCT) can be valuable in explaining the psychological process whereby one makes this reconstrual. Described as an application of a Kantian theoretical model, PCT was developed by a practicing clinician as a means of developing, ordering, and explaining clinically significant processes. PCT accepts the primacy of interaction with the world and the resulting experiences over a totally independent, factual "reality."

By construing, Kelly means "placing an interpretation"[21]: a person places an interpretation on what is construed. Many constructions may have been acquired in infancy, before language development, and are nonverbal and outside one's consciousness. Dimensions of appraising self are explicitly taught to the child, who is likely to incorporate them, for a time at least, within his or her own construction system. As social experience widens, the child meets other dimensions from the peer group, older children, and adults. Whatever the world may be, one can only come to grips with it by placing one's own interpretations on what one sees.

Coming out, then, in PCT, is the process whereby gay men and lesbians grow to elaborate the construing of coming out or of being gay. Personal change, in PCT, is not a change of reality but a change of one's reconstruction of the environment. B.M. Dank defines it as reconstruction of the "cognitive category" homosexual.[22] Thus, Dank's interviewees placed themselves in the cognitive category of homosexual. But most people who eventually identify themselves as homosexuals require a change in the meaning of the cognitive category of homosexual before they can place themselves in that category. Dank's subjects, in effect, said, "I am homosexual but not deviant," or "I am homosexual but not mentally ill." The cognitive category of homosexual now becomes socially acceptable, and the individual can place himself or herself in that category and yet preserve a sense of self-esteem or self-worth.

In PCT, it is clear that persons change themselves by changing their constructions. To do so first requires information as to the possible alternatives. What are the sources of the gay construct for homosexuals? Like all constructs, according to Kelly's theory, the constructs applied to homosexuality derive from experience, i.e., through successive interactions with a real universe. In the case of constructs concerning homosexuality, constructs may be derived through successive interactions with that part of the real universe which is the gay subculture. Direct and indirect contact with gays provides information about homosexuals that challenges the straight image of the homosexual. Interaction with other homosexuals facilitates the learning of a vocabulary that not only explains but justifies homosexual behavior. Dank's interviewees identified numerous types of physical settings in which they gained their knowledge of homosexuals and homosexuality (see Table 1). Conspicuously minor in Table 1 are situations of negative public labeling, i.e., being arrested, that some labeling theorists consider so prominently. Given the research findings on the development of sexual orientation and self-concept discussed about, it seems quite unlikely that labeling of any kind can be considered significant contributing factors of the genesis of a homosexual orientation. Hence, a homosexual identity seems to arise out of self-labeling rather than as a result of labeling by others.[23]

Dank's findings support Goffman's more general conclusion on how the stigmatized come to know themselves:

> It is important to stress that, in America at least, no matter how small and how badly off a particular stigmatized category is, the viewpoint of its members is likely to be given public presentation of some kind. It can thus be

Table 1

SOCIAL CONTEXTS IN WHICH RESPONDENTS CAME OUT[24]

Social Contexts	N	%
Frequenting gay bars	35	19
Frequenting gay parties and other gatherings	46	26
Frequenting parks	43	24
Frequenting men's rooms	37	21
Having a love affair with a homosexual man	54	30
Having a love affair with a heterosexual man	21	12
In the military	34	19
Living in a YMCA	2	1
Living in all-male quarters at a boarding school or college	12	7
In prison	2	1
Patient in a mental hospital	3	2
Seeing a psychiatrist or professional counselor	11	6
Read for the first time about homosexuals and/or homosexuality	27	15
Just fired from a job because of homosexual behavior	2	1
Just arrested on a charge involving homosexuality	7	4
Was not having any homosexual relations	36	20

> said that Americans who are stigmatized tend to live in a literarily defined world, however uncultured they might be. If they don't read books on the situation of persons like themselves, they at least read magazines and see movies; and where they don't do these, then they listen to local, vocal associates. An intellectually worked-up version of their point of view is thus available to most stigmatized persons.[25]

This conclusion tends to be supported in the related experiences of gays attempting to find themselves. Books and other media are almost universally recognized as important.[26]

The importance of Goffman's statement is that it makes clear the communicative nature of the experience through which constructs are defined and redefined. After this is made explicit one can understand the communicative component of all experience and can look beyond the strictly verbal channels Goffman talks about. But for the time being these verbal channels serve well.

On the basis of the foregoing, lesbians and gay men in America, on coming to a sexual awareness, are faced with the necessity of redefining reality, i.e., the nature of homosexuality, if they are to accommodate themselves. In Kelly's terms, new sets of constructs must be applied to the phenomenon of homosexuality to replace the constructs provided by society at large. These new constructs are found and their application learned through experience with the gay community, i.e., through communication. Now, coming out can be examined from a constructivist view of communication, with

> an emphasis upon the reciprocal and emergent creation of meaning as a joint product of a socially shared code for the expression of thought (historically and socially affirmed structures) and the individual interpretive and behavioral processes (individual structures) by which strategies are enacted and expressed meanings are translated into subjective understandings.[27]

This is a more radical statement than that made by studies documenting common and often peculiar usages of verbal and nonverbal symbols with the gay community. These studies demonstrate only an expanded vocabulary; they do not necessarily demonstrate a language code representing a shared reality in the sense of PCT. Our view of coming out has important implications: Within this view, coming out becomes not an autonomous natural process like aging but a purposive human endeavor subject to critical scrutiny. As suggested at the outset of this essay, we intend not only to try to understand coming out but also to reach some tentative evaluation of how well it serves its functions in the gay community. For both of us, the function of coming out is expressed by a statement from Kelly: "Man, to the extent that he is able to construe his circumstances, can find for himself freedom from their domination."[28] To this end we now turn to data that corroborate the theoretical stance outlined here toward coming out, and provide more specific information as to how homosexuals in America are reconstructing their worlds to accommodate their sexual selves.

Survey of a Sample of Lesbian and Gay Male Professionals

Kelly introduced the Role Construct Repertory Test (Reptest) as a means of sampling the important constructs that an individual uses to give structure to her or his environment.[29] The Reptest recognizes the freedom of the individual to construe the world in a personal way (and the freedom of the researcher to construe that data in a personal way)! A similar procedure is Delia's Political Construct Differentiation Index.[30] Completion of the instrument required subjects to

> think of the characteristics which political figures have that you like and dislike. You should attempt to think of those characteristics which *in general* are important to you. We are not asking for the qualities which any specific political figure has. List below in the left-hand column a quality which you like very much in a political figure. Then in the right-hand column list the quality which political figures have which is the opposite of that good quality. Continue to do this until you have listed most all of the qualities that you feel are important.

After listing, subjects were asked to rate "the importance of each construct for you personally." These judgments were made on a scale of 0 (for no importance) to 5 (of very great importance).[31]

To study the model presented here, those who attended the 1978 Gay Action Caucus of the Speech Communication Association and who entered their names on a mailing list were sent a questionnaire based on the Reptest design. Of the forty-eight questionnaires sent out, twenty (or 41 percent) were returned.

The questionnaires sought the dichotomous constructs individuals apply to the phenomenon labeled homosexual and the phenomenon labeled gay, as well as each individual's degree of identification with those constructs. Table 2 presents a breakdown of the returned questionnaires according to sex and affectional preference.

Table 2

RESPONDENT SEXUAL IDENTIFICATION

	Male	Female
Straight	0	1
Bisexual	4	1
Gay-Lesbian	9	5

Initially, the data tended to confirm our view that coming out is a process, that there is a gap between assuming homosexual behavior and assuming the identity "homosexual." In our sample the average difference between "first same-sex experience" and "considered self homosexual" was seven years. The average age of some coming out events for our sample is presented in Table 3 as a way of suggesting a trend in the ordering of events and their separateness. Not every individual conformed to this trend even in the ordering of events, but we believe it to be representative. Our data conform very closely to that collected on gay members of the American Psychological Association provided in Table 3.

Table 3

AGE OF COMING OUT EVENTS[32]

Experience	Age*	N
Aware of homosexual feelings	10.6	19
First same-sex experience	15.8	19
Understood term homosexual	16.2	18
Considered self homosexual**	22.8	18

*Inexact ages were assigned values, e.g., 4 to 5 years was assigned a value of 4.5, and early teens was assigned a value of 14.
**Also to be read as "gay," "bisexual," or "lesbian."

In making this seven-year transition, respondents to our survey also tended to confirm Goffman's view of a literarily redefined world in a rather literal sense. Table 4 presents a breakdown of sources listed by respondents from which they had acquired positive information about being gay and which had a significant impact on changing their feelings about themselves.

Table 4

RESPONDENTS' SOURCES OF INFORMATION

Source	Males	Females	Total
Friends	12	5	17
Gay and lesbian literature	11	5	16
Scholarly articles and research reports	5	1	6
Lovers	3	2	5
Gay liberation and/or feminist movement	1	3	4
Television and movies	3	0	3
Counseling	1	1	2
Rap group	1	0	1

"Literature" ranks second only to "friends," and when combined with "scholarly articles and research reports" clearly dominates the sources of information. Although Table 4 is not exhaustive in terms of responses received, it does present the most commonly mentioned and readily categorizable sources of new constructs regarding homosexuality for the females and males participating in this study. Many of the categories —"friends," for example—are so variable that it would be impossible to predict what kinds of constructs would be likely to arise. But on the basis of individual responses it is possible to note some trends, particularly in "literature."

"Literature" was used here to designate material, whether fiction or nonfiction, emanating from gay or lesbian sources. This category includes novels, periodicals, poetry, and so on. J. Gurko and Sally Gearhart have asserted that the literature of gay males tends to emphasize the physical-sexual aspects of homosexuality, while lesbian literature tends to be more politico-philosophic.[33] Certainly, this seems to conform with the reading habits of our sample. When citing specific authors, works, or periodicals, gay men mentioned John Rechy (2), the *Advocate* (3), *Blueboy* (1), *Screw* (1), and *After Dark* (1). Rechy's work has been classified as part of a "new genre of homosexual pornography" distinguished from run-of-the-mill skin books by its high stylization; [34] the *Advocate* has earned its reputation as a long-lived source of gay news, but it has never been particularly radical, and its "Trader Dick" section attests to a heavy emphasis on male sexuality; *Blueboy* is a glossy skinmag; and *After Dark* is a closet case that has long presented homosexuality via the arts—especially its "tasteful" nudes and sensuous photographs of dancers. Lesbians mentioned Colette, Gertrude Stein, Kate Millet, A. Rich, *Sisterhood Is Powerful, Our Bodies, Ourselves,* and material by the group Radicalesbians. The nature of this material is more generally familiar for two reasons: (1) There is considerable overlap with the feminist movement and its wider audience, and (2) lesbians seem to produce a higher concentration of generally recognized literary works than gay men do.

This difference in the reading sources of gay men and lesbians tends to be maintained in other areas as well. Fifty percent of the lesbian or bisexual women indicated involvement in either the gay or feminist movement, or both, while only one of thirteen male respondents (7.7 percent) mentioned such involvement. Gay men had greater responses in the areas of "scholarly articles and research reports" and "television and movies." This is probably due largely to the fact that there is more in these areas for gay men. Because of historically greater visibility, gay men have been the subjects of a far greater number of studies than have lesbians,[35] and gay men have also been more ready subjects for the mass media, now that the curtain has been lifted.

Perhaps the most important finding of this survey lies in the consistency between the constructs presented in the sources used by lesbians and gay men to seek new constructs, and the constructs they actually applied to homosexuality. In redefining reality, naming can become very important. In modern times blacks, women, and homosexuals, each in turn, have sought to rename themselves. It is easier to bring new constructs to bear on a phenomenon if first the phenomenon is given a new name. Within the gay community this attempt at renaming has taken the force of rejecting "homosexual"—a label that defines only the sexual acts that are performed and not whole persons—in favor of "gay" or "lesbian"—labels that, we feel, express a consciousness, a life-style, or an outlook apart from any sexual act.[36] As expected from the sources used for new constructs, this renaming has had less effect on the males in our sample than on the females. More than half the males either used the same or similar constructs to describe both homosexual and gay, or they stated that they saw no difference. In contrast, only one third the women failed to make a distinction between homosexual and gay—or, as most added, lesbian. Males tended to describe homosexual and gay in more sexual terms than did females. Males used terms like "hot," "fem," "gorgeous," "trade," "leather number," "hunky," "sexual," "sensuous," "enemas-enjoying," "lecher," "chicken," "tease," "tail queen," "well-hung," and "dirty old man." Women, however, used almost no patently sexual terms, except for the standard sexual labels that were also used by men, e.g., "gay," "dyke," "lesbian," "homosexual," etc. The actual terms women used were more complex and made more distinctions between homosexual and gay-lesbian. Although these terms are examined more closely when we discuss the differences, just in passing it is interesting to note that perhaps consistent with the more politico-philosophic sources of constructs, women on the average generated a greater number of constructs than men did (fifteen compared to thirteen).

The evidence presented thus far suggests the importance of sources of information in determining the constructs one uses to define roles. This would tend to legitimize pointing to the gay and lesbian press as an efficacious disseminator of value. But before any questions of evaluation can be undertaken, the central and prior question of reidentification must be dealt with. The question of coming out is more than "What are the sources of alternative constructions of homosexuality?" or even "How effective are sources of alternative constructions of homosexuality?" The real question is "How effective are sources of alternative constructions at creating reidentification, at providing constructions that one can identify with self?"

Because each respondent listed his or her own constructs, it is impossible to compare these constructs in a systematic way. What we are more concerned with is whether or not the respondent has created a system of constructs with which he or she can identify. Note that this question is different from the question of self-esteem; we cannot be certain either from the degree of identification the respondent has with the construct or by the terms used in the construct whether the construct is favorable or not. In the first case, persons may have a high identification with constructs they perceive to be undesirable, resulting in some form of self-hate. Mart Crowley's *Boys in the Band* is the classic presentation of this response by male homosexuals. In the second case, the apparent evaluation in the terms used is unacceptable, because that reflects society's evaluation. Sometimes minority groups explicitly seek to change not behaviors and the labels for these behaviors but the way these behaviors and labels are viewed. Thus, "nellie" applied to a male or "butch" applied to a female might be perceived as good or desirable. The data in Table 5 present the mean degree of identification with or the ability to see oneself in the system of constructs that one has for the concepts homosexual, and gay or lesbian. Table 5 is broken down by sex and affectional preference according to the

Table 5

CONSTRUCT IDENTIFICATION

	SM	BM	GM	SF	BF	LF
Homosexual	—	3.0	3.7	1.0	3.0	2.7
Gay or lesbian	—	2.9	2.9	1.0	4.7	3.4

Note: If respondents indicated that they made no distinction between homosexual and gay or lesbian in terms of constructs, it was assumed that there would be no difference in identification with these constructs in either case.

two concepts, and the means are calculated on a scale of 1 to 5; 1 is very weak identification with the construct system one has, and 5 is very high identification with the construct system.

The data in Table 5 tended to support what we would expect from self-labeling and from sources used for constructs. Men who labeled themselves bisexual tended to have a lower identification with either homosexual or gay than did men who labeled themselves homosexual or gay. The fact that there were no responses from straight males is suggestive in itself. The one straight female in the sample had the lowest degree of identification with her constructs, as could be expected. The only surprise is that women who labeled themselves bisexual had a higher degree of identification with both homosexual and lesbian than did self-labeled lesbians, and had by far the highest degree of identification with lesbian than did any other group with any set of constructs. This may be because the most radical lesbian consciousness is a political separatist consciousness almost divorced from sex. It is more radical than that of lesbians within the gay rights movement, and it is more radical than that of straight women with the women's movement.[37] The very notion of separatism requires a higher degree of polarization and the need to clearly seek a strong identification. The most radical of radical lesbians might find the label lesbian itself restrictive and sexist, and may prefer bisexual, as less limiting.[38]

With regard to the sources used in garnering new constructs, we noted that both gay men and bisexual men who tended to use more sexually oriented sources had a higher identification with the more sexually defined concept homosexual than with the more political concept gay. However, in keeping with their political sources, both bisexual women and lesbians tended to identify more strongly with the politico-philosophic concept of lesbian than with the more sexual concept homosexual, and to exhibit a greater differentiation in their identification along with a greater differentiation of the concepts themselves.

The question of self-labeling itself becomes important if we can demonstrate a connection between the label one chooses and some characteristic(s) of the sources one used for construct formation. With the men in the sample one of the determining factors in self-labeling seemed to be age. The men who labeled themselves as bisexual had the highest average age of any group in our sample (47.8 years). Is there any evidence of changes in sources over time that might account for this fact? Two studies by J. Darsey suggest that there have been distinct discursive periods for homophile liberation in America. One study shows a marked discontinuity in the discourse of Mattachine Midwest between the pre-Stonewall period and the post-Stonewall period.[39] (This refers to the period immediately contiguous to the Stonewall rebellion in 1969.) Another study is a survey of the entire movement over the course of its history (1948-77), in which six distinctive eras are identified.[40] It is suggested that homosexuals were making different claims about themselves in each of these eras (and, presumably, because of the interactive nature of message construction, heterosexual society was saying corresponding different things about homosexuals in each of these eras as well).

To see if this view of discourse revealed any pattern in self-labelings and in subsequent constructs and identification, we calculated the years in which various respondents had their first same-sex experience, the year in which they first understood the term homosexual, and the year in which they first considered themselves homosexual. The most obvious differences were among the men. Our sample of women was smaller, and the women tended to have a closer alliance with feminist literature, thus not reflecting the patterns of homophile literature. Using Stonewall as a rough divider (cell size becomes impossibly small if we break it down any further) we noticed that among the men, four of the ten who did their coming out in the periods before Stonewall identified themselves as bisexual. In contrast, none of the three men who faced reidentification after Stonewall identified themselves as bisexual. The suggestion is that this oldest group of men had to seek reidentification at a time when the constructs being provided for "homosexual" were too oppressive and too far removed from the experience to create meaningful identification. As a result, these men tended to paint the bleakest picture of homosexuals, to have the lowest identification with these constructs, and to be unable even to accept the label. They also had a tendency not to have kept abreast of the recent gay movement and the attempt to redefine "gay" from its early use as a secret code to a label of positive self-affirmation, and therefore made little distinction between the two.[41]

The men most apt to make a distinction between homosexual and gay fell into a middle-age group—men who were coming out in the periods immediately contiguous to Stonewall, the most radical discursive periods. These are men who were inclined to have had some involvement with the movement, and movement politics and consciousness. They tended to identify more with gay than with homosexual. The youngest group does not continue this trend, however. Radicalism in the movement has declined. Politics has given way to social and sexual concerns, and since this group has never really had to bear the painful associations with the word homosexual, they find no need to make sharp distinctions between this word and "gay," and tend to use the same generally sexual and optimistic constructs for both.

We have attempted to make the case that coming out is essentially a communicative process, and in this section we suggest that coming out, although it must ultimately be an individual confrontation, is not highly particularistic; there is sufficient commonality in the experiences of gay men and lesbians within similar discursive periods to make comment on the process of coming out meaningful (rather than Joe's coming out or Alice's coming out). We have further argued that a significant source of this commonality in experience derives from a common heritage of reidentification techniques largely transmitted in the literature of lesbians and gay men. On the basis of this argument, we may ask of gay and lesbian literature a question similar to what a Plato or a Tolstoy might ask: "How does it benefit its society?"

Teach Your Children Well: Reflecting on Heritage

Coming out, as we see it, should have two criteria: First, it should enable self-acceptance; it should help a person identify in a positive way with what she or he is. This does not mean that coming out should be a course in homosexual chauvinism; gay is good, but it is not necessarily inherently any better. Clearly, this is an area where the messages provided for those who are coming out, looking for new constructs, could be improved. The scores for identification reported in Table 5 tend to be only moderate, reflecting some ambivalence regarding group identity. Homosexuals are not asking for complete identification; they do not want a completely homogeneous (sub)culture—the San Francisco Castro Street clone carried to its logical conclusion—but it is clear that distance created by depreciation and hate is unhealthy and harmful both to self and to others. In a fairly typical example of disownment of one's "own" and thus oneself, Merle Miller relates, "I once belonged to twenty-two organizations devoted to improving the lot of the world's outcasts. The only group of outcasts I never spoke up for publicly, never donated money to or signed an ad or petition for were the homosexuals. I always used my radio announcer's voice when I said 'No.' "[42]

Men, on the whole, achieved a higher degree of identification with their construct systems than the women in our sample. But before we can hand out any merit badges for achievement, there is a second criterion we must invoke, a second function that coming out, in our view, should serve: The concepts used in homosexual literature should liberate and allow the individual to define himself or herself in terms that encourage the exploration of his or her potential. The constructs with which the men in our sample chiefly identify are basically restrictive and unidimensional. The constructs that male homosexuals find in their literature encourage them to define themselves in sexual terms. The sexuality itself we find no fault with. In fact, we see the celebration of one's sensuality as a healthy antidote to the repressive puritan heritage about which H.L. Mencken said, "There is only one honest impulse at the bottom of Puritanism, and that is the impulse to punish the man with a superior capacity for happiness—to bring him down to the miserable level of 'good' men, i.e., of stupid, cowardly, and chronically unhappy men."

The problem with the sexual definitions adopted by the men is that, although these definitions create fairly strong degrees of identification, and although they do encourage homosexuals to embrace an integral part of themselves that is often maligned and denied expression, their exclusivity makes them unnecessarily restrictive. Not everyone can identify with "hunky," or "gorgeous," or "young stud," or "hot number." The criticisms that have been leveled at the youth and beauty cult in terms of its superficiality and its exclusivity are really extensions of the argument implied by the first criterion.[43] Such constructs limit the number of people who can identify with them. But for those who can aspire to identify with them, they are even more pernicious. In their lack of breadth, these construct systems encourage people to define themselves in terms no larger than their gonads; being gay becomes a twenty-four-hour-a-day occupation. One can get a glimpse of this mentality in John Rechy's *The Sexual Outlaw.* As L. Clarke and J. Nichols describe this failing;

> a difficulty with coming out is that it frequently becomes a dead-end experience rather than a continual process. Coming out too often stops abruptly with the discovery of social institutions like gay bars and clubs, the acquiring of a few new friends, and going to parties or dances.[44]

As judged by this second criterion, the constructs available to the women in our sample were clearly superior. On the whole, the women were able to present more complete, more integrated pictures of themselves than were the men in our sample, and by defining themselves in such terms, they suggested an ability to explore more personal dimensions than the men. The women did not choose to define themselves within the narrow parameters of sexuality; in fact, some lesbian literature tends to downplay the sexual component of lesbianism. This is consistent with the marked absence of sexual terminology in the construct systems of our female respondents.

By way of summary, then, what can be said? The tendency toward divisiveness between gay men and lesbians has increased in recent years. Some of this divisiveness is based on the kind of issues addressed above, with regard to construct systems. Lesbians find gay men to be sexual and superficial, and gay men find that lesbians have raised their consciousness to the point of unrelenting rage and defensiveness. We would argue that each group has much to offer the other based on their common problems in facing the reconstrual or reidentification of self. On the one hand, gay men could learn breadth of definition from lesbians, thereby releasing themselves from the oppression of their own limited definition of themselves. Lesbians, on the other hand, could learn to create construct systems that encourage higher degrees of identification from gay men, and if part of that identification is a delight in the sensual, then that would be good too. More importantly, both lesbians and gay men must become aware of the nature of coming out as a heritage handed down through communication. This realization squarely places the responsibility for the quality of this experience on gay men and lesbians themselves.

Chapter 3

Lesbians, Gay Men, and Their "Languages"

Joseph J. Hayes

Why research gay slang? What questions would one try to determine? Is there anything to find out? These are the sort of questions I hope to answer in this essay; I also hope to add some new ones.

Thinking in terms of academic disciplines, I believe there are two principal reasons for this work: (1) to place the undeniable existence of a gay slang—an out-group dialect or register—in its rightful place in all those disciplines that concern themselves with language and speech; and (2) to end the academic hegemony of white males. Almost all research in the areas of linguistics, speech, rhetoric, and communication is based on the assumption that white, heterosexual, male speech constitutes the norm for American speakers of English. This will no longer do. To dismiss the language and language behavior of out-groups as "deviant" from the artificial norm of men's speech can no longer be an honored practice among serious researchers, no more than it is possible today to speak of any country's system of language as primitive (as compared, say, with European languages).

Several other groups have begun to make similar efforts. In her book *Language and Woman's Place,* Robin Lakoff[1] draws on her own language and that of her circle of friends to point out a number of political and social meanings to certain traits she identifies as particular to women (such as tag questions). Several years ago a number of black linguists received a boost from a State of Michigan Supreme Court decision that recognized black English as a dialect on a par with white dialect, and instructed the school districts in question to begin teaching both. A California linguist, Ernie Smith, wants to give the name Ebonics to the whole study of black English. There is also a current revival of interest in Yiddish, Romany

(Gypsy), and other folk or ethnic languages and dialects, along with a recognition of their influence on modern American English. What are these scholars of women's, black, and ethnic English seeking in their work? A rightful place for the way many Americans speak in the currently all-male club, but without the sycophant's eagerness to point out that we're really all the same, when we know that we aren't.

Thus, the gay scholar not only shows how this language exists and operates within the various gay communities, but shows how it shares similar traits with other language, dialect, or register groups. For instance, Stephen Murray has explored the similarity of ritual insult exchange among black, Jewish, and gay men: ritual insult as personal self-defense; defeating the persistent feeling of inadequacy within the dominant group's norms; seeking self-aggrandizement through display of verbal ability and the need for quick thinking and rapid repartee as survival skills in an oppressed group.[2] In sum, gay language is at last being explored along with other language phenomena, particularly those of out-groups, and not as a special case apart from any other social phenomena. We are finally coming to discover truths about language, not perpetuating folk beliefs.

Historical Bias

Both inside and outside the academy there is a tendency to view the idea of *a* homosexual as having unvarying meaning beyond time and history, whereas, in fact, homosexuality, as the term is used today, is itself a product of history—a cultural artifact designed to express a certain concept. The term itself was not even coined until 1869, by the physician Benkert. Although there is thorough documentation that homosexual *behavior* is both universal and timeless in some variety or other, evidence of a homosexual *identity* has been found only in recent and specific phenomena. Homosexuality exists everywhere, but only in certain cultures or under certain circumstances is it *structured* into a subculture or made an official institution of a closed community (e.g., the courts of some monarchs, nunneries, the Greek gymnasium). Elsewhere it seems to lack any structure whatsoever.

Homosexual slang, therefore, is something that must have grown out of one of these communities, subcultures, or institutions, and can only be understood within the context of one of them. One might say, then, there are no words pertaining to homosexuality that have an unvarying meaning beyond time and history; rather, they are a product of that history —cultural artifacts specifically invented to express a prior and particular concept or act. In classical Greece, for instance, there was no single word for homosexual or heterosexual.[3] It was believed that every male responded to both male and female stimuli, and would act differently and have different types of sexual experiences at different stages in life. Thus, Greek words for homosexual types and behavior express phenomena that vary from time to time and place to place (e.g., Attica and Sparta). Unless we understand the rich detail of the complex ritual of Greek courtship, seductions, ideals, and taboos, we have no understanding of what words mean and how we are to apply them to various aspects of Greek sexual life. To speak of a gay *language,* therefore, is to speak of the usage of a smaller number of people than the total population of all those who express homosexual behavior.

Sources of Our Knowledge

Our knowledge of how various lesbian and gay groups use language is hampered by the universal contempt and oppression in which gays have been held, urging them toward secrecy of congregation and caution in committing anything to writing. As always, the records of the dominating group are generally not to be trusted. Nevertheless, we may first try some speculation, to get a sense of the possible varieties of gay language that may have existed, by examining a few historical groups or individuals.

Among American Indians there is a lengthy history of an institution, variously named, but most commonly called *berdache.* The berdache is a male who, at his usual name-calling time, would receive instructions, often from the moon, to put on the dress and take up the chores of a woman. He spoke a language known to all, but sometimes used language employed only by the berdache.[4] There is documentation of a woman chief who wore male attire and used male speech.[5] Among the Gros Ventre Indians there are separate men's and women's languages. Young Gros Ventre, who speak more in English than in the tribal language, are afraid of making a mistake and using the wrong language, thus being ridiculed for effeminacy or mannishness, which are almost always connected by Americans to homosexuality.[6] Among Native Americans there is a time-honored homosexual dialect, of the berdache or cross-gender chief—important to the transmission of wisdom and prayer, and other shaman duties—of long duration in their culture. More recently, with increasing exposure to whites, these dialects are becoming a source of shame for reservation Indians eager to avoid any further contempt (the accusation of homosexuality) from whites.

From religious writings and chronicles, particularly of the Hebrews, we know of the existence of widespread temple prostitution as part of the religious obligations of many peoples of the ancient Near East. Is it possible that there existed a special gay language for the gods, perhaps a set of prayers, to establish a relationship to the gods?[7] We know also of the Sacred Band of Thebes, the fiercest and bravest army of Western history, composed exclusively of male lovers. Did they have a military-erotic code, involving a formal or ritual language?

Finally, there is the case of Sappho, the most praised poet who ever lived. She was especially lauded for her extreme sensitivity to language and for the brilliance and subtle nuance with which she could capture the various emotions of love and of jealousy and sorrow at separation. She was so widely copied in every corner of what was then the known world that it is difficult not to wonder if what are now taken as conventional ways to express feelings about love might not have had their origins in lesbian affection. However, there is ample documentation of the conversations, writings, and speeches of Oscar Wilde.

These few examples show how uncertain it is to speak in historical terms, and why I have limited my study to the past hundred years. Without fully understanding the historical context we cannot make sound linguistic judgments. My experience of contemporary American society indicates that we are in a period of rapid transition, engaged in sorting out what words we need for the particular purposes that we can identify (i.e., a nonsexist vocabulary or codes for nonverbal signaling, like the gay male pocket handkerchief code). This process suggests that other gay subcultures may have had this need, too, and history provides some examples. As soon as homosexuality ceases to be a normal pastime and becomes a sin or a crime, then civil and canon law need a criminological vocabulary to describe it. Similarly, religious texts (the Bible, the Koran, sermon literature), medicine, social science, personal memoirs or journals, gay literature, and gay scholarship all have need of a lexicon. Yet all but a few sources are judgmental and prejudicial; almost all assume heterosexual behavior to be the norm against which all others are measured. The language of these codes and disciplines transmits and enforces an arbitrary standard of behavior by comparing *a* view of homosexuality to a universal, widespread, persistent form of coercion to a norm called heterosexuality.[8]

A major caution, then, for a study of gay culture is the need to recognize that the terms which ought to denote a group or status are instead the end of a long historical narrative, in which each use of the word evokes all prior narratives for it. Wayne Dynes and Warren Johansson set this principle forth quite cogently in "Eros, Myth and Stigma: The Historical Semantics of Sexual Intolerance."[9] The historical bias, or dilemma, can be summarized by two points: Whose language are we talking about, and how are its users affiliated? The users may be a dyad (e.g., code in the correspondence of Stein and Toklas or of Woolf and Sackville-West), a private (and often coded) journal of a single person (as Walt Whitman), or a large and diverse group, such as may be presumed true of the readership of the widely read periodical *The Advocate*. For my own purposes I am speaking of two "communities" of speakers—American lesbians and gay men—who share only certain common characteristics. As a social group, they came into existence in late nineteenth-century Europe, noticed almost exclusively in urban areas and defined mainly by their erotic behavior.

With the understanding that any discussion of lesbians and gay men, and of any special form of communication among them, is directed at only a segment of the total group who practice homosexual behavior; that time and place make vast changes in the way homosexuality is viewed; and that language does not always work to express these facts, but sometimes to conceal or neutralize them, I would like to discuss three areas of contemporary concern: labels, nonverbal language, and the oppressive aspects of gay slang. These areas were chosen because they have generated the largest numbers of articles, letters, and disagreements about language both from within and outside the communities.

Labels

Labels are language at the core of our identity, and they may be the most powerful of all language behavior toward gay people. Thomas Szasz says that the power to define sickness (i.e., homosexuality as a mental illness) is equal to the church's power to define sin, the priestly function having been assumed by psychiatrists in our society.[10] The power of the label is something gays are very aware of, and this power helps to explain why labeling has occupied so much of their thinking in the past ten years. Here are some general considerations about labeling that might guide discussions of the subject:

Labels never remain static; new ones always come to be preferred. When I was young it was polite to refer to one racial minority as *colored*; as a teen-ager, the polite term was *Negro.* As an adult, I am encouraged to use the word *black,* which used to be a term of insult when *colored* was preferred. Currently, there are strong feelings about the use of *female, lady,* and *woman,* when referring to adult biological females. Among my friends, *woman* is the only acceptable term.

Labels may change connotation. *Lesbian* began as a term of contempt in English slang—and is still used that way sometimes—but is used only in an ameliorative sense by modern lesbians. Conversely, *homosexual* was coined by Benkert to replace the pejorative connotations of words like *invert* or *unspeakable.* Currently, however, there is opposition to the use of the term among some gays, who see it as a pejoration, connoting illness, criminality, and an overemphasis on genital relations.

Perhaps the biggest enemy of gays in this business of names is the habit of silence, the unspeakability of gay behavior, described most famously by Augustine as "that horrible crime against nature not to be spoken of among Christian men." Thus, in E.M. Forster's novel *Maurice* the hero can only get a name for these feelings he has from a charlatan, an American hypnotist who tells him he has "congenital homosexuality." Prior to this, Maurice had consulted the old family doctor and, after much fumbling, could only describe his complaint thus: "I'm an unspeakable of the Oscar Wilde sort."

Yet in the search for new names to describe feelings of love and sorrow, jealousy and passion between members of the same sex, gays often forget the singular lack of success that neologisms have had when there are already well-established words in the language. At the time that *homosexual* was coined and picked up widely in medical usage, the following words were in direct competition with it: *invert, sodomist, pathic, bisexual, catamite, androgenic, contrasexual, homogenic, intersexual, morphadite, Platonist, shame, similisexual,* and *urning.* It is much easier to make over old linguistic garments than it is to get masses of people to try on new ones. Presently, most activist lesbians have cast off the terms homosexual and gay as being male-marked (i.e., female homosexual or gay woman), in favor of *lesbian,* which is quite clearly and solely female-marked. Moreover, some lesbians have decided to rehabilitate a formerly debased term, *dyke,* and turn it into a word that connotes strength, defiance, and self-affirmation.

However, because gays have never been a neatly categorized group, type, or subculture, Western gays have always had as a central intellectual concern the need for good definitions and accurate labels that reflected the view of homosexuality as seen out of their own particular life's window. Here are some representative responses of gays to the existence of labels, showing dislikes and preferences:

In an article titled "The Homosexual Question," Eric Bentley[11] notices that all the terms used to describe homosexuality are histories of ideologies and that they assist the dominant social order in promoting and maintaining itself: If there were no homosexuals, there would be no heterosexuals, since heterosexuality is mainly that which is not homosexuality. Homosexual is a descriptive term only in a sexist society; it describes what is *un*heterosexual. The essential difference is that gays celebrate sex as self-justifying, but Bentley feels that labels currently used by gays —*homophile, gay*—are sex-limited or vacuous in some way: they take away the gay contribution to the campaign against nonmissionary sex.

Kevin Burke and Murray Edelman suggest that dominant groups rally behind certain words the better to manipulate: language as a means of social control.[12] *Dyke* is not just a label, but calls to mind all the past stories about dykes: the label as a short, running narrative history. Thus most existing terms for gays keep circulating folk myths and prevent persons from questioning or from penetrating the surface. What is, in fact, a metaphor gives the aura of a denotative definition. This process is not dissimilar to the smug announcement of the judge who admits to no personal definition of pornography but "surely knows it when he sees it."

Not everyone wishes to bring about change. When queried on the use of *gay* as a synonym for *homosexual,* two thirds of Houghton Mifflin's *American Heritage Dictionary* panel of word advisers decided that *gay* was not "appropriate for formal speech and writing."[13] Gay activists don't always like labels, either. Jill Johnston, writing in *MS.* magazine, asks that *lesbian* no longer be used as a label only for a sex act.[14] She feels that it more accurately defines a "political choice which women make to be free of the female role." And so is born the notion of the *political* lesbian.

Although many lesbians and gay men feel that current definitions are oppressively restrictive, others wish for more denotative definitions. Anthropologist J. Rogers Conrad feels that social science research is hampered by lack of an empirical definition.[15] Considering homosexuality as a statistical category, community, subculture, disease, and label, he finds each of these designations lacking. He proposes instead Carol A.B.Warren's notion of *status,* in particular a *key status,* that entity which, like the keystone of an arch, supports and relates to all of one's other statuses. In a similar vein Michael Davidson, in his book *Some Boys,* objects to adult-minor relations being described as *pederasty.*[16] Although Davidson offers no term of his own, he points out that biblical passages make no allegations about offending *boys* and that the Greek word has not a thing to do with sodomy. Finally, psychiatrist Thomas Szasz wonders why society arbitrarily applies derogatory labels to common forms of behavior.[17] Why do we apply a disease concept to homosexuals and alcoholics, but not to masturbators or nicotinics (i.e., smokers), when the first of each set equally practice nonprocreative sex and the latter equally abuse the body's tissues? Objective medical phenomena are not used to define diseases but to stigmatize persons.

Inside the gay communities many lesbians and gay men feel that the attempt to ameliorate and rally behind formerly pejorative terms has not been entirely successful. Some gay men look on *gay* as just another attempt to make homosexuals bland and acceptable: "Gay is a bought up word meaning Right-wing, upwardly mobile man whose chief goal is to achieve the same status as white, heterosexual man."[18] Similarly, Thomas Dotton writes: "Movement gays want to persuade people that gay is a 'homosexual whose heterosexuality is expressed through homosexuality.' . . . In coming out, *gays* transfer the sick label to transvestites, transexuals and fetishists, themselves to emerge purified and made mediocre."[19]

Rita Mae Brown early recognized the different purposes in labeling that came from inside or outside the lesbian and gay communities.[20] In a society where sex roles are rigidly defined and dominated by male supremacy, the label lesbian functions to hold women in line, as a scare term (as it did in the early days of the National Organization for Women [NOW]); a woman who belongs to no man in a sexist society is invisible, pathetic, inauthentic, and unreal. But *inside* the lesbian community, when *women* give women a new sense of self, as a woman-identified woman, then *lesbian* becomes a label that declares equality, visibility, and an emergent new self.

The discussion about women and their relationship to labels occupied a great deal of space in the lesbian-feminist press from 1968-73, although it has been a continuous concern in the gay press for the past hundred years. The issue is so critical to all aspects of American lesbian life that when the newspaper *The Lesbian Tide* changed its logo from *lesbian/feminist* to *feminist/lesbian* (thus changing its context from homosexual to feminist), almost half the issue was devoted to explaining the deliberations leading up to and the main reasons for making the change.

Since the flurry of interest in terminology began in the nineteenth century, brought about by the entrance of homosexuality—formerly a private behavior—into the arena of law and medicine, an unsettled debate, marked at all times by strong feelings, has been in continuous play. Although it is difficult to extract dependable generalizations from the subject, two facts seem to stand the test of time:

—that labels are inescapable and ever-changing; they will be proposed from outside and urged from within.

—that few lesbians and gay men remain neutral on the subject; they line up from one end of the spectrum ("I wish to be associated with no label") to the other ("I wish for a precise, empirical, and universal definition").

Nonverbal Behavior (Paralanguage)

Especially during the period between the Kinsey reports (1948 and 1953) and the emergence of a gay liberation literature (c. 1968-71), almost all books on homosexuality or homosexual behavior included some remarks or descriptions on dress, gestures/mannerisms, or the rituals of gay bars, baths, or sex pickups. Similarly, few of the lesbians and gay men I know don't wonder at some time about how readily they recognize one another, and often proffer their own ideas about how this happens. On the sinister side, there is frequently a great deal of interest in developing a lesbian/gay iconography to be used as a means of recognizing those who wish to stay concealed during times of oppression (e.g., election years) or who wish to protect themselves where the law does not (e.g., in employment discrimination). The literature on the subject generally falls into four categories: (1) historical signals used for recognition, (2) ethnographies of nonverbal behavior, (3) efforts at "scientific" measurement and description, and (4) as an important political question within lesbian and gay communities.

Historical evidence—from satirical poems, both Greek and Roman comedies, police reports, travelers' guides to overseas low-life—reveals that dress has been the principal mode of nonverbal communication and that it served as a means of mutual recognition. In ancient Rome gay men were said to wear green or yellow trim on their togas and were thus called *galbanati* (from Latin *galba,* yellow). In nineteenth-century Europe and early twentieth-century America, the tie was a primary signal. In Paris gay men signaled with green ties; in Frankfurt, with black ones; and in America, with red. Men's attire has always been a salient feature among some lesbians, although the Paris salon of Natalie Clifford Barney included the wearing of Greek-inspired designs, in honor of Lesbos. There was even an ill-fated attempt to form a utopian colony on Lesbos (modern Mytilene) in which the Aeolian style was to be imitated as much as possible. Later, smoking tobacco was said to imply lesbianism.

Recently, urban gay males have created an extraordinarily elaborate sexual signal system out of the rear-pocket display of a colored handkerchief commonly known as a bandana (modern bandanas come in more colors than blue or red). This custom seems to have originated in nineteenth-century Colorado mining towns, where men with pocket bandanas played "follower" and those without played "leader" at Friday night dances where there were few or no women present. There exists today perhaps the most elaborate set of clothing signals among gay men of any time in history (although the upper-class Victorian dress code and the whims of certain monarchs may equal the current era in complexity).

The largest number of modern descriptions of nonverbal behavior comes from the ethnographers, almost all of whom are social scientists. Their work deals almost exclusively with gay males and the way in which they manage sexual contact and conduct in bars, truckstops, baths, parking lots, subways, and tearooms (toilets). For the most part these works set as their goal a description of how the system operates, many vacillating between pornography and how-to manuals. A few of the better efforts discuss the social and political implications of both the institutions and the individuals' behavior.[21] The authors do not disagree much among themselves; rather, they seek to get an accurate description and, more recently, to place their conclusions in the context of related situations, whether or not they're sexual. Not many of these ethnographies have contributed much to language behavior, except perhaps in the form of chronicle-writing. Patricia Nell Warren's *Front Runner*[22] might be said to bear a similar relationship to ethnographic writing as Shakespeare's history plays do to Holinshed's *Chronicles.*

Possibly the newest discipline to be brought to bear on the subject of gay nonverbal behavior is semiotics, the science of the measurement and description of signs. At present only two works are available. Hal Fischer's *Gay Semiotics: A Photographic Study of Visual Coding Among Homosexual Men* provides photographs and texts to present his "urban archetypes": classical, natural, western, urban, and leather.[23] A second work, *The Gay Picture Book,* contains only photographs and would necessitate an informant for interpretation.[24] The semiotics of urban gay male dress and display is a subject worthy of further exploration.

In *Kinesics and Context: Essays on Body Motion,* Ray Birdwhistell devotes a chapter to masculinity and femininity as "display."[25] He draws on seven societies for his information: Chinese, middle-upper-class London, Kutenai, Sushwap, Hopi, Parisian, urban American. Male and female informants easily detected male and female movements, but no position, expression, or movement carried any universal meaning of its own. Nonverbal behavior seems, therefore, to be culture-bound. All of Birdwhistell's informants could easily detect the message, "I wish to be considered a lesbian or a gay man," but no message could be discerned or defined that read "I am gay" if not sent out voluntarily. This observation poses a difficult problem, since many straight and gay people would deny the ability to conceal that message at all times. But the lack of a universal signal and the lack of confidence in discernment—however tentative—are worth noting, because this is the only large-scale study available. Of course, many still cling to the folk-belief, perpetuated even in insiders' memoirs of the forties and fifties, that there is an iconography of stereotypes, or "How to Spot a Homo."

In a more controlled area of investigation, Richard Dyer has done some interesting work in film iconography: How do directors convey the presence of a lesbian or a gay man—or their equations, an effeminate man and a mannish woman—to the audience?[26] What are the verbal/visual/aural signals? For men, Dyer suggests the following attributes: overconcern with appearance, association with decadent good taste, and fastidiousness in speech, gait, eating, etc. For women, he describes a sense of smart chic (lesbianism as the dallying pastime of the idle rich), mannishly cut clothes or men's clothes outright, a dressed-down appearance, and a very undemonstrative gait and manner of address. Dyer points out that we are to read personal style in a psychological sense and to read physical mannerisms as a whole way of life.

Finally, novelist Rita Mae Brown suggests that sexism and patriarchal attitudes can have a direct effect on body language.[27] With men, she observes, women tend to lower their shoulders, pull in their bodies, and tighten their jaws and upper back muscles. She describes this as "protective tension," an attempt to reduce the amount of space occupied. She urges lesbians to use up, and to project and push forward into more space than lesbians habitually do now, not to "stay in their place."

The form and meaning of nonverbal behavior are probably more important to gays than to straights. Gays are more sophisticated in its use, depend on it more, and know better how to manipulate it for their own ends. Moreover, their necessary involvement in role-awareness and role-playing makes them aware of how little important communication is actually put into words. Sophistication in nonverbal language also makes gays aware of the dangers that lurk everywhere in the use of spoken language.

Language That Separates and Oppresses

In speaking about labels and about stereotypes for spotting lesbians and gay men, there is an underlying assumption that the words gays use or have used about them are, more often than not, value-laden. A code language that once protected a minority at a certain time and place may cease to have any real value after awhile, and may continue to bind gays to destructive and divisive values. Gay men might have to ask if the silent language of dress—most manifest in the clone look—might actually be a language trait preventing, rather than assisting, the liberation of the physical and the spiritual body. Lesbians face an even more difficult task in sorting out which words from the old culture actually oppress women and which seem to but in fact do not. I would like to touch on some of the kinds of problems that the mere existence of a gay language poses, and what steps have been taken to remedy them. Most of the source material for this section comes from the comments of women and non-English speakers of English-language countries, persons that might be referred to as double minorities in the field of speech and language.

When an International Gay Association was finally formed, in the winter of 1978, the British information officer for Esperanto International complained that IGA's choice of English as their official language showed "language imperialism," since English is the language of the world's most aggressively imperialist nation—the United States. In a more democratic spirit, the information officer should have chosen a "progressive" language, like Esperanto. In a 1975 letter to *The Body Politic* (Toronto), English-speaking gays were called on to put French-speaking gays on a par with them by issuing all materials bilingually, so that language would not become yet another tool used against gays.[28] Indeed, one of the most insidious forms of oppression against groups outside the mainstream is preventing them access to language, which self-appointed guardians—such as scientists, doctors, priests, and publishers—control, in manner and mode, according to what they consider permissible. As one embittered gay cried out to the professionals, "We can't use your words because they're not scientific [dismissing our ideologies] or in good taste [washed of the taint of our sexuality]."

Finally, the question must be asked: Should lesbians and gay men have a special language at all? In the 1980s will they need *any* kind of gay language, verbal or nonverbal? The person who has addressed this question with the most carefully reasoned arguments is Julia Penelope (Stanley), who presents an epitome of the lesbian argument against gay slang.[29] She poses what I think is the central question: What is the relationship between gay language and gay culture?

She answers first by pointing out that there is no homogeneous community composed of lesbians and gay men. There are areas of common concern and common oppression, but is there *a community*? First, there is no common gay language that provides its speakers with a lexicon expressing values and experiences important to a unified culture, because one does not exist. Lesbians and gay men are included within a single reference group—*homosexuals*—because they have been persecuted, ostracized, and cast out of society for their same-sex loves. This association, then, is based on mutual persecution. In a true community there would be a well-established set of terms—argots, cants, slangs—used to maintain group cohesion, as is found in psychological jargon, sports terminology, or self-help groups. How much, can we say, of gay language is cohesive and supporting?

Julia Penelope feels that gay language functions more to exclude and oppress the lesbian than to bind her to a community of men and women. She believes that few lesbians are familiar with many terms in gay slang, only a few such as *camp, dyke, gay, faggot, queer, drag queen, come out, bring out, closet, straight, butch, femme.* But the greatest portion of the gay lexicon refers to gay male sexuality and associated activities: *fist-fuck, glory hole, basket, size queen, clone.*[30] In our culture, men are the coiners and users of slang; thus gay slang is a male domain. It is designed for the expressive needs of men, not women, who have no use for it. Rather than uniting the lesbian and gay male communities, Julia Penelope feels that gay slang serves to divide them.[31] In her view, gay slang is another vehicle for self-hatred and self-oppression, rather than functioning as a language that speaks *for* gays and enables them to speak to themselves. Moreover, she insists that the language and culture of gay males is a distorted imitation of the dominant society that condemns and oppresses them, the macho male hetero hegemony.

In truth, most terms were not coined by gays but were borrowed from underworld and criminal groups—thieves, addicts, prostitutes. From prostitutes come *trick, trade, rough trade, seafood,* and *number.* Many terms for sex acts are borrowed from heterosexual males: *go down, blow-job, 69, ball, get it on,* and *get laid.* Lesbians, too, have borrowed many terms from the vocabulary of heterosexuality. Since the culture we grew up in is sexist, racist, and classist, Julia Penelope says, we will have become the same as our culture by incorporating their language as ours. In one sense only *camp* and *closet*—respectively, a flaunting of stereotypes and a concealment of the true self—can be said to be uniquely gay. What does this say about gays' relationship to American society? For one thing, it suggests that the mere existence of a gay slang is one of the factors that holds homosexuals to conform to corrupt social values and prevents them from pressing ahead into a political existence based on their *own* lives, not as a distorted reflection of others.[32]

Among gay activists the most commonly heard solution to these problems is that the use of gay slang must be stopped altogether. Yet other gays, because the language was formed originally as a protective reaction and so continues to support the fear of heterosexual power, suggest that they should strengthen themselves and overcome centuries of (self-) hatred by reclaiming and flaunting the worst of the terms of abuse—dyke and faggot—and give them *their* meanings. For the first time these words would take on a political meaning. Thus, lesbians would continue to ask for their own terms; perhaps all homosexuals might find terms to help them cohere.

An answer to the charge of the separating function of gay language has been offered by Louie Crew.[33] Crew states that cross-gender identification ("Hey, sis!"; "O! get her!") does not trivialize or mock women, but acts as a defiance of heterosexual culture, which defines all males as feminine who do not want sexual intercourse with a woman—something like, "I'm queer and proud!" He sees it as a conflict: Cross-gender references may improve bonds with other males (our "sisters"), but it is done at the expense of putting down women by acting out all the large, pejorative stereotypes. He feels that if gays shy away from any attempt at gender-linked humor, they will end up with nothing but neuter blends, something like a gay *New Yorker* style. Some gays say the sooner they stop using gay slang altogether, the sooner they will cut off the last ties to the ghetto and to second-class status. Others say that if they abandon gay lexicon—and that is happening at an astonishing rate in the United States—they will have committed mass cultural suicide, akin to the attempt of the Maoist Chinese to eradicate all links to the feudal past by allowing only Western art and music. Yet their most powerful leader wrote poetry and encouraged massive use of wall posters, as if to recognize that the Word is, finally, both vital and ineradicable.

At a certain point in its existence the language of an oppressed group is not heard. But gradually it filters into the mainstream. Currently, we find words like closet and gay, the disco revival, Bette Midler's career beginning at New York's Continental Baths, *Rubyfruit Jungle* put on supermarket book racks by its mainstream publisher, obviously lesbian-inspired fashions touted as The Look for Fall, and even Ronald Reagan speaking out against Proposition 6—all these phenomena making *gay* increasingly indiscernible from fashionable or common customs.

Yet gays are left, finally, with a dilemma. If their language is really hetero-male derived, then they must abandon it utterly, without so much as a moment spent on nostalgia. But if they should forget to preserve the record of a gay language, they will lose the ability to read Walt Whitman, Gertrude Stein, Frank O'Hara, Victoria Sackville-West, and François Villon, and they will be cut adrift from their heritage and culture. I think new forms of language that help delineate male-male and female-female experiences in their uniqueness need to be explored. The misfortunes of past oppressions of language must be recognized for what they are. Above all, I think gays have to be very practical each day as they make dreams for the future. It might be nice someday to have neuter pronouns like *um* and *ums,* but in the meantime we ought to be practicing how to make do with the ones we've got.

One of the bitterest and longest battles has been waged over whether the words homosexual and homophile are, in themselves, obscene or offensive to public taste. Only recently, after a ten-year legal struggle, did various gay groups in the San Francisco Bay area win the right to be listed under the heading Homophile Organizations, in the Pacific Bell Telephone Yellow Pages. This was not just a case of "would rather not" on the part of the telephone monopoly, but a long, expensive fight, bitterly fought through every imaginable legal angle. Other Yellow Pages and regular listing battles are still in litigation. Related to this is the problem of library classification and access. The request to remove, as the principal heading, phrases such as Sexual Deviation, Sexual Perversion, or Sodomy from library subject catalogs has not met with much success. Similarly, the libraries' policy of treating anything pertaining to homosexuality as obscene and assigning it to the Limited Access or Special Section collections of the library is usually difficult to have modified. This practice is especially pernicious, since few people seeking information about a subject that confuses them, or in which they hope to find confirmation for their own growing self-identity have the courage to request a book out loud in a crowded catalog room.

The lesbian and gay communities are most immediately involved in three areas of concern. The question of self-labels is by no means satisfied, and the current political climate in the United States pushes some toward timid retreat and others toward a more defiant boldness; a consensus seems farther away than ever. The origin and effects of in-group humor are beginning to be examined more closely. Gay men's *camp* is coming under closer scrutiny, particularly with regard to its political implications and what some see as its dependence on the mockery of women. Above all, many thinkers are recognizing camp as a more complex process than earlier treatments have allowed; there is even a book-length treatise on the subject in the works.[34] More recently, there have been a number of articles on lesbian humor.[35] Several lesbians have pointed out that humor usually needs a scapegoat to work, and that the lesbian's position at the bottom of the sociopolitical order causes her to make herself the scapegoat of her own humor. The lesbian both initiates and receives the brunt of the joke.

There is a general phenomenon at work in gay communities that fascinates me. In reading the anthologies, journals, and newspapers directed at a lesbian audience, I couldn't help but notice how much emphasis there is on conversation and on the values of good conversations. Similarly, the large number of experimental literature panels at professional meetings seems to suggest that lesbians are in the forefront in linguistic experimentation in fiction and poetry, especially in the area of speculative fiction. Conversely, since the mid-70s gay men have been evolving an astonishingly elaborate system of nonverbal languages in terms of dress, display, adornment, management of space, and uniqueness of style in housing, furnishing, and dance—all as if to become as independent of verbalizing as possible. It would seem that lesbians are joyously abandoning woman's traditional role of "suffer and be still" and that gay men are equally eager to give up their traditional occupation of the central language space. But these are only speculations, and we must see where they lead before proclaiming them a trend.

Part II

Inside the Gay Community

Chapter 4

Gayspeak

Joseph J. Hayes

In this essay I examine some aspects of language use in America's largest subculture, homosexuals.[1] It is not my purpose to offer a descriptive analysis of syntax, morphology, or phonology, but to analyze the social functions of language in this particular group. I wish to see the ways in which the language used by gay men reflects and affects the relationships between dominant culture and subculture, and, in turn, to evaluate the relationships between normative and special dialects in the way they influence the self-image of their speakers.[2] To facilitate a discussion which must include lexicon, usage, imagery, and rhetoric, I call the language of this community Gayspeak.[3]

Since any special language must be evaluated within a contextual framework, I have divided the body of my essay into three sections in order to account for some specific behavior patterns in the subculture, which are directly reflected in language use: the secret, the social, and the radical-activist settings.[4] At the conclusion of this analysis of social context I offer some hypotheses on the effects which the normative and special dialects have on each other and their users, and some comments on the unique functions of language in gay culture.

In this analysis I have drawn primarily on observations of my own language and that of other gay people. I have listened over a long period of time to a wide range of people talking in bars, clubs, meetings, and social gatherings, and to the voices of novelists and periodical writers. These people are my informants; their linguistic behavior forms my "data." My analysis explores the linguistic behavior of the gay community within the three settings listed above. The criteria for such an analysis come from the behavior of each speaker toward other gays and toward the dominant culture, as well as from language differences. It is important to understand, however, that any member of the gay community may function in any one or all three of these settings. They are not exclusive to any individual or subgroup.

In the *secret* setting, gays are covert in expressing their gay identity, separatist (from the straight world especially, but often from the gay community as well), apolitical, and conservative. They are often painfully self-conscious about the stigma imposed on them by the straight world and take great pains to avoid any mannerisms or language which would stereotype them. The *social* gay setting is the most traditional one. It is best known to the dominant culture, since its linguistic behavior is often the butt of comments and jokes. The central meeting place for social language is the gay bar or club, and as the name suggests, gays in this setting frequently engage in social activity with other gays, either privately or in gay meeting places. Gays who frequent the social scene, however, may be open about their subcultural identity with friends or fellow workers in the straight world. Gays in the third setting, the *radical-activists,* are currently the most visible in their behavior. Although they may not have formal ties with the gay liberation movement, they are usually highly political and freely expressive about their identity. Because of their association with the counterculture they are sometimes alienated from people who move only in the secret and social settings, although radical gays may themselves move in the secret or social setting at various times.[5]

The Secret Setting

The gay who is in a covert setting may be distinguished from one in a social or activist setting by his refusal to use any Gayspeak or only as much as is necessary for making social contacts. Even in a gay social group or alone with a friend the secret gay may refuse to refer to his subculture life in any but the mildest euphemisms. This typical exchange of two men at a straight social gathering might serve as an example:

Mr. X: You certainly have on a colorful tie!

Mr. Y: Yes, I really like gay apparel.

The information, "I am gay and I believe you are, too," has been transmitted in what amounts to code language. In this setting, guarded use of Gayspeak allows people to hint at their sexual orientation, but never in a way which jeopardizes their ability to pass. Even among friends the secret gay may eschew gay terminology, preferring to call his lover of many years his *friend,* his circle of gay acquaintances the *kids,* and all gays *members of our book club* or *people of our faith.* The simple question, "Is he?" in many contexts asks any or all of the following questions: "Is he gay?", "May I use Gayspeak in his presence?", "Do you want him to know that you (or both of us) are gay?", "Is he straight but hip to the scene?", "Would he be available as a potential sex partner?"

Another prominent feature of secret Gayspeak is the tendency to avoid specific gender reference. In describing a weekend trip, a gay person might begin: "I went to the mountains with this person I know and they enjoyed the view from the summit." Gays may also become adept at switching gender reference when there is a perceived threat. Chatting on the telephone in a public office, the covert man or woman may refer to Elliott as Ella or to Jill as Joe in order not to arouse suspicion.

In questions which anticipate a specific gender response, this person may respond vaguely as follows:

X: Who'd you go to the movies with last night?

Y: Oh, this friend of mine.

Similarly, we find in the film *Sunday, Bloody Sunday* a middle-aged gay physician who has been accosted by his aunt at a family Bar Mitzvah. She asks when he's "going to give us all a nice surprise." He responds pointedly, if lamely: "I haven't found the right person yet—."[6]

Secret gays may also use innuendo in referring to other gays, calling them *artistic, liberal-minded, understanding,* or *sensitive.* People with *tendencies—artistic tendencies, unusual tendencies*—are hinted to be gay. This usage may have developed from a standard locution on employment or security-clearance forms: "Have you ever had homosexual feelings or tendencies?"

For gays in a secret setting, the development and maintenance of a code language form a protection against exposure. As certain words or phrases pass into general usage or become generally familiar, some gays must develop new phrases or employ more arcane synonyms, in order to maintain secrecy. They are always on stage and usually on guard. However, it must be remembered that the language habits in the secret setting are used by most gays whenever they perceive a threatening situation.

The Social Setting

Unlike the covert gay, for whom Gayspeak helps to maintain a rigid separation between minority status and mainstream acceptance, the gay who is in a social setting uses language to express a broad range of roles both within and outside the subculture. Social Gayspeak emphasizes the importance of acting in language behavior. If I were to summarize the social setting simplistically, I would say that it employs a vast metaphor of theater, which includes role stereotypes, clear notions of approved sexual behavior, and the rewards and punishments that are assigned according to one's ability or failure to use the symbols assigned by sex role. "Scanning the possibilities"—being always on the alert for contexts in which various modes of expression are either allowed or appropriate—requires one to perceive the total spectrum of distinctions between what people say and what they do.[7] Thus, the humor in Gayspeak, especially camp, is often cynical because it is based on a serious relation to the world. In the social setting, Gayspeak suggests that there is always a vast gulf between what people pretend to be and what they are.

Closely related to the acting behavior is the habit of categorization. Although all speakers make categorical distinctions, gays do so along specific parameters: "The important point is that everyone (and every kind of sexuality) be accounted for by some linguistic category of the gay world. Words, then, function to separate outsiders from insiders, to account for ambiguous persons within sociable or sexual interaction, and to describe the primary, close, and unique relationships of insiders with one another."[8] In the social setting people are not only typed by the usual distinctions (height, weight, race), but by sexual preference (*bottom boy*: anal receptor, *suck queen*: fellator), intimacy of relationship (*auntie, sister, husband),* rank within the subculture (*queen bee*: social arbiter, *nelly number*: effeminate and insignificant), and eccentricities within the norms of the subculture (*leather*: motorcycle crowd, *drag*: transvestites, *S/M*: sadomasochists). In general, a person's occupation, status within the dominant culture, or family are not described in Gayspeak except as they have some bearing on events in the subculture.

As we would expect from the process of categorization, the richest features of social Gayspeak are found in the lexicon, particularly in compound constructions. Perhaps the most widely employed stem word for building compounds is *queen.* The more traditional meaning of the term implies effeminate behavior in a man. In its wider context, however, it may be used to build a limitless series of images: to describe sexual preferences —*dinge queen* (one who prefers blacks), *size queen* (one who likes men with large penises); to describe a subculture type—*queen mother* (older man who serves as counselor or social arbiter), *queen of tarts* (a pimp for hustlers); to make fun of a man's hobbies or interests—*Chippendale queen* (likes antiques), *poker queen* (likes to play cards); or as an all-purpose term of derogation—*Queen Mary* (large or fat), *Queen of Spades* (black with high status).[9] There is no limit except each speaker's imagination, and neologisms are constantly being coined. In all the forms I have cited, *queen* refers simply to gay man. In certain instances where the speaker refuses to consider any event or person outside the terms of Gayspeak, *queen* may simply refer to all men in general.[10] Thus, a gay man noticing the impeccable clothes of a public official might observe, "Oh, she's such a neat queen!" (one obsessed with cleanliness and order). He does not mean that the mayor is gay; rather that the speaker is gay and that he recognizes in the mayor a stereotyped trait of the gay community, that all gay men are fastidious housekeepers or dressers.

As is true of American slang in general, social Gayspeak has an especially large number of synonyms for sexual organs and sexual acts. To the extent that the dominant culture defines gays largely in terms of specific sexual practices and the imagined role and behavior changes that these acts must bring about, the subculture reflects this labeling in the richness of its vocabulary for proscribed sexual acts. It is outside my scope here to resolve the chicken/egg question of whether the sexual vocabulary developed in response to outlaw status or whether it merely generated itself.[11]

However, as an adjunct to the acting skills of "scanning the possibilities," social Gayspeak has developed an important cluster of images from stage and film. Famous Hollywood stars of the thirties and forties figure importantly, especially if the roles they play are campy or treat of tragic love. A melodramatic loser, for instance, is a *Stella Dallas.* A man who is suspected of actually enjoying his constant misfortune becomes a *Camille* or a *Sarah Bernhardt* (sometimes *Sarah Heartburn).* Stars such as Mae West, Bette Davis, and Carmen Miranda are mimed along with some of their famous scenes or routines probably because they exaggerate the various stereotyped roles that women play in general society. Gayspeak has, thus, an idea of acting within acting. Mimicking the tone, diction, rhetoric, and speech mannerisms of these camp heroines would seem to show the subculture's perception of how seriously the dominant culture takes the language by which it maintains rigid images of sex stereotyping. At its very core, camp is the art of the put-down, especially of one's self and culture. Behind the irony of camp, however, is the awareness of the roles played outside the culture as well. By pretending to be a vamp or a sexpot, gay men manifest an implied awareness that language may be used as a means to reshape attitudes toward social roles. Through camp, stereotyped behavior is revealed as nothing more than another form of playacting.[12]

Some articles have offered evidence to show the extent to which women's language makes use of the expressive as opposed to the instrumental mode.[13] This is certainly true of gay men's language to some extent. There is a difference, however. The metaphor of acting in Gayspeak implies that the process of trivialization, when put on or off at will, is a form of mockery, perhaps a flaunting of "abnormality." What would appear to be a trivialization of the world, because social Gayspeak is often frivolous, comic, precious, or fleeting, amounts to a trivialization through parody of the dominant culture.

With these general remarks behind me, I wish to turn to the specific features of traditional, social Gayspeak. The most useful place to start is with a written sample of social Gayspeak. Below is a paragraph from *Data-Boy,* a biweekly tabloid distributed free in Los Angeles gay bars. It demonstrates an awareness of role playing and of the effectiveness of "pose," both of which are trademarks of social Gayspeak:

> FLASH: Remember all the rains just before Christmas? Well, it didn't seem to stop any of the "girls" from finishing their last minute shopping. Xmas Eve there they all were just running pitter-patter up and down the Blvd. with their smart umbrellas and raincoats. All but one! This one was standing in front of Fredericks (*sic*) of Hollywood in his white levis and jacket just posing

> up a storm and mentally picturing what he would look like in the lovely creation in the window. And you know, he was right? It is a lovely outfit, Mr. T., but the silver rivets around the collar are a bit too much.[14]

The style, of course, imitates the breathless and heavily allusive "items" published by the late Hollywood gossip-columnist, Louella Parsons. The main image of this "item" describes the contrast between the hypermasculine hustler on Hollywood Boulevard, in his "butch" Western outfit, and the display window of one of the world's most famous purveyors of exaggeratedly "feminine fashions," especially lingerie. "Louella" treats ironically the styles of posing in both cultures in this "scene." The writer himself, and the special milieu of his item, refer to the shoppers as *girls,* silly creatures on unimportant errands which they treat seriously. In addition, the *girls* are very interested in clothing and decoration, as all women are supposed to be. These stereotypes are the vehicle for the irony. Just as the men shopping on Hollywood Boulevard are self-consciously dressed in their *smart umbrellas and raincoats* (a rarity in southern California) and the mannequins in the windows show off their "naughty" lingerie, the hustler *posing up a storm* against the storefront is shown to be excessively concerned with his own clothing and decoration, carefully dressed in his hustler's uniform, levis and matching jacket. Decoration with rivets may signify counterculture, leather/SM, or "ultra-feminine" intentions, but all decoration, says "Louella," is a pose. Exaggerated femininity or masculinity are made indistinguishable by the juxtaposition of the mannequin in the window and the one on the sidewalk.

Notice also that the language "Louella" uses qualifies the action in order to make it trivial. The shoppers are not simply running errands, but are *running pitter-patter up and down the Blvd.* Their walk is dainty and their direction chaotic. The shoppers are also *just running* and *Mr. T.* is *just posing;* there is no great significance to either action. The window displays a *lovely creation* and the hustler wears a *lovely outfit.* The adjective *lovely* is considered women's language by many people.[15] The silver collar rivets are not startling, but a *bit too much.* The tone is finally precious, "feminine," and belittling. No one must take himself too seriously, and "Louella" has only scorn for the hustler who tries to do so.

The narrative has an oral quality which is a mark of the social community's emphasis on verbal wit. The style is rather deprecating of both self and audience, self-conscious in its pose, and reductive in treating its subject. It also avoids bluntly obscene language as well as any terms considered to be "masculine." In social Gayspeak, "masculine" statements are often reserved for irony.

Social Gayspeak is the version best known to the public. It is the one employed in films such as *The Boys in the Band, Staircase,* and *The Gay*

Deceivers, and in plays like *Norman Is That You?* It is also the basis for humor directed specifically at gays in shows and articles. At both political extremes within the community, however, social Gayspeak is considered to be a mark of stigma.

Since all special dialects are subject to influence from the normative one as well as from the special dialects from communities to which gays might also belong (e.g., blacks or Chicanos), Gayspeak is constantly changing. Radical-activist gays have been especially concerned with bringing about changes in the features of Gayspeak and in its use. What makes this particular language setting so interesting is the conscious attempt by radical gays to manipulate the relationship which language and behavior bring to bear on each other. Finally, it is this area which shows us the more recent developments in the use of Gayspeak.

The Radical-activist Setting

The rhetoric of gay liberation is often indistinguishable from the rhetoric of the general counterculture. It is distinguished from the rest of the gay community, however, by its deliberate reevaluation of Gayspeak. As is true of the counterculture at large, the gay activist believes that a change in the way people use language can bring about a change in society's structures and values. If language can create attitudes and modes of behavior in a subculture, they argue, then a change in Gayspeak can bring about changes in the dominant culture. Julia Stanley summarizes the relationship clearly:

> Thus, although gay slang is the vocabulary of people who are themselves outcasts from the straight culture, it is also sexist, classist, and racist, and the existence of terms that reflect such attitudes binds us to the same value system that makes us outcasts. Such a conflict within the gay subculture will not be resolved easily. . . . [16]

The first strategy is to avoid any special jargon at all. This attitude links the radical group with the secret group. While the more conservative secret group wishes to distinguish itself from the gay subculture, the activists, who also wish to distinguish themselves from gays in a social setting, avoid Gayspeak not to hide their gay identity but rather to stop both the process of alienation and ghettoization and to reject the value system which Gayspeak has incorporated from the mainstream culture.

As the feminist and black movements have worked out a new set of values for the terms woman and black, the task of value redefinition occupies a central position in gay liberation theory. In an article on the general subject of his personal identity, Allen Young describes the process of redefinition in its largest context:

Saying "I am gay" has the important element of *self-definition* to it. It is not the negative definition of others (homo, lezzie, queer, pansy, fruit) but a positive term we can call our own. (Even if the term is not an ideal one—there have been objections to the trivializing aspects of the word "gay" from within our community—still it is the one most generally favored by gay people.) . . . The term homosexual does not comply with the need of self-definition, because the term was given to us by doctors and other "scientists" who have not generally been our friends. "Faggot" and "dyke" are used in a special way, turning terms of put-down into proud affirmation. . . . The affirmation of gay identity allows us to get together and achieve *unity* with others of like identity. This has obvious advantages for our sexual and social needs, but it also means we can share life experiences which cannot be shared with people who are not gay. . . . This leads quite naturally to the discovery of gay media, international communications and understanding among gay people, and perhaps most important, action against our oppressors. The price of suppressing one's gay identity, the price of closetry, is a very high one to pay.[17]

A similar attempt at definition is found in D. Cartier's "A Dyke's Manifesto." In asking the question, "where does the woman from a dyke-masculine background fit into the women's liberation movement?", the author describes her response to the position of the lesbian in the general feminist movement:

Crap on society, I say, when I walk into a bar and see the rigid faces of women who have forgotten or who never learned how beautiful it is to be loved as a woman by a woman. Anger and rage when I look over the years at the unreality of being ostracized from straights and men because I am a woman, and alienated from other women, and my very identity, because I played to win on a losing side.

These are my sisters who like myself are just beginning to recognize that their real strength and beauty lie in being their own self-denied women. These are my sisters who have come to realize that that little gun is a crippler and the very chain that separates us from an honest love for other women like ourselves.

It's a strange sort of sisterhood because we have enemies on all sides and inside. Our enemies are society and its sex-roled oppression that has alienated us from half of ourselves and the women we purport to "love." Our enemies . . . are ourselves and internalized illusion that what this society says is "strong and right" is really crap—and was never us to begin with.[18]

Like the style of the social setting, gay radical rhetoric often has a "spoken" quality to it, although this tone resembles the rhetoric of political conflict (the "speech") more than "gossip." The language attempts to dramatize and intensify rather than trivialize. Terms of *anger* and *rage* —the *crippler gun,* the *chain, enemies*—and the images of deceit, alienation, sell-out, delusion, and ostracization give Cartier's passage a vivid and aggressive tone. The situation discussed is termed significant and dramatic. In this sense, radical Gayspeak, like its other versions, is also a form of acting. Since Cartier's piece is meant to be taken seriously, it adheres to a "masculine" tone, that is, it does not qualify the action, dwell on decorative elements, or use ironic parody. This tone is employed by both men and women. The writer creates a persona who is neither arch nor coy. She wishes to convey strength and determination. Like other radical-activist writers she has learned from the subculture to use "male" language to make "power" statements.[19]

However, the frequently expressed belief that the dangers of *posing* are as inimical as those of *passing* makes many activists distrustful of all language. For them words are very important; but the use of language as a tool for changing behavior is occasionally met with suspicion. In a humorous column on radical rhetoric, Rita Goldberger reflects the gay world's heightened awareness of euphemism and cant:

> *Movement* people do not "gossip." They "discuss intra-*Movement* personal dynamics." They do not "cruise" because cruising is sexist. And *Movement* women do not "trick," they have "short term," but "meaningful" relationships. . . .
>
> One last word that is necessary of a *Movement* person's vocabulary is "high." One meaning of "high" is "stoned." . . . *All Movement* people get "high" because getting "high" is illegal and therefore very radical. . . . However, when used with the word "consciousness," "high" takes on a new connotation. Someone with a "high consciousness" is someone who is politically aware and understands her oppression. One can tell how "high" a person's consciousness is by how many meetings she goes to and how often she uses the word in this article. Thus, to demonstrate a "high" consciousness, *one does not really have to change one's ideas, but merely one's vocabulary.*[20]

Thus, radical gays are committed to the notion that "language uses us as much as we use language."[21] Many radical gays feel that Gayspeak holds them to the ghetto, either because gays subsume in their dialect the contempt manifested by the straight world or because it reflects the oppressive values of that world. By making over pejorative terms (*faggot, dyke*) radical gays are attempting to turn back these terms into symbols of defiance of the dominant culture. From other stigmatized groups, radical gays have learned to put their special dialect to use as a focus of pride and identification. Radicalesbian provocateurs label themselves The Dyke Patrol. A group of Berkeley gays picketed a San Francisco gay bar called The Stud to urge a name change to The Fairy (from straight machismo to gay affirmation). A Boston quarterly calls itself the *Fag Rag*. Just as Black is Beautiful, Gay is Good.[22]

Indeed, one important way to distinguish radical from social Gayspeak is by the differences in understanding of contextual meaning. Kinship and rank terminology may serve as a representative example. The circumstantial nature of relationships in a stigmatized community seems to act as an impetus to the creation of alternative structures modeled on the dominant community. Since the acting nature of social Gayspeak emphasizes caricature and exaggeration, these kinship terms are intended to be parodic. A gay man might refer to his *sisters,* who are his close friends with whom he enjoys the confidentiality and close ties that the siblings of the idealized family enjoy. His *mother* is the person who first introduced him to gay society (a *father* for gay women). An *auntie* affords him the indulgences, kindness, and general entertainment that a visiting relative might provide for her adored nephews. A gay *son* or *daughter* may have been housed or educated by an older member of the community. In many larger cities, elaborate costume balls are held to elect an *emperor, empress, princesses,* and a *royal court.* In the spirit of Mardi Gras and King Momus, the strictest etiquette is observed, but in a spirit of merrymaking.

Except in the egalitarian sentiment of *sisterhood* and *brotherhood* radical gays abjure the use of these kinship terms as "elitist" and "sexist," as well as a waste of time better spent on social work or political activity. They perceive the use of social Gayspeak as inimical and serious, a manifestation of ghetto sycophancy. In their concern for the values implied in social Gayspeak, radical gays seem to have a more restrictive understanding of contextual meaning than gays in the social setting. The lexicon of social Gayspeak may be "elitist" or "sexist" only if the social context is taken seriously. If, as I suggested, the acting metaphor of social Gayspeak presents language as potentially comic or parodic whenever it deals with sex roles or stereotypes, then gays in the radical setting can properly be accused of a failure to understand social Gayspeak.

An Overall Perspective

Gayspeak has some unique aspects which make it especially interesting to the study of language behavior. It is always acquired as a second dialect or register, yet its features are not generally known to the mainstream community. Unlike black English or Chicano Spanish, which are the normative dialects in their own communities, Gayspeak is not ever used by many gays, although they are normally exposed to it in late adolescent or early adult life. While most bidialectals learn the dominant culture's language at least by their early school years, gays learn to acquire the special dialect well after learning the normative one, usually at the time of entry into the gay community. Within that community, moreover, there is much debate about the value of Gayspeak. For some it is a source of pride and self-affirmation; for others it is an embarrassment or a threat.

Gays who remain only in the secret setting face problems in understanding and using social Gayspeak. Since the development of some Gayspeak was brought about by the need to remain covert, the secrecy of the language makes it difficult to acquire for people who wish to come into contact with the gay subculture. The process of coming out is both aided and inhibited by the existence of Gayspeak. Since there has been a manifest conspiracy of silence in all media when dealing with the subject of homosexuality, except in a degrading or lurid fashion, the language used to describe the gay world relies almost solely on stereotypes. For even the most secretive gay person, it is almost impossible not to become familiar with some Gayspeak. Yet it is the knowledge of Gayspeak which may potentially expose the covert gay to the straight world and is treated by many gays as a mark of the ghetto mentality. Certainly, this is a situation of "damned if you do, damned if you don't." In the short run, a knowledge of Gayspeak may ease the transition into the gay world during the coming-out process. In the long run, however, Gayspeak has a potential for harm.

As the radicals point out, much of gay lexicon is sex-linked. The association of women with passivity and men with aggression finds exaggerated expression in the subculture. No one has ever satisfactorily determined to what extent language influences our behavior. But there is a danger that Gayspeak may develop in men the *belief* that they are sexually abnormal, weak, silly, passive, and unstable creatures. To the extent that the speaker is aware that these poses are ironic, it can be a healthy antidote to repression. To the extent that linguistic behavior determines psychological behavior, it can be dangerous.

Inevitably, the gay who moves in more than one setting must evaluate how his use of language will affect intragroup prestige and standing. The queen, whose social status is low because of his "feminine" traits is often marked by his witty chatter. The "strong silent type," however, is much sought after because his apparent verbal inabilities are taken to be a sign of masculinity. In our society, silence is frequently associated with power. Women are often denigrated for "chattering," or in the male view, trivializing the world by talking about it too much. However, outside the sexual marketplace, linguistic "cleverness" may be a valuable skill, especially if one is good at the brand of repartee called dishing.

The final problem for the secret gay is the passing of Gayspeak into the mainstream language. When code language appears in normative language it threatens those who seek protection behind it, because once-secret signals are now open to public scrutiny. Lakoff suggests that gays always use the dominant culture's language, whereas the dominant culture abjures minority language.[23] I do not think this is true for gays in the radical setting or to the extent that the language of gay activists has been absorbed into everyday speech. As the taboo against talking openly about sex has abated somewhat recently, many terms from Gayspeak have entered the language, just as terms from black English relating to drug usage have done.

Films such as *The Boys in the Band* have made Gayspeak words like *auntie, butch, cruise, drag, queen,* and *gay* more familiar to the general public. There has also been a cross-fertilization in the political realm as well. The process of coming out or the trap of being in the closet, for instance, are discussed widely in weekly newsmagazines and film reviews. One may come out to the women's movement or be a closet radical. One might also come out as a member of a party to which one does not nominally belong. A film motif might be described as closet Gothic. The controversial Madalyn Murray O'Hair appealed to American "closet atheists" to "come out of the closet."[24]

In the course of this essay I have suggested that the straight world's narrow focus on abnormality and sexual "deviance" is incorporated to some extent in Gayspeak. To put the case somewhat simply, I feel that Gayspeak reflects this pejoration in two ways: extreme euphemism, even to the extent of denying Gayspeak altogether, and extreme dysphemism, a mark of the parodic nature of Gayspeak. In Gayspeak this is the difference between *dropping your hairpins,* giving subtle hints about your sexual orientation, and *throwing your beads* (or *pearls*), being dramatically open about your gayness. An alternative response in the gay community comes from the radical group, which attempts to reverse the pejoration by redefining certain terms to give them positive values. Perhaps ironically, the proudest affirmation of one's personal identity and the most paranoid repression of it in the gay community are achieved principally through the existence of Gayspeak.

Final Observations

A proper conclusion must certainly include a perspective on problems in current and future research. Until recently, research on the gay community has followed principally one interest: the investigation of the etiology of "abnormality." As a result, we have little phenomenological or ethnographic information about gay life. We do not know, for instance, much about the ways that gay people in various contexts and settings view each other. Nor are there data for distinguishing between male and female language in the gay community. Are the differences related to class, sex, adaptation, or position in the dominant culture? Why is male Gayspeak so full of pejorative terms for women while the reverse is not true?

When linguists write about black English, Chicano Spanish, or women's language, some assume that all speakers come from the same class. Is the bond of a subculture stronger than the class structures developed by the main culture? This question is important in discussing Gayspeak since there is such a strong stigma attached to being gay. We also need to study the use of nonverbal language in the gay community and its relationship to the spoken dialect.

We can only guess how widely Gayspeak is used. Who employs it? Can we discern patterns in those people who will not use it other than to serve their desire to remain covert, appear more masculine or feminine, or to avoid the oppression of a ghetto mentality?

Finally, we need to examine Gayspeak in greater detail precisely because its speakers come from all races, classes, and occupations, and because it exists in many languages. In pursuing the answers to some of the questions I have raised, researchers will bring us closer to a complex and sophisticated model for understanding the reciprocally affecting influence of language and behavior.

Chapter 5

"Gayspeak": A Response

James Darsey

Of course the first thing to do was to make a grand survey of the country she was going to travel through. "It's something very like learning geography," thought Alice as she stood on tiptoe in hopes of being able to see a little further.

—*Lewis Carroll*
Through the Looking Glass

The burgeoning of such groups as the Gay Academic Union, the gay caucuses of the American Psychological Association and the Modern Language Association, and now the Caucus on Gay and Lesbian Concerns of the Speech Communication Association (to name a few) suggests a growing belief that the study of gay- and lesbian-associated phenomena (psychology, literature, language, or other behaviors) is a legitimate and discriminable area of study. If this were not so, there would be no need for the academic activities of such groups; they could be merely political advocates within larger organizations and communities. The creation of new academic communities is justified only to the extent that it can be shown that valuable insights are impeded by the structure of current academic communities. This essay attempts to provide some preliminary views on what areas are the legitimate province of a legitimate gay studies,[1] especially gay language and communication studies. No one would like to play chess from the perspective of one of the pieces, yet gays risk the consequences of just that unless they make some attempt to reflect on their claim to academic uniqueness. They, like Alice, must occasionally stand on tiptoe to get the lay of the land if they are to be effective.

The claim I pursue here is that it is profitable for those involved in shaping gay studies to think of scholarly endeavors as either generic —those that are concerned with broad, generalizable classes of phenomena—or idiographic—those that are devoted to establishing and understanding the unique characteristics of an event, person, or group. For example, a study that demonstrates the unique effects being black has on behavior is idiographic. In contrast, a study that uses a black ghetto population as an example of the effects of lower socioeconomic status on behavior is generic. Similarly, a study that uses gays as a source of data does not necessarily say much about gays. For instance, a study of the rhetoric of Mattachine Midwest that I prepared several years ago says something about agitative rhetoric but little about gays[2]; it was properly included in an extant tradition of scholarship that has such questions as its concern; it was a generic study.

It seems apparent to me that gay studies, if there is to be such a thing, must concentrate on the idiographic, that is, precisely what no one else is going to study. The traits that are unique to gay men and lesbians must be isolated, and their impact on various phenomena, such as language usage, must be studied. Unfortunately, at the present time, we often lack the basic knowledge to make that distinction—the distinction between the generic and the idiographic. If we fail to make and use this distinction, we run the risk of failing our essential function in gay studies. If we confuse this distinction, we run the risk of creating outright falsehood.

A close examination of "Gayspeak" (chapter 4) by Joseph Hayes[3] clarifies the nature of the idiographic/generic distinction and its importance, and suggests some possible directions for future research.

Joseph Hayes and the Nature of Gayspeak: A View from Across the Hall

Joseph Hayes deals with the "social functions of language" in the gay subculture. Within his scope he includes "lexicon, usage, imagery, and rhetoric," all under the rubric of Gayspeak.[4] To facilitate analysis Hayes divides Gayspeak into three social contexts: the secret, the social, and the radical-activist settings. In the secret setting Gayspeak is apparently a restricted language code used to identify other gay people without jeopardizing one's own identity.[5] The other function attributed to secret Gayspeak is evading the inquiries of others concerning one's identity and the nature of specific relationships.

From Hayes' description the latter function is simply filled by lying about the nature of these relationships, activities, and attachments. There does not appear to be any peculiar linguistic usage. For example, a college student with a roommate of the opposite sex, unbeknown to his or her parents, might employ the same tactics Hayes claims to be peculiar characteristics of Gayspeak. One wonders if this example provides any insight into the social functions of language in the gay subculture.

The former function—identification—is more interesting. Hayes maintains that "for gays in a secret setting, the development and maintenance of a code language form a protection against exposure."[6] In other words, Hayes sees this activity as analogous to the highly popularized citizens' band codes—a code specifically created to facilitate communication within an in-group while excluding members of an out-group. In making this assumption, Hayes ignores the full implications of the term he uses to describe the gay community: subculture.

Cultures and subcultures have histories. Some histories may be more highly developed and explicated than others, some long and some short, but all cultures and subcultures have continuity in time. To have a history means that the events that constitute this history are defined in terms of people, places, things, and times. Often these events have significance to the culture of which they are part but not to other cultures. More to the point, an event that is significant to a particular subculture may go largely unnoticed by the larger, surrounding culture. In other words, *cultures and subcultures have a host of events—including people, places, things, and times—that largely attain significance only within that culture or subculture.* These events, people, places, things, and times have symbolic referents (names) quite aside from any nonexternally grounded attempt to create a "secret code." For example, several years ago there existed in Atlanta a gay bar known as Bayou Landing. The surrounding straight culture was largely unaware of the bar, but it was known by virtually every active gay male in the Southeast. Thus, using Hayes' scenario, two strange men at a straight social gathering, after the preliminary nonverbals, might engage in some conversation. The discussion would be directed to Atlanta (considered a gay city), further to places to go there ("Oh, really? Where do you go when you're there?"), and finally, someone would drop the name Bayou Landing. Appropriate recognition of the name serves to fill all the functions Hayes describes.[7]

The same kind of interaction could take place with events (the Stonewall rebellion), people (a local gay person, a national figure like Franklin Kameny, or a literary figure like Christopher Isherwood), literary works (*Teleny, City of Night*), gay publications (*The Advocate, Christopher Street*), or places (San Francisco, Polk Street, The Gold Coast). Hayes' citation of certain cult heroes and heroines is a further example of this.[8] Mae West may be part of the subculture because she wrote plays with lesbian themes[9] as much as for any exaggeration of "the various stereotyped roles that women play in general society."[10] Bette Midler started her career in the gay baths of New York and became a gay idol. Montgomery Clift owes much of his gay following to gay identification with his own homosexual torment, and Tennessee Williams' plays have a loyal gay audience, partially because of Williams' own homosexuality and his use of homosexual themes.[11] Sometimes heroes and heroines are part of the gay subculture because of a real or believed participation in this subculture's history.

This cultural view of Gayspeak grants it new dimensions for which Hayes cannot account. The difference in origin between what Hayes presents as a code expressly created for limited communication, and what I have presented as a code growing out of a history with significance limited only to an in-group might be expected to create differences in function as well.

In the secret setting, for example, Hayes sees Gayspeak limited almost in contradiction to his definition and certainly more limited than the historical/cultural view would dictate. The question Hayes presents —"May I use Gayspeak in his presence?"[12]—is never really raised. If, by its nature, Gayspeak "allows people to hint at their sexual orientation, but never in a way which jeopardizes their ability to pass,"[13] the question Hayes presents is not really important. A better way to conceptualize it is the question "Would it be profitable (friendship, sexual encounter, etc.) for me to use Gayspeak in his presence?"

In the social setting none of the questions Hayes presents in the secret setting are relevant. All these questions are tacitly answered by participation in the group. The situation is no longer one of being identified, resolving doubts, and making contact. Social-setting Gayspeak, then, serves a distinctly different function than does secret-setting Gayspeak.

Small-group theorists give insight into the function of social-setting Gayspeak in talking about the social rewards of groups.[14] Extending this notion of rewards, one can begin to understand why a heavily stigmatized group would create social climates that build a defense against the attacks of a larger, surrounding culture. In keeping with current sociological thought on the topic, *stigmatized groups socialize in an effort to create an alternative social reality to the one held by the oppressing society of which they are a part.*[15]

This effort manifests itself in social-setting Gayspeak through the use of camp. Hayes talks of camp in general terms. Vito Russo describes it particularly as it relates to and reflects the gay subculture:

> Since camp flourishes in urban cliques and is something of a secret code, it has become one of the mainstays of an almost ethnic humor which has been formed for defense purposes over the years. Because camp seeks to comfort and is largely a generous rather than a selfish feeling, it has also operated in a human sense, aiding people in forming images with which they feel comfortable in a hostile culture.[16]

Except for the appearance of certain words believed to be peculiar to the gay subculture (apparently because they describe acts or relationships largely restricted to that group), most of the characteristics Hayes ascribes to the social setting are more properly characteristic of camp. The sexism (use of *queen* and *she*), the exaggeration, the trivialization, and the self-deprecation are all qualities of camp.[17] This distinction is important, because camp is neither exclusive to the gay subculture[18] nor universal within that subculture.[19] Gayspeak in the social setting, then, may not be Gayspeak at all, but camp.

If the predominance of camp in the social setting grants insights into the function of social-setting Gayspeak, then the marked absence of camp in the radical-activist setting may indicate something about a difference in function. Russo says: "Camp, because it deals only frivolously with the roles we've been assigned and entails no criticism of them, is totally apolitical."[20] The exclusion of, even contempt of, camp in the radical-activist setting rests on this apolitical nature that is dysfunctional to the distinctly political function of the radical-activist.

> We perceive our oppression as a class struggle and our oppressor as white, middle-class, male-dominated, heterosexual society, which has relentlessly persecuted and murdered homosexuals and lesbians since the oppressor has had power.[21]

This excerpt from the introduction to "a collection of the experiences and philosophies of *radical* lesbians and homosexuals"[22] illustrates the radical-activist stance, which is anything but a frivolous treatment of the gay person's status in America. In fact, implicit in the radical-activist stance is a rejection of such an orientation, often accompanied by scorn for those who participate in the social setting.[23]

In a like manner the secret homosexual is the philosophic antithesis to the radical-activist. The idealized version of the radical-activist never worries about his ability to "pass." This type of behavior is injurious to one's goals.[24] With this orientation, use of a restricted language code—as Gayspeak is defined in both the secret and social settings—is philosophically repugnant and counterproductive. Wide-scale change in the sociopolitical sphere is not facilitated by communicating with only a few. An elaborate language code is necessary for effective sociopolitical dialectic. Thus, the Gayspeak of the radical-activist is not the Gayspeak of the social or the secret setting.

Perhaps the most important statement made by Hayes about the radical-activist Gayspeak is that it "is often indistinguishable from the rhetoric of the general counterculture."[25] This observation is further supported by a notion of an undifferentiated radical-revolutionary rhetoric developed in an article by James Chesebro, who specifically includes gay liberation in his study as an example of a cultural revolutionary group.[26]

Here Hayes falls prey to the same criticism raised in connection with the social setting. He is exploring a phenomenon that is not exclusively a product of the gay subculture, nor universal within that subculture. Perhaps his insights are more applicable to radical-revolutionary rhetoric than particularly to a type of Gayspeak. This argument gains impetus when one realizes that this mode of Gayspeak is so different from, and even critical of, other modes that it is doubtful they have anything in common, except the fact that all three are used by members of the gay subculture.

Substantively, then, Hayes has made a basic confusion between the generic and the idiographic. In an attempt to tell us something about the unique behaviors of the gay subculture, he has stumbled into larger areas of behavior with no compelling evidence that they are in any way uniquely employed by gay persons. Each of the three settings serves a different, sometimes antithetical function, and even on a linguistic level, Hayes fails to provide us with any words or word patterns that have a constant function and usage across settings which might indeed illuminate something uniquely and universally gay. Rather than a singular Gayspeak that appears in three settings, it seems that a more appropriate conception is Gayspeak_1, Gayspeak_2, and Gayspeak_3, the latter two being subsets of generic behaviors (linguistic and otherwise) known as camp and the rhetoric of the radical-revolutionary, respectively. An artificial association of the three results in a confusing picture of linguistic behavior in the gay subculture, with little clear indication of its importance and no clear directive as to where we go from here.

Future Directions for Gayspeak

The above analysis is not intended to minimize the contribution of Hayes' work. In fact, it may be seen as a tribute to the breadth of Hayes' work, since it seeks to reduce it to more manageable portions. Very little of the substance of Hayes' essay has been contested; it has only been put into a new framework.

Given this body of data as a starting point, where do we go from here? Those who are interested in using gays as data for more generic concerns might expand the notions of camp and radical-revolutionary rhetoric. Consciousness-raising is still another, quite new setting in which gays participate but which is also characteristic of women's and men's liberation.[27] Many fields have ignored the gay subculture as a valuable source of data. In an earlier paper, I commented on the paucity of articles in speech communication that acknowledge the existence of the gay community.[28] Those who are interested in pursuing the idiographic approach—creating a distinctive area of gay studies—will indirectly benefit from the encouragement of this generic work.

There are also immediate possibilities for those interested in the idiographic aspects of the gay community. As claimed earlier, this depends on isolating distinctive qualities of the gay subculture and looking for the effects of those qualities on behavior.

Both on the basis of the foregoing analysis and on outside documentation, the secret setting seems to be the area in which gay persons claim their greatest distinctiveness. The issue of identification never materializes for other similarly oppressed groups. Stuart Byron explicates the view that the "particular problem of homosexuality itself—the thing about the state of being gay which distinguishes it from other 'oppressed' conditions . . . is that one can hide one's minority group status: 'staying in the closet' is a phrase that has little application to women or blacks or chicanos."[29]

For students of language and communicative behavior such isolation suggests questions like the following: How does this ability (for anonymity) affect language use? Does "identification" create unique patterns of interpersonal satisfaction of following up a hunch, feeling of mutual membership in a clandestine community, sexual encounter), and if so, are they distinguishable from the interaction patterns?

The issue of concealed identity also raises a host of questions concerning different levels of membership and the effect of varying degrees of involvement with the subculture on interaction patterns. The gay community has a remarkable latitude in the degree to which its members identify themselves as such, ranging from the married businessman who stops off at a local tearoom on the way home from work and hustlers who just "let the 'Johns' do them" to the radical-activists who assert their sexuality as an integral part of themselves that cannot be compromised. Ironically, those who least identify themselves as members of the subculture are those most in need of some unique form of communication. Presenting oneself as gay (or at least as desirous of homosexual contact) is often a necessary prerequisite for identifying others as gay. Only when the conditions of wanting to identify (i.e., be identified) and not wishing to "jeopardize one's ability to pass" are simultaneously present is there a need for unique modes of interaction. The radical-activist and even many regular participants in the social setting are seldom confronted by both exigences at once.

One potentially fruitful line of pursuit would be the exploration of how nonverbal modes of communication supplement verbal modes, particularly in secret-setting identification rituals. Hayes represents the process linguistically through the following exchange:

> Mr. X: You certainly have on a colorful tie!
> Mr. Y: Yes, I really like gay apparel.[30]

The problem with this representation is that it lacks context; Hayes gives no hint that any but linguistic cues have been employed here. Martin Hoffman, however, describes something of the intricate, subtle nonverbal type of behavior that usually predetermines the safety and desirability of any further interaction:

> It is not true that the majority of homosexuals are recognizable on sight by the uninitiated. It is often true, however, that they can recognize each other. This is not because of any distinguishing physical characteristics, but, rather, because when cruising, they engage in behavioral gestures which immediately identify themselves to each other. A large part of cruising is done with the eyes, by means of searching looks of a prolonged nature and through the surveying of the other man's entire body.[31]

This emphasis is confirmed and extended to almost the level of mystique in a letter from a veteran of the gay community to one who was then a young initiate pondering the increasingly apparent ability to recognize and be recognized by other gay men:

> Well, let's take it from the top. First of all (this is going to be in very plain, subculture language), there is a definite difference in straight and gay males (as well as many females). I don't mean mannerisms. I mean things like attitudes, degree of sensitivity and awareness, perception, etc. This is, of course, not particularly logical nor rational, but is, nevertheless, my observation. These things are not visible or perceptible to the majority of straights. Of course, there are individuals (straight) who are trained by profession or are for some reason sensitive or perceptive enough (interest being stirred by some sort of contact previous) to "spot" gays (who don't necessarily have outward mannerisms). However, I maintain the old saying that "it takes one to know one." Tacky but true.[32]

The importance of the nonverbal is carried even further when one realizes the pervasiveness of object language cues in the gay subculture. Some of the artifact displays[33] are widely known even in the larger heterosexual community; pinky rings, for example, commonly make the wearer suspect. Gay persons have an elaborate set of object language symbols that not only indicate membership in the homosexual community, but also sexual preferences.[34] Wearing an exposed key chain is an old indicator of interest in S & M (sadism and masochism). A cowboy-type handkerchief (bandana) has also been used as an indicator of sexual preference. This is worn in the back pants pocket—one side for "active" and the other for "passive"—or around the neck—if one will "swing both ways." The color of the kerchief determines the type of sexual activity. What is significant about these object cues in relation to Hayes' essay is that they usually are the basis for and precede any verbal interaction. An excerpt from a short story written by a hustler illustrates the use of behavioral cues and object language:

> The newcomer was dressed the same as I was—black leather jacket, engineer's boots, and—this season's high fashion—light tight chino pants

> instead of Levis. The Chinos showed you off better if you had anything to show. He had no cap on and his black hair was tumbled. But somehow he didn't seem to me to be a hustler. He wore the "uniform" as if it were his working clothes, and his body sort of settled into it. With the hustlers and the leather crowd you could generally tell it was all a masquerade, a drag, a play-pretend dress-up costume party for itty-bitty boys, with everyone more or less self-conscious.
>
> I slid onto the empty bar-stool next to him. He turned and grinned.
>
> "Hi," he said.
>
> "Hiya," I said, gruff. You just didn't speak to strangers the way he had. You stared and sized 'em up first. This cat must have been real green.[35]

Although the above evidence is not intended to be conclusive, it does give some perspective within which the linguistic components can be viewed as part of a complex exchange. These examples also give some insight into the extra-linguistic behaviors that are peculiarly gay and will make potential researchers in gay studies aware of possibilities in these areas.[36]

Another area in which work obviously needs doing is nonmale, nonwhite gay communication. Homosexuality more thoroughly transcends other minority memberships than does any other identification: Blacks can be gay; Chicanos can be gay; Native Americans can be gay; women can be gay. In a sense it can be viewed as an additive process—e.g., a black female homosexual. Most of the work to date deals only with the white, male segment of the subculture. This essay exhibits the same male bias that Hayes notes in his essay.[37] Persons interested in gay studies need to overcome this bias and be aware of the interactions among subsections of a subculture. What unites them? How do traditional divisions on one level and common oppression on another affect interaction?

Related to this problem of minority membership is the lack of role models in the gay community. Unlike blacks, Chicanos, Native Americans, or women who have someone with whom they share their identity and oppression, gay persons generally do not have gay parents. In fact, they usually have no role models at all until they have managed to find their own way into the gay community. How does this affect language use and interaction patterns? In fact, how do people learn Gayspeak at all? With no role models until they have already penetrated the gay community to some extent, the process of acquisition is itself problematic. These are the kinds of questions and problems to which persons interested in promoting gay studies as an idiographic area of study must devote their attention.

Excitement, Shortsightedness, and a Trip Down the Rabbit Hole

In the above comments I have intended to suggest that gay studies must develop a clear understanding of its unique purpose—to inform us of gay persons qua gay persons. Every eleventh-grade poetry class studies Walt Whitman as a poet. But gay studies has the responsibility of studying Sappho, Whitman, Dickinson, Ginsberg, Auden, and so on as *gay* poets and the responsibility of establishing that there is validity in doing so, or there is no reason to use gayness as a division of study. The issue is, of course, larger than poetry.

The gay subculture provides an excellent example for the necessity of giving such an overview and outlining the research possibilities. With most communicative bodies, including that of the black rights and the women's liberation movements, the activity is aboveboard; it is there to be observed by anyone who cares to look. Not so with the gay subculture. Much of the significance of Hayes' remarks lies in the fact that the uninitiated may be involved in a gay exchange and never know it. This has a tremendous significance for future research unless we are to leave it all to those who already possess a familiarity with the cues and symbols, and hope that they also possess the training and methods.

Essentially, the problem I have raised here is one of definition. Especially for a young and burgeoning area, it is important for those developing the area to be somewhat introspective; to actively consider the area's purpose, substance, and province; to define. Earlier I said that my criticisms of Hayes' article would reflect most obviously the infant state of gay studies. I hope that it is now apparent why. Ethnic and minority studies are a relatively new idea. Psychologists hypothesize that such studies are a result of a newfound determination for gays to be themselves that they achieved through countless repetitions of "the gestalt prayer" as they negotiated the 60s. Now that gays have decided to be themselves and to be proud of who they are, they are desperately searching to find out who they are and what it is they are proud of. In the 80s they are all looking for their roots.

Gay studies is the newest of the new. As an inaugural venture, Joseph Hayes has provided a great service by supplying future scholars with a wealth of data that requires further exploration and, more than that, by providing a backdrop against which gay studies can begin to find itself. He has given gay persons that grand survey of country they must travel through which Alice sought by standing on her tiptoes. But just as Alice's broad survey failed to provide an understanding of the forest, where even names were lost, or of the shop, which eventually faded into a rowboat, a closer examination of Hayes' broad view reveals that things are not always what they seem at first glance. Although it is vitally important to keep gay studies grounded in phenomena, it is also important in gay studies to be reflective. Without such an examination gay men and lesbians may find themselves calling hills valleys and doing all the running they can do just to stay in the same place.[38]

Chapter 6

Recognition Among Lesbians in Straight Settings

Dorothy S. Painter

When first pursuing systematic knowledge concerning a lesbian speech community, a number of years ago, I was asked *how* lesbians identify one another in nonlesbian settings.[1] My immediate response was, "I don't know." It is not that I did not know because I lacked insight into the phenomenon; it was that *knowing* and *seeing* were not explicable interpretive procedures. Three key informants and approximately fifteen other lesbians were asked about identification; in all cases the answer was, "I don't know." One of the informants explained, "I don't know how I do it. I just know, that's all." The answer did not seem to lie in a practiced and learned set of systematic cues, but rather in a combination of factors.

The purpose of this essay, then, is to examine from a theoretical perspective how lesbians identify one another in straight settings. Identifying others as lesbians is chosen as a subject for study inasmuch as it is a highly complex communicative and interpretive activity. As such, through investigation, insight into a common, everyday activity can be found. Besides providing insight into how lesbians accomplish peer identification, it is felt that in a more general and theoretical sense this essay provides groundwork concerning how inexplicable types of identification are done by all persons, gay and straight.

At first glance the organizational framework of this piece seems neither logical nor linear. The organization is one of an internal logic-in-use from a member perspective in that interpretive procedures and external cues are presented in the order they are necessary for a member of the lesbian speech community to identify others as lesbians. The first section, incorrigible propositions, is a discussion of those underlying instances of lesbian social knowledge that are not questioned or questionable by lesbians concerning the ability to do identification. Lesbians can identify one another because *they believe* they can identify one another.

The questions at the ends of the sections work to show how identification cannot be explained using only information from that section, and how numerous features of the interpretive process are dependent on one another for identification to occur.

The second section, nonverbal and verbal cues, allows one to experience some of the subtle cues that are occasionally present to aid the lesbian doing identification. However, for many of the cues to be heard as "proof" of lesbianism, the identifier must already possess an internal sense that the speaker may be a lesbian.

The third section, "a sense of the familiar," explicates the theoretical stance that may explain the internal sense that one is a lesbian. Theoretically, it is argued that members of hidden groups become attuned to one another and are capable of identifying others who are like or similar to themselves.[2] Finally, it is suggested that much identification is accomplished by the omission of cues usually expected to be present, not by reading cues that are present.

The process engaged in by lesbians to identify one another in straight settings can be viewed as an interpretive procedure. For identification to occur, the following conditions are necessary:

1. One must believe unquestionably that identification is possible.
2. Either cues must exist that can be interpreted as evidence to support the identification, or cues that would normally be interpreted to deny the identification must be missing.
3. One must possess an intuitive sense or feeling of familiarity concerning the individual that works reflexively to provide a context in which the cues may be interpreted.

Before examining lesbian identification procedures in straight settings, it should be understood that existing outside the lesbian community compels the lesbian to engage in and be aware of numerous complex communicative procedures. Studies that discuss how lesbians exist in straight social settings usually focus on the difficult and complex process of "passing."[3] Passing is a necessary way of life for the majority of lesbians if they are to hide their true identity from the straight majority. However, passing can lead to a sense of isolation. The primary reason for lesbians to engage in identifying work is to lessen their sense of isolation by being able to "see" others like themselves. One lesbian explained, "Just knowing that there are others (lesbians) out there makes me feel more in touch with the world."

Lesbians *must* engage in interpretive work outside the lesbian community if they are to be able to see and identify other women as lesbians.

Lesbians' ability to pass as straight makes lesbian identification by lesbians more difficult than it would be if passing was not necessary. Lesbians must be able to identify others as lesbians while the women are working to pass as straight. The ability to see others as lesbian does not mean that the other passing lesbians are not skillful passers. They are. The passing lesbians' ability to skillfully pass is constituted by the inability of straights to identify them as lesbians. To exist in the straight community lesbians must be bicultural and bidialectal. They must be able to speak, act, and interpret as straight to pass; at the same time they must use lesbian social knowledge to interpret and identify others as lesbians.

Incorrigible Propositions[4]

Before one can begin displaying the interpretive work done through incorrigible propositions or the interpretive work necessary to constitute incorrigible propositions, some discussion concerning awareness and perception is requisite. The adage "things are as we perceive them" when heard as "things are as we talk about them" helps to explain a verbally reflexive view of social reality.[5] Since occurrences are reflected on, interpreted using group (lesbian) social knowledge, and then talked *about,* they become *real* through the talk, not through their happening. In this way a woman does not "become" a lesbian through some specific act, but through how that act or set of acts are talked about and interpreted using the social knowledge of the community. This type of self-perception, or awareness, is the first, crucial step that the potential lesbian takes in the process of becoming. If one must be aware to begin the process of becoming, awareness—by definition—is the first instance of lesbian social knowledge that is an incorrigible proposition members share.

Awareness can be viewed as the most crucial and first bit of lesbian social knowledge that is required, and often sufficient, for a woman to switch from being a potential lesbian to becoming a lesbian. It is the natural starting point for becoming, because one cannot become that of which she is not aware. Consequently, a potential lesbian cannot become a lesbian until she becomes aware of a possible lesbian reality for herself.

Awareness can be viewed as an example of Harold Garfinkel's consistency proposition. Garfinkel states, A is always A, although it can be mistaken for B.[6] When a lesbian (A) mistakes herself for a nonlesbian (B), this mistake occurs because she is unaware of her A-ness. Awareness is crucial for viewing oneself as a lesbian, because members view a lesbian as having *always* been a lesbian, although some time may have existed when the lesbian was not aware of her lesbianism.

Examples that conversationally show the importance of the incorrigible proposition of awareness can be found in much lesbian talk. One woman describing a friend stated, "She's gay, but she doesn't know it yet."

A lack of awareness concerning one's true sexual orientation is applied not only to others, but also to aware lesbians to explain the time before they came out. The following example is representative of such talk. A member is speaking: "I went to Middle State University for four years. It was OK, I guess, but I sure wish I'd known that I liked women then. (*Pause*) What a waste of four years." Of primary interest is the way events are talked about reflexively. The speaker does not say (nor have I heard any lesbian say), "I wish I would have been a lesbian then." In every instance the speaker refers to the time before she *knew* she was gay. Consequently, turning back to Garfinkel's consistency proposition, a lesbian is reflexively viewed as having always been a lesbian. But at some time she may have mistaken herself for a straight woman. Time when she was "mistaken" about her sexuality is viewed as time before she became *aware* of her lesbianism.

The concept of awareness explains how one can be viewed as a potential lesbian and/or speech community member. Members view potentials as lesbians who are not aware of their own lesbianism. Lacking awareness explains why some lesbians come out relatively late in their lives, often after having a straight marriage and children. Straight women do not "become" lesbians; lesbians who are living straight life-styles realize they are lesbians and come out.

The shared social knowledge of awareness within the community is used to explain events differently from the way these events are explained from a straight perspective. Members believe straights think lesbians recruit straight women and persuade them to become lesbians. The idea of persuasion conflicts with the social knowledge shared by members. Based on lesbian social knowledge, members know that straight women are and have always been straight; lesbians are and have always been lesbians. When one appears to change, one has become aware. All the awareness, however, is done reflexively. Since all awareness is accomplished reflexively, "what" happened in a woman's past is of secondary importance to "how" it is talked about. Through the reflexive sense-making process, lesbian talk can be used to constitute a sense of shared past experience among members and to reinforce shared lesbian social knowledge.

Awareness is necessary to support the lesbian social knowledge that states members can recognize other lesbians outside the community. Although members claim almost 100 percent accuracy, when asked how recognition is done, the most common answer is, "I don't know." When confronted with the idea that the woman the member "sees" as lesbian may not view herself as lesbian, one member stated, "Just because she doesn't know it, doesn't mean I don't know it." The member who views a woman outside the community as lesbian can believe the view correct because of the importance of awareness. Awareness is viewed as complex; consequently, failures may be viewed by members as reinforcements of the complexity. Identifying lesbians outside the community seldom results in failure, because the identified women cannot usually be asked about their sexuality. One member explained:

> Can you imagine walking up to someone and saying, "Ah, pardon me, but I just noticed you're a lesbian?" People would flip out; so many of them are in the closet. I mean, the worst that could happen is that I find out they're married or something. Then I know they just don't know. You know, most of them gotta be gay.

The shared social knowledge of awareness works as a self-fulfilling prophecy of lesbianism. If the identified woman is later seen within the community, the member can claim she knew all along. If the woman is later seen living what is perceived to be a straight life-style, the woman is not aware. The member is always correct, and this gives her a sense of superiority over straights and potential lesbians. Both successes and failures can be interpreted by members as evidence of the importance of awareness, since even potential lesbians cannot "see" their own lesbianism until they become aware. All lesbians are, by definition, aware; they can talk about some period of time before they came out and share a similar social knowledge of this experience. Members believe in awareness because they can give accounts of the time before they came out in terms of awareness and its importance. A member clarified the importance of awareness by stating, "Sure I was gay; I was just too dumb to know it."

In conclusion, lesbians see others as lesbians because they believe that they *can* see others as lesbians. Lesbian social knowledge is used to interpret verbal and nonverbal behavior such that the reality of one's lesbianism is not tied to external acts, but instead to the unquestioned and unquestionable propositions of the community itself. The woman, whether she perceives herself as a lesbian or not, is verbally constituted as a lesbian through the indexical use of members' talk. This theory leaves one important question unanswered, however. Why are some women perceived to be lesbians while others are not? That is, why are some women perceived and made sense of differently than others?

Nonverbal and Verbal Cues

This section could provide the most concrete identification if the above questions were answerable. It might be possible to explicate subtle differences in voice tone, posture, kinetics, eye contact, and proximics (to name a few characteristics) if one were to videotape a number of gay and straight women and then to play back these tapes in slow motion again and again, coding them in a blind study. All this seems to be too much trouble for the little information it might yield, considering all the other confounding factors that one could not control.[7] Working to identify small "twitches" on tape is particularly useless to this discussion, since the lesbian, in her everyday life, does not use sophisticated, mechanical techniques and must rely on brief, often momentary scans of the environment for information to process.

The crucial phrase in the above paragraph is "*if* the above questions were answerable," because for the lesbian in her everyday life they are not. Lesbians do not possess a repertory of verbal and nonverbal cues they can explicate or knowingly use to interpret lesbianism. Consequently, coding movement on tape is a meaningless activity, since the purpose of this essay is to discuss how lesbian identification is achieved from a lesbian perspective.

What lesbians do possess is an intuitive sense or feel concerning who is and who is not a lesbian. This is not to imply that lesbians do not occasionally send out or interpret direct cues as a means of signaling or making sense of one's lesbianism. Using direct verbal and nonverbal cues to do being a lesbian, however, is not identifying work; it is producing an acceptable account of one's lesbianism. Ways of doing these accounts are briefly discussed, not because they are a primary means of doing identification, but because they are a means of checking out one's intuitive sense of another's lesbianism.

Checking out one's intuitive identifying work may be accomplished by reading other women's prolonged eye contact or by hearing a key word used in conversation to identify lesbians. One key word is the name of the bar where the fieldwork was conducted. The informal name of the bar is also a man's name. Consequently, a member can use the name conversationally, *as if* it is the name of a person. If a woman present is a member and wants another woman to know she is a member, she can respond to the *name* by smiling, saying, "Yes, I've been there" or "We have a friend in common." These phrases are not the only ones that can be used; anything is appropriate as long as the message is: "I know what you are talking about, and I want you to know that I know."

Members use the words "the bar" during conversation as a way of identifying members. "The bar" is heard as "Harry's," the lesbian bar. "The bar" frequently is offered by members as an answer to the question, "Where do I know you from?" If the woman who asked the question is a member, the question can be heard as, "Are you a member?" The answer "the bar" is a yes answer. If a nonmember hears the answer "the bar" and asks for clarification, the member can easily provide a plausible-sounding answer, such as, "I met some new people in a bar the other night, and I really thought she was one of them." Consequently, the identifying question/answer pair can be used with minimal risk of being identified as lesbians by nonmembers. Social knowledge necessary for identification is member knowledge and is lesbian speech community specific.

Another verbal cue to one's lesbianism is the use of nonspecific gender reference. The words person, friend, and they, when a singular individual is being discussed, are used to avoid direct reference to gender. For example, when asked what she did on a given night, a lesbian might respond: "I went to a movie with a friend." The following question/answer pair might occur between a mother and her unknown lesbian daughter.

Mother: Have you been going out much?

Daughter: Well, I have been seeing this one person.

In this case, the use of the word person is not an attempt to cue mother to daughter's lesbianism. It is an attempt to pass.[8] The lack of gender reference in gay persons' speech, however, is so common that another gay individual would hear the daughter's answer as an indicator of lesbianism.

Another study also examines gay talk as it is used by gay persons to accomplish identification (see chapter 4).[9] In "Gayspeak" (chapter 4), Joseph Hayes presents as an example of a sharing of identity through talk an exchange between two men in a straight social setting:

> Mr. X: You certainly have on a colorful tie.
> Mr. Y: Yes, I really like gay apparel.[10]

Since most of my research has been conducted in a lesbian speech community, I do not claim to possess expertise concerning the talk of gay men. However, given that the use of the term gay has been widely publicized in the media in recent years, it is doubtful that the above dialogue could now occur, not because it would not identify one as gay, but because it would not allow one to pass. The importance of doing confirmation of identity through talk with other gay individuals is that the talk functions to constitute the individual as gay *only* to other gay persons, while permitting one to pass as straight among straight persons.

Nonverbal cues are more difficult to discuss as indicators, given that they are open to a wider range of interpretations than verbal messages. The primary problem for assessing the use of nonverbals is that, although I believe nonverbals comprise the majority of communicative cues used to determine lesbian identity, they cannot be listed and named. The brief shifts of body and facial movement that serve as guides for seeing lesbianism are perceived and interpreted by lesbians *intuitively*. When a lesbian sees a woman who exhibits such cues, she does not check off lesbian characteristics, add them together, and see if the total is high enough to warrant the mental interpretation of "lesbian." The lesbian sees another woman and simply thinks, "Lesbian."[11]

When a number of lesbian members were pressed to explicate a list of nonverbals that lesbians exhibit, the initial response was reported as confusion, which was followed by a reported period of frustration. Comments during the first stage included:

"I don't know."

"I just see it; I don't think about it."

"You know, I've thought about it a lot. I really wonder. (*pause*) But I don't know."

Later answers include:

"Well, I don't know. (*pause*) There's something about the eyes."
Question: "What if you can't see their eyes?"
(*almost shouting*) "I don't know. I just *know*!"

"They just *look* like dykes."[12]
Question: "How do dykes look?"
"Like me!"

As seen from the above conversations, little information can be gained from asking lesbians directly how they "see" other lesbians in straight settings. It is not felt that they were withholding information, since many of these women had answered other questions concerning themselves, their relationships, and their life-styles. In addition, all the women knew I could also identify lesbians in straight settings. In summation, lesbian social knowledge does not provide specific answers to the above questions. To be a lesbian, one must be capable of seeing and identifying other lesbians in straight settings, not explicating the procedures for doing so.

A Sense of the Familiar

So far throughout this discussion what has been displayed is that lesbians see other lesbians intuitively. Intuitive knowing differs from other types of knowing and seeing, which accomplish identifying work inasmuch as features *cannot* be explicated. Intuitive knowing is not the type of interpretative work that is used in much everyday identifying work. For example, if asked how one identifies a piece of furniture as a chair, individuals could explicate at least some of the characteristics of chair-ness, even though they do not usually need to do so to see a chair as a chair. In addition, although chairs share a number of common features with tables (four legs, a flat surface parallel to the floor), chairs and tables are rarely confused with each other. As women who are perceived as lesbian and are then seen to be living a straight life-style are still perceived as lesbians, tables that people sit at are still perceived as tables.

One crucial difference exists, however, between those things that are identified through interpretation of nameable features as opposed to unnameable features. Nameable features are subject to reexamination and reidentification. That is, if a piece of furniture is initially identified as a table and is later seen being used as a chair, the individual has the option of reinterpreting it as a chair. This reidentification is not possible with unnameable features, inasmuch as the features (data, evidence) cannot be reexamined. The only way a woman initially identified as a lesbian can be viewed as a nonlesbian is for the identifying lesbian to say, "I was wrong." As the section on incorrigible propositions shows, this is rarely, if ever, done due to the unquestioned and unquestionable proposition that lesbians can identify other lesbians.

Understanding that lesbians identify one another in straight settings through the interpretation of unnameable features, the question remains, "*How* is the identification accomplished such that the observed woman is constituted as a lesbian?" It should be noted that the identifier's contact with the perceived lesbian may be minimal. "Contact" may include having a brief conversation with the woman, meeting her in a public place and exchanging a few words, seeing her sitting in a lobby as one walks by, passing her on the street and exchanging no words, seeing her waiting for a bus from a distance of a half block or more, seeing her picture in the newspaper, or hearing her voice on tape or on the telephone. In such cases the lesbian does (and can) identify *some* women as lesbians.

The intuitive sense that lesbians use to identify one another can be described as a sense of the familiar. By a sense of the familiar I mean that even though specific features cannot be named, the lesbian perceives an element of sameness that might be verbalized as "she's like me." More specifically, a sense of the familiar is more personal than, but in some ways similar to, typifications.[13] Concerning the typification of objects, Alfred Schutz writes:

> What is newly experienced is already known in the sense that it recalls similar or equal things formally perceived. But what has been grasped once in its typicality carries with it a horizon of possible experience with corresponding references to familiarity, that is, a series of typical characteristics still not actually experienced but expected to be potentially experienced.[14]

Schutz continues with an example of seeing a dog. Although this particular dog may not have been seen before, it possesses a number of features that typify it as belonging to the class of similar objects known as dog. Moreover, all the features that contribute to dog-ness need not be perceived for their typicality to be experienced. The unseen features are assumed to exist such that they "show the same typical features though with individual modifications."[15]

It is the et cetera filling in of unseen features that a sense of the familiar shares with the idea of typifications. Features that are not seen are known to exist, inasmuch as they are necessary features for seeing an object as being of a particular type. Features that are not seen and do not necessarily contribute to the identification of the type are not considered. This explains why even though some dogs have long ears, not every dog must have long ears to be identified as a dog, and every animal that has long ears is not identified as a dog. Similarly, although many lesbians have short hair, one need not have short hair to be identified as a lesbian, and all women with short hair are not identified as lesbians.

The crucial difference between typifications and a sense of the familiar is that despite the fact features are not normally named to typify an object, they can be named if a particular situation necessitates it. This might occur on a dark night when one sees movement in one's backyard. If the object is identified as an animal, and it is small and covered with fur or hair, specific features are searched for in an attempt to determine if it is the neighbor's cat, a stray dog, a wandering raccoon, a large rat, or another identifiable animal. It is the ability to name and identify specific features that distinguishes typifications from a sense of the familiar. Naming features and types is based on their immediate sense of relevance. Schutz states:

> It is always the system of relevance that chooses from the vocabulary of my vernacular (and also from its syntactical structure) the relevant term, and that term is the typical pre-experienced generalization interesting me (or my interlocutor) in the present situation.[16]

The inability to name features in intuitive knowing, or in experiencing a sense of the familiar, does not lessen the importance of relevance. Contrarily, for features to be intuitively perceived, they must be highly relevant to the individual. Not only must they be relevant, but also necessary for the identifying interpretation to occur. Specific, although unnameable, features are perceived and interpreted by lesbians because it is relevant and necessary for lesbians to be able to identify one another. These features are not perceived or interpreted as indicators of lesbianism by straight women, because identifying lesbians is not relevant or necessary for them.

Another way to discuss the use of unnameable features is to consider the process as membership categorization for verbal typifications for which the devices cannot be named.[17] Using this perspective, when a woman is seen by a lesbian, pertinent features are considered in conjunction with the context of the perception to determine her relationship to other known members of specific categories, one of which is lesbian.

A woman may be viewed as a member of more than one category, such as teacher, mother, volunteer campaign worker, and lesbian. Straight women could see the perceived individual as belonging to any category except lesbian, and in doing so would rely on past knowledge about the individual or typifications to do so. Lesbians could also rely on past social knowledge or typifications to identify the individual as a member of one of these categories. Lesbians also possess the interpretive ability to *sense* that the woman is a lesbian. Further, it is suggested that other teachers might be capable of sensing a familiarity about the woman that would lead to an intuitive identification of her as a teacher, without dependence on typifications or past social knowledge. The same may be true for other mothers and campaign workers. The primary difference, however, is that being a teacher, mother, or campaign worker is not normally viewed as deviant and therefore does not need to be hidden. Consequently, although members of specific groups may be capable of intuitively identifying one another, it is not *necessary* that they be able to do so, inasmuch as category membership is not hidden.

What is being suggested is that through a highly selective and discreet learning process, members of specific, often hidden, groups learn to identify one another as members, not based on nameable features, but instead by being attuned to the familiar and the unfamiliar. Just as a tree, when viewed on two different days, is not the same tree, due to the process nature of existence, so too a lesbian is not the same lesbian when perceived on two different occasions. Furthermore, two different lesbians may be viewed as *the same lesbian* on separate occasions, when individual differences are not taken into account and the primary focus of one's interpretive work is on the identification of members of the lesbian category.

This attunement may work to explain how undercover police officers often can identify one another even when the individuals are not known to one another. As one officer commented, "I don't know what's different about them; I can just 'make' (identify) another cop." Another example may help to display how sensing the familiar intuitively operates among members of categories other than lesbian. Lesbians are perceived as having qualities of lesbian-ness, just as religious sisters and priests have qualities of religious-ness. A friend who is a religious sister told me that when she presents a paper on a religious topic at a convention, she always scans the audience for other religious. Since I had attended several of these programs, I realized that the religious did not wear religious habits or other typically identifying clothing that could serve as obvious cues. When I asked why she did the identifying work, she said that other religious knew more about what she was talking about than other audience members, and they made her nervous. Accepting that she engaged in this identifying work for a presumed need, I asked how she identifies them. She said, "I don't know. I just can. My last audience had two sisters, a priest, and a possible priest." The word possible works to show that the identification of the two sisters and the priest was not questioned (or perhaps questionable). The idea of a possible priest may be similar to a potential lesbian, or a lesbian who is in the process of coming out or is not aware of her own lesbianism.

If reports from informants are accurate, being attuned to sensing familiarity in particular individuals involves seeing not only what is there, but also what is not present but usually would be assumed to be present. Among women this may entail "normal" forms of social posturing used to attract males. That is, the lesbian, who does not engage in subtle verbal and nonverbal patterns in straight settings to attract members of the opposite sex, notices or identifies other women who are also not engaging in these types of behaviors. Being cued by what is missing or how the woman is *not acting* would help to explain why lesbians have difficulty when attempting to name interpretive cues. The cues may be cues of omission. Although sufficient data are not available to adequately support the concept of lesbian identification through omission of behavior and features, two lesbians have stated that the only women they confuse with lesbians are religious sisters. A lack of engagement in social behavior to attract males is the primary similarity between these two groups.

The lesbian who is passing as straight in the straight community can be viewed as attempting to hide her lesbianism by not acting and talking as a lesbian. However, she may not work to present herself as straight in terms of performing typical straight female behavior. Lack of behavior is nonspecific enough to pass unnoticed and unnamed by straight individuals. Among lesbians it may be unnamed and unnameable, but it is not unnoticed.

Discussion

How one begins to study and interpret features that exist only through their omission is an area worthy of thought. It may work to help explain diverse concepts such as love at first sight, instantly and definitely sensing a strong like or dislike or trust for some individuals, and being able to sense friends and enemies. An intuitive sense of identification is useful and practical. During times when some individuals could be viewed as dangerous to one's well-being (because they carried clubs or sharp sticks), possessing a well-developed intuitive sense of "our group versus their group" could underlie one's ability to survive (and pass along this trait to the next generation). The ability to "go with the gut" and not contemplate may exist in all individuals. It may simply be embedded so deeply in one's deep structure that one cannot do enough of an infinite regress to get back to one's basic interpretive procedures. One is left knowing that one sees *it* but not knowing *what* one sees or *how* one sees it. Through a sense of the familiar, one glimpses a sense of what one is, and an invisible bond is formed that reaches out and allows one to re-member oneself through another.

Chapter 7

Communication Patterns in Established Lesbian Relationships

Connie L. Day and Ben W. Morse

Relationships between persons are formed daily. Many such relationships are temporary and short-lived, while others are marked by some degree of permanency or even marriage. In the latter instance it is usually the case that man and woman meet and form a relationship. Such is *not* the case for relationships formed by a small, yet significant, percentage of our population. The Institute of Sex Research estimates that homosexuals constitute 10 percent of the U.S. population.[1] As with heterosexual couples, homosexual couples establish and utilize rules and procedures to help pattern their relationships.[2] Communication acts that define a relationship are termed the relational dimension of the message.[3] That is, messages contain not only information, but impose behavior and define the relationship. That aspect of the message which defines or redefines the relationship has been titled relational communication.[4] While much of the work in relational communication stems from marriage research, one study contends that it is useful to consider relational control messages in nontraditional pairs.[5] The purpose of this study was to examine the relational control postures of lesbian dyads.

Rationale

Relational communication refers to that aspect of a message which defines a relationship. Important aspects in relational communication theory are complementarity, symmetry, and transitory. These pertain to whether both members of the dyad are competing for control of the relationship, whether one gives the control that another seeks, or whether one party of the relationship is not trying to define the relationship.

A message may suggest one of three relational control alternatives: (1) "one-up" messages assert dominance, (2) "one-down" messages signal acceptance or submission, and (3) messages that avoid acceptance or assertion of dominance are "one-across." All relational messages provide a barometer of how control of the relationship progresses from moment to moment. M. Parks extends this analysis when he suggests, "Relational definitions . . . are not the products of single individuals."[6] Rather, how one defines the relationship is contingent on the partner's definition of the relationship. Thus, at the dyadic level of exchange the three message types form a 3 x 3 matrix.[7]

This matrix shows three types of symmetry, two types of complementarity, and four types of transitory. Complementary statements are either one-up/one-down or one-down/one-up message pairs. These are presented in the middle cell of the first column and in the top cell of the second column. In complementary messages, differences between members of the dyads are maximized.[8] It is important to note, however, complementary relationships are not necessarily unbalanced in the sense that one member of the dyad is forced into submission. While the relationship may appear unequal, control of the relationship is usually given up rather than usurped.

		Person 1		
		One-up	One-down	One-across
Person 2	One-up	Competitive symmetry	Complementarity: tending toward one-up	Transitory: neutralized control to dominance
	One-down	Complementarity: tending toward one-down	Submissive symmetry	Transitory: neutralized control to submission
	One-across	Transitory: dominance to neutralized control	Transitory: submission to neutralized control	Neutralized symmetry

Matrix of Relational Communication System States

Symmetry has generally been viewed as competitive. It has been pointed out that members of a dyad struggle for control over the ability to define the relationship.[9] But it is possible that a dyad consists of two individuals who are both trying to force the other to define the relationship. Interactions that are symmetrical are one-up/one-up, one-down/one-down, and one-across/one-across. In the matrix these cells form the diagonal from top left to bottom right.

Transitory exchanges are those found in the bottom cells of the first two columns and the top two cells of the last column of the matrix. Simply stated, transitory exchanges are neither symmetrical nor complementary. Rather, transitory exchanges represent a time during which at least one member of the dyad is not trying to define the relationship. The term transitory suggests that dyads in such a state are in the process of moving from one steady state to another. In relational communication such is not the case. It has been demonstrated that the transitory state can be an end state.[10] The term does not describe the nature of the state, but the question of relational definition for at least one member of the dyad. For the member emitting one-across messages, the question of relational definition is neutral, and the state is one of neutralized control to dominance, neutralized control to submission, submission to neutralized control, or dominance to neutralized control. Similarly, the term neutralized symmetry refers to symmetry in name only. While neither member is concerned with the definition of the relationship and therefore emits messages that match each other, there is no struggle for control.

In summary, relational communication statements by individuals can be characterized as one-up, one-down, or one-across. When the relationship becomes the unit of analysis, nine system states are producted: (1) competitive symmetry, (2) complementarity—tending toward one-up, (3) transitory—neutralized control to dominance, (4) complementarity—tending toward one-down, (5) submissive symmetry, (6) transitory—neutralized control to submission, (7) transitory—dominance to neutralized control, (8) transitory—submission to neutralized control, and (9) neutralized symmetry.

Early characteristics of lesbians established a dichotomy which has permeated research—that of the butch who assumes the manly role and that of the femme who assumes the feminine or submissive role.[11] These characterizations not only perpetuate stereotypes of masculinity and femininity, but also suggest that lesbian couples mirror a butch-femme dichotomy. According to these stereotypic descriptions of mannish-type and feminine-type lesbians, it seems logical to conclude that the communication of members in a lesbian dyad would be one-up/one-down, thus characterizing complementarity.

But a controversy exists between research that support the butch-femme dichotomy and opinions of lesbians concerning role orientation. Based on their personal experiences and social experiments, D. Martin and P. Lyon, founders of the oldest lesbian organization in America (the Daughters of Bilitis), assert that the butch-femme dichotomy is a misconception.[12] They state that while the lesbian is believed to embody all the worst masculine attributes of toughness, aggressiveness, overemphasis on sex, and the need and desire to dress as a man, and lacks emotion, sentiment, and stability, this stereotype is incorrect. They posit that because of the absence of role models and because the traditional (husband/wife) marriage is endorsed by society, the young lesbian usually gets involved in the butch-femme syndrome at first but seldom continues searching for relationships which mirror that syndrome. They contend that a lasting, successful lesbian relationship cannot be based on society's exaggerated male-female, dominant-passive roles, as depicted in earlier writings. Rather, current, successful lesbian relationships mirror positions of equality.

In support of this contention, an experiment was conducted which revealed that "hardly a single myth about the stereotyped truck driver image, masculine ways or severe neuroses seemed to hold water."[13] Although lesbians scored more masculine in their interests on the Minnesota Multi-Personality Inventory (MMPI), researchers doubt that even this is a lesbian characteristic in these "days of shaken sex roles." It appears that all women are moving away from the traditional male/dominant, female/submissive social roles.

In 1974 D. Rosen reported that of twenty-six lesbians questioned, thirteen considered themselves both masculine and feminine.[14] On administering the Adjective Check List by Gough,[15] Rosen reported that adjectives such as adaptable, healthy, individualistic, and practical were among those checked most frequently by lesbians. These results clearly disconfirm the butch-femme dichotomy and support the belief that members of lesbian quasi-marital unions (LQMU) are more concerned with maintenance of individuality and relational equality than with who is in control.

Given the idea that masculine and feminine sex-role development progresses independently, researchers tested the incidences of sex-role outcome within homosexual and heterosexual adults using a four-fold typology of (1) both masculine and feminine (androgynous), (2) masculine, (3) feminine, and (4) undifferentiated (neither masculine nor feminine).[16] Results indicated a higher incidence of masculinity within the homosexual female group. However, although not significant, there was also a higher incidence of masculinity within the female heterosexual group in comparison to the three other categories of feminine, androgynous, and undifferentiated. Androgynous marked the second highest rate of incidence for lesbians, while heterosexual females were second highest in the undifferentiated category. Feminine marked the lowest incidence for both groups of women. This indicates that sex roles, as previously conceived, are disintegrating, with a trend toward masculinity. Perhaps more important is the high incidence of lesbian androgynous individuals. This also denies the previously dismissed stereotypic butch-femme dichotomy.

According to available data, a couple may learn to function at different points along the masculine-feminine continuum. As J. DeLora and C. Warren pointed out, several kinds of masculine-feminine role combinations may occur: neither partner may appear masculine, one partner may appear more masculine, or both partners may appear masculine.[17]

Another group of investigators found that in response to the question of whether the women's liberation movement had helped or hurt them, 80 percent of lesbians questioned agreed that it had helped.[18] They explained that for the first time women are being considered as persons, not as "mere appendages to men." The women's movement has had some impact on the breakdown of the butch-femme dichotomy. Why the change has occurred is not as important as the fact that it has occurred, and for lesbians entering quasi-marital unions, traditional and stereotyped role expectations are becoming obsolete. It follows from the previous section on relational control that redefined role expectations precipitate alteration in communication patterns. The butch-femme dichotomy strongly suggested relationships characterized by complementarity. However, current lesbian research suggest that role differentiation based on traditional and stereotyped masculinity and femininity is no longer a concern of lesbians.[19] The breakdown in role expectations and the nature of lesbian relationships imply that lesbians in quasi-marital unions will emit a greater volume of one-across messages. This will result in LQMUs being typified by the transitory state or neutralized symmetry. Accordingly, the following hypotheses were tested:

H_1: A significant portion of first-order LQMU exchanges will be transitory.

H_2: Among those first-order LQMU exchanges that are transitory, a significant portion will be neutralized symmetry.

H_3: A significant portion of second-order LQMU exchanges will be transitory.

H_4: Among those second-order LQMU exchanges that are transitory, a significant portion will be neutralized symmetry.

Research Method

This study solicited the help of ongoing lesbian dyads. Dyads varied in length of the relationship, reflected different professions, and represented diverse economic and social statuses. Twelve pairs were used in the study. The twenty-four participants ranged in age from late teen to midlife. Length of the relationship was based on length of cohabitation. A minimum of one year cohabitation was required for a couple to be included in this study. All subjects were from the greater Dayton and Cincinnati areas.[20]

Each LQMU dyad was asked to discuss one or two predetermined topics. One topic dealt with nuclear energy and the other addressed government spending.[21] Discussions were taped, transcribed, and coded. The relational coding procedure employed provided an index of the relational control posture of the pairs.[22] The relational coding procedure was three-fold: (1) messages were categorized by response made and grammatical format; (2) control directions were assigned to each message on the basis of format and response; and (3) control codes were combined to form exchange codes for sequentially ordered message pairs.[23]

A three-member panel coded the main study transcripts. Each coder was instructed according to prescribed procedures.[24] Then, coders were asked to code practice transcriptions. Percentages of agreement between coders were calculated. A reliability figure of .79 was attained.

All data were gathered by the experimenter in the pairs' homes. The general sequence of events was five-fold. First, the experimenter determined which of the two topics would be used during a warm-up discussion and which topic should be taped. Determination was made prior to entering a couple's home and via the toss of a coin. Second, dyads were asked to discuss one topic for approximately ten minutes. This warm-up exercise ensured that a conversational mode would be reached by the pair prior to the taped discussion. Third, the discussion topic to be taped was presented, and the couple was allowed ten minutes to talk. Simultaneously, the pair was instructed to include emotions, impressions, expectations, problems, and solutions in their discussion. A set of standardized probes was employed by the experimenter if the couple sought direction in the discussion or if fifteen seconds of silence elapsed. Fourth, the experimenter replayed the taped discussion and allowed the dyad the opportunity to request potentially revealing segments to be erased (no dyad requested erasure of any taped discussion segment). Fifth, the experimenter administered a self-report questionnaire to secure demographic data and thanked the pair for participation in the study.

Discussion and Heuristic Value

A Markov chain analysis was used to test the hypotheses.[25] Acceptance of H_1 indicated that members of the lesbian pairs emitted a significant portion of one-across messages in first-order exchanges that resulted in transitory system states.[26] As Parks stated, one-across messages are viewed as falling at the midrange of a dominance-submission dimension.[27] The transitory exchanges are neither complementary nor symmetrical in nature. In other words, the relationships of individuals who engage in transitory exchanges are not unbalanced in the sense that one member asserts control over the other. Nor is a struggle to define the relationship present. Acceptance of H_1 is incongruent with literature positing that butch-femme relationships are typical.[28] Butch-femme relationships have been characterized by one-up/one-down messages, resulting in complementarity. Clearly, this study demonstrated lesbian pairs are transitory.

Transitory relationships are those in which the question of relationship definition is neutral for at least one member of the relationship. Acceptance of H_1 is supportive of and congruent with later research,[29] which posited that butch-femme dichotomy is becoming obsolete.

Confirmation of H_2 further denies the credibility of viewing lesbian pairs from a butch-femme perspective.[30] A significant portion of messages emitted by the couples were found to reflect neutralized symmetry. Parks asserts that neutralized symmetry is a result of a dyad functioning within some mutually accepted norm or contract. Further, neutralized symmetry implies that one-across messages are being emitted by both members in a dyad, meaning that neither member is concerned with asserting control or defining the relationship. In short, lesbian pairs appear to be equalitarian rather than complementary or symmetrical.

H_3 and H_4 both deal with second-order exchanges. Examining second-order exchanges permitted the analysis of relationship posture as opposed to examining individual message types. This entailed dividing all discussions into groups of three interacts to determine if two messages could predict a third message.

Acceptance of H_3, that a significant portion of the couples' exchanges were transitory, illustrates that not only do LQMU members emit significant portions of one-across messages, but that the response to a one-across message is likely to be another one-across message. Again, this refutes the likelihood of lesbians emitting one-up/one-down messages.[31]

H_4, which proposes that a significant portion of lesbian pairs' exchanges would be neutralized symmetry, was confirmed.[32] Second-order neutralized symmetry existed when all three interacts in a three-message exchange were one-across. Acceptance of H_4 supports three assertions: (1) lesbian pairs emit a significant portion of one-across messages, (2) one-across messages are emitted in response to other one-across messages, and (3) the system state of neutralized symmetry extends to second-order exchanges.

Results lend support to the assertion that lesbian couples do not communicate in a one-up/one-down fashion which constitutes complementarity. Nor is there an obvious struggle for asserting control of the relationship definition. Rather, members communicate in a fashion characterizing neutralized symmetry. Seemingly, members experience relational equality in their communication exchanges.

This study demonstrates that lesbian communication patterns are characterized by transitory and neutralized symmetry. This appears to reflect the status of lesbian relationships as being equalitarian. Thus it may be that the model of relationship maintenance lesbians are practicing is one of equality. It does appear that they reject the traditional model of heterosexual marital unions.

Chapter 8

Gay Masculinity in the Gay Disco

James W. Chesebro and Kenneth L. Klenk

Being a man or being masculine is an issue for many males in our culture today, and gay males are no exception. Arthur M. Schlesinger, Jr. has aptly captured the issue:

> What has happened to the American male? For a long time he seemed utterly confident of his manhood, sure of his masculine role in society, easy and definite in his sense of sexual identity. . . . Today, however, men are more and more conscious of maleness not as a fact but as a problem. The ways in which American men affirm their masculinity are uncertain and obscure. There are multiple signs, indeed, that something has gone wrong with the American male's conception of himself.[1]

Schlesinger has concluded that the American male now faces a "crisis of masculinity."[2]

Masculinity is even more difficult to affirm if a male is identified as a homosexual, for several reasons. First, homosexuality frequently functions as an overwhelming stigma that diminishes the energy which might be devoted to the formation of a humane ethic of masculinity. As detailed in the Introduction, in a 1978 poll, for example, 70 percent of Americans believed that homosexual acts are "always wrong even if the individuals involved are in love."[3] Moreover, when specifically asked, of UCLA's entering freshmen in 1979, 39 percent of the females and 56 percent of the males believed that "homosexual relations should be prohibited."[4] In this regard, Americans typically believe that homosexuality can be eliminated by concerted social action. In a 1977 Gallup poll, for example, 56 percent of a random sample of Americans believed that "homosexuality is due to upbringing and environment."[5]

Not surprisingly, these negative conceptions have functioned as a self-definition for some homosexuals. For these persons, homosexuality is a stigma. The stigma can become overwhelming and totally consume efforts at self-definition. Erving Goffman has pointedly observed that the stigma of a sexual act may go far beyond the province of the act itself, and it is the stigma that becomes the " 'master status determining trait' that lies at the heart of a person's public and inner identity."[6] After interviewing 686 San Franciscan males in 1978, Alan P. Bell and Martin S. Weinberg reported that 80 percent of their respondents said they possessed a "relatively low" or "moderate" self-acceptance of their homosexuality.[7]

Recently, however, many males preferring same-sex relationships have rejected these societal definitions. Since the Stonewall riots in New York, in June 1969—which gave rise to the gay liberation movement—some gay males have claimed and sought to obtain societal support for an alternative conception of their identity and meanings associated with same-sex relationships. These individuals typically identify themselves as gay, assert a commitment to a gay ideology, and overtly espouse a sense of pride and power in being gay.[8] Indeed, when males identifying themselves as homosexuals have been distinguished from those viewing themselves as gay, Carmen De Monteflores and Stephen J. Schultz have reported (and G. Weinberg,[9] and Stephen F. Morin and S.J. Schultz[10] have concurred) that the homosexual male "internalizes negative stereotypes" while the gay male "rejects the negative societal stereotype associated with being homosexual" and defines himself as "healthy."[11]

Nonetheless, a healthy form of masculinity is particularly difficult for many homosexuals to affirm, because many homosexuals have yet to identify themselves with a gay orientation. An external definition of homosexuality as a stigma is internalized by these males; the internalization entails self-hate conceptions that overwhelm and reduce the attention which might be devoted to the development of healthy forms of male bonding and group self-definitions. Moreover, while a person's sexual orientation is logically independent of a person's sexuality, a homosexual preference is frequently associated with a particular mode of sexuality. Accordingly, the traditional John Wayne image associated with masculinity is culturally defined as inconsistent with the limp-wristed, lisping, hairdresser stereotype of the homosexual.

Second, masculinity is even more difficult to affirm if a male is identified as homosexual, because manliness has traditionally been defined by a male's sexual union with the opposite sex and, concomitantly, by division or separation from other males sexually. In this sense it is unbecoming a man, if not completely inconsistent—to claim to be a man and a homosexual simultaneously. In rather vivid personal terms Bruce Werner explains:

> When you go to bed with a person of the same sex, you take a giant step in total contradiction of everything you've been brought up to believe in. It flies in the face of every tacit truth that has been drilled into our heads from day

> one. To begin with, the entire concept of masculinity in the traditional sense comes into play. A man has to "make it" with a girl, with her on the bottom and him on top, drilling away, making her completely subservient to his will. She is "fulfilled." He "has his way" with her.
>
> If that man, instead, gets it on with another man, then both of them cannot "have their way." One is going to "lose." Even if one just goes down on the other, the one who simply stands or lays there may well question his masculinity. And if that guy responds in any way at all, he becomes an active participant, and "less than a man."[12]

Third, masculinity is extremely difficult for homosexuals to affirm, because being a man or being masculine traditionally involves particular forms of nongenital behavior that are antithetical to being gay. The idealized form of male sexuality, argues Alan E. Gross, has traditionally included "goals and success," "control and power," and "aggression and violence" as interrelated and defining themes of manliness.[13] These themes create a transcendent style or standard for behavior in male bonded groups. Robert A. Lewis describes this traditional mode:

> Although males report more same-sex friendships than women do, most of these are not close, intimate, or characterized by self-disclosure. Many barriers exist to emotional intimacy between men, some stemming from the demands of traditional male roles in our society, such as pressures to compete, homophobia, and aversion to vulnerability and openness, as well as from the lack of adequate role models.[14]

These traditional modes of nongenital masculine behavior constitute, especially, problematic norms for gay males. Same-sex relationships involve overt, intimate, and self-disclosing sexual acts, often including declarations of liking or loving. The requirements of the sexual act, then, function as one influence on the social atmosphere in gay environments. Traditional masculine themes—goals, success, control, power, aggression, and violence—are therefore inappropriate for gay relationships; nongenital demonstrations of affection are far more consistent with the sociosexual conditions established by gay relations. Traditional masculine themes of nonintimacy are accordingly rejected in gay relationships. It is in this context that Nick Benton has argued, "Our commonality is *not* homosexuality. Our only unity is the common, but deeply personal experience of resisting, usually in isolation and terror, the pressures of becoming a *man* from the ongoing society."[15] More universally, Bell and Weinberg report that the "stereotypically 'masculine' image" was sought by only "about one-quarter of the [686] respondents" they interviewed in San Francisco.[16]

Given these three conditions, a particularly unique environment seems necessary in which gay males might be able to develop a mode of masculinity specifically suited to the demands of their internal social system and yet responsive to heterosexual interactions. Such an environment apparently needs to be predominantly gay at this point in time to minimize the stigma associated with homosexuality. Moreover, such an environment apparently needs to be predominantly all male as well in order to minimize opposite-sex interactions as a central definition of masculinity. Finally, such an environment apparently needs to be predominantly social in order to minimize the competitive modes associated with traditional nongenital masculinity. The gay disco appears to meet these requirements. In this context it might also be noted that the gay disco is a profoundly rhetorical environment and is therefore theoretically capable of generating new life-style conceptions. Music and dance—the major environmental features of the disco—are themselves modes of communication. In addition, discos are social environments in which talk and the absence of talk also establish, mediate, and alter interpersonal relationships of all forms. The disco, as is true of bars or pubs in general,[17] functions as a major courting environment—courtship being a thoroughly verbal and nonverbal communicative activity. Finally, the gay disco is a relatively private symbolic enclave. While the literature of gay liberationists provided major reconceptions of same-sex relationships, these were predominantly public strategies designed to deal with the attitudes, beliefs, and actions of heterosexuals. Because this approach has been described in research literature (see chapters 4 and 15),[18] and because this political movement is no longer actively formulating or directing dimensions of gay life-styles, this essay focuses on the creation of a symbolic world view as it occurs in a natural or everyday communicative setting: the gay disco club.

Our investigation proceeds along two major lines. First, the ethnographic methods used in this study are identified, followed by a brief ethnographic sketch of the object of concern, the gay disco as a sociocommunicative environment. Second, the identity of gay males as men, as gay, and as members of a community is examined. Particularly, gay masculinity, as defined in the gay disco, has been selected as the central foundation for exploring these issues. Our intent is to capture the frame of reference of gay males in these discos as they perceive their sociocultural values and modes of interaction. However, we ultimately view this symbolic system as paradoxical. Not viewed as necessarily pathological or illogical, the notion of a paradoxical world view,[19] as maintained toward the close of this essay, is likely to be a useful concept for examining the symbol-using activities of a host of contemporary communication systems.

Ethnological Methods and the Gay Disco as an Ethnographic Communication System

Our research strategy has been variously labeled naturalistic, field, qualitative, ethnographic, and action research.[20] The objective of such examination is to analyze the symbolic parameters of an ethnographic unit as a system, while simultaneously preserving the meanings of a community as they are experienced by members of that community.[21] In such field studies data are not obtained in laboratories or by way of focused questionnaires, but are collected in the settings created and maintained by the community members being studied. Thus everyday communication[22] constitutes the substance for such a study, and every method of investigation should be intentionally designed to preserve the identity of the community by eliminating the reactive influences of the research design and its execution whenever possible.[23] In this study four unobtrusive and nonreactive field methods were employed: simple observation,[24] open-ended interviews,[25] participant-observation,[26] and content analysis.[27] There are reasons to believe that the use of these multiple measurement classes may generate reliable, valid, relevant, and significant data.[28]

The foundation for the patterns of symbol-using reported here was initially shaped by our observations and understandings arrived at through direct, immediate, and personal experiences in gay discos for the last several years. However, the formal use of ethnographic methods for the particular results identified here began in February 1978 and continued through April of the following year. Simple observation and participant-observation functioned as the primary data collection methods during this period. We have found it useful to supplement these observations with transcribed audiotapes of open-ended interviews with six gay bartenders from these clubs. We have singled out gay bartenders for this special consideration, because they function, in gay clubs, as more than service workers; they are frequently the first sources of information for those who are in new clubs; they make direct contact with more members of the clubs by virtue of the service they render; and they are frequently employed because they are liked and respected by a significant number of local gays. In addition, employing content analysis techniques, we have also drawn freely from episodic archives and private records of the gay community, particularly from publications designed solely for gay male readers such as *Blueboy* (the largest circulating monthly gay male magazine in the United States) and from regionally circulated gay activist literature when it applied to the nature and function of issues generated by the gay disco. Finally, we have readily employed published focused interviews with gay males when these interviews allowed gay males to describe their relationships in detail without interruption.[29] We have used these materials to construct the intersubjective reality of gay males as it emerges in gay discos.

We find Thomas S. Frentz's and Thomas B. Farrell's " 'language-action' paradigm" a useful organizational base for specifying our field of investigation. Frentz and Farrell posit a "deductive" paradigm that moves from a consideration of "context" to "episodes" to "symbolic acts."[30] Correspondingly, we find it appropriate to first identify the contextual "form of life" or "those partially linguistic and partially nonlinguistic constellations of activities which fix the meaning of concepts and expressions."[31]

The life form we explore here finds its immediate contextual enclave defined by the perimeters of the gay disco club. The largest gay discos in San Francisco, Minneapolis, New York, Washington, D.C., Houston, Philadelphia, and Los Angeles—representing seven major cities in the East, West, South, and Midwest—constitute the foundations for our conclusions.[32]

Although geographically removed from one another, the clubs share several common characteristics. All these clubs are advertised as gay clubs, and virtually all their members, based on our interactions, identify themselves as gay. In addition, these are male clubs; during our formal sampling periods, males persistently constituted 92 to 97 percent of those within these clubs.[33] Also, almost half these clubs are private; new members must be endorsed by a current member of the club, must pay a membership fee, and must present their membership cards whenever seeking admission. Even if not officially private clubs, these clubs operate as enclaves apart from the straight world. Besides their membership restrictions, the clubs typically operate from midnight until early hours in the morning, are located in secluded regions of the cities (Philadelphia's DCA club is located at the junction of two alleyways and is hidden from sight on all sides, while New York's 12 West is located between two warehouses in the dock area), and advertise solely in gay newspapers. All the clubs are large, with 500 to 2,000 members present on a typical Saturday night. These clubs are also discos; music blares constantly, and 30 percent of those present are dancing at any given time during the evening. In this context it should be noted that disco originated in these clubs; dancing itself has been described as the major sport of gay males.[34] Beyond these commonalities, five of the seven clubs serve alcohol; all maintain dazzling light shows; drugs are an evident phenomenon; and clothing styles vary from the denim and leather sometimes associated with S/M to the chic dress associated with the Gucci style to the clean-cut look associated with the college student to the natural look of the radical gay liberationist.

As one enters one of these gay discos a barrage of images converge on the senses simultaneously. "Dance, Dance, Dance" or "If My Friends Could See Me Now" or "O Happy Days" might be screaming from giant speakers. The refrain is answered by hundreds of half-naked men, their backs glistening in the hypnotic lights, swirling around the room. Raised arms with clenched fists punch out the rhythm that dares the dancers to keep up with it. The smell of sweat hangs heavy in the barn-sized room. A body-to-body wall surrounds the dance floor. Beyond this human wall, narrow and irregular paths are created and vanish as crowds form and re-form, creating different social constellations and networks. Crowds and dyads come into existence as people move throughout the clubs. Other groups form more stable signposts throughout the night. Smoke, conversations, moods, lights, and music seem to increase in tempo and volume as the evening passes. The males are being entertained visually by others and by responses to their own images—a form of visual entertainment is hyped by lights, music, and overcrowding; the experience is not unlike what one might imagine interactive three-dimensional, tactical, audio, and olfactory television to be. There is indeed a kind of fever that fills these Saturday nights. The collage has been vividly interpreted by Clarke Taylor:

> I am somewhere in lower Manhattan, somewhere in the middle of the night. I am surrounded by beautiful people lost in the soaring sound of Donna Summer. Boogie fever. I am bathed at one moment in blue moonshine, at another in sunset. I may choose my mood, even my sex. I know everyone; I know no one. I am touched, felt, found, and I am alone. I am a product of this environment, no more, no less. I am having the time of my life without knowing the time, and I am peering in at my life, which I cannot define. These are the perimeters of my experience in a strange and foreign, and even primal land: disco madness.
>
> In the light of day I know I've experienced Les Mouches, New York's newest and most elegant disco (if Halston were to design one, it would look like this), but I might have been in similar time and space in Washington, Atlanta, Miami, Los Angeles, San Francisco, Chicago, or even Monterey. Disco transcends the geographical, even the spiritual boundaries of our ordinary lives.
>
> And disco works its magic not only for gays (although gays all but invented the phenomenon), but for other minorities, and the straight middle class, and even the rich and famous—as though they needed yet another escape from the real world.[35]

Overall, these are the clubs where, in Erving Goffman's words, "direct participation" in a "type of commercialed action" occurs. Goffman appropriately labels such action "fancy milling." While commercialized and conspicuous, such interactions can create socially shared objectives as well as generate new relationships and new life-style guidelines. As Goffman initially explains:

> [One's] mere presence in a large, tightly packed gathering of reveling persons can bring out not only the excitement that crowds generate, but also the uncertainty of not quite knowing what might happen next, the possibility of flirtations, which can themselves lead to relationship formation, and the lively experience of being an elbow away from someone who does manage to find real action in the crowd.[36]

As Goffman might put it, these gay discos constitute backstage arenas, at least from a heterosexual perspective. Gay discos are back stages in the sense that they are intentionally hidden or private environments designed solely for one type of male; at the same time, for the gay males in these clubs, they function as front stages. Gay males entering these discos engage in ritual interactions designed to create and confirm a public "presentation of the self."[37] These presentations are public, for the verbal and nonverbal symbols of the individual males in these clubs are validated or invalidated by a massive crowd, of whom—given the size of these clubs—only a few can be personally known. We are particularly interested in these gay discos when they are conceived as front stages designed to create and confirm such public presentations of the self, and specifically, we focus on the verbal and nonverbal symbols that are employed to create a sense of a socially shared identity for the members within these clubs.

Whether intended or not, we argue that gay males employ the structure of the gay disco and the social processes within these clubs to create a symbolic system which fosters the development of a particular mode of masculinity. We assume that this mode of masculinity—as is true of all forms of masculinity—is a product of the verbal and nonverbal stylistic choices invoked to provide the male gender with a distinct sense of identity.[38] In this view there is nothing inherent in the male physiology or psychology which determines that the traditional goal-success-control-power-aggression-violence syndrome must characterize any male's sense of being as a male. The entire concept of sexuality, as well as any specific mode of sexuality, is socially constructed by selective symbol-using.[39] More broadly stated, this theory of symbolic determinism posits that symbols are creatively generated by human beings: symbol-using is an active, rather than passive, process by which human beings selectively create figure-ground relationships and thereby transform the chaos of reality into an ordered system that defines the nature of social reality, and the identity and appropriate styles for human interactions, whether these interactions be sexual or otherwise.[40]

Paradoxical Symbol-using in the Gay Disco: Unbecoming Men

The formation of masculinity described here emerges from a world view or perspective of reality that is profoundly paradoxical in nature. This paradoxical world view[41] provides the foundation for a redefinition of masculinity, a mode of masculinity we can ultimately refer to as *gay masculinity*. Particularly, two different concepts are associated or linked that are perceived as inconsistent by the mainstream of the culture. However, these two contradictory concepts are unified and transformed for gay males by the more encompassing and transcendent notion of gay masculinity. Each concept is described here separately, followed by a discussion of the implications created by unifying these two components.

The Virility Component

One concept asserted in the gay disco is an exaggerated, if not flagrant, form of masculinity in appearance. In these discos, gay males acquire and display all the trappings of the most masculine traditional man. The concern for the traditional rugged look partially accounts for the denim and leather that are so evident in the gay disco. But denim and leather are only symptoms of an entire nonverbal image. An extreme case of this composite image includes an explicitly displayed, muscularly developed body; a flannel shirt; a leather vest; denim or leather pants; construction or cowboy boots; a spread-legged stance, with thumbs carefully locked in belt loops; and a slow-speaking, low-keyed style (images of Marlon Brando emerge), typified by the overall image of the tall, dark, and silent type. Andrew Kopkind reaffirms the existence of this image and also offers a possible explanation for the choice of such an image:

> A famous case of feedback is found in the "Christopher Street clone" look that began to be popular with homosexual men in the Village about six or seven years ago. In its classical cold-weather form, it consists of a T-shirt under a plaid flannel shirt under a gray hooded sweatshirt under an antiqued leather jacket. Pants are jeans; shoes are light brown leather workboots; socks are, ideally, of gray wool with hunter's orange bands at the top and toe. And the hood of the sweatshirt must *always* fall back over the collar of the cracking leather jacket.
>
> The clone uniform was never really designed as a whole, but collectively invented as an exact replication of a "butch" male icon, at a time—shortly after the first flowering of gay liberation—when male homosexuals were able and eager to assert the reality of their masculinity. Before 1969, gay males were "not men," that is, "sissies" or "nellies" or "fairies." The first lesson of liberation was that it was legitimate for men to love the masculinity in themselves and others of the same sex, and the sweatshirt-and-leather look was the medium to communicate that message.[42]

Similarly, in our interviews with those in the discos, the quest for males with a "more masculine image" continuously emerged. One patron overtly remarked, "It is a very relaxed atmosphere. I find it very relaxing. Mainly because I go with a lot of other men, and not with a lot of screaming queens, and I'm not with a lot of women." Likewise, consider this exchange between several of the bartenders who work in these discos:

L: Lacoste tops are too dressy for 12 West. You loop them through your belt loop. It's all part of the look: jeans, workboots, keys, and shirts through the belt loops. I got that down pat.
W: That would make me laugh as much as queens.
L: But if 1,500 people are doing it, it is the norm.
K: They love costumes; 12 West is pure environmental disco—they manipulate you.

Thus, while the endorsement of traditional trappings of masculinity is pervasive, the identification is incomplete. As one bartender notes above, such extreme identifications "would make me laugh as much as queens." Likewise, another of these bartenders recognizes that these styles are in fact costumes and a product of external manipulations.

Underscoring the recognition that virility is but one component of gay masculinity, the limits of the macho image have been assessed in detail by gay critics of the gay discos and by the members of the discos themselves. These assessments cluster, constituting three recurrent scenarios.

First, the virility image is perceived as a force that could potentially destroy the individuality of gay males. Within the gay discos the word clone is a common and frequently employed term applied to those who appear to accept the virility image too seriously or unconsciously. In greater detail James Tyson focuses on the socially shared meanings of such interactions:

> "Costume gayness" robs us of our individuality. I'm thinking of the workman's boots, the jeans (preferably torn), the bomber jacket covering a Windbreaker, the hood of which remains outside the jacket, the short hair and the mustache. When you're a man, it's comfortable to be masculine, but *contrived* masculinity is as silly as *calculated* effeteness.[43]

Second, the costume is not intended to promote sexism. The trappings are typically viewed as relatively insignificant and harmless affectations compared to the power-oriented acts of traditional heterosexual males that have been rejected by gay males. The issue is consciously and forcefully addressed by one regular patron of the discos:

> Is my macho showing? My army boots, my lumberman shirts, my leather jacket—do these make me a sexist? I frequent backroom bars in New York City, the bars on Folsom St. in San Francisco, drink beer from phallic-shaped bottles, understand that my first impression of others are always sexual.
>
> Let us not mistake macho garb for sexist garbage.[44]

Third, and finally, the costume is but a preliminary stage from a form of heterosexual mimicry to a more personal and profound sense of what gay masculinity ultimately ought to be. Kopkind traces this transition, at least that portion of the trend which has emerged thus far:

> Before long, it became necessary (and boring) to repeat the same message over and over again, a subtle but sure modification of the butch icon began to take place. Gay men all over town (and around the country) trimmed, shaped, and refitted the shaggy casualness that was the real essence of the original straight image. The T-shirts were tightened, the flannel shirts were fitted and crisped, the leather jackets were newer, the jeans were snugged around the buttocks. And, of course, hair styles became increasingly shorter

and moustaches more carefully shaped. What emerged was a *deliberate* new style which does not say, "I am a straight construction worker" but rather "I am a post-liberation gay man!" The marvelous historical irony of that process is that men now adopt the uniform to prove their gayness rather than imitate the straightness they once envied.[45]

While these three dimensions of the virility image are each rejected in particular ways, the virility component of gay masculinity ultimately has a profoundly distinct context and meaning for gay males. The overriding distinguishing issue is male bonding. For the gay male, the all-male group can be sharply distinguished from the norms controlling all-male heterosexual groups. For the traditional heterosexual male, being masculine has implicitly required that males, especially in all-male groups, adopt an indifferent attitude toward the feelings, moods, and interpersonal needs of other males. As George Leonard cogently argues, " 'Be a man' often means turn off your feelings, wreak your will upon others, and act always under the traditional system of rationality."[46] Others argue that this solely rational relationship among heterosexual males has led to "our tragic adventure in Vietnam"[47] and to the early death and high suicide rates of males.[48] Moreover, Benjamin Boshes has suggested that heterosexual males are becoming increasingly destructive when interacting with one another.[49] We explore the approach of gay males to male bonding as we consider the second major component that defines gay masculinity.

The Affectional Component

In the gay disco a solely rational conception of masculinity is rejected. By purpose and design the disco is a nonrational institution. At least temporarily, traditional patterns of sensibility are intentionally destroyed. The flickering strobe lights, combined with other unexpected lighting "creations," constitute what are called light shows; discos are frequently evaluated by their light shows. Yet these light shows distort perceptions. The strobe light, for example, creates the illusion that people are moving in jerky and segmented progressions. Likewise, the blare of the music—at decibel levels harmful to the human eardrum—dominates the disco and creates an isolated enclave virtually immune from outside noises. Furthermore, rather than attempting to eliminate overcrowding, the successful disco overcrowds—one's personal space may be literally defined by only the ground beneath one's feet. Thus, traditional patterns of sensibility in terms of sight, sound, and space are drastically altered, giving the never-never land effect that may also be associated with the nonrational.

While the structure of the disco may contribute to the kinds of human interactions that occur within these discos, it also becomes evident that emotionality banishes rationality in the social processes of these discos. The masculine male in these gay discos must be capable of being interpersonally sensitive to other males' feelings, enjoyments, moods, sentiments, and social and, possibly, sexual needs. Consequently, the norms controlling male behavior in the gay disco are not to be found in any other all-male environment.

Forms of noncompetitive "play" dominate male interactions in the gay disco. For example, the dance floor is typically located in the center of the room and is designed to be the central activity of the room; patrons generally face the dance floor at all times; the dancers are a form of visual stimulation and entertainment. As mentioned earlier, 30 percent of the males are dancing at any given time. Although the dance is a symbolic ritual, the decision to dance with another male is a statement of preference, both affectionally and sexually. In addition, given the location and placement of nondancers, the dance is also an overt public statement of the dancers' affectional preference. The dance also functions as an erotic physical display of the body for both dance partners and for observers, for the undulations, pulsations, and vibrations of most disco dances mimic the sexual act. The mood and tone of the dance floor, then, are aptly reflected in this sequence of songs played during a one-hour period: "If My Friends Could See Me Now," "O Happy Days," "At the Discotheque," "Macho Man," "East Meets West," "Love's Coming," "I Can't Turn You Loose," "Hit and Run," "Little Sister," "Cherchez La Femme," "Risky Changes," and "How Much, How Much I Love You." Such songs certainly contribute to the intensity of the dance, for the typical disco song has 127 beats per minute. The beat and words of the music contribute to the emotional high, an almost euphoric intensity when the sound level of the music is considered with the lighting and overcrowding effects.

For the nondancers in these discos, modes of interaction likewise focus on predominantly emotional rather than rational issues, conveyed in dramatic rather than logical styles. Overall, the physical presentations of nondancers—as is true of the dancers—function as sources of stimulation, entertainment, and fantasies for one another and for the dancers. The presentations of selves in these discos involve a host of different stylistic features. Sexual displays are evident, varying from the shirt unbuttoned to the navel to tight clothing that emphasizes body shape to more overt forms of crotch display. Moreover, rather than avoiding physical contact with other males as heterosexual males are likely to do, the overcrowding in gay discos ensures that male touching will occur, even if these touches are initiated or experienced as accidental. As one member of these discos puts it, "It's crowded, and you can feel a stranger standing behind you, his body near you. The crowd pushes—contact! It's a ball." In this context it is not surprising to note that most males circulate in these clubs and that constant motion—either when walking or while dancing—tends to be the norm. This is not to suggest that some do not find their spots and defend these territories for an entire evening; however, at any given time more people are in motion while walking or dancing than are at rest.

Conversations in gay discos are also likely to deal with what most would consider emotional topics (feelings, moods, sentiments, personal experiences) in the style of the dramatic storyteller, in which events and experiences are cast in a conflict-resolution form that clearly identifies good guys and bad guys. Consider the ways in which the drama of the narrative culminates in a moral precept in this exchange:

P: Hey, did Charlie tell you what happened to him last night?
H: He's always getting into messes!
J: Even when Charlie and I were together, he had a knack for trouble.
P: But, really, he's a good egg, but last night he left us—remember, early. He went to the other side of the club on one of his little subtle searches.
H: Yeah, he was after that guy with the construction boots.
P: Well, he met him. They talked some, and then Charlie came back, kind of upset 'cause the guy seemed to lose interest.
J: Depressed is the word.
P: But, after we left the club, Charlie saw him outside. They did that kind of quiet stare. Charlie walked down the block; this guy followed slowly. They talked again and went to Charlie's.
J: See, I try to tell him not to cruise in the bar. It's not the place. This place is for seeing and getting someone's attention—later is for the hot stuff.
H: Yeah, true.
W: Yeah, but did you ever wonder who makes these little rules?
P: Who knows?

Four major topics emerged in the conversations we taped and later transcribed. Sex and romance among gay males were discussed 47 percent of the time, followed by recountings of gay-heterosexual interactions (29 percent). Gay discos and gay politics were discussed 18 percent and 6 percent of the time, respectively. Thus, emotional topics rather than more rational issues dominate these conversations.

For both dancers and nondancers, alcohol and drugs also serve as stimuli that shift the emphasis of interactions from the rational to the emotional. The drug amyl nitrite serves as a convenient example, especially given its widespread use within these discos by both dancers and nondancers. Amyl nitrite is a clear, yellow liquid compounded of nitrous acid, 3-methylbutyl ester, and isopentyl nitrite. The drug is inhaled; it has a peculiar ethereal, fruity odor. Typically carried in an ampule or bottle, the container can be passed to others easily and can be inhaled directly from the bottle, even while dancing. The drug is called a "popper" because of its immediate, powerful, but short-term effect. It produces an euphoric, intensive high for a maximum of fifteen seconds, although a lingering aura may last a minute or two longer. The popper is consistent with our conception of the gay disco as a nonrational environment, for it produces a kind of goof with an overt sense of palpitations and mental confusions that are antithetical to more logical interactions. In gay discos poppers are commonly observed, communally shared, and a frequent topic of conversation.[50]

Virility and Same-sex Intimacy—Implications of the Union

Overall, when defined in the context of the gay disco, gay masculinity may thus be understood to be a merger of two components: virility and same-sex affection. A logician could technically argue that these two concepts are not inherently paradoxical. When independently defined these two notions may exist simultaneously. Strictly speaking, virility is but the precocious development of secondary sex characteristics in males, while a same-sex affectional preference highlights only a priority for tenderness and fondness for males by males. The two concepts, understood in this way, possess no self-contradictory themes. However, such reasoning follows the kind of rigorous guidelines only a logician is apt to use. In the context of the American culture the concept of virility is a more encompassing social idea. Socially defined, virility includes the goal-success-control-power-aggression-violence syndrome that Alan Gross argues is the predominant characteristic of "the male role and heterosexual behavior"[51] in all-male bonded groups. This mode of interaction is inconsistent with the emotionality associated with the principle of same-sex affection. As Robert A. Lewis argues:

> Cultural prohibitions in America, as well as in many other Western nations, frown strongly upon the demonstration of intimacy between men, such as adult males openly sharing affection in public. As a consequence, many American males in adult life have never had a close male friend nor known what it means to love and care for a male friend without the shadow of some guilt or fear of peer ridicule. Because of these restrictive norms, even those who have male friends usually have experienced little trust, little personal sharing, and low emotional investments in these friendships. There is more than a little irony in the keen observation that many American men report their closest male relationships as those discovered through war or sports, i.e., when they are bonded together to kill others.[52]

The paradox thus emerges: Culturally defined, virility and same-sex affections are mutually inconsistent.

The ambiguous nature of the phrase unbecoming men aptly illustrates the paradox. For most Americans, it is inappropriate or unbecoming for a virile male to be part of a same-sex affectional relationship. In this sense it is unbecoming to men to show affection to members of their own sex. For gay males, however, the desire or natural inclination is to show affection for other males. For these gay males, it is necessary to destroy the sociocultural conditioning which traditionally demands that males maintain nonintimate relationships in all-male groups. The gay male must dismantle the conditioning that precludes male intimacy; the gay male must pass through a process of unbecoming men in the sense that he must reject the nonintimate dimensions traditionally associated with manliness. At the same time, for a variety of reasons (i.e., to pass in heterosexual environments, to compensate for previous concepts of the gay male, and so forth), gay males adopt some of the trappings of traditional masculinity that suggest they would do nothing, at least in appearance, unbecoming or inappropriate to the male role. Not only does the phrase unbecoming men carry with it the paradoxical connotation of maintaining the appropriate decorum associated with manliness, but it also underscores the necessity to initiate major changes in terms of what manliness will be understood to include and not to include.

For the gay male, the decision to adopt a virile mode cannot be viewed as merely a stylistic affectation. The existence of known masculine gay males has a special meaning to others; gay masculinity conveys a message to others, particularly to heterosexual males. The gay male who is known as both gay and masculine challenges the sensibilities of heterosexual males far more than the effeminate gay male. Under experimental conditions researchers have consistently reported that effeminate gay males are more tolerated and less aggressed against than more masculine gay males.[53] In this sense, gay males known to be gay would wisely anticipate that the decision to adopt a virile image will have social implications. Gay masculinity is not only an inconsistency or paradox for heterosexual males, it is also a symbol that challenges the traditional social hierarchy which has conventionally placed the white heterosexual masculine male at the top of the sociosexual hierarchy. In this context the assertion of a virile gay identity is a political act that confronts the sociosexual power structure. In the 1960s, rhetorics of confrontation were presumed to be predominantly discursive and products of the mass demonstration. In the 1980s, rhetorics of confrontation may be decidedly nonverbal and interpersonal in nature. Rather than diminishing its significance, this transformation in the rhetoric of confrontation may generate a more powerful influence on the sociosexual system. Nonverbal confrontations are frequently more amorphous and therefore more difficult to recognize and analyze than verbal challenges. Likewise, interpersonal confrontations posit a more direct challenge to the personal and immediate life-style than mass demonstrations against political institutions or elected politicians.

Three other implications of this analysis also seem warranted. First, for heterosexual males dealing with traditional conceptions of masculinity as a problem, this essay implies that the lack of intimacy among males may contribute to the difficulties currently associated with conventional modes of manliness. Barriers to nongenital intimacy among males seem to include excessive competition, homophobia, an aversion to vulnerability and openness, and a lack of role models of affection-giving between males.[54] Coping devices for the development of nongenital intimacy among males are available.[55]

Second, applications of the concept of a paradoxical world view employed here might be profitably applied to other social actions. For example, it appears that several radical political movements[56] might be explicated with the concept of a paradoxical world view. In addition, the issues associated with urban communication look to be explainable with the concept; particularly, the coping devices used to prevent information overloads[57] might be viewed as the devices that also create loneliness, anomie, and social disengagement in urban centers.[58] Finally, the use of paradoxical world views may also clarify the ways in which bureaucracies create mass quiescence.[59]

Third, this analysis also suggests that the development of a concept such as gay masculinity may be instrumental in identifying the nature of sex-role rigidity and androgyny. In this view, stereotypical sex roles are not defined by the existence of any particular substantive feature. Both feminine and masculine stereotypes are currently defined by noting that each gender is persistently associated with certain adjectives not commonly linked with the other gender. Barbara Westbrook Eakins and R. Gene Eakins reason that:

> there are various popular beliefs about what women and men do and don't do. Such beliefs are stereotypes or overgeneralizations about the sexes. . . . Females were characterized by both sexes in terms such as *sophisticated, poised, well mannered, tactful, pleasant, sociable, modest, gentle, affectionate, kind, sentimental,* and *lovable*. . . . The stereotype of males held by both sexes involved a straight-forward uninhibited social style, rational competence, and vigorous action.[60]

Such an analysis gives the impression that one is approaching males and females stereotypically if women are assumed, for example, to be more lovable than males. Substantive descriptors, such as lovable versus rational, are not the issue. Stereotypes exist whenever any descriptor or set of descriptors are consistently associated with one gender or are consistently employed by one gender. Nonstereotypical thinking occurs only when the complete range of human actions are believed to be available to both genders. Similarly, nonstereotypical actions occur only when the complete range of human actions are choice-items for both genders. In this regard it seems more useful to conceive of the androgynous to be those who employ different styles of interactions as circumstances change, rather than assuming that the androgynous employ both masculine and feminine strategies. The issue here is not which styles are employed, but whether the complete range of styles are employed and varied as circumstances are altered. The range of strategies employed, rather than the type of strategies utilized, is the mark of the flexible, adaptive individual. Such a view suggests that both masculinity and femininity are socially constructed presentations that should be freely selected and altered as circumstances require. In this framework, male and female bonding are assumed to be enduring and recurrent cross-cultural phenomena. Such bonding creates special styles of interaction. However, these styles should be selected from the complete range of viable human options. The measure of such freedom is ultimately determined by the actual number of different kinds of interaction styles selected.

Conclusion

This essay has constructed the intersubjective reality of males who identify themselves as gay in the sociocultural environment specified by the gay disco. Employing ethnographic techniques, the issue of gay masculinity is explored as the central foundation for understanding the identity of gay males as men, as gay, and as members of a linguistic-thought community. This identity is created and mediated by the rhetorical figure of paradox employed as the organizing construct, world view, or perspective of reality unifying a host of different attitudes, beliefs, and actions associated with gay males. Ultimately, gay masculinity has been conceived as an association between two concepts typically viewed as incompatible—virility and same-sex affectional relationships. The association creates social tension between gay males and heterosexual males, and may in fact challenge the sociosexual hierarchy that characterizes the American culture. Implications of this association appear to affect the traditional conceptions of masculinity held by heterosexual males, to provide a framework for examining a host of other social actions, and to alter understandings of what sex-role rigidity and androgyny mean.

Chapter 9

Gay Fantasies in Gay Publications

John D. Glenn

To understand the world view of any group, be it a minority, majority, or political and social collective, we tend to look first at the documents formally prepared for the uninitiated, such as statement of goals, charters, constitutions, by-laws, and membership requirements. While such documents are useful, focusing attention exclusively on prepared statements excludes a number of equally significant communicative modes that shape and define the communication system of the group in question. Ernest G. Bormann has suggested fantasy theme analysis as a critical method for examining social groups and movements. Specifically, Bormann proposes that an investigation of the in-group fantasies of a social collective can reveal values, attitudes, and even whole frames of reference that would otherwise be ignored. Moreover, Bormann argues that these in-group fantasies may "chain out" to create a "rhetorical vision"; a vision, "constructed from the concrete dramas developed in a body of discourse," that enables the critic to examine "the social relationships, the motives, the qualitative impact of the symbolic world as though it were the substance of social reality for those people who participated in the vision."[1] Bormann further posits that these fantasies may be predictive of a group's future, for as fantasies chain out, they may move from the small group to the larger minority and, ultimately, to the entire culture. Thus, fantasy theme analysis may be useful, not only in providing a critical method for discovering a group's "hidden agenda," but also to predict a group's evolution, development, or phases.

Such a phasic progression of visions is evident in the fiction written by and for "America's largest sub-culture"[2]: the gay community.[3]

A comparison between short fiction stories that appeared in nationally distributed publications targeted for a primarily gay male audience during the years 1970 and 1979–80 yields these major conclusions[4]: (1) The fantasies of the gay community have undergone a major change in the 1970s. (2) An ideal conception of romance, predominant in the fictions of the early 70s, had given way by the late 70s and early 80s, to a more realistic exploration of all dimensions of sex. (3) These changes constitute an effort to change from a heterosexual model to a more completely gay ethic that is, at present, incomplete. This incompleteness provides, in part, a justification for the claim that the 1980s will see the emergence of a third phase in the gay community's evolution: the merger of virility with affection.

This essay employs a three-fold analysis. First, the seven fantasies of the early 1970s are described. These seven fantasies are cast as elements of an inductive argument which provide a warrant for claiming that the overall and unifying vision of stage one is a *romantic* vision. Second, the seven fantasies of the late 70s and early 80s are described; these fantasies constitute stage two in the evolution of the gay community. As with the early 70s fantasies, these later seven fantasies supply an inductive argument for the claim that the unifying vision for the late 70s and early 80s is a vision of *carnal virility*. Third, the implications of this are identified. These implications contain the essence of the thesis developed in this essay, namely that the gay community has significantly shifted from a heterosexual model for interpersonal relations and is in the process of creating its own unique gay ethic. The 80s will undoubtedly be affected by this shift, and I foresee the emergence of a third vision: *virile affection*. However, before dealing with these and other implications, let us first examine the vision of the early 70s.

Vision #1: Romance

Romance is, at best, an ambiguous concept, carrying with it a variety of connotations. These connotations include an idealized love that is faithful and pure. "Chivalrous," "heroic," and "adventurous" are also commonly used to characterize the romantic. Moreover, romantic central characters are pictured as fighters against the outrages of injustice. Daring all odds, these characters emerge victorious over evil. Such a romantic vision emerges from the seven fantasy chains, common to all or to a majority of the fictions examined from 1970.

Being gay is being different. In these fictions, being gay is something that produces conflict and confusion, and requires maturity to be dealt with successfully. In "The Talsen Interlude" the central character, Kert, is captivated with a feeling for Gary that,

> he couldn't explain. The more he tried to define the sensation, the more irritated Kert became with himself as he fought the creeping realization that perhaps they had been more physically attracted than his chauvinistic male

> ego wanted to admit. Kert's inner turmoil was beginning to ruin his power of concentration.[5]

In "Fantasex," Tom is likewise overcome with a passion that "ravishes his senses; in no remembered spring has he felt like this."[6] Larry, in "Larry and the Lieutenant," also admits that his relationship with Mary Ellen had been a "farce-phase of his life and was over."[7] Later, Larry forces himself "to look at the lumbering Ciminelli, wondering if the idiot suspected he was gay."[8] In this fantasy theme being gay is treated as if a visible deformity is the issue. The self-discovery of one's gayness or coming out is portrayed not only as a painful process, but also as an important growth process. Recognizing the meaning and implications of coming out is cast as necessary for the realization of who one is, a process that, if denied, results in rejection of one's basic personhood and therefore a failure to achieve maturity.

Being gay is socially difficult. In this vision being gay is something that results in externally imposed pain and ostracism. In "Larry and the Lieutenant," Ciminelli thinks that "fags should be drummed out of the service for being fags."[9] In "The Talsen Interlude" Kert's mother refers to Kert's affection for Gary as "plain unhealthy and unnatural."[10] And Kert "stormed out the screen door in humiliated rage, cursing himself for what he was sure was a sick and perverted feeling."[11] In "False Glory," Robert's grandfather writes, "If you know what the Bible tells us about the disgusting sin against nature . . . to suffer this shame you have brought upon our good family . . . I no longer consider you my grandson."[12] And Robert's father writes, "I pray that you love and the love that is given to you will make the price you must pay seem as pennies. For the future, live in a large city where Maywood's small-town brand of crucifixion cannot touch you."[13] And in the "Pumpkin Coach," Laddy and Marv "had carefully arranged their meetings and partings to avoid giving Loreen any excuse to contest the divorce or make a stink."[14]

This fantasy represents a period in which gay males listen to the negative heterosexual interpretations of being gay and internalize these interpretations. However, in these stories this is only a *period*—an early period at that—and a period that is to be overcome. This fantasy is an early, temporary, heterosexually generated fantasy.

Being gay requires one to excel in any endeavor according to the standards of excellence established by society. This fantasy reveals the frequently employed strategy for assimilation of the minority group into the larger culture. For instance, the black movement, in its early stages, believed that one way to secure change was simply to adopt the standards of the established white society. Likewise, in this fantasy gay males are described as adopting the standards of the established heterosexual society. Bob and

Roger save the lives of twenty-eight GIs and are awarded the Bronze Star for gallantry in action. Larry receives the honor of being the best recruit during his boot camp training. Kert and Gary are straight A students, and stars of the football team. All the characters are bright, good-looking, and driven to achieve. The message that comes across in this fantasy is that to prove oneself in the face of adversity one must be superior to the adversary on the adversary's terms. To gain favor for an unpopular cause, one must demonstrate worthiness by accepting society's evaluation of what is and is not worthy. There is no honor, in this fantasy, in being the best hairdresser or interior decorator.

One can be gay and still be masculine. James W. Chesebro and Kenneth L. Klenk give three reasons why masculinity has been a problem area for gay males (see chapter 8):

> First, homosexuality frequently functions as an overwhelming stigma that diminishes the energy which might be devoted to the formation of a humane ethic of masculinity. . . . The stigma can become overwhelming and totally consume efforts at self-definition. . . . Second, . . . manliness has traditionally been defined by a male's sexual union with the opposite sex and, concomitantly, by division or separation from other males sexually. In this sense, it is unbecoming a man—if not completely inconsistent—to claim to be a man and a homosexual simultaneously. . . . Third, masculinity is extremely difficult for homosexuals to affirm, because being a man or being masculine traditionally involves particular forms of nongenital behavior that are antithetical to being gay.

In this fantasy each character is described in terms such as muscular young body, strongly built physique, lean and hard, broad-shouldered and narrow-hipped, rugged good looks, chiseled features. Words and phrases traditionally used to describe a he-man, or characterizations that connote health, vitality, and virility. Stereotypically, the gay male is a mincing queen or a sissy. He is, stereotypically, half a man because of a same-sex affectional preference. Real Men do not and cannot, in this masculine mystique, love one another. The notion of masculine gay males has been traditionally seen as a contradiction in terms.

This fantasy attempts to overthrow these preconceived stereotypical notions, denying or at least seeking a reinterpretation and reevaluation of this apparent contradiction. To be gay is therefore, in this fantasy, to be healthy, vital, and masculine. The prescription is clear: one need not deny his masculinity or his sexual preference. In this context the occupations of the characters become extremely important in this fantasy. Six of the characters are accordingly soldiers, one is a farmer, two operate an electrical supply business, and two are white-collar professionals—all are "manly" professions. Soldiers and farmers are stereotypically seen as "more than mere men." They are the "backbone of our country" and "our way of life." In a phrase, these are the occupations cast as the epitome of masculinity. By denying the stereotype the fantasy is ultimately a confrontational strategy.

Emphasizing the occupations of the characters and their geographic location serves as a fifth fantasy: *Gay men are everywhere.* From the rice paddies of Vietnam, to boot camp in southern Georgia, to small-town New Jersey, to farms in the Midwest, to the summer playground of Fire Island; indeed, from sea to shining sea, gay men will be there, and in occupations that are typically viewed as masculine. The message is clear: "Come out! Your brothers are everywhere." There is less to fear than originally thought. By openly coming out the beginnings of a national community can be established. No more must one move to a large city for support and safety. The fantasy that one is isolated and more prone to danger in a small town is shattered. As more people come out, the gay community will strengthen, this fantasy asserts, offering support and sanction across the country.

To be happy and gay requires love in a committed relationship. In this fantasy not only are heterosexual relational models posited as the ideal mold from which to cast a gay relationship, but also loving, committed coupling is seen as necessary for the achievement of personal wholeness. Larry rejects Bert's overtures and opts to wait for the lieutenant, whom he loves. After their love has been realized Larry is ecstatic and can endure any hardship. Gary is filled with overwhelming joy when he realizes that Kert loved him and wanted him to have something special that would signify their love to the world. Bob and Roger use their love for each other as protection against the dangers of combat. Marv's love for Laddy enables him to extricate Laddy from an uncomfortable situation, and together they can overcome their financial problems and the problems of a messy divorce. Of the eleven characters, five are couples. This fantasy might be viewed as a mini-Gothic romance; the characters are portrayed as battling all odds for the realization of their love for one another. Their love is not socially sanctioned and potentially necessitates personal sacrifice. A committed union, then, is necessary to overcome the obstacles; together the characters can face anything and realize their full potential.

Looking at the last two paragraphs of each story to see how the drama is resolved reveals the seventh fantasy chain: *Gay is good.* Each short story resolves itself on a positive or optimistic note. Laddy and Marv walk hand in hand into the sunset. Larry knows the lieutenant has not said good-bye, that they will be able to continue their relationship. Kert is filled with joy. Tom is overcome with passion. Each story, through this fantasy, tells the reader that self-exploration and self-realization of one's gayness is a process—at times painful but on the whole a positive step toward growth and maturity.

The seven fantasies are unified and given greater significance through the rhetorical vision of romance. As Chesebro has written of romance:

> While romantic agents are superior to others only in degree, the situations they face seem to contain almost overwhelming elements of unknown danger and risk as well as requiring remarkable levels of human power, intensity, dedication, and capacity. Clearly, romantic agents must be intellectually superior to others and be capable of exercising superior control over their environment.[15]

Clearly, then, these fantasies fulfill the criteria for a romantic vision.

Being gay, as illustrated by the above fantasies, results in a socially imposed stigma of the gay person as abnormal, unnatural, and immoral. Society thinks such a person is bad and should be punished, and touts the divinely inspired "Holy Word" as justification for its crusade of oppression. The gay male is told it is bad to be gay but that if he must, he had best live in a large city, where anonymity can be preserved and where safety can be maintained through numbers. Small towns, with their high degree of visibility and rarified moral fiber, are not safe places. In choosing homosexuality over heterosexuality the gay male, in the romantic vision, is pictured as a dark horse racing against oppression, prejudice, and provincial mentality. Additionally, the gay male is given contradictory messages: be gay and realize the potential of self; be gay and realize the rage of society.

The romantic vision is, moreover, a call to come out, a call to become political, a call to fight stereotypes and oppression—the first steps toward the creation of a social movement. For gays, the late 60s and early 70s were years of political harassment; years when vice squads regularly practiced techniques of entrapment to purify their cities of moral corruption; years when coming out of the closet was condemned by society and staying in the closet was condemned by those gays who were politically active. June 27, 1969, the night of the Stonewall riots, saw "the forces of faggotry"[16] unite and "the New Homosexual born."[17]

The romantic vision promotes the image of the birth of the new homosexual: the gay male. This vision acknowledges the social and political realities of the time. It was difficult to be gay, particularly in small towns. But the only way to overcome the difficulties was to come out. Showing the world that one's gayness was not an isolated abberation, but a healthy, vital, masculine aspect of one's personality. Showing the world that gay males could be loving, caring, committed men. Moreover, the vision is filled with idealized love and optimism: Love conquers all; good wins out over evil. The vision implies that by setting the right example oppression and bigotry can and will be overcome. A romantic conception of gay males and their relationships constitutes the controlling vision of the early 70s. This vision differs radically from the vision of the late 70s and early 80s. For the end of the decade is characterized by the vision of carnal virility.

Vision #2: Carnal Virility

The phrase carnal virility evokes a number of implications. The word carnal suggests desires and appetites of the flesh or body: sensual, animal, earthy. Virility suggests masculine vigor, force, and potency as they pertain to male sexual functions.[18] For one to be described by the phrase carnal virility implies that one is a supermale, concerned with intensive sexual exploration. The vision of carnal virility accounts for the seven fantasy chains common to the fictions examined from the late 70s and early 80s.

Gay males are obsessed with physical appearances. Every story has graphic descriptions of the physical appearances of the main characters. Blond. Blue eyes. Milk white complexion. Olive complexion. Broad nose. Sultry eyes. Sensual lips. A thick, tangled mass of curls. Bull-like neck. Washboard belly. Granite muscles. For example, Barry from "Midnight Sailor" is described as follows:

> His sailor whites clung snugly to the tapered muscularity of his body, the shirt outlining his chiseled pectorals, and the rippled stomach. The blue-ribbed flap stood out slightly over his broad shoulders in back, while in front hair curled thickly from the v of his collar.[19]

Each partner conjures images of the macho superman. There is also an element of earthy pride in the descriptions. Each character is a man who is proud of his body and takes care of it.

Gay males are sensuously, not romantically, oriented. In this fantasy the exploration of and desire for heightened sexual satisfaction takes precedence over romantic involvement. For example; "He is pivoted on his knees in a manner to reduce me to screaming and ecstasy."[20] Many such vivid, if not graphic, examples of these sensuous encounters dominate these magazines—they are, in fact, one of the major themes of these articles.

Gay males are powerful sex machines. As Marc Fasteau writes, describing the traditional male image, "The male machine is programmed to tackle jobs, override obstacles, attack problems, overcome difficulties and always seize the initiative; his most important positive reinforcement is victory."[21] In this fantasy gay males are ready for sex with anyone, anywhere, anytime. For example: "Racing toward an eruption, their bodies were a single, penetrating motion, like a movement when every instrument is the same, or a piston driving with unrestrained power."[22] Or: "When I went to the baths one night, I just stretched out and scores of people piled on top. Finally, I got bored with the operation and switched on Auto-Pilot."[23] As with any machine, performance becomes a measure of quality, and according to this fantasy, the number of sexual encounters becomes a measure of one's worth.

Gay males are free and independent, shunning commitments. Even when characters are paired, the relationships are open, allowing each partner the freedom of sexual exploration. For example: "I began to ask him questions about his life but he smiled and rolled over and said, 'Let's just have sex.' "[24] Or: "They called themselves lovers, but Martin wondered if they ever had sex without anyone else involved."[25] In none of the stories was there mention of a monogamous relationship. Sex is not to be confused with love or commitment, and therefore becomes viewed as sport. Of the four practicing gay typological groups discussed in Alan P. Bell's and Martin S. Weinberg's *Homosexualities,* the two individually largest groups were open-coupled and functional, groups that rated high on numbers of sexual partners.[26] This particular characteristic should not be viewed as unique to the gay community, however. Chesebro has argued that sensuous noncommitment has characterized the entire American society during the late 70s, and is part of a larger social problem.[27]

Viewed as sport, a fifth fantasy emerges: For gay males, *the chase or the game of conquest becomes second in importance only to sexual release.* To facilitate the playing of the game this fantasy pictures gay males as having developed a set of rules or symbols unique to their culture. Signals that become important to potential partners as indexes of one's particular proclivities or preferences: an earring, a colored bandanna, an outfit of leather, a meaningful glance. For example: "For no more than a second their eyes have met and the signals have been sent."[28] Or: "Sometimes I just come here and watch them all follow each other or cruise or play whatever games they happen to be playing."[29] And from another story: "The ritual commenced."[30] In "The Poker Game" Rice and Antonelli play five-card stud, gambling for the privilege of sex.[31]

As in any sport, there are amateurs and there are professionals, technique being the characteristic that separates the two. As technique improves, newer and more bizarre ways are created for the attainment of sexual gratification. Be it whip, boot, or blindfold, any imaginable fantasy can and will be realized, contingent only on one's imagination. The masters of technique refer to their "toys" and "playrooms," further emphasizing the gamey side of sex. As one story puts it:

> The Dungeon was aptly named. Its decor suggested the basement of a crumbling old castle: heavy timbers, cobwebs, chains, and dank stone walls. An Iron Maiden stood implacably beside the cash register, and ancient instruments of torture were scattered here and there, as though they had just recently been laid down by some long-dead sadistic torturer. The overall air of the place was gloomy and foreboding, but the customers really went for it.[32]

Gay males consider straight men to be in need of enlightenment. In one story a gay male proclaims, "I felt sorry for him, for all straight men. What a burden they carry."[33] And Rico gasps, "No woman ever felt like this."[34] In this fantasy, gay is portrayed as better than straight and, once tried, will illuminate a missing and vital aspect of every man's sexuality. Further, straight males are seen as being oppressed by the constraints of traditional male sex-role stereotypes.

Gay males have their own geographically identifiable community. Baths, bars, and appropriate city streets are the places in this fantasy and in reality where gay men meet one another. From one story, Barry had waited restlessly to come "to this place by the river. An area so well hidden and so well known, where love could be won nightly on your back or on your knees. Love that lasted as long as it took to reach orgasm."[35] These are the places where all the preceding fantasies culminate in search of orgasm. This is a fantasy of territorial possessiveness, for it is a world segregated and known only to the initiated. It is a world, according to this fantasy, where gay males become lusty, earthy animals seeking to assert and to explore the limits of their virility.

Carnal virility becomes not only an apt but also a compelling vision of the late 70s. Admittedly, there are dehumanizing aspects to this vision; sexual exploration and gratification become substitutes for romance, and love becomes an evening of necessary passion. However, there is also a very human side to this vision. Gay males are rejoicing in their physicalness, asserting their newly formed identity, and rejecting the externally imposed heterosexual ethic.

Implications of the Evolving Fantasies in the 1970s

There are three implications of the evolving fantasies in the 70s. First, the fantasies of gay males underwent a major change during the past decade. Gay males abandoned not only the heterosexually imposed model for relationship formation, but also the negative, heterosexually imposed stigma of homosexuality and being gay. Vision #2, Carnal Virility, indicates that gay males are exploring at least one aspect of their identity to its fullest. While vision #2 may be seen, in part, as dehumanizing, it is so only when viewed from a traditional heterosexual conception of "proper" behavior. Moreover, carnal virility indicates that the gay community is still at an incomplete phase of its evolving identity, exploring one facet of what is surely a multifaceted and complex system.

Second, the 70s, in which two phases were identifiable, can be viewed perhaps as a setup for the 80s, into which has passed some of the style and content of the earlier two visions. If the two visions of the 70s are viewed as incomplete phasic stages in the evolution of a gay community, then we should expect to see at least one additional phase. Vision #3, if correctly predicted, would be Virile Affection. As Chesebro claims, "the gay community gains its identity as a cultural system by virtue of this socially shared sense of affection or fondness and tender attachment among its members. The gay community is, in fact, the only cultural system unified by such a human sociosexual emotion."[36] This third vision, if correct, would see the more complete emergence of a uniquely gay ethic—a gay ethic that recognizes and rejoices in the diversities among people and their ways of life; an ethic that denies any apparent or stereotypical inconsistencies in same-sex affectional relationships; an ethic that fills the word gay with pride, power, and affection.

Third, by looking at rhetorical visions as phases of an evolving group's development, Bormann's original concept of fantasy theme analysis can be modified. Perhaps this modification will allow the critic to look at any group and its changing visions over time, and enable the critic to predict new phases in the group's evolution. Virginia Kidd employs such a phasic analysis of visions as she examines advice on interpersonal relations in popular magazines over a twenty-year period.[37] For the rhetorical critic, the use of phasic visions becomes a powerful critical and analytical method for the study of the relationship between fantasy and reality, a relationship that leaves an important question unanswered: Does the reality of the gay community create and maintain the fantasy, or does the fantasy of the gay community create and maintain the reality?

Part III

Homophobia

Chapter 10

Male Homophobia

Stephen F. Morin and Ellen M. Garfinkle

The fear of homosexuality has been described by several writers on men's issues as a powerful and central dynamic in the maintenance of traditional male roles.[1] It is often assumed in analyses of the male role that the fear of homosexuality is stronger in men than in women, and that this fear interferes more with the development of intimate relationships between men than between women. This essay examines these assumptions and specifically assesses the link between the fear of homosexuality and the experience of the male role.

Definitions and Conceptualizations of Homophobia

Homophobia has been conceptualized both from an external or cultural perspective and from an internal or psychodynamic perspective. Each perspective offers different insights into its origins and dynamics.

Cultural Perspectives

From a cultural perspective, homophobia is defined as any belief system which supports negative myths and stereotypes about homosexual people. More specifically, it can be used to describe (a) belief systems which hold that discrimination on the basis of sexual orientation is justifiable; (b) the use of language or slang, e.g., "queer," which is offensive to gay people; and/or (c) any belief system which does not value homosexual life-styles equally with heterosexual life-styles.

The cultural perspective on attitudes toward homosexuality is evident in the origin of the term homophobia. W. Churchill[2] uses the word homoerotophobia to describe the fear of erotic or sexual contact with members of the same sex and gives particular emphasis to the continuum defined more than a decade earlier that described the extent to which various cultures placed restrictions on homosexual contact.[3] Churchill concluded that attempts to repress homosexuality are the direct result of socialization practices of "sex negative" cultures. He argued that contemporary American society is such a sex-negative culture, and pointed out that attitudes toward male homosexuality have reached such phobic levels that any behavior which is suggestive of homosexuality is strictly condemned and avoided.

Considerable support for Churchill's view has been found in recent cross-cultural research. For example, one group of investigators found that males who were rated high in homophobia were more constricted than low-homophobia males in their view on sex-appropriate behavior for men, and had a greater tendency to suspect any male who exhibited so-called "feminine" characteristics of harboring homosexual tendencies.[4] Further support for Churchill's contention that homophobic attitudes are related to general cultural values regarding sex-appropriate behavior can be found in studies which compare attitudes of Brazilians, Canadians, and West Indians.[5] Brazilians, who were found to have the most conservative attitudes toward sex-appropriate behavior of the three cultures studied, showed the most homophobic attitudes; West Indians, who demonstrated moderately conservative attitudes toward sex-appropriate behavior, were intermediate between the highly sex-negative Brazilians and the less sex-negative Canadians. Similarly, the finding that the attitudes toward homosexuality are more negative among those people reared in the strongly sex-negative subcultures of the midwestern and southern regions of the United States than those reared in other regions of the country is also consistent with Churchill's view.[6]

Other writers have conceptualized homophobia in terms of a generalized, cultural belief system regarding the relationship between the sexes. G.K. Lehne uses the term homosexism to describe "sexism between individuals of the same sex (although they may differ in sexual orientation)."[7] This same general belief system has been called "heterosexual bias"[8] or "heterosexism,"[9] in that it specifically argues the superiority of heterosexual over homosexual life-styles.

A number of studies have found that the need to preserve a double standard between men and women is a more basic component of homophobia than is sexual conservatism.[10] It has also been noted that negative attitudes toward homosexuals are associated with the belief that men are more potent than women.[11] Using a multiple regression analysis, it was found that the best single predictor of homophobia is a belief in the traditional family ideology, i.e., dominant father, submissive mother, and obedient children.[12] The second best predictor of homophobia was found to be agreement with traditional beliefs about women, e.g., that it is worse for a woman to tell dirty jokes than it is for a man. In addition, traditional religious beliefs have been found to be predictive of both traditional attitudes toward women and negative attitudes toward homosexuality, particularly in men.[13] Again, this correlational data supports Churchill's contention that cultural learning regarding appropriate roles for each sex is a powerful force associated with fear, dread, and hatred for homosexuals, particularly male homosexuals.[14]

Personal Perspective

As an individual personality dynamic, homophobia refers specifically to "the irrational fear or intolerance of homosexuality,"[15] or to "an irrational, persistent fear or dread of homosexuals."[16] In this context, the term homophobia is used to describe a specific phobic condition, rather than a generalized cultural attitude.

The use of the term homophobia to describe a personal rather than a cultural dynamic was first popularized by George Weinberg.[17] He described the phenomenon of homophobia as an irrational fear on the part of heterosexuals of being in close proximity to people they believe to be homosexual. For example, support of such statements as "I would be uncomfortable if I knew I were sitting next to a homosexual on a bus" would represent a homophobic attitude. In an important attempt to clarify the dynamics of homophobia among homosexuals themselves, Weinberg postulated the nature of this phenomenon as a self-hatred which results from the internalization of others' irrational fears. Studies that have investigated attitudes of homosexual men toward homosexuality have found that homosexual men have internalized many societal beliefs regarding homosexuality, but they do not hold these beliefs to the extent found in heterosexual men.[18]

The personality correlates of homophobia clearly suggest that those people who are afraid or intolerant of homosexuals are afraid or intolerant in a great many other social and interpersonal situations as well. Those who are more negative in their attitudes toward homosexuality have been found to be more authoritarian,[19] more dogmatic,[20] more cognitively rigid,[21] more intolerant of ambiguity,[22] more status-conscious,[23] more sexually rigid,[24] more guilty and negative about their own sex impulses,[25] and less accepting of others in general.[26] All these personality characteristics might be expected of any highly prejudiced group of people.

In addition, there is ample evidence that heterosexual men do, in fact, have classical fear reactions in response to homosexual men. Ironically, the bulk of this evidence has been supplied by researchers gathering baseline data in attempts to "cure" men of their homosexuality by the use of classical conditioning procedures. The basic theoretical assumption underlying such treatment programs is that male homosexuality represents a learned phobia to women. The data, however, do not support this assumption.

An instrument called the "phallometer" was developed to measure penile volume changes in response to viewing pictures of male and female nudes.[27] As hypothesized, both homosexual and heterosexual male participants responded to their preferred sex pictures with increased penile volume. Homosexual men, however, responded no differently to female stimulus pictures than to neutral pictures. The surprising result was that heterosexual men had decreased penile volume in response to pictures of nude men. This behavioral manifestation of a specific aversion was hypothesized but not found among the homosexual participants.

This aversion response of heterosexual men to pictures of nude males has been replicated in a series of studies, all of which fail to find support for the theory that homosexual men fear women. Using penile volume measures, homosexual men were found to have no aversion to (a) pictures of nude, adult females;[28] (b) auditory or written descriptions of heterosexual intercourse;[29] or (c) pictures of the vulva, the face, or the breasts of a mature female.[30] Researchers found that the homosexual participants' verbal ratings of the experience of arousal and pleasantness were not only significantly higher for slides of males than for slides of females, but were also higher for slides of females than for neutral slides.[31] In addition, all the homosexual participants' pleasantness ratings were positive. Heterosexual participants, however, found only the slides of nude females to be sexually arousing, and rated the slides of the nude males as unpleasant.

These findings suggest that homosexual men do not fear women, but that heterosexual men may have some sort of fear of their own sexual impulses toward men. In order to clarify the dynamics of the fear of homosexuality it is important to differentiate between the fear of others and the fear of one's own impulses.

Fear of Others Versus Fear of One's Own Impulses

We conceptualize homophobia as occurring on several levels with different dynamics associated with each level. The motivations for homophobia are so many and so individual that all of them could not possibly be explained with the same interpretation. With this qualification in mind, a few of the motivations will be considered.

Superficial fears regarding gay men appear to be rooted in the general belief systems by which people are socialized in our culture. Acceptance of stereotypes which view homosexuals as sick and dangerous seem to be particularly associated with negative attitudes, suggesting that a sense of threat is related to rejection of male homosexuals. D. Steffensmeier and R. Steffensmeier found that the more a person agreed with the stereotypes which view homosexuals as sick and dangerous, the more rejecting he or she was, and male participants were found to be more rejecting of male homosexuals than were female participants.[32] We interpret these findings to mean that males are more likely than females to view the male homosexual as a sexual failure and more likely to perceive him as personally threatening and dangerous. Similarly, the belief that homosexuals are dangerous and the belief that homosexuals should be subject to legal and social restrictions not placed on the rest of society are the major factors which account for attitudes toward male homosexuals.[33] These same beliefs appeared to be secondary in accounting for attitudes toward lesbians.

Most of the superficial fear regarding male homosexuality can be attributed to ignorance about or lack of direct experience with gay men. The stereotype which describes male homosexuals as sick or psychologically disturbed seems to carry with it the belief that gay men are unpredictable or untrustworthy. The "dangerousness" stereotype connotes that male homosexuals are a threat to others (e.g., male homosexuals are child molesters) and they are a threat to one's personal safety (e.g., male homosexuals are hypersexual and are sexually aggressive toward unwilling partners). The evidence that homosexual men average 1.3 orgasms per week compared to an average of 3.0 for heterosexual men[34] casts serious doubts on these stereotypes of hypersexuality.

One approach to understanding fear of homosexuality in others is to relate this fear to basic species-specific reactions. For example, ethologists note that many lower species and many young children have a basic dread of others whom they perceive to be different from themselves.[35] From this perspective, cultural prohibitions and negative stereotypes may, at least in part, be rooted in this primitive species characteristic of fear of difference.

At the level of personal motivation, homophobia may be regarded as an expression of anxiety regarding one's own sexual impulses. Some writers feel that these feared impulses are homosexual in nature. According to this hypothesis, a man who is basically afraid of his own latent homosexual feelings attempts to reassure himself and convince others that he is really a "healthy, normal heterosexual" by actively and vigorously suppressing all homosexual impulses. Homosexual feelings create such great anxiety in these men that their existence cannot be tolerated. Fear of homosexuality in such persons might then be understood as the projection of the fear of one's own homosexual impulses onto the expression of the homosexual impulses of others.

Other writers shift the focus away from fear of latent homosexual impulses to anxiety or fear surrounding expression of sexual impulses of any sort.[36] According to this view, people who are uncomfortable about their own sexual feelings express their discomfort in the form of negative attitudes toward others whom they perceive to be more openly expressive of their sexual impulses, including homosexuals.

This explanation is in basic agreement with Freud's (1916–58) theory which relates paranoia to the projection of unconscious and unacceptable impulses, and has also found support in more recent research. For example, Churchill concluded from his cross-cultural and cross-species study of homosexual behavior among males[37] that prejudice against homosexuality in others is a function of one's negative attitudes toward one's own sexuality, implying that it is an antisexual factor which accounts for negative attitudes toward homosexuality. M. Brown and D.M. Amoroso concluded that antihomosexual subjects were more disapproving of various sexual practices and reported greater personal sex guilt than did subjects who were not opposed to homosexuality,[38] and K. Smith found that antihomosexual attitudes correlate with greater personal rigidity and personal sex guilt.[39] Similarly, D.F. Berry and F. Marks found that "antihomosexual prejudice as a social defense is not unlike paranoia as an individual defense in terms of the motivational dynamics and life's experiences which give rise to the projection process."[40]

Pervasiveness and Manifestations

Survey Studies

The most recent data on attitudes toward homosexuality suggest that the majority of Americans (56%) think that homosexuals should have equal rights in terms of job opportunities.[41] At the same time, however, this general philosophy of equal rights was found not to apply to hiring homosexuals in certain sensitive positions. For example, a significant proportion of the respondents would deny to a homosexual the right to be an elementary school teacher (65%), a member of the clergy (54%), a doctor (44%), or a member of the armed forces (38%). Although the majority of respondents (53%) felt that a homosexual could be a good Christian or Jew, fewer (43%) felt that homosexual relations between consenting adults should be legal, and even fewer (14%) felt that homosexuals should be allowed to adopt children.[42]

These data suggest considerably more positive attitudes than were expressed in 1970 in data collected by the Institute for Sex Research.[43] At that time, the vast majority of respondents (84%) believed that "homosexuality is a social corruption that can cause the downfall of a civilization." Three quarters of the respondents would deny to a homosexual the right to be a minister (77%), a schoolteacher (77%), or a judge (76%), and two thirds would bar the homosexual from medical practice (68%) or government service (67%).

Other surveys have found similar results, with homosexuals generally perceived to be either sinful[44] or sick.[45] A recent survey conducted by *Psychology Today* on the subject of masculinity included questions pertaining to attitudes toward homosexuality.[46] Although this study is based on an unusually large sample, it should be noted that the respondents were markedly younger, more affluent, less religious, better educated, and more liberal than the average American. Despite this liberal bias, 70% of the heterosexual respondents (both male and female) reported believing that "homosexual men are not fully masculine."

Demographic analyses of attitudes toward homosexuality have produced some conflicting results. E. Levitt and A. Klassen,[47] as well as Gallup,[48] found that those who were more negative in their attitudes were more likely to be rural, white, and male. While Levitt and Klassen found no significant age or educational differences, Gallup found both age and education to be significant factors. Studies conducted on professional samples suggest that although attitudes are likely to be more favorable in these groups than in the general population, a significant amount of myth and stereotyping remains despite high levels of education and training.

Behavioral Studies

Direct behavioral measures have generally revealed more convincing evidence than have survey studies regarding attitudes toward homosexuals. In one study, researchers explored attitudes using a methodology in which interpersonal distance was measured by the participants' arrangement of stick figures.[49] They found that participants placed themselves significantly farther from marijuana users, drug addicts, obese persons, present homosexuals, and past homosexuals, in that order. Participants expressed little optimism about the possibility of a homosexual changing to a heterosexual orientation, and former homosexuals evoked even greater social distance than did current homosexuals. Interestingly enough, former homosexuals were thought to be less trustworthy than current homosexuals.

Another group of investigators used chair placement as a measure of social distance to determine the effects of perceiving a person to be homosexual on establishing interpersonal space.[50] Participants were interviewed under two conditions by either a male or female experimenter regarding their attitudes toward homosexuality and other issues. They found that in the experimental condition where the experimenter wore a "gay and proud" button and was introduced as working for the Association of Gay Psychologists, participants positioned their chairs significantly farther away from the experimenter than in a neutral condition where the experimenter wore no button and was introduced as a graduate student. Males reacted with about three times as much social distance in interaction with a male experimenter who was perceived to be homosexual than did females in interaction with a female experimenter who was perceived to be homosexual.

An additional and important finding in the latter study was that the participants reported more positive attitudes toward homosexuals when they perceived the interviewer to be homosexual, while at the same time positioning their chairs at a greater distance. As we conceptualize it, body language speaks more loudly than words. In that the bulk of what is currently known regarding antihomosexual attitudes is based on questionnaire and interview techniques, these findings must be interpreted cautiously.

Another study found a clear relationship between expressed negative attitudes and aggression toward homosexuals.[51] Using loss of money which resulted from a participant's negative evaluation of an experimental confederate as a measure of aggression, they found that heterosexual male participants who scored high on a measure of negative attitudes toward homosexuals were: (a) significantly more aggressive toward homosexual than toward heterosexual targets; (b) highly aggressive toward target homosexuals regardless of the type of prior interaction with a target homosexual; and (c) significantly more aggressive toward homosexual male targets who were perceived to be similar to, rather than different from, them in personality. Those who conducted this study speculated that such aggressive reactions toward homosexuals are accounted for by the dynamic of personal threat.

Are Men More Homophobic Than Women?

Although homophobia is found in both women and men, it appears to be more exaggerated and more powerful in males than in females. Research on sex differences in homophobia has been hampered by the failure of many studies to (a) use females as well as males as participants, and (b) differentiate between male homosexuals and female homosexuals as the target group to be evaluated. Lack of sophistication of both research methodology and the conceptualization of the construct under study have also contributed to the absence of definitive evidence regarding sex differences in attitudes toward homosexuals.

Of those studies which have investigated sex differences in antihomosexual attitudes, eight reported that males are more negative or threatened by homosexuality than are females.[52] Six studies have found no significant differences in antihomosexual attitudes of men and women.[53]

Those studies which failed to find significant sex differences in attitudes toward homosexuality have tended to assess the more general, cultural beliefs about homosexuality, rather than the more specific, individual attitudes which might relate to the element of personal threat in an interaction with a homosexual person of the same sex.[54] The remaining studies which failed to find significant sex differences used more sophisticated measures, but still remained on the level of assessing global, cultural beliefs rather than specific, personal attitudes.[55]

The element of same-sex interaction is a crucial variable in negative attitudes toward homosexuals. One investigation found "a pattern of more negative descriptions of same-sexed homosexuals than of opposite-sexed homosexuals."[56] In addition, participants expressed both significantly more personal anxiety with respect to same-sexed homosexuals than with respect to opposite-sexed homosexuals, and also greater preference for opposite-sexed (as opposed to same-sexed) homosexuals.

Another study found behavioral confirmation of the hypothesis that same-sex interaction is crucial to the presence of negative attitudes toward homosexuals.[57] Using chair placement as a measure of social distance, they found that male participants reacted with approximately three times more social distance when being interviewed by a homosexually labeled male experimenter than did females who were interviewed by a homosexually labeled female experimenter.

Other authors have emphasized the male homosexual's violation of the male sex role as a crucial element in the finding that men appear to hold more negative attitudes toward homosexuals than do women. Steffensmeier and Steffensmeier found that male subjects are significantly more rejecting of homosexuals than are female subjects, and that male subjects are "especially rejecting" of male, as compared to female, homosexuals.[58] The authors argued that male homosexuality is defined as being more incongruent with the culturally sanctioned sex role than is female homosexuality, and that male homosexuals are thus more susceptible to censure and rejection than are their female counterparts. In other studies, a direct correlation between the degree of sex-role stereotyping and antihomosexual attitudes among male subjects was found.[59] As a result of two inquiries, it was found that antihomosexual attitudes correlate with the need to maintain traditional masculine and feminine sex roles and with the need to preserve double standards between the sexes. F.A. Minnigerode found that men were significantly more negative in their attitudes toward homosexuals than were women.[60] Also, those subjects who were classified as antihomosexual showed significantly greater sexual conservatism and were significantly more antifeminist than those subjects who were classified as prohomosexual. Minnigerode interpreted these findings to indicate that both antifeminist attitudes and sexual conservatism, i.e., attitudes which do not depart from or challenge the traditional definitions of sex roles, independently contribute to antihomosexual attitudes.

Support for the theory that violation of sex-role norms is a more salient factor in contributing to negative attitudes toward male homosexuals than toward female homosexuals can be found in the feminist analysis of the different values placed on the male and female roles in American culture. Many have argued that American culture clearly values the male over the female role.[61] Thus, women who break with the traditional sex-role expectations may not be judged as harshly as men who break with a more valued role. This hypothesis is consistent with the observation that female homosexuals are less likely to be defined as a social problem, less likely to be negatively stereotyped, and less likely to be rejected than are male homosexuals.[62]

Homophobia and the Male Role

It is commonly believed that gay men do not fit the cultural criteria for masculinity, and being gay is strongly associated with the violation of sex-role stereotypes in American society. Research on attitudes toward male homosexuality and beliefs concerning the male role reveals that the typical male homosexual is seen to be quite different from the typical male heterosexual in consistently negative ways. Using a semantic differential technique, Rodney G. Karr (see chapter 1) found that a sample of 100 men rated the "typical male homosexual" on an evaluative factor as less good, less honest, less fair, less positive, less valuable, less stable, less intellectual, less friendly, and less clean, as well as more shallow and unhealthy than the "typical male heterosexual."[63] On a masculinity factor, homosexuals were rated as more delicate, more passive, more womanly, smaller, softer, and more yielding than heterosexual men. These data indicate that the male role is a distinct and powerful one, and that gay men are seen to deviate from this role in significant ways. It is apparent from these findings that the fear of being labeled a homosexual can operate as a powerful force in keeping men within the boundaries of their traditional roles.

Behavioral validation of the way in which fear of the homosexual label operates to maintain traditional role behavior supports the attribution studies. Karr arranged an Asch-type experiment in which one experimental confederate was labeled as a homosexual by a second confederate in the experimental condition, and not so labeled in the neutral condition.[64] Participants performed a nonverbal communication task and then were asked to rate the other members of their group, including the confederates, on a number of dimensions. On a masculinity factor, the homosexually labeled confederate was rated as significantly less masculine, smaller, weaker, softer, and more passive, more yielding, more delicate and less powerful than the same confederate when not labeled. It is interesting to note in this context that many gay men have described their own self-contempt as neither stereotypically masculine nor feminine, but rather as more typically androgynous, or expressive of characteristics of both sexes.[65] The perceived homosexual in the Karr study was also rated as less friendly, less happy, less funny, more unpleasant, more tense, and less handsome than the same confederate when not labeled.

Karr's participants also ranked the confederates on a scale of "most preferred" to "least preferred." The same man was rated as among the most preferred when not labeled but among the least preferred when labeled as homosexual. Additionally, there was clear evidence that participants perceived their groups less positively and group problem solving was less effective when a homosexually labeled person was present.

A surprising and extremely interesting finding in Karr's study was that the confederates who actually performed the labeling were all perceived as significantly more masculine and more sociable when they labeled someone homosexual than when they did not. Karr suggested that men who demonstrate ability to simply identify another man as a homosexual are rewarded and reinforced by other men in our culture for possessing that "skill."

Homophobia thus appears to be functional in the dynamics of maintaining the traditional male role. The fear of being labeled homosexual serves to keep men within the confines of what the culture defines as sex-role appropriate behavior, and it interferes with the development of intimacy between men. Homophobia limits options and deprives men of the potentially rewarding experiences of learning from and being close to one another.

Can Homophobic Attitudes Be Changed?

There is a great deal of controversy over the extent to which attitudes toward homosexuality can be changed. Again, this is a complex issue, related to the variety and intensity of the motivations supporting homophobic belief systems. It has been suggested that "many middle-class heterosexual (college age) males have not adopted firm attitudinal decisions about alternative life-styles."[66] It would appear that for the vast majority of people, beliefs about homosexuals are simply an unchallenged part of their socialization experiences.

Few people have systematically tried to change people's attitudes toward homosexuality, but in those few cases where it has been attempted, change has been surprisingly rapid and rather extensive. Stephen F. Morin reported dramatic changes in attitudes resulting from a single course on homosexuality offered to graduate and undergraduate students in psychology.[67] Consistent with Weinberg's predictions,[68] improvements in attitudes toward homosexuality showed a significant positive correlation with independent measures of the student's own self-esteem. Subsequent research has indicated that exposure to as little as one article can significantly change a person's reported attitudes toward homosexuality in either a positive or a negative direction, depending on the content of the article.[69] The relative ease with which homophobic attitudes can be altered has come as a surprise to many. It is important to note, however, that these are changes of surface attitudes, and have not been subjected to tests of behavioral validation.

Sex education in the United States does not seem to have eased the public's prejudiced attitudes toward homosexuals. Of the respondents in the Levitt and Klassen[70] sample who had received sex education (27%), only 40% had homosexuality even mentioned in that training. Of that 40%, only two thirds were told that homosexuality was always wrong, and only 1.5% were told that it was not wrong at all. If sex education is to have any impact on attitudes toward homosexuals, it would appear that significant changes will have to be made both in the curriculum and in the attitudes of the sex educators.

In training psychotherapists to work with gay clients, we have noted one type of behavioral change in attitudes toward homosexuality. Part of the training process has involved providing experiences in which individual therapists may begin to challenge their own homophobic attitudes. For example, when the male therapists went on an excursion to several gay bars, many reported significant changes in their perception and attitudes. Typical observations were: "I felt like such an outsider; there were so many of them and so few of us"; "I initially felt uncomfortable watching two men dance . . . but later, after a few drinks, it didn't upset me at all"; "I was amazed at how many of the men appeared more masculine than myself"; and "During the night, I moved from feeling like a voyeur to feeling like a participant."

Many of the men had to deal with being asked to dance. Most said yes, but some said no. For most, it was a major decision. Few men reported receiving sexual advances, and many expressed disappointment and surprise that they were ignored. Most reported, with some amazement, an appreciation of what women must experience in heterosexual bars. Some expressed the recognition that being looked at as a sex object was not a totally pleasant experience. Many of the women in the training classes have been overwhelmed by the men's lack of insight into women's experiences.

At the end of the evening of bar-going, it was not unusual for the men to embrace when saying goodnight. Almost all reported that this single venture into the gay subculture broke down more of their homophobic attitudes than did all of their reading and discussion on the subject. Similar changes in attitudes have been reported in the experiences of men's groups.[71]

Close personal interaction with gay men of similar status appears to be a crucial experience in altering homophobic attitudes and behavior. Further, people consistently report feeling better about themselves as their homophobic attitudes decrease.

What Heterosexual Men Can Learn from the Experiences of Gay Men

It is clear that heterosexual men can learn a great deal about their own internalized sex-role stereotypes from becoming familiar with the experiences of gay men who have creatively violated the traditional sex-role stereotypes. Further, much can be learned about improving and/or expanding heterosexual relationships from the experiences of nonrole-stereotyped relationships which have evolved among gay men and women. For example, gay couples have the advantage of beginning their relationships on an equal biological status. Many of these relationships are worthy of the attention of those who are interested in developed relationships which incorporate more equality and more satisfaction for both partners.[72]

Recently, one of us (Morin) was involved in a training session for counselors in which two men from the group were asked to role-play being lovers. Specifically, they were to role-play going to see Morin as a therapist because of severe anxiety over losing their heterosexual friends if their relationship were discovered. Fortunately, one of the most outspoken homophobic men volunteered for the exercise. When the couple was asked in therapy why they had chosen to be lovers in light of all the persecution they would experience, the homophobic man replied, "Because we love one another and because I'm gay." Later, this man reported that he felt a sense of great relief and exhilaration in saying that he was gay. It was like admitting to the worst possibilities and finding nothing bad happened to him. Similar experiences have been reported by women in the feminist movement as they have come to terms with lesbianism.

It would appear that as the men's "consciousness focusing" movement progresses, those who desire more intimate and more rewarding relationships both with other men and with women are going to have to challenge their own male homophobia. The irrational fear of being close to other men and of the label "homosexual" has been a long-standing dynamic which has kept many men imprisoned in traditional roles. Acceptance and appreciation of gay men within the men's movement is essential to its growth. Gay men have a vital part to play in the development of new definitions of the male role.

Chapter 11

The Pathogenic Secret

Larry G. Ehrlich

For the gay man or woman who feels like the only person in the world, the knowledge that millions of individuals share a similar life-style can be surprisingly unsupportive. Even the discovery of "others" across town or a member of the "fraternity" right next door can be an undependable edge against the feelings of isolation and disaffection that result from negative labels superimposed by the most insensitive quarters in one's environment. And even for homosexual men and women who, against the odds, have discovered and sustained meaningful, love-filled relationships, moments of anomie and discontent can intrude what is by almost any reasonable definition a strong and supportive personal sanctuary. The personal, social, and professional appetites of gay men and women are not significantly different from their heterosexual counterparts; the requirements for survival in personal, social, and professional arenas are, however, dramatically dissimilar.

The struggle for a positive self-image in the gay community has been keynoted by confrontations with the more outrageous critics of the homosexual life-style. The technical losses in Eugene, Oregon, Wichita, Kansas, and Dade County, Florida were in fact "victories." The referenda in various sectors of the country have induced dialogue and a sense of collegiality in the gay community. While the conversations in the streets of the gay community are exceptionally important, the self-encounters resulting from the debates in the political sphere are equally significant. The history of oppressed minorities and subcultures, including the contemporary campaign for gay rights, has been one of circling back—returning to do battle with oneself, a struggle more devious and dangerous than any created by one's detractors.

The degree of introspection evidenced in the gay community is obviously not unique to the homosexual experience. Only a fool would suggest that the heterosexual world is devoid of sensitivity, insight, and caring souls. Strong support is, however, available to suggest that the unique challenges of sustaining a balanced personality in an era of repression lead the gay man and woman, more frequently and more predictably, to the threshold of introspection. While the search for compatriots and supporters is high on the political agenda for any disadvantaged community, the most important of the cultural dialogues about alternative life-styles may well be the quality and direction of the intracultural dialogue in the gay community. The campaign for social and political franchises will have been for naught if members of the homosexual community do not draw positive and reinforcing conclusions about themselves. A humane and sensitive culture will be one in which not only the purveyors of bigotry and intemperance are harnessed by legal injunction, but one in which all people, including gays, are intellectually and emotionally emancipated. The real challenge for gays will be to express themselves as well after liberation as before. The aspects of the homosexual experience which represent potential blocks to growth and productivity in an era of liberation are worthy of consideration by any profession that embraces the centrality of meaningful, sustained interpersonal communication.

The Uniqueness and Meaning of Self-disclosure for the Gay Male and Lesbian

Surviving as a gay in a heterosexual context often rests in having a command of the art and science of self-disclosure. The individual decision to share information about one's most inner thoughts and desires can become all-consuming—and, occasionally, overpowering—to most gays who live, work, and survive in an environment that is at least neutral and more often than not hostile. One survey reported that 70 percent of the individuals polled felt that homosexual acts were *always* wrong even if the individuals were in love.[1] Gay men or women who might wish to share the knowledge of their life-style with individuals in their environment are understandably intimidated by a repressive attitude that has shown little indication of abating in the last decade.

Literature on the importance of self-disclosure suggests that personal growth and development is in part a function of being able to appropriately invest one's *self* in interpersonal encounters. Gerald M. Phillips and Nancy J. Metzger have identified disclosure as a type of currency, "a very valuable prize to most people. . . . When someone confides in us, it makes us feel important because someone gave us so much power over his life. It is safer and more productive to contemplate weaknesses with a trusted friend, apparently, than to try to handle them alone."[2] In many instances the option of disclosure is effectively precluded for gays.

A "philosophy for disclosing" rests in the hope that the risk of shared intimacy will not be abused. The disclosing individual wishes to impress the potential friend with a high level of trust, and at the same time wishes to psychologically disarm one's critics with candor. The necessity with which members of the homosexual community are called on to disclose themselves is not matched, at least in quantity, by the requirements of a heterosexual life-style. Unless a member of the straight world is closeting some sort of heinous behavior, the requirement of disclosure that can sear through the soul of a gay individual is essentially unknown in the heterosexual world. Information expressed by heterosexual lips that might be considered mundane and pedestrian would be grist for the rumor mill if expressed by a member of the gay community, e.g., one's life mate, celebration of anniversaries, social outlets, and so on. In the best of circumstances the healthy gay learns to share information in the most productive manner possible. Tempering tact with discretion, disclosing gays can skate clear of unsuspecting homophobic responses. Gay men and women may have to sanitize pronouns to protect their worst critics from their own intemperance. However, with good fortune, like any individual, gays can grow and be nurtured in a community in which friendship and companionship is measured partially by a healthy degree of mutual disclosure.

The alternative to interpersonal sharing—a strategy of nondisclosure—can easily become the communication style forced on gays by a nonsupportive environment. Frivolous self-disclosure can be counterproductive; the absence of any intimate exchange can be a dangerous personal vice. Any individual, straight or gay, who feels compelled to live a lie may reach a point at which the "fiction" shared with one's associates becomes reality even to the author. Nondisclosure can be an instinctive response to a homophobic environment. However, a strategy of selective deceit can also erode one's ability to communicate with one's gay brothers and sisters. The closeted homosexual is the personification of the nondisclosing philosophy. Ultimately, an individual, gay or straight, embraces an interpersonal style and negotiates the demands of disclosure. The most tragic of oppressed individuals are trapped against their intellectual and emotional instincts by the onus of the "pathogenic secret."

The concept of the pathogenic secret has been credited to Viennese physician Moritz Benedikt. A pathogenic secret is personal information intentionally withheld that induces a state of physical and psychological dysfunction. The pathogenic secret is characterized by the withholding of relevant data when the demands of the social situation militate in favor of expression. The gay man or woman who has an opportunity to identify his or her homosexuality in a nonthreatening environment but is muted by a pattern of secrecy, is typical of the personality most susceptible to such dysfunctions. In many cases the reason for keeping the "secret" is a real or imagined fear of rejection by the proximate or remote participants in the encounter, e.g., "If I tell him, my parents might find out." Regardless of the reasons for the lack of candor, the ultimate result is the progressive debilitation of a productive member of society. The virulent nature of homophobia in America renders some members of the gay community especially susceptible to the pathology of nondisclosure.

The correlation between effective interpersonal communication skills and the parameters of the healthy personality are well established in the literature of communication studies, and are buttressed by research in the social and behavioral sciences. The classic work of Jurgen Ruesch and Gregory Bateson in *Communication: The Social Matrix of Psychiatry* establishes the primacy of communication behavior in culturing a healthy personality. Ruesch argues that "people are mentally healthy only when their means of communication permit them to manage their surroundings successfully."[3] The give-and-take of interpersonal communication provides a litmus test of one's powers. A communicating individual is a healthy personality, because ongoing effort to influence one's environment is a consummate act of optimism. An individual who is no longer willing to take the risk of change and acceptance has been sidetracked from the possibility of growth inherent in interpersonal contact. According to Ruesch, psychopathology is defined in terms of an interruption of the communication process. An individual who holds tenaciously to a pathogenic secret has reduced the arena of contact to an audience of one—the self.

Information about oneself that is persistently repressed over a period can induce the dimensions of stress, thereby fostering the worst consequences of the pathogenic secret. Sidney Jourard has noted that the energy and time used to conceal information distracts the individual from more rewarding and meaningful encounters. In some respects it might be easier for gay persons to disclose themselves to a fellow advocate or an avowed homophobe than to the less polarized personalities, the somewhat nondescript individuals representing most of the encounters encompassed in a lifetime. The vagaries of the supercritic and the detractor are easy to chart. But the nonpublic, apparently uncommitted encounters represent a substantial threat. Because one doesn't know where the average Joe is coming from, the most conservative instinct—not to risk rejection—is just as psychologically damaging as a homophobe with bludgeon in hand. The gay who wishes to disclose but succumbs to "passing" in a fairly neutral environment may turn on herself or himself, and by confirming loss of self-confidence, court the price of the pathogenic secret. Gays share the frustration recorded by Jourard when he wrote, "I am beginning to suspect that I can't even know *my own soul* except as I disclose it."[4]

H.R. Ellenberger has identified a "no-exit" aspect to the pathogenic secret.[5] To Ellenberger, the frustration of not being able to disclose substantial portions of oneself, such as sexuality, is exacerbated by the feeling, albeit untrue in most cases, that there is *no* chance that this vital information can ever be unlocked to another living being. The first step toward reducing the dissonance caused by nondisclosure, confession and revelation, is effectively precluded by the psychological mind-set of the individual. The no-exit aspect of the nondiscloser is the essence of personal pessimism about life in general. The philosophy of pessimism may be nothing more than a form of adolescent escapism, a world in which the probability of pain, loss, defeat, and despair is effectively held at bay.

The trap of no-exit funnels gay men and women into spates of hedonism that are furtive and ill-fated attempts to find self-validation, precluded by their incapacity to share themselves with the nonhomosexual world. "An individual's sense of worth rests both upon the validation given by the self and that provided by society. The gay person is usually excluded from social validation except from within the gay community."[6] In exchange for a nonhostile territory, gay men and women, often in desperation, trade meaningful but hurt-filled encounters for the safer environments of hedonism, for which the gay community-at-large is criticized. If repressed hope for self-fulfillment has been effectively erased, the world of the narcissist and the hedonist may be all that remains for individuals who feel trapped in a world of unfair rules. Caged by an attitude of no-exit, many gay men and women approach a feeling described by Clark E. Moustakas: "It seems that loneliness is sort of a cunning thing. It kind of knows 'torture' methods of its own. Sometimes it can begin to convince you that false truths are right, or it can let you see your friends having fun without you, and that can hurt."[7] The disaffected have reached an exceptionally dangerous stage of loneliness at no-exit, a condition amplified by the pathogenic secret. The pathological nondiscloser can quickly create a world of containment, a personal repertoire of roles and expectations that progressively escalates the individual into a nonproductive world of fantasy. As the nondiscloser is seduced further into the world of fantasy, the option to pursue a meaningful and productive life wanes.

Homophobia and Self-disclosure

Susceptibility to the pathogenic secret can be evaluated in the gay community as a response to a traditionally homophobic society. The term homophobe has yet to be enshrined in traditional dictionaries; the impact of homophobia in the culture is carried ultimately in everyone's emotional lexicon. Most individuals have little difficulty offering their gut feelings about homosexuals in their midst. Homophobes are individuals with an inordinate fear of men and women who profess, or are suspected of, sexual attraction to members of the same sex. G.K. Lehne describes homophobia as "an irrational, persistent, fear or dread of homosexuals."[8] W. Churchill used the term homoerotophobia to identify the "fear of erotic or sexual contact with members of the same sex."[9] Homophobes occasionally miss the distinction between illusion and reality. According to George Weinberg, "the fear . . . of being in close proximity to people they *believe* to be homosexual,"[10] can precipitate the rage of homophobia. The prevailing attitudes about sex, in general, have become so repressive in contemporary society that "attitudes toward male homosexuality have reached such phobic levels that any behavior which is suggestive of homosexuality is strictly condemned and avoided" (see p. 118).[11]

The more crass manifestations of homophobia are not well documented in the general press. America's homophobia has been recently broadcast from an embarrassing international platform. U.S. Immigration and Naturalization Service (INS) officers held a Mexican citizen incommunicado for twenty-four hours because officials at San Francisco International Airport discovered dresses in his luggage. Immigration authorities detained the man as a suspected homosexual but released him after it was discovered he was a dress designer. The woman's ensemble that had precipitated the detention was intended for a hostess in the Bay area.[12]

The actions of the INS have escalated to such outrageous proportions that Sen. Alan Cranston (D-California) has announced his intention to introduce legislation to eliminate the antihomosexual provision of the federal immigration code. Cranston feels that the restrictive immigration code is "intellectually, morally and medically unsound," and concedes that efforts to remove the discrimination will be difficult because of a "lot of medieval thinking on this subject in the Congress."[13] The discrimination by homophobic American officials was the subject of ridicule by a major media caper conducted by Dutch gay activists at Amsterdam's Schipol Airport. The Homo Squad and the Dyke Section—Dutch gays masquerading as immigration officials—approached unsuspecting American tourists and asked them: "Are you homosexual?" The media stunt was reported to have had a major impact on American tourists subjected to reverse discrimination.[14]

When members of the gay community attempt to participate in the symbolic charitable and social aspects of the community, the response of the homophobic mentality is almost comical. In Tucson the U.S. Marine Corps refused to accept donations of toys and cash for their Toys for Tots program because the contributions originated through the local gay community. The holiday spirit was sorely absent as Houston police officers arrested a gay activist for operating a public address system without a permit on a vacant lot in the city's Montrose section. A Houston gay present at the yuletide program declared: "I have never been to a choir concert that was raided. With all the major crime in Houston, to put ten or twelve officers out on a Christmas carol program is a pretty bad scene."[15]

Homophobia, unfortunately, has not been limited to silly and furtive raids on holiday parties. The most vulgar of the gay-haters have littered the nation's streets with the blood and tears of gay men and women. Attacks against persons and property have come from the community-at-large as well as from members of the law enforcement community. In Denver, harassment from police has been so bold that a program entitled Datacall, which is supported by the National Gay Task Force, has been established to document threats to gays. One act of intimidation in Denver involved three men who were ordered into a police car, where their heads were shaved with battery-powered clippers. Reportedly, the police released the three men with the admonition: "Go back and tell the rest of the faggots that this is just a warning."[16]

Physical threats from homophobes are matched by the psychological threat represented by active and violent intolerance. Unspoken and implied threats of violence can be equally damaging. The nonvocal homophobe is a special kind of coward. The homophobic silent majority, in many instances, passes under the guise of disinterest or mock tolerance. Unwilling to engage in public dialogue about their greatest fears, muted homophobes do their greatest damage in an indirect and deceitful manner. Rumor, innuendo, and gossip—the mainstays of the homophobe's lexicon—have rarely been considered strategies in the arsenal of sensitive and humane individuals.

Homophobia is also evident in the choice of profession that the public in general feels appropriate for individuals of a homosexual life-style. For most individuals the choice of a profession is a thoughtful decision that weds the instincts and talents of an individual to the best-suited profession, a marriage of self and calling that will foster security as well as interpersonal growth and development. The homophobic mind-set, in many cases, categorically denies some professions to individuals because of their sexual preference. A Gallup poll reported in the *San Francisco Chronicle* indicated that many people are willing to restrict the range of professional options for gays. Sixty-five percent felt that it was inappropriate for a gay to be an elementary schoolteacher; 54% felt it was improper for a gay man or woman to be a member of the clergy; 44% preferred that medical doctors not be homosexual; and 38% would exclude gays from the armed forces.[17]

The chronology of homophobic discrimination in the United States is a record of a social disease that has strongly influenced gays' view of themselves and their faith in the future. The Weinberg–Collins research published in the mid-1970s documented the extent of psychological differences evident in the attitudes of homosexuals as compared to general samples of the population. Thirty-four percent of the homosexual research sample felt that "no one cares what happens to you," compared to a 23% response from the general population. Forty-eight percent of the gay population viewed human nature as basically "uncooperative"; only 27% of the heterosexuals studied considered their environment to be unhelpful. And when asked if most persons could be trusted, 53% of the gay group answered "No," contrasting with a 23% negative response from the straight environment.[18] It is evident from the Weinberg–Collins survey that one's sexual orientation, especially if recognized as deviant from the community norm, can impact on self-concept, one's feelings about the viability of meaningful interpersonal communication, and the attitude with which one relates to others in general. Gays have a greater chance of isolating themselves because of the suspicion, in many cases with good reason, with which they approach their immediate environments. A legacy of personal oppression can easily manifest itself in an increased susceptibility to the pathogenic secret.

A comprehensive profile of homophobic individuals is elusive. Except for the inordinate fear of homosexuality, homophobes are not restricted to any particular professional, social, religious, racial, economic, or ethnic background. Homophobes are fairly consistent in their basic mind-set. Homophobes usually do not limit their intemperance to the gay community; the mentality that hates gay finds little difficulty hating blacks, Jews, Chicanos, Iranians, etc. Efforts to chart the demographics of homophobia have been haphazard. E. Levitt and A. Klassen conclude that homophobes are more likely to be "rural, white and male."[19] Occasionally, research conclusions are contradictory. Louie Crew's analysis of homophobia in the academic world concludes that a female chairperson was much more likely to be hostile to a gay person than a nonfemale administrator.[20]

Homophobia as an Institutional System

The very institutions to which gays might turn to temper the pains of discrimination are the most obvious bastions of homophobia: the church, the family, and one's peers. Organized religion, the family unit, and educational institutions have demonstrated an impressive degree of insensitivity regarding homosexuality. Criticism of nonmonolithic social institutions obviously runs the risk of overgeneralization; the exceptions to general repressive traditions are, however, more the exception than the standard.

Gay men and women are products of a society that has an exceptional regard, if not fear, of religious dogma. Colonial America was founded in the name of freedom of religion. But exclusion of gays from religious prerogatives has been as consistent as the manner in which the culture has been manacled by a spirit of puritanism. Self-proclaimed theologians have consistently translated select passages of scripture to the advantage of their world view. The amount of guilt that organized religion has been able to heap on the gay community is astronomical. One of the greatest challenges gay men and women encounter involves mitigating the sense of loss, guilt, failure, disappointment, and despair that results from rejecting the homophobia of the church. Traditional organized religion in the United States has preached compassion but has rarely practiced charity. Contemporary religious practices represent a major psychological threat to the gay community. "Regular church attendance is correlated with negative attitudes toward homosexual relations among Methodists, Presbyterians, Lutherans . . . but active church attendance for Baptists and Episcopalians . . . has been correlated with less prejudice."[21]

In one Midwestern seminary a bishop has been able to effectively thwart the ordination of a man who had openly proclaimed his homosexuality. The very institution that purports to offer consolation, warmth, and understanding has proven itself to be heartless and insensitive. While the recent addition of gay parishes, fellowships, and religious caucuses is a positive contribution to the homosexual community, gays are still inclined to be influenced by feelings of existential guilt, resulting from their recognition of being excluded from the church's community.

Most homosexuals would be willing to leave their sexuality at the doorstep of the cathedral; critics of homosexuality are not. Occasionally, there is hope for a renaissance of humanity in the church in America, but the more predictable reaction of Religion on the Right in America is illustrated by the Baptist minister in Watertown, New York who put a sign in front of his church: "God Says Death to Homos." The intemperate minister of the Word believes that gays should be exterminated by the government.[22]

The church would be an ideal interlocutor between the homophobic community, and the homosexual who feels psychologically under seige. As confessor and shepherd, the church should be in a unique position to counsel tolerance and pilot gays away from self-destructive paths of self-criticism and self-indulgence. "Men do experience existential guilt. Everyone carries the burden of failed potentiality—the pursuit of a career, in interpersonal relationships, even in play and creative enjoyment. But few men *discuss* failed potentialities."[23] The church has sadly missed its function as listener in guiding bigotry toward the light and gays away from the paths of the pathogenic secret.

A life force equally as powerful as the church if not more so, is the primary family unit. The fear of disclosing their homosexuality to their parents and guardians has driven gays to lives of extreme isolation or artificial marital relationships, and tragically, to suicide. The possibility of appearing to be a failure in front of the folks can drive an individual into the depths of the pathogenic secret. The importance of the family in the scheme of human needs has been well established in the literature of sociology and psychology. Abraham Maslow's hierarchy of prepotent needs attests to the importance of a sense of belonging. Only the primary requirements of food and water and shelter transcend the importance of attachment to a family unit. The validation of self, and personal fulfillment are dynamos of behavior that develop *after* a sense of belonging is established. Gay men and women who fear ultimate rejection by their parents also forgo the opportunity to reach a state of self-actualization.

The sense of guilt and shame that is induced by religion is duplicated by one's relationship to the primary family unit. The wrath of disappointed parents is not as psychologically damaging, ultimately, as the feeling that one has failed to live up to their expectations, i.e., to be an average, normal individual. Parents instinctively monitor their own actions for proof of the cause for their child's homosexuality. And their feeling of remorse for having failed fuels a hatred, and hostility, toward their child. By clogging the channels of communication at first encounter, parents render themselves impotent in loving, counseling, and guiding their son or daughter through the treacherous waters of a very misunderstood life-style. Rather than sharing their fears, hopes, and desires with Mom and Dad, the homosexual son or daughter is isolated and catapulted toward the stance of the pathogenic secret.

A nineteen-year-old told his parents of his intention to live life openly as a homosexual. The disclosure was particularly gutsy, because the young man had never experienced a physical relationship with another man. The parents' response was immediate and reactionary. The young man was ordered from the home for his willingness to share himself with his parents. In a matter of minutes, the young gay's life was converted from one centered around his primary home to one of self-containment and potential isolation. The institution that should be the antithesis of the pathogenic secret in this case provided a vivid rationale why so few gays come forward willingly.

The university is another social institution that would be expected to represent an environment contrary to the pathogenic secret. In its most classic sense the center of learning provides a free and open forum in which to test attitudes, ideas, and beliefs without fear of recrimination. The university, as described in Louie Crew's *The Gay Academic,* has faltered as badly as the church and the family in providing a forum for the free, unfettered discussion of alternative life-styles. The university has been an institution that has meekly abided discussion of gay liberation but has carefully avoided activism.

The university has been inaccurately considered to be the center of liberal thought. Student attitudes, including views regarding homosexuality, have taken a decided turn toward conservatism during the last decade. A survey published by the American Council on Education in conjunction with UCLA entitled "The American Freshman: National Norms for Fall, 1979" describes the incursion of conservative thought. The report notes that 39 percent of the women and 56 percent of the men felt that "homosexual relations should be prohibited."[24] "Whether the recent resurgence of conservatism in North America, decline in college attendance, and more fundamentalist religion will signal a renewal of homophobia in the population is difficult to determine. Certainly organized opposition to homosexuals has become more vocal in the late 1970's."[25]

Voices of conservatism in the church, in the home, and at the university have prevailed and flourished because advocates of the gay life-style have been reluctant to express an alternative view. Gays young and old and in every profession suffer from a lack of attractive role models. Oppressed gays will be able to leave their closets when they recognize a positive alternative to their life of stress mired in the world of pathogenic secrets. The liberating aspect of attractive gay role models was poignantly identified in a letter from a young man to Dave Kopay, the former professional football player who confirmed his homosexuality in December 1975.

> You did more for me in that one 45-minute television interview than I've been able to do in almost a year of soul-searching and selective conversation. I'm a 19-year-old guy with a semi-steady girl, an exclusively heterosexual past and—until recently—a presumably heterosexual future. Recently a guy I've known at school for about a year and a half has begun making rather blunt overtures—sexually—in my direction. Shit. All these big words. He's been putting "the move" on me. And I've been casually sidestepping them. Which is fine except I'm not at all sure I want to sidestep them. So it's been really bugging me. I've talked it over with him, tried to explain to him, but I don't know how or what to say to my girl, my one real love right now. Last night, we had our closest yet to a discussion of it—and although it never came out, I think she now realizes what the problem is. I got home and turned on the TV feeling really down and man—*there you were!* I just sat there and didn't move for an hour. I hung on your every word. You seem so at peace with yourself and able to articulate things I've been trying to tell myself and others for months now. Man, you almost made me cry and that isn't too usual for me. I called the guy today and I'm gonna see him for a long talk next weekend. I need that much time to prepare myself because I guess it'll be a turning point in my life. So something's gonna happen for the first time in quite a while—although I'm nervous as hell—I feel good about myself, my sexuality. It's me and I have no reason or right to deny it. I love you and I thank you.[26]

The pathogenic secret and its capacity to destroy is irrelevant to the young man who wrote Kopay, but the luck and enlightenment reflected in his letter are unique. The opportunities to meet and evaluate oneself in reference to positive role models is exceptionally limited.

Homophobia and Sexism—Common Causal Foundations

The ascendancy of the homophobic mentality can be seen as the "psychopathology of the average." When one scratches beneath the crass and rude behavior of the gay-hater, one usually encounters a rather frightened and pathetic kind of norm. Antigay attitudes can be extensions of the age-old battle of the sexes. Advancement of gay rights is incorrectly seen as an assault on male privilege. The average heterosexual male, trapped by traditional male roles and barely holding his own against the efforts of the women's humanist movements, is infuriated by the gay male's social iconoclasm.

Homophobic individuals have been trapped by the definition and norms placed on them by their own environments. The traditional mold of the family unit has little latitude for the concept of a homosexual family. Men and women who are parents and now lead exclusively homosexual lives are viewed as pariahs who deceived the sanctity of the family and knowingly superimposed their preferences, even though repressed, on unsuspecting mates. The gender-bound expectations promulgated by the society influence a man's or woman's ability to respond to representatives of life-styles who reject the narrow definition. Traditional society has encouraged men to repress their emotions and has thereby destroyed a constructive channel of expression. If a gay man gets in touch with his emotions and demonstrates them openly, the interdiction of society's norm about restrained sensitivity for men is as threatening as the thought of sleeping with another man. The instinct of the individual bound by such narrow distinction is to hate those who destroy the security of the label. But the greatest fear of contact with gay men and women may be to discover that labels are only averages. Through contact with oneself and individuals of the gay community, heterosexual associate and homophobe alike will reinforce the Masters and Johnson scale of sexuality, which suggests that reality is most likely somewhere between one and six.

Chapter 12

Androgyny, Sex-role Rigidity, and Homophobia

Paul Siegel

It has by now been well documented that affixing the homosexual label to a real or hypothetical person will result in the derogation of that person.[1] Equally clear is the finding that scholarly writings[2] or extraordinarily successful careers[3] will be viewed as less impressive when attributed to females.

There seems to be an interplay among these findings. One clue is that, once labeled gay, an object person will be judged with far less disfavor if that person is perceived as fitting that part of the gay stereotype which dictates that homosexuals imitate the mannerisms of the opposite sex. Thus, effeminate gays are more tolerated[4] and less aggressed against[5] than are their butch counterparts.

A related finding is that feminism (and presumably, lesbianism) is devalued even by subjects who claim to support the women's movement. Women rated as physically unattractive are also likely to be labeled feminists.[6] Further, it has been demonstrated that unattractive women who are labeled feminists will be judged to have become feminists for a host of maladaptive (e.g., shyness and discomfort in the presence of men) rather than altruistic (e.g., a need to promote human values and equality) reasons.[7]

A number of researchers have shown that negative attitudes toward women and toward feminism are highly correlated with negative attitudes toward homosexuality.[8]

Sandra Bem describes the androgynous individual as one who successfully integrates masculine and feminine personality components,[9] and has convincingly established that androgynous persons are indeed highly competent in both traditionally masculine and traditionally feminine tasks.[10]

Numerous investigators[11] have attacked Bem's Sex Role Inventory

(BSRI) on psychometric grounds. Others[12] have questioned the BSRI's validity on the grounds that it fails to correlate with a number of measures that "should," intuitively, be among its correlates. These researchers have been concerned with measures of attitudes toward women, toward feminism, and toward homosexuality.

The purpose of this essay is to explore three constructs—homophobia, sex-role rigidity, and androgyny. The former two correlate very highly with each other, but the latter has not served well as a predictor of either of them.

Negative Attitudes Toward Homosexuals: Dimensions and Levels of Homophobia

When George Weinberg first coined the term homophobia, it was treated as a unidimensional variable and was not defined with great precision.[13] For Weinberg, homophobia was the irrational fear of heterosexuals of being in close proximity to homosexuals. Weinberg also suggested that gay persons themselves could manifest homophobia, but that it would then be transformed into self-hatred.

Dorothy Riddle has proposed a "phase theory" of negative attitudes toward homosexuals.[14] The four stages she identifies are *repulsion, pity, tolerance,* and *acceptance.* Repulsion is the most strongly felt reaction, expressed in the belief that gays are disgusting and vile creatures, and in blaming gays themselves for their state.

Pity, the second level, still involves the belief that homosexuality is wholly inferior to heterosexuality. Here, however, the gay person is seen as victim. Riddle notes that many myths we hold about sexuality generally tend to perpetuate pity-level homophobia. To the extent we believe in the vaginal orgasm, for example, we will pity the lesbian, who will never obtain full sexual satisfaction through the prerequisite deep penetration by the penis.

If we are functioning at the tolerance level, we view homosexuality as an adolescent phase. That is, we tolerate it because we expect people will grow out of it in time.

Riddle undoubtedly intends to convey a measure of irony in her selection of a positively valenced word, acceptance, for her final level of negative attitudes toward homosexuals. To "accept" homosexuality, within this model, is merely to acknowledge its existence nonjudgmentally. But it is also, Riddle notes, to deny the political reality of gay oppression. Statements such as, "I do not think of you as a lesbian, but just as I do anyone else," and "What you do in bed is your business—why make such a fuss?" ignore the fact that many Americans *do* make it their business what gays do sexually. That bumper stickers advising the reader to "Kill a queer for Christ" were not uncommon in Dade County, Florida indicates to

Riddle that mere acceptance is insufficient to safeguard the basic rights of lesbians and gays.

To date, the most impressively systematic approach to assessing prejudice against gays was conducted by James Millham and his colleagues at the University of Houston.[15] Using a factor-analytic design, Millham uncovered several independent clusters that serve to partially explain negative attitudes toward homosexuals. Among Millham's factors are the following:

1. *Dangerous-repressive:* This is the belief that homosexuals are dangers to society, and that it is therefore society's right, or obligation, to repress homosexuality.
2. *Moral reprobation:* Here we find a strong feeling that gays are sinful or immoral.
3. *Cross-sexed mannerisms:* This is the equating of homosexuality with sex-role inversion. Gay males are judged effeminate, lesbians are viewed as overly aggressive or masculine.
4. *Personal anxiety:* This is the subjective experience of discomfort in the presence of homosexuals, or with the topic itself.

It is crucial to note that only the last factor—personal anxiety—seems at all related to Weinberg's original conception of homophobia. That is, it is clearly possible to hold very strong antigay attitudes without presenting a phobia, in any meaningful sense of the word. We have long taken as truism that those who are most antigay must be terribly insecure about their own sexuality, afraid that homosexuality might somehow rub off, if one approached too closely. Millham's findings seem to belie this myth.

Indeed, the fact that the dangerous-repressive dimension emerged at all as an independent cluster

> raises serious doubts as to the validity of tying the roots of repression of homosexuals to such concepts as homophobia and moral indignation. It is possible that advocating legal and social repression of homosexuals is related to a more general repressive style with respect to deviance generally, rather than to a particular characterization of homosexuals.[16]

Perhaps cognizant of this conceptual problem, a number of writers have suggested reevaluating the utility of such a misleading label as homophobia. A.P. MacDonald points out that the word is not only inaccurate in suggesting that all prejudice against gays is based on fear, but that it is also "politically inexpedient," as it can cause unnecessarily defensive reactions in a reader who is seemingly being called "ill."[17] And Stephen F. Morin prefers terms such as "heterosexual bias" or the more succinct "heterosexism" to describe the view that heterosexuality is preferable to homosexuality.[18] My own decision to retain the admittedly troublesome homophobia label is mostly a simple reflection of its pervasiveness in the literature. Even Morin continues to use the word, not only within the context of his writings, but in the title of at least one of his articles (see p. 117).[19]

Behavioral Manifestations of Homophobia: Devaluation, Avoidance, and Aggression

Homophobic response has been demonstrated in a number of studies. In her doctoral dissertation, Terri Levy showed a group of 106 mental health workers a videotape of a one-on-one therapy session involving a female client.[20] Half the mental health professionals were led to believe that the client was lesbian, while the other half were told she was heterosexual. When the subjects were asked to assess the psychological adjustment of the client, the "lesbian" was seen as more defensive, less nurturant, less affiliative, less autonomous, and less self-confident than the heterosexually labeled client. The lesbian was also seen as manifesting less self-control and harboring more negative attitudes toward men. Subjects' reactions to the heterosexually labeled client were completely positive. Indeed, many of the mental health workers wondered why this woman was in therapy at all.

Whereas Dr. Levy's dissertation shows us that many persons will devalue gays, based on the homosexual label alone, William Hensel's dissertation goes a step further.[21] In Hensel's study, students were presented with a written description of an imaginary fellow student. When the object person was labeled gay, not only did subjects devalue the so-labeled person, but they also avoided contact with him. That is, they chose not to exercise the option of meeting him "after the experiment."

Studies in social distancing conducted by Wolfgang and Wolfgang[22] and by Morin and his colleagues[23] further support the contention that many people will choose to avoid homosexuals. In the former study, subjects were asked to imagine (and to indicate, using stick figures) at what distance they would feel comfortable talking informally with a homosexual. And in the latter study, actual inverviews were conducted by a homosexually or heterosexually labeled interviewer. In both studies, subjects maintained their distance from known homosexuals. Interestingly, Morin's subjects reported more positive attitudes toward gays when presented with a homosexually labeled interviewer than when presented with a heterosexually labeled interviewer. The verbal and nonverbal components of the interview, as such, carried contradictory information. (The contradictions were dramatic indeed. The ratio of distance maintained from homosexual: distance maintained from heterosexual was larger than 3:1!) Morin concludes that a social desirability factor must have been operating, and that actions speak louder than words.

Finally, C. San Miguel and James Millham found that homophobia is often manifested in *aggression* toward homosexuals.[24] Subjects were led to believe the experiment concerned development of interviewing skills, and that their evaluation of the skill of the (confederate) interviewer would determine whether or not that person would receive the full amount of money possible for participation in the study. Thus, subjects were told they had a degree of power over the confederate.

All subjects had been pretested for attitudes toward homosexuals. When the confederate was labeled homosexual, those subjects who had scored high on the pretest homophobia measure chose to withhold more money from the confederate than did low scorers. Moreover, when the experimenter arranged for a mildly unpleasant initial interaction with the confederate (the subject ostensibly losing an opportunity for bonus participation points, due to the confederate's poor performance in a *Password* game), all groups of subjects (homophobic or not) "aggressed" significantly more against the gay-labeled than against the straight-labeled confederate.[25]

The implication of the San Miguel and Millham study seems to be that, in the best of times, there will always be homophobic persons who aggress against gays. In the worst of times, everyone will behave as does the homophobe. More succinctly, homosexuals make convenient scapegoats.

Keeping the Woman in Her Place: Dimensions of Sex-role Rigidity

Sex-role rigidity was developed as a construct by MacDonald to refer to a strong personal investment in maintaining traditional distinctions between acceptable masculine and feminine behaviors.[26] Thus, many persons attempt to prevent sex-role confusion by adherence to some or all the following dimensions:

1. *Equality in business and profession:* This is the belief that there are "men's jobs" and "women's jobs," and that anyone who engages in sex-role–inappropriate employment is highly suspect.
2. *Personal habits, masculine/feminine:* Little girls should be brought up to be ladylike; little boys, to be aggressive. "It is infinitely more disgusting to hear profanity from the lips of a woman."
3. *Social-domestic work:* The woman does the cooking and cleaning; the man effects major household repairs.
4. *Power in the home:* As head of the household, the father should have final say in decision-making.

Homophobia and Sex-role Rigidity

Homophobia has been associated in survey studies with a number of variables, including authoritarianism[27] and sexual conservatism.[28] Along with the simple dichotomous variable of having previously known a homosexual (see chapter 10),[29] the best predictor to date of homophobia is sex-role rigidity, as measured by MacDonald's Sex Role Survey.[30]

Sex researchers tell us that sexual orientation (gay or straight) and sex-role identification (masculine or feminine) are generally unrelated phenomena. Why should it be, then, that people tend not to be prejudiced against sex-role deviants without being also prejudiced against homosexuals?

Perhaps the answer to this question can be found in the cross-sexed mannerisms dimension of Millham's Homosexuality Attitudes Scale.[31] This factor is characterized by the mistaken belief that gender identification and sexual orientation are related, despite the overwhelming evidence to the contrary.[32] This belief is referred to by MacDonald[33] and by M. Storms[34] as the sexual inversion myth.

(It is probably worth noting that the appearance of *Homosexuality* as a bona fide heading in *Psychological Abstracts* is a relatively recent phenomenon. It was not yet a decade ago that readers were cross-referred to *Sexual Inversion.* The myth thus perpetuated seems rather benign when compared to that implicit in the indexing policy of the *Readers' Guide to Periodical Literature,* which only recently stopped referring readers to an alternative heading, Sexual PER*version.*)

A.P. MacDonald and R.G. Games suggest that "sex role confusion" is indeed the crux of the relationship between homophobia and sex-role rigidity.[35] Briefly, they view the state of sex-role confusion, the inability to comfortably fall back on traditional delineations between masculinity and femininity, as highly threatening. To the extent that gays are perceived as transgressors of sex-role prescriptions, they will produce sex-role confusion in the observer.

This sex-role confusion hypothesis can also serve to explain some consistent findings of differential levels of homophobia, reported by Morin (see chapter 10): (a) men are more homophobic than women; (b) male homosexuals elicit more homophobia then do lesbians; and (c) gays who are perceived as somehow similar to us are especially threatening.[36]

That men are more homophobic than women is no great surprise. Each dimension of the Sex Role Survey, as we have seen, suggests an underlying assumption that masculinity is better than femininity. Men should have the power, the better-paying jobs, and the rule of the home. Men, being on top, have more to lose. It is especially in the male's interest, then, to maintain traditional sex-role boundaries. Add to this scenario the sex-role inversion myth regarding homosexuality and we can understand that gay persons are particularly threatening to men.[37]

If we carry the inversion myth a step further, we will be able to suggest an explanation for the finding that gay males make people more uncomfortable than do lesbians. If gays are perceived as cross-sex typed, then lesbians are perceived as trying to be men. And this should be excusable. At least they are erring in the right direction. But gay males, perceived as wanting to be females, force us to question the male superiority assumption. To do so is extremely threatening, creates intense sex-role confusion, and therefore a higher level of homophobia.[38]

Finally, we seek to explain the finding that gays who are perceived as similar to us produce the very most homophobia in us. The typical experimental design involving a similarity manipulation will find subjects presented with bogus personality profiles, interpreted to suggest that the subject and the (gay-labeled) confederate are extremely similar personality types.[39]

Sensing that the sex-role confusion hypothesis could only be invoked very tentatively in bogus similar personality manipulations, Storms attacked perceived masculinity/femininity more directly.[40] He provided his subjects with a brief paragraph describing John, a college-age peer. On some forms John was described as having stereotypic feminine interests (majoring in fashion design, being "into" dance, and wearing flowery shirts, tight European slacks, and stacked-heel shoes). Other forms described John as traditionally masculine (majoring in business, being "into" IM sports, and wearing sweaters, jeans, and hiking boots).

Storms' results served to confirm the sex-role confusion hypothesis. When John was labeled gay, he was far more disliked if he appeared masculine than if he appeared feminine. The reverse was true if John were labeled straight.

To best see how the sex-role inversion myth explains the finding that similar (or macho) gay males are especially threatening, let us assume the stance of one of the experimental subjects asked to judge a gay-labeled confederate. If I, as a heterosexual male who views himself as fairly traditionally masculine, am presented with a highly effeminate (dissimilar) gay male, I can effectively dismiss him: "Here is a man who will never enjoy male privilege, because he acts like a woman. He clearly never had a choice in the matter. Thus I need only pity him. I need not rethink my belief in the inherent superiority of the male."

If, however, I am forced to perceive a gay person as highly similar to myself, especially in terms of masculinity, then I will have some inconsistencies with which to wrestle. After all, here is someone who can "pass," thus enjoying all the benefits of being male. But he has *chosen* to give it away. This perception forces me to reassess my assumptions. The process is itself highly threatening.

An alternative explanation for the high degree of homophobia directed toward similar gays may be found in the personal anxiety dimension of homophobia. Certainly, the larger amount of personal anxiety will be elicited by a highly similar gay person. "There but for the grace of God go I" becomes a meaningful theme. If I cannot easily discern differences between the gay person and myself, I am forced to conclude that my own heterosexuality is a fragile thing, that I could just as easily be homosexual.[41]

Androgyny as Sex-role Flexibility

Bem's dramatic reconceptualization of masculinity and femininity,[42] discarding traditional practice of dealing with the two as opposite ends of a single continuum, resulted in the BSRI.

The BSRI consists of sixty adjectives—all positive. Twenty were prejudged by a sample of men *and* women to be especially admirable in males. Twenty others were similarly selected as particularly admirable in females. The remaining twenty items were viewed as equally important for both males and females.

An individual's BSRI scores are gathered by having the subject report on a seven-point scale (from 1—"never or almost never true"—to 7—"always or almost always true") how that subject feels an adjective applies to himself or herself. High masculinity scores reflect having given high self-report ratings for the twenty masculine adjectives. Similarly, femininity means high self-report ratings from the twenty feminine adjectives.

Bem derives an androgyny score as a function (student's "t" ratio) of the difference between one's masculinity and femininity scores. For Bem, then, to be androgynous is to endorse masculine and feminine qualities equally. This can mean either that I view myself as highly masculine and highly feminine, or as low in both dimensions, or somewhere in between. The only requirement is that the difference between my masculinity and femininity scores be a small one.

More recent research has produced impressive behavioral validations for the androgyny concept.[43] Specifically, androgynous individuals were found to perform at levels superior to their nonandrogynous counterparts in both masculine and feminine tasks. They exhibited the best of both worlds. Further, it was shown that strongly sex-typed subjects (that is, very masculine males and very feminine females) go to great pains to avoid situations in which behavioral demands appropriate for the opposite sex are made of them. Even when offered money, for example, highly masculine men would prefer not to be photographed tidying up a ball of yarn.

Androgyny and Homophobia—Any Relation?

A number of investigators[44] have attempted to extend MacDonald's sex-role confusion hypothesis by demonstrating a negative correlation between androgyny and homophobia. Since androgynous (and, for that matter, cross-sexed) individuals are themselves sex-role deviants, they should surely accept the perceived sex-role deviance of others, or so the reasoning goes.

Without exception, these investigators have failed to confirm their hypothesis. Typically, a suggestion is offered in discussion sections that something must be wrong with the BSRI itself.

Indeed, there has been quite a furor in the literature over just what androgyny means, and how it can best be operationalized. One group of researchers, for example, feel that only those subjects who score very high on both masculinity and femininity should qualify for the androgyny label.[45] More recently, J. Moreland and his colleagues have subjected their sample's BSRI scores to factor analysis, and have concluded that androgyny is far more complex a variable than a simple difference between masculinity and femininity.[46] Moreland also noted that numerous "masculine" and "feminine" items did not load on the appropriate dimensions, but were instead "contaminated" by forming new dimensions with supposedly neutral adjectives. Concluding that androgyny is something quite apart from masculinity or femininity, they argue that it would seem a "contradiction to define empirically the androgynous person on the basis of his/her endorsement of attributes labeled with the very constructs these individuals have transcended."[47]

Thus, many researchers see the noncorrelation between androgyny and homophobia as an indictment against the validity of the androgyny measure. This may be the case. But more can be said on this issue. Let us assume, for argument's sake, that Bem's inventory *does* measure androgyny.

In their early research on the psychology of deviance, J. Freedman and A. Doob found that deviants are far less likely than "normals" to aggress against other deviants, especially if the sources of deviance for judge and judged are similar.[48] Using this reasoning, we would expect androgynous persons to be very tolerant of gay persons. Or would we?

Are we not assuming the sex-role confusion hypothesis to prove the sex-role confusion hypothesis? To predict, a priori, that androgyny brings tolerance of homosexuality, we must assume both (a) androgynous individuals see themselves as deviants, and (b) androgynous individuals share the mainstream sexual inversion myth regarding the masculinity/femininity of gay males and lesbians.

Recall the trend of San Miguel and Millham's results.[49] They found that perceived similarity of subject to gay-labeled confederate actually *increased* the aggression against that object person. (Of course, their similarity manipulation did not involve a measure of perceived deviance, only of personality scores.)

Storms showed that masculine gay males are more devalued than feminine gay males.[50] Also of interest is his finding that feminine straight males are more devalued than masculine straight males. Storms did not administer the BSRI to his subjects, so his results cannot be interpreted in terms of androgyny as an intermediating variable. Yet, this notion of deviance is again salient. The norm for straight men is to be masculine, while the norm for gay men is to be feminine. Deviation from either norm leads to devaluation.

Getting back for a moment to the BSRI itself, can we reasonably call a person scoring in the androgyny range a deviant? Probably not, at least not in a pejorative sense. Remember, all the adjectives comprising the scale are very positive ones. Can we be risking much by incorporating only the most admirable qualities of the opposite sex into our own self-concepts?

Perhaps those most nearly eligible for deviant status are the cross-sex-typed respondents (i.e., masculine females and feminine males). And there is some weak evidence that these cross-sex–typed subjects do in fact behave more acceptingly toward gays and toward women.

Thus, in Weinberger and Millham's study, of the bare few correlations involving the BSRI that did reach significance, it was the cross-sexed, and not the androgynous, subjects who emerged more tolerant. (The specific factors on which cross-typed subjects scored very low were *Power in the home,* from the Sex Role Survey; and *Moral reprobation* and *Personal anxiety* from the Homosexuality Attitudes Scale.)

And, in an argument for the retaining of her own operationalization of androgyny,[51] Bem points out that liberal attitudes toward women, as measured by J. Spence and R. Helmreich's Attitudes Towards Women scale,[52] are very much affected by one's score on the BSRI—at least for men. Feminine males are the most favorably predisposed toward women, masculine males the least so.

Clearing Up the Muddle—Guidelines for Future Research

A number of conceptual problems have been identified in attempting to correlate Bem's BSRI with commonly used measures of homophobia. Among these is a degree of uncertainty regarding who is the truly androgynous individual. Another is whether this truly androgynous individual is also a sex-role deviant, or is merely a compromise between the traditionals and the cross-typed respondents, the latter group being the only real deviants. Finally, we have begun to address the assumption that a deviant will be more accepting of the deviance of others.

Solutions to the first two kinds of problems will be psychometric. We are still not sure what androgyny is or how to measure it. Future research in this area should do at least two things. First, it should reopen the question of allowing subjects who score *low* on both masculinity and femininity to qualify as androgynous. Second, it should address the concern that, by constructing scales of exclusively *positive* adjectives, it allows individuals to be labeled androgynous even though they do not "risk" much by also functioning as deviants.

Concerning the final muddle, regarding the kinds of thought processes that might be embraced by androgynous persons when asked to judge homosexuals, we need carefully constructed designs to examine the interplay between situational and personality characteristics. Employing androgyny as an independent variable in a study of aggression (such as San Miguel and Millham's) would be a reasonable first step. We also need to be more ingenious in our dissimilarity manipulations, to ensure that the person being labeled dissimilar is indeed perceived as such. This is especially true when dealing with the androgynous subject and a perceived masculinity/femininity manipulation. We must know how the androgynous subjects view themselves before we can begin to predict if a confederate will be perceived as similar or dissimilar.

Chapter 13

Gay Images on Television

Steven A. Simms

Review of the Literature

Since the late 1930s, researchers have been examining the enigmatic conditions surrounding stereotypes. Two theories that are related have been posited: the "Kernel of Truth" theory and the "Just a Shell of Information" theory.[1] These theories indicate that stereotyped characteristics offer only a piece of information concerning the subculture in question. The theories also consider stereotyped characteristics to be signs, means of identification, and not ends in themselves. Stereotyped attributes are symbolic representations of the culture in question. Stereotyped attributes can be assumed to be the consensus of generalized characteristics that are due to faulty thought processes.[2] These thought processes become perceptual habit[3] and are based on information available to society, concerning the minority or life-style in question.[4]

The current problem with stereotyped characters portrayed in the media is the audience's perception of those characters as real or unreal.[5] Are viewers perceiving these stereotyped characters as representative of the respective subculture? Some rationalize the presence of stereotyped characters in the media as "simple," ethnic humor. William Raspberry, a *Washington Post* columnist, best refutes the ethnic humor rationalization:

> The mistake is too often made that ethnic jokes are essentially innocent because they amount to nothing more than commentaries on ethnic idiosyncrasies. . . . When you show that you believe the stereotype to the degree that you make it tough for a man to get a decent job or home or education, don't expect him to laugh at your jokes based on the stereotype.[6]

Other areas of concern related to the stereotype problem are outlined in the surgeon general's report on television and social behavior. The report indicates that by the time a child is in first grade, he or she exhibits preferences for particular characters and shows.[7] It also indicates that stereotypes appear primarily in situational comedies and action dramas, with a majority of young children preferring situational comedies.[8] Some children are able to filter out stereotyped mediated messages due to a reference group. For example, a child can distinguish that all mothers are not like the mother who dusts her furniture while wearing a chiffon gown by observing his or her own mother engaged in housecleaning activities. Likewise, a black child can observe that black men are not of the caliber of Jack Benny's Rochester by observing men around them. Concern should be exhibited for children who lack the specific reference groups.[9] As a white child views a black character on television, this child can interpret the black character as being representative of the black culture if the white child does not associate with black children. Some research reveals children can perceive television characters in application to the real world, which exemplifies the reference group issue.[10] This discussion of stereotypes recognizes there are impressionable children viewing a medium —television—that is peppered with stereotypes for which there is no reference group for feedback.

Researchers are attempting to isolate the variable(s) that dictates the audience's perceived authenticity of stereotyped characteristics. John Brigham has found that certain segments of society consistently give a low evaluation to the character of other segments of society.[11] Brigham administered an ethnic character evaluation test to a group of white subjects (the test evaluated the character of various subcultures—blacks, Italians, Germans, and other ethnic groups). The results indicated noncollege whites from rural areas consistently evaluated the character of blacks lower than any other subgroup in the sample. Brigham also noted the Archie Bunker syndrome: those who evaluate one minority low tend to evaluate other minorities low also. Perhaps an explanation for Brigham's findings may be reflected in a study by R.M. Williams: Williams has found that increased social contact among various subcultures within society lowers ethnic prejudice.[12]

Bradley Greenberg has made progress in assimilating fragmented facts to begin developing a theory for explaining the stereotype enigma. Primarily relying on the social contact or reference group variable, Greenberg found that white children who are further removed from a particular ethnic group will use television's depiction of this group in their own descriptions of it.[13] He discovered this when examining television's representation of stereotyped black characters.

Current research has examined the effects of stereotyping women, blacks, and other minorities.[14] Due to media hype and the sexual revolution, a concern for the homosexual stereotype has emerged. National statistics estimate that 9 percent of the nation's population is gay.[15] The gay community expresses the invalidity of the wrist-flapping, feminine, gay male stereotype as depicted on television—specifically television situational comedies. To solidify Greenberg's and Williams' findings, this research examines the stereotyped homosexual character as depicted on television.

Developing a stereotype theory that can be utilized in explaining why people believe stereotypes is vital to finding a theory that can be all-inclusive among the various stereotypes as depicted on television. All previous literature indicates the reference group variable to be the factor in determining the viewer's perceived authenticity of the stereotyped character. Using the homosexual stereotype, this research tested for the reference group or social contact variable and the quality of that social contact. This research also considered other demographic variables as secondary predictors.

Hypothesis: Heterosexuals who have had social contact with homosexuals will more likely identify a television stereotype of a homosexual more so than heterosexuals who have had no gay social contacts.

Methodology

To ascertain the audience's perception of the gay stereotyped character in reference to the social contact variable, two groups were shown a popular television situational comedy, *Barney Miller,* that depicted two homosexual characters. In a twenty-three item close-ended questionnaire designed around the situational comedy, the two groups were asked to evaluate the show and the characters' interactions.

One of these groups was made up of homosexual experts (n = 45); the other, heterosexual college students (n = 95). The homosexual expert group was utilized to determine if the researcher's perception of a homosexual stereotype was accurate. Homosexual subjects were contacted through the Gay People's Alliance, an Illinois State University student organization, and the University of Illinois' gay student organization, the Gay Illini. The heterosexual group was a random sample made available through Illinois State University's general education course, The Fundamentals of Speech 110. Four classes were surveyed. The situational comedy had been previously taped on a videotape cassette. The tape—unedited except for commercials—was shown to both groups on a black and white television monitor. After the show each group was asked to fill out the questionnaire.

The questionnaire was divided into three sections: (1) background information, (2) media habits and attitudes, attitudes and perception of the situational comedy and its characters, and information concerning interpersonal relationships, along with (3) a few basic demographic variables.

Both groups were asked if homosexual characters were present in the show and to indicate the identity of these characters. They were also asked if the gay characters were representative of the gay community as they perceive the gay community. Another question ascertained whether or not the subjects thought the gay characters were stereotyped. The heterosexual group was asked to evaluate their attitudes toward the gay community as well as the quality and quantity of their interactions with gays. The homosexual group was asked the same questions but in reference to the straight community. All groups were asked to indicate which straight characters' interactions with the gay characters best exemplified and atypified society's general reactions toward the gay community. The entire evaluation process was pretested with a group of both junior and senior Mass Communication students attending Illinois State University (n = 19). After the pretest some wording modifications were made to clear up ambiguity in the questionnaire.

Results

The analysis was conducted through two stages. Initially, frequencies were examined to note any general trend in differences of opinion between homosexual and heterosexual groups. Certain data modifications were made for the second wave of analysis and key variables using one-way analysis of variance (ANOVA) and t-test statistical tests. Data were significant at $p \leq .05$.

Media Habits and Attitudes

The two groups differed slightly in media habits. It is evident that television is an important source of entertainment for both homosexuals and heterosexuals. A majority of homosexuals (55.1%) and heterosexuals (57.4%) indicated they viewed television three to four hours daily. A significant number of respondents from both groups (heteros, 41%; gays, 51%) indicated a combination of the print media as their major information source. The next closest source of information for homosexuals was friends (12%); radio ranked second for heterosexuals (12%). As major entertainment sources, the heterosexual group chose television (41.4%) and radio (25.3%). The homosexual group's major entertainment sources were books (32.7%) and television (24.4%). When asked their opinion toward stereotypes in general as depicted on television, the homosexual group responded they were "somewhat" offended (79.6%). Forty percent of the heterosexuals responded with "somewhat" offended, while the majority of heterosexuals (52.6%) found stereotypes in general "not at all" offending. Most heteros found stereotypes in general "humorous" (62.1%), while only 20% of the gays thought stereotypes were "humorous." The plurality of gays (32.7%) found stereotypes in general, as seen on television, "not needed."

Perceptions of the Show and the Characters' Interactions

Ninety-five percent of the heterosexuals and all the homosexuals were able to correctly identify the two homosexual characters that appeared in the *Barney Miller* show. The mannerisms of the two gay characters were indicated by both groups to be the key to initially recognizing these characters as homosexuals (mannerisms were specified as feminine walk and other feminine gestures). On a six-point scale (ranging from highly representative to highly unrepresentative), the plurality of both groups (31.6% heteros; 32.7% gays) thought the homosexual characters were partially representative (3) of the gay community. To determine the stereotypic nature of the two gay characters, a five-point scale was used (1 = stereotyped; 5 = not stereotyped). Eighty-three percent of the gay sample and 48% of the heterosexual sample thought the characters were stereotyped. Of the straight characters, Wojo (a young white detective), and the Inspector (white, and in his late fifties) were the ones most offended by the gay characters and were indicated by both groups to represent society's reactions to the gay community. Barney (the captain of the detectives) was indicated by both groups as the straight character that atypifies society's reactions to the gay community.

The final stage of frequency analysis indicated 64 percent of the heterosexual sample "never" associates with the gay community. This gay contact variable was assimilated into an independent variable representing the heterosexuals with gay social contacts (n = 26), the heterosexuals with no gay social contacts (n = 52), and the homosexuals. The heterosexuals who did not respond to the question asking how often they dealt with the gay community were omitted from the final analysis.

Analysis of Variance Among Heteros with Contact, Heteros Without Contact, and Gays

A one-way ANOVA using the gay social contact variable as the independent variable and the five-point stereotype scale that evaluated the stereotypic nature of the television gays as the dependent variable was conducted to test the hypothesis. The hypothesis was upheld when it was found that heterosexuals who had social contact with the gay community were more likely to identify the television gay characters as stereotyped than heterosexuals with no gay social contacts (see tables 6 and 7, pages 159–60). This latter group's mean score was statistically autonomous from the gay sample.

One-way ANOVA was also utilized with the heteros—both with and without gay social contacts—and the gays as the independent variable, and the six-point representativeness scale relating to the television gay characters' representativeness of the real gay community as the dependent variable. The heterosexuals' average mean score (3.48; 3 = partially representative) was shown to be statistically different from the homosexuals' mean score (4.32; 4 = partially unrepresentative) when the least-significant difference test was made (see tables 6 and 7).

When a one-way ANOVA was made using the heteros with and without gay social contacts and the gays as the independent variable, and the dependent variable relating to attitudes in general toward television stereotypes, it was found through the least-significant differences test that all three groups' mean scores were statistically different. A lower mean indicated a negative attitude toward stereotypes depicted on television. The gay samples' mean was 1.93; the heterosexuals with gay social contacts, 2.34; and the heterosexuals with no gay social contacts, 2.65 (3 = not at all offended by stereotypes in general on television; 2 = somewhat offended).

An analysis of variance utilizing the t-test was made between the heterosexuals with and those without gay social contacts, and the dependent variable measuring the quality of gay social contact when that contact is made. A statistical difference was found to exist between the two groups ($t = -7.88$; 75 df; $p \leq .003$). A lower mean indicated open communication between heteros and gays. The heterosexuals with social contact scored 2.34; the heteros with no social contact scored an average mean of 3.7 (1 = comfortable; 2 = at times uncomfortable; 3 = mostly uncomfortable; 4 = avoidance).

Discussion

Research indicates that stereotypes affect people's perception. Greenberg, testing the social contact variable in reference to the audience's perception of the black stereotype, found that those viewers who lacked contact with the black culture more readily believed television's depiction of this culture. This study supports Greenberg's findings but in reference to the homosexual stereotype depicted on television.

The gay sample, in evaluating the television gay characters, felt that the characters were partially unrepresentative of their culture and that they were very stereotyped. The heterosexuals with gay social contacts more readily agreed with the gays' evaluation of the stereotypic nature of the television gays, as compared to the heterosexuals with no gay social contacts. Both groups of heterosexuals indicated the characters as partially representative of the gay community. It was also noted that heterosexuals with gay social contacts feel more at ease around gays than those with no gay social contacts. Finally, this study indicates homosexuals are most offended by stereotypes in general on television, followed by heterosexuals with gay social contacts, who felt somewhat offended by stereotypes. The heterosexuals with no gay social contacts felt the least offended by stereotypes in general as seen on television.

Table 6

MEAN SCORES OF ATTITUDES TOWARD STEREOTYPES, REPRESENTATIVENESS OF CHARACTERS, AND STEREOTYPE SCALE FOR HETEROSEXUALS AND HOMOSEXUALS

Groups	Attitudes Toward Stereotypes in General on Television*	Stereotype Nature of Television Homosexuals**	Representativeness of Television Gays to the Gay World***
Heteros with social contact (n = 26)	2.3462_{a}	1.68	3.5769_{a}
Heteros with no social contact (n = 54)	2.6538_{ab}	1.9298_{ab}	3.3889_{a}
Gays (n = 45)	1.9388	1.25	4.3265
Average among groups	2.315	1.6308	3.782

*Scores ranged from 1 = very offended to 3 = not at all
**Scores ranged from 1 = very stereotyped to 5 = not stereotyped
***Scores ranged from 1 = highly representative to 6 = highly unrepresentative
[a]Means significantly different from gays
[b]Means of heteros with no social contact significantly different from heteros with social contact

Table 7

ANALYSIS OF VARIANCE BETWEEN ATTITUDES TOWARD STEREOTYPES, REPRESENTATIVENESS OF CHARACTERS, STEREOTYPE SCALE FOR HETEROSEXUALS WITH AND WITHOUT GAY SOCIAL CONTACT AND HOMOSEXUALS

Factor	Source	df	Sum of Squares	Mean Squares	F Ratio	Prob.
Opinion of stereotypes	Between	2	12.9313	6.4657		
in general on television	Within	124	42.4700	0.3425	18.878	.0
	Total	126	55.4013			
Representativeness of the	Between	2	23.9673	11.9837		
television to gay society	Within	126	249.9542	1.9338	6.041	.0031
	Total	128	273.9214			
Stereotype nature of	Between	2	12.1176	6.0588		
the television gays	Within	127	110.1588	0.8674	6.985	.0013
	Total	129	122.2764			

Given the nature of stereotypes found in past research, especially the male homosexual stereotype, this study is added support for the "Kernel of Truth" theory. With the heterosexuals indicating the television gay characters as being partially representative of the gay community, and the gay sample indicating partially unrepresentative, both groups concede that stereotyped traits do exist in the homosexual community. The gays indicate this to a lesser degree than the heterosexuals. A small number of gays do assume a stereotype role in their culture.

This research indicates that experience is the best teacher in learning about subcultures that exist in American society. The majority of heterosexuals with gay social contacts indicate there are gays who do behave in a stereotyped manner, but because of their experience with the gay community, label a television gay as stereotyped. However, heteros with no gay social contacts indicate that all gays are not like television gays, but at the same time they are not sure if those television gays are stereotyped. In other words, heterosexuals without gay social contacts cannot recognize a stereotype that is supposed to be recognized as a stereotype. Network comedy series use stereotypes because they are funny and the audience can quickly associate the stereotype with its respective culture. This philosophy of entertainment must be challenged when the stereotype is not being recognized as a stereotype and is merely reinforcing preconceived ideas of the viewing audience. It is easy for heterosexuals with gay social contacts to modify their preconceived images of the gay male when they are exposed to the gay community. Heterosexuals with no gay social contacts cannot recognize the stereotype as a stereotype and, consequently, their perception of the real world is distorted. Ultimately, the consequences are ineffective communication among people.

This research has indicated the reference group or the social contact variable to be the best predictor in explaining why people believe stereotype portrayals. Future investigation should take into consideration that one question cannot necessarily tap a person's preception of a particular phenomena. An attempt should be made to understand secondary predictors that affect a viewer's perception of stereotyped characters. Understanding the secondary predictors as well as the effect of the social contact variable will enable researchers to construct scales that more accurately measure and predict a viewer's perception of stereotyped characters.

Part IV

Institutional Forces Shaping the Public Images of Gay Males and Lesbians

Chapter 14

Images of the Gay Male in Contemporary Drama

James W. Carlsen

> *Who was it that used to say, "You show me a happy homosexual, and I'll show you a gay corpse."*[1]

Introduction

Michael, the guilt-ridden and self-destructive central character in Mart Crowley's landmark play, *The Boys in the Band,* in a sorrowfully mocking way made the preceding statement in tears to Donald, his close friend, at the end of a birthday party and the end of a play. For Michael, this evening was more a vicious and emotion-letting ritual than a celebration of joy. For the American theater, in 1968, the image of the gay male moved from the closeted underground world of half-light, innuendo, and persona non grata to the publicly spotlighted, openly candid, and legitimate dramatis persona.

The Boys in the Band was not the first play to attempt to characterize effectively the homosexual, but it did provide a turning point for the theatrical display of the gay male in his own world. Despite some criticism of an unnatural picture of gay life in its worst fashion, the play was significant—as Clive Barnes, of *The New York Times,* stated in his opening night review—because it "takes the homosexual milieu, and the homosexual way of life, totally for granted and uses this as a valid basis of human experience."[2] For some, however, this portrayed experience satisfied the tastes of gay-haters, but William M. Hoffman, in the introduction to his recent book, *Gay Plays: The First Collection,* suggests that "*The Boys in the Band* can also be read as an indictment of homosexual self-hatred."[3] In the words of the character Harold, the self-proclaimed, thirty-two-year-old, ugly, pock-marked Jew fairy, to Michael:

> You are a sad and pathetic man. You're a homosexual and you don't want to be. But there is nothing you can do to change it. Not all the prayers to your God, not all the analysis you can buy in all the years you've got to live. You may very well one day be able to know a heterosexual life if you want it desperately enough—if you pursue it with the fervor with which you annihilate—but you will always be homosexual as well. Always, Michael. Always. Until the day you die.[4]

Whatever the critical verdict may be on this play, there can be no doubt that a significant subculture in our society became dramatically visible through Crowley's diverse character portrayals. Using *The Boys in the Band* as theatrical precedent and prologue for its historical time frame, questions arise as to how contemporary drama has pictured the homosexual and in what ways are playwrights creating realistically perceived and dramatically valid portraits of the gay male. Through an examination of selectively representative plays,[5] this essay responds to these questions and provides insights into the images of the gay male as depicted in contemporary drama.

Pre-*The Boys in the Band* Perceptions

To better understand the contemporary role assigned to the gay male, it is necessary to be aware of the pre-*The Boys in the Band* theatrical perceptions of the homosexual. Historically, the dramatic tradition of Western civilization, for one reason or another, has offered little in its desire to identify openly and honestly the gay male. It has been suggested that it was not until 1591, in Christopher Marlowe's *Edward II,* that a homosexual character was portrayed in a major role.[6] In this case the image of a homosexual king of England in the fourteenth century provided an uncommonly sophisticated acceptance and treatment of homosexuality as in integral aspect of the drama. Shakespeare, in such plays as *As You Like It, Antony and Cleopatra, Twelfth Night,* and *Troilus and Cressida,* made allusions and references to homosexuality. Oscar Wilde, one of the most noted and reputable playwrights who was gay, did not create gay characters, in the strictest sense, and was not, one would consider, a gay playwright. This opinion is in contrast perhaps to that of Eric Bentley, who when asked in an interview what has been the most significant piece of gay theater responded, "*The Importance of Being Earnest,* because it is by Oscar Wilde (and his best play)."[7] Further amplifying this statement George Whitmore, contemporary American writer of gay literature, supports Bentley by suggesting that *The Importance of Being Earnest* is "the paradigm of gay theatrical style—swift, witty, subversive."[8]

This controversy over the questionable gayness of Oscar Wilde's playwriting indicates a need to clarify what is meant by a "gay play" and "gay theater." Hoffman delineates the distinction by stating that "while the subject and the characters of a play will determine if a play is gay, the manner in which a play is acted and directed will determine if a production is 'gay theatre.' "[9] This essay focuses on plays with characters or themes that reflect an inherent male homosexuality.

Probably the most significant play since *Edward II* to deal openly with homosexuality, was produced in 1927, written by Jane Mast—more commonly known as Mae West—and was entitled *The Drag*. Two recent books, *Lavender Culture* and *Gay Plays,* document Mae West's bold, if not totally successful, emergence as a playwright of modern gay plays—*Sex* (1926), *The Drag* (1927), and *Pleasure Man* (1928).[10] The rare and mostly unavailable play *The Drag* was labeled "a homosexual comedy in three acts" but, in an almost prophetic way, is considered to be "an *extremely* serious melodrama that borders on a plea for tolerance of homosexuals."[11] Despite progressive attempts by Mae West to create naturalistic and legitimate dramatic renderings of the gay male, such plays were banned and the playwright jailed; in general, society was unwilling to accept the existence of the homosexual and his sensitive depiction on stage.

The overall repressive attitudes that existed before the socially and theatrically liberating events of the late sixties manifested themselves in playwrights' views of the homosexual. Although dealing with alleged lesbianism and not with the gay male, a classic example of false accusation as a way to introduce homosexuality was evidenced in Lillian Hellman's 1934 play, *The Children's Hour*. In the forties and fifties Tennessee Williams, an openly professed homosexual, wrote some of the most poetic and complex character studies in the American theater, but he has often been accused of distorting his characters to present a disguised image of both male and female characters. There are those, however, who defend Williams' portrayals and suggest that he himself has been falsely accused.

> Williams was as outspoken as anyone could possibly have been in the forties and fifties, and portrayed or mentioned homosexuals in many plays. His gays *are* gay. It is true that sometimes Williams was oblique, especially in *Cat on a Hot Tin Roof* (the relationship of Brick and Skipper), but few were as honest as Williams during that period.[12]

Although they were not ideal, well-adjusted personalities, the young husband of Blanche who committed suicide prior to the events portrayed in *A Streetcar Named Desire* (1947), and Sebastian in *Suddenly Last Summer* (1958) were two homosexual portraits presented by Williams in a repressive period in which homosexuality was a taboo topic.

Two commercially successful plays in the fifties that dared to mention elements of homosexuality did so through innuendo and false accusation. *Tea and Sympathy* (1935) by Robert Anderson developed a situation in which a "sensitive" young man was caught in homosexual false accusation.

Arthur Miller's *A View from the Bridge* (1955) depicted the incestuous desire of Eddie Carbone for his niece, Catherine, and resulted in a resentful gay accusation of Rodolpho, Catherine's boyfriend.

What was most revealing about the theatrical images during that period was not necessarily what was said, but what was *not* said or rather *how* it was said. This kind of melodramatic posturing in hushed and whispered tones whenever the subject of homosexuality arose undoubtedly reflected societal attitudes and was exemplified in *Tea and Sympathy*. In the following brief moment—presented with the playwright's stage directions—Laura, the older, sympathetic woman and wife of Bill, the headmaster of a boys' school, inquires about Tom, the "sensitive" young man.

> LAURA: (*hardly daring to suggest it*) But, Bill . . . you don't think Tom is . . . (*She stops. Bill looks at her a moment; his answer is in his silence.*) Oh, Bill![13]

Although more appearances of gay male characters were evident in the late fifties and early sixties, Don Shewey, in an article on gay theater, suggests that the "gay content was still largely between the lines and often as not gays were ultimately seen as unhappy and pathetic."[14] Examples of such recognized plays in this category were Shelagh Delaney's *A Taste of Honey* (1959), and Edward Albee's *Tiny Alice* (1965) and *Malcolm* (1966).

The year 1964 was important in the evolution of gay plays for the beginnings of two vanguard playwrights, Robert Patrick and Lanford Wilson, and for the off-off-Broadway success of their plays, *The Haunted Host* and *The Madness of Lady Bright,* which were first performed at the Caffe Cino.[15] Both plays, although different in tone and characterization, made a sincere attempt to present a candid picture of the gay male. The honesty with which Robert Patrick approached the gay life-style was refreshing, and provided a positive contrast to the innuendo, hushed whisper, or false accusation in many of the plays in the fifties. This openness and lack of sexual self-consciousness was revealed in *The Haunted Host* when Jay, the extravagant, Greenwich Village homosexual, was questioned by Frank, a straight, young man who was visiting.

> FRANK: *Are* you a homosexual?
> JAY: I'm *the* homosexual![16]

With the progression and further development of plays with gay themes in the late sixties, theatrical images of the gay male were becoming more diverse (but still somewhat stereotyped) and were beginning to convey the complexity of the homosexual personality, which much of the heterosexual society did not comprehend or want to accept. Charles Dyer's portrait of two aging, homosexual barbers in *Staircase* (1966) represents the universal problems of aging and of a long-term relationship. *Fortune and Men's Eyes* (1967), by John Herbert, explored another aspect of homosexual life in a frank and sometimes brutal prison drama.

Post-*The Boys in the Band* Portraits

The commercial success of *The Boys in the Band* and the more willing acceptance of homosexual subject matter by a mass audience were combined with the liberating effects of the Stonewall riots of 1969 to herald a new era for the gay male in contemporary drama. If *The Boys in the Band* suggested that homosexuality was no longer a forbidden or closeted topic for the legitimate, mass audience theater, then different boundaries and guidelines became evident to the writer of plays with gay themes or characters.

> On the one hand, it enabled writers to deal with homosexuality on a more honest, open level without suffering instant doom; but on the other hand, it opened the doors to a flood of sensationalized plays using homosexuality as a kinky novelty. This dichotomy exists to this day.[17]

Despite newly founded acceptance by audiences, another influence on the reception of plays with a gay orientation was a pervasive negative response by theater critics. In some cases ill-received plays were the victims of homophobic reactions of critics rather than of valid criticisms of the dramatic integrity of the works. Allan Pierce suggests that "reviewers are careful not to offend the often naive and primitive tastes of white, straight, middle America."[18] In an examination of fifty years of reviews of plays with gay themes or characters, Pierce revealed that "the critics have generally been abrasive to the healthy homosexual sensibility. Rather than fostering mass enlightenment, theatre critics have by and large acted as narrow-minded, prejudiced fag haters and baiters."[19] Examples of contemporary plays receiving less than favorable reviews from New York critics who exhibited a homophobic bias by their tone and language would include *And Puppy Dog Tails* (1969) by David Gaard and *Find Your Way Home* (1974) by John Hopkins. The critics' use of condescending and belittling name-calling manifested itself in such homophobic terms as "faggots," "fags," "deviates," and "fairies."[20] More often than not, this critical approach revealed a personal fear and sexual insecurity of the reviewer rather than an attempt to evaluate honestly and sincerely the dramatic image of the gay male.

In 1970 the gay male became not only more accepted in mass-audience theater, but was openly spotlighted. Unfortunately, as with a certain unfavorable bias of critics, this new acceptance occasionally carried with it a sensationalized, stereotyped, or patronized concept of the gay male. The comedy *Norman, Is That You?,* by Ron Clark and Sam Bobrick, is an example of a play with the tendency to stereotype and patronize the gay life-style. It was unsuccessful in New York, but apparently its view of coming out and the broadly comic characters involved in the process successfully pleased the community and dinner theater audiences in the rest of America who felt safe and secure with this portrayal of homosexuality.

However, a positive outgrowth of the openness and relative freedom to present the gay male in the seventies resulted in the desire of playwrights and directors who were gay to combat sensationalism and exploitation of homosexuality onstage by speaking for themselves through their creativity. Playwright/director Doric Wilson, in 1972, founded TOSOS—The Other Side of Silence—as "a place where authors and artists who want to deal with their gayness can have their work done, and done well, and done away from the marketplace where sensationalism is the rule of the day."[21] *Lovers,* an original musical by Peter del Valle and Steve Sterner, was the successful first production, in 1973. Other gay theater organizations whose concern was to develop new plays for those with a shared homosexual vision were sponsored in San Francisco, Los Angeles, Chicago, and Minneapolis.

All this activity created an environment in which plays of various forms and styles, whether on Broadway or in gay theater workshops, could deal openly with homosexuality. More important, the image of the gay male was beginning to escape from the straight, narrow stereotype of an effeminate, unhappy, or sick personality to a character whose identity was unrestricted and disparate. The motivations and behavior of the gay persona, then, depended on the particular setting and circumstances of the dramatic situation, as should be true of any characters in any play. Even with an open and upfront gay orientation, the intentions and backgrounds of plays emerging during this period were various and multipurpose. A few examples of successful plays with such diversity are *P.S. Your Cat Is Dead!* (1972), by James Kirkwood; *Tubstrips* (1974), by A.J. Kronengold; *The Ritz* (1976), by Terrence McNalley; and *The West Street Gang* (1977), by Doric Wilson.

The West Street Gang and *A Perfect Relationship* (1978) were published in 1979, in a volume entitled *Two Plays by Doric Wilson,* and dealt with the attitudes and mores of contemporary gay life. Wilson has said that both plays are about "an intense commitment to noncommitment," and as Felice Picano stated in his introduction, "a statement which is not a paradox if you've been to any urban gay meeting place lately."[22] This collection of comedies undoubtedly documents Wilson's position as a significant and continually emerging writer of gay theater. Robert Chesley, in an article on the playwright for *The Advocate,* confirms this appraisal.

The two plays stand out far ahead of the bulk of theatre dealing with gay topics. Not only are they right-on about the issues of present-day gay life, they are very funny and provocative. Wilson is first and foremost a skillful and experienced playwright: he knows theatre, he knows audiences, and he knows gay men. If you go to his plays, you will see yourself and your friends voicing the attitudes and opinions of urban gay culture—and you may even have reason to think a bit more about these attitudes and opinions (as well as about yourself and your friends). Wilson's satire can be devastating.[23]

The West Street Gang, subtitled "a polemical satire in two acts," was first performed for the Spike Bar in New York's West Side, and was clearly a sociopolitical play focusing on the attacks on gay men by youth gangs. But it also commented on aspects of the gay movement: the police, Anita Bryant, and *The Village Voice.* Because of its more domestic, intimate setting and circumstances, *A Perfect Relationship* differs from *The West Street Gang* in tone and style. The central characters, Greg and Ward, roommates for eleven years, live on Christopher Street in Greenwich Village and pride themselves on their liberated homosexual life-style; but such freedom, with its comically combative role-playing, blind the love and hide the commitment of the two roommates. The following dialogue concerning who will cook dinner and therefore be the most "domestic" humorously illustrates how each character tries to define himself and his "masculinity."

WARD: You can make a souffle—don't deny it. I've seen you.
GREG: That was an omelet. Lots of men make omelets.
WARD: With strawberries?
GREG: That recipe came from *Popular Mechanics.*[24]

Not only do the actions and dialogue of Greg and Ward promote and establish self-imposed perceptual identities (as is often the case in gay culture), but they also present images, sometimes misinterpreted and distorted, to the outside, heterosexual world. This is the case with Muriel, a flighty, straight woman and Greg and Ward's subleasor, who makes these observations to her many boyfriends throughout the play.

Gay men have boodles of money.

They have their own restaurants and bars and everything.

Gay people like to sound cynical. They think it's sexy.

They drink beer just like you.

Gay people like to play games.[25]

In both Doric Wilson plays there exists beneath the comic creations the element of truth, and we are presented with images of real gay men honestly involved in real gay life situations. The playwright, then, with his understanding of gay culture and his theatercraft, has effectively displayed "real gay men facing specifically gay-related problems for whose solutions they have no moral or cultural referents as guides. They have to find the answers to questions they are being forced to ask themselves for the first time."[26]

Diverse portrayals of the gay male and his sexuality were clearly represented by two contrasting and critically successful theatrical efforts of the late seventies—*A Chorus Line* (1975), by James Kirkwood and Nicholas Dante, and *Streamers* (1976), by David Rabe. *A Chorus Line,* an award-winning and tremendously popular musical, allowed one of the major characters to tell his poignant and emotion-filled story as a drag queen early in his career and his personal frustrations with this situation. *Streamers* presented a powerful and brutal portrait of homosexual passion and homophobic reaction in a military setting.

A further extension in the liberation of the legitimate theater to show characters who were gay without sensationalism or stereotyping was evident in *The Shadow Box* (1977), by Michael Cristofer, and *Fifth of July* (1978), by Lanford Wilson. In *The Shadow Box* the characters Brian and Mark share a love within a setting and theme of death and dying: Brian, who is terminally ill, is visited by Beverly, his former wife, who meets for the first time Mark, Brian's lover. Mark is somewhat uncomfortable with Beverly's intrusion into Brian's cottage at this time, and in a humorously awkward scene, Beverly introduces herself.

> BEVERLY: Oh, sorry. Sorry. Introductions first. That way you'll know who you're throwing out. (*She extends her hand in a handshake.*) I'm Beverly. No doubt you've . . .
>
> MARK: Yes.
>
> BEVERLY: That's what I figured.
>
> MARK: Brian's wife.
>
> BEVERLY: Ex-wife.
>
> MARK: Former.
>
> BEVERLY: Yes. Former. Former wife. He prefers former, doesn't he?
>
> MARK *(shakes her hand):* Yes. I figured it was you.
>
> BEVERLY: You did?
>
> MARK: Yes . . . it wasn't hard.
>
> BEVERLY: No, I guess not. *(She smiles.)* And you're . . . uh . . .
>
> MARK: Yes.
>
> BEVERLY: Yes. I figured.
>
> MARK: Mark.
>
> BEVERLY: Great. Well.
>
> MARK: Well. *(Pause)*
>
> BEVERLY: Well, now that we know who we are . . . how about a drink?[27]

The previous dialogue suggests the oftentimes delicate and sometimes problematic situation of a heterosexual confronting a homosexual lover relationship. And this, of course, is compounded when there is a mutual love interest and previous partner, as in the case of Brian. The openness with which Cristofer creates this sensitive meeting is further demonstrated later in the scene, when Beverly, in a state of intoxication, insists that Mark join her in a drink. This provokes Mark's protective concern for Brian and Beverly's misconceived and stereotypical notions of a gay man.

MARK: I mean, it's sort of a delicate situation, right now. He's had a very bad time of it and any kind of, well, disturbance . . .

BEVERLY: Such as me? Oh, you get used to it. You just have to think of me as your average tramp.

MARK: . . . any disturbance might be dangerous, especially psychologically and . . . I sound like an idiot, the way I'm talking. But you don't seem to be understanding a goddamn word I'm saying!

BEVERLY: No. I am. I am. You know, you don't *look* like a faggot.

MARK: Oh, for Christ's sake!

BEVERLY: No, I mean it . . . I mean, I didn't expect . . .

MARK: Well, you'll get used to it. You just have to think of me as your average cocksucker. All right?

BEVERLY: Good. Now we're getting someplace. Are you sure you wouldn't like a drink?[28]

As with *The Shadow Box,* the element of homosexuality in Lanford Wilson's *Fifth of July* is not presented for its own sake, but rather is one of the integral aspects of the drama. In this case the dramatic situation is set in rural Missouri and portrays Ken, a legless Vietnam veteran, and his lover, Jed, who exist within circumstances where their homosexuality is not emphasized, but rather the diminishing dreams and ideals of the 1960s.

One of the most recent and significant plays to deal forthrightly with male homosexuality is *Bent,* by Martin Sherman, which opened in New York at the New Apollo Theatre on December 2, 1979. The story is concerned with particular circumstances surrounding the persecution of gays in the Nazi concentration camps. Not only is the play forceful in its depiction of another oppressed minority in Nazi Germany (homosexuals wore a pink triangle, just as Jews were forced to wear a yellow star), but it also painfully highlights the conflict between avowing one's sexuality and love for another man, and giving up such personal commitments in order to survive. Max, the central character, in proving his desire to survive, states, "I make deals, I stay alive." And this is confirmed when his lover, the dancer, is beaten brutally by the Nazis on the train to Dachau, and Max agrees to punch the already limp dancer, which results in the ultimate death of his lover. In terms of playing a homosexual in the legitimate theater, it is significant that Richard Gere, a notable and highly acclaimed film actor, accepted the controversial role of Max, and such casting, coupled with his critically praised performance, enhances the credibility of serious and honest presentations of the gay male onstage. Edwin Wilson, in *The Wall Street Journal,* reviewed *Bent* as a play with three concerns: survival, the holocaust, and homosexuality.

> In addition to writing about survival and the Holocaust—two subjects that are related—Mr. Sherman has written what might be considered a third play about homosexuals. Despite his callousness, Max has shown at several points that he cares about his male lovers. . . . But whenever anyone expresses love for Max, he lashes out, demanding that no one should love him. "Queers aren't meant to love," he exclaims.
>
> In the last act, which takes place at Dachau, when Horst (a fellow prisoner) is killed, Max cradles the body in his arms and finds the ability to express the gentleness and the love he has not expressed before.[29]

Clearly, Max is not as insensitive and uncaring as circumstances might have suggested, and this translates into the positive message that "it is all right for homosexuals to be tender with one another and express their love."[30]

Conclusion

From pre-*The Boys in the Band* perceptions of homosexuality that approached the subject through silence, innuendo, false accusation, or stereotyping, to the more open, candid, and honest portraits of the late seventies, the image of the gay male in contemporary drama has achieved a level of dramatic validity and social acceptance not imagined a few years ago. With changing attitudes in society and with greater freedom and activity for writers, a sensible environment for the exploration of gay characters or themes can be achieved. This is not to suggest that portrayals of gayness onstage should abound without dramatic integrity, social awareness, or critical evaluation, but that efforts should transcend dishonest, distorted, or sensationalized attempts. The gay male is a complex, multifaceted personality, with attitudes, beliefs, and values that are affected in both similar and dissimilar ways to that of any other individual. And characters in a play should reflect such distinctive and idiosyncratic traits, allowing for honest and unbiased portrayals. The motivations and actions of the gay persona should and must be determined by the dramatic situation, not some preconceived or preconditioned myth and stereotype.

Despite the positive evolution in the creation of plays that portray the homosexual with openness and human sensibility, as is chronicled by the previous examination, effective and more fully developed renderings need to be pursued. Until society and its theater refrain from homophobic and insensitive reactions to and depictions of homosexuals—real life or stage personae—and until gays are willing to accept themselves and their artwork without apology, there will be a need for constant reexamination of theatrical images and continual critical appraisal of dramatic perspectives on the homosexual experience.

Chapter 15

Views of Homosexuality Among Social Scientists

James W. Chesebro

Scant attention has been paid to the role and function of sexual preference as a variable in the communication process. Within the last twenty years only two published essays have explored this issue within the discipline of speech communication. One essay, published in 1973, identified and described the small-group techniques of radical gay militants in consciousness-raising sessions that preceded public confrontations (see chapter 18).[1] A second and more recent essay, in 1976, examined the verbal terminologies used by gay people in "secret," "social," and "radical-activist" settings (see chapter 4).[2] Overall, however, given the size of the population involved and its more public declarations since the June 1969 Stonewall riot in New York, little academic concern has been devoted to the variable of sexual preference and the role of gay people in the communication process.[3]

This essay deals with only one word—homosexuality—and the ways in which this word has developed the connotations it has. Attention is devoted particularly to the ways in which social scientists in their published essays and books have transmitted connotations of this word to others.

Social scientists have published massive quantities of analyses cast as "research," "data," and "factual information" regarding same-sex relationships. The analyses, frequently posited as definitional and descriptive, have "seeped" into the popular culture in amorphous and often unpredictable ways (television talk-shows and the like). However, the definitions and descriptions are read with an almost desperate fervor by those for whom sexual preference emerges as a question, if not a problem. Likewise, anxious parents and concerned friends turn directly to these studies to deal with the new experiences, feelings, and attitudes of those coming out. Indeed, these studies appear "objective," for their tone and mood are "scientific." The style is detached and didactic: people are treated as "subjects," "data" are "collected," and "findings" and "conclusions" are "reported." In all, an "unbiased" stance is promised. Indeed, for some, the social scientist has emerged as the "neutral arbitrator of conflicts" in our culture.

Rhetoricians, however, ought to be cautious whenever such claims of objectivity are implied. Irving J. Rein notes, for example, that definitions themselves may not provide descriptions of reality; they are more likely to function as strategies which only manipulate the image of a group of people.[4] Even in the physical sciences, the objective stance has been questioned. As Werner Heisenberg aptly observed:

> Science no longer is in the position of observer of nature, but rather recognizes itself as part of the interplay between man and nature. The scientific method of separating, explaining, and arranging becomes conscious of its limits, set by the fact that the employment of this procedure changes and transforms its object; the procedure can no longer keep its distance from the object. The world view of natural science thus ceases to be a view of "natural" science in its proper sense.[5]

Dealing directly with the rhetoric of the social sciences, Herbert Simons argued:

> Yet, in the classical, nonpejorative sense, "rhetoric" refers to reason-giving activity on judgmental matters about which there can be no formal proof. The classical conception permits, and even encourages, the eulogistic sense of rhetoric as *good* reasongiving on matters of judgment. And, in the final analysis, that is what defenders of science *mean* by "scientific objectivity."[6]

Given this initial perspective, the findings and analyses of social scientists are treated here as if they were persuasive messages which, consciously or not, create a social conception of same-sex relationships and the people within those relationships. Ernest Bormann's method of fantasy theme analysis,[7] has been employed to identify the major content and stylistic themes within social scientific discourses. Particularly, the objective of this analysis was to specify what Bormann identifies as "fantasy types" or "recurring scenarios in a body of discourse" in order to allow identification of the ways in which these fantasy themes are "integrated" to create a "coherent" and "shared" overview or "rhetorical vision."[8]

Two major recurring fantasies permeate the rhetoric of social scientists as they deal with same-sex relations. A third fantasy has recently begun to emerge, but it is dealt with only briefly at the end of these first two sections because it has yet to attain the technical status of a recurrent fantasy theme or fantasy type. The essay closes by identifying the rhetorical vision that most appropriately accounts for the two major fantasies specified. This rhetorical vision, it is claimed here, is paradoxical; an alternative concept and referent for social scientific research is therefore outlined for those examining same-sex relationships. Specifically, the word "gay" and its referents are posited as a more viable research base for same-sex social science analyses.

Fantasy #1: The Homosexual as Degenerate

Degeneracy, as a concept, generates a host of symbolic connotations. Most commonly, degeneracy is treated as a kind of "character, structure, or functional . . . condition" of a "peculiarly corrupt and vicious state." Particularly, the degenerate condition is associated with those who are "degraded from the normal moral standard," "debased by a psychopathic tendency," "sexually perverse," and show "signs of reversion to an earlier culture stage."[9] Moreover, degeneracy is also associated with deterioration, debasement, decadence, degradation, retrogression, demoralization, decay, decomposition, erosion and corrosion, and consumption and waste.[10]

My reading of the discourses of the sampled social scientists has led to the belief that the most appropriate entitlement and transcendent term for a major theme of their conception of same-sex relations is *degenerate.* This unifying theme of degeneracy emerges when same-sex relations are cast as particular and discrete collective actions characterized by secretive, lonely, isolated, unemotional, demeaning, esoteric, dehumanizing, and neurotic behaviors. Pointedly put, this viewpoint reinforces, and perhaps creates, the image of the homosexual as degenerate.

The scientific fantasy of the homosexual as degenerate is dramatically illustrated in the first chapter of Martin Hoffman's book, *The Gay World,* a book recommended by several gay rights organizations. Hoffman offered a scenario between two characters, David and Tom, which Hoffman claimed functions as an excellent foundation "to our study of the gay world—its character, its internal structure, and the problems which are generic to it."[11] David is described as "a typical young urban homosexual male."[12] In greater detail, Hoffman offered this account of David:

> David came to San Francisco from Kansas City when he was 20 years old. His father was a dentist and his mother a housewife. He has no brothers, but has a sister three years older than him and one two years younger.
>
> He first noticed an erotic interest in boys when he was around 12 years old, but did not consider having sex with them until he was 18. At this time he became involved in a theatrical group in his home town and he was introduced to a number of homosexuals. From them he learned the terminology of the homosexual community and was introduced to a few novels about the subject. He was befriended by someone whom he describes as a "gay mother," who sort of took it upon himself to instruct David in the ways of the

> gay world and told him that eventually he would "come out," i.e., define himself as homosexual and enter the homosexual world. This person was not sexually interested in David, but there was someone whom he described to David as being an admirer of his. At a party, his admirer kissed David, who liked it and got an erection. But when the seducer learned that David was still a virgin, he decided not to have sex with him, not wishing to be the first one to introduce him to homosexual practices. . . . David went to college at the age of 19 and had his first homosexual experience, with his college roommate, whom he had a crush on. His first sexual experience consisted of necking and allowing his roommate to perform fellatio on him. He now says that he will engage in almost any kind of sexual activity, but he has found out that his preference is to play the passive role in anal intercourse.[13]

Though cast as an objective and understanding perspective, this analysis describes the individual homosexual in pointedly selective and unappealing terms. Stereotypical descriptions emerge (San Francisco, theatrical groups, a "gay mother," and so forth). The cultural setting is cast as extremely isolated, if not lonely ("come out," "enter the homosexual world," and so forth). Human responses are described solely in behavioral and dehumanizing terms ("got an erection," "perform fellatio on him," and so forth). The pattern of interaction is implied to be promiscuous ("seducer," "He now says that he will engage in almost any kind of sexual activity," and so forth).

Nonetheless, this scenario and the particular features characterizing it represent the recurrent, not the exceptional, strategies used by social scientists to create the fantasy of "the homosexual as degenerate." Particularly, the degenerate scenario is created by five themes, which define homosexuals as (1) a relatively stable, precise, and discrete subculture which, therefore, does not function as part of the "mainstream of American life"; (2) a cluster of identifiable types—a stereotyping strategy regardless of the evaluation of the stereotypes; (3) located in particularly undesirable settings—while aesthetic standards may vary, I have found the word sleazy to function as a critical term describing these settings; (4) engaged in sexual acts that are described in behavioral, nonemotional, and therefore dehumanizing terms; and (5) destined to face predictable psychological problems.

In this scenario, then, those persons preferring the same-sex relationships have been cast as a relatively precise subculture existing apart from heterosexuals. A host of terms such as "the world of the homosexual,"[14] the "velvet underground,"[15] and "the homosexual world"[16] have been used to describe the cohesive nature of this collective. Lawrence Hatterer noted that "there is no completely satisfactory term to describe the collective aspects of homosexuality." Nonetheless, he observed that the "term 'world' is being used" as well as the "terms 'subculture,' 'society' and 'community.' "[17] More directly, D.W. Cory and J.P. LeRoy argued that homosexuals "are a society within a society."[18]

Likewise, members of this "subculture" have been cast as distinct from the norms of the American culture. Members of same-sex relations have been identified as "sexual heretics,"[19] "sexual outlaws."[20] and by a set of more derogatory terms such as faggot, queer, fairy, fag, homo, pansy, fruit, boy, and queen. However, in the writings of social scientists, this array of terms is typically replaced by the word homosexual. Wardell B. Pomeroy, of the Institute of Sex Research at Indiana University and coauthor of the famous Kinsey studies, posited a relatively common behavioral definition of homosexuality. He suggested that, "*Homosexual behavior* is defined as sexual activity between two persons of the same sex."[21] In this context, Edmund Bergler argued that a homosexual acts "in contradistinction to a heterosexual who is sexually attracted only to members of the opposite sex."[22] By their choice of sexual partners, then, homosexuals are, in this view, set aside from heterosexuals.

Homosexual types are clearly stereotyped in the rhetoric of social scientists. Although one author has argued that a homosexual defines "himself to *some* extent, as homosexual, in all other respects he is a typical American,"[23] others have tended to identify types of homosexuals; their typologies are approximately the same. One team of authors identified three types: the effeminate male (viewed as "representing only a small minority of the minority—a group within a group"); the muscle man; and the male prostitute.[24] Arguing for a similar set of categories, another author claimed that among the range of "recently emerging urban homosexual subcultures" are "such groups [as] the leather-jacketed 'butch,' or sado-masochistic, group to the male prostitute or 'hustler,' the 'queen,' who appears overtly feminine or who is a transvestite, the 'piss elegant' member of the wealthy upper class or pretender to top social status, or the 'closet queen,' who regularly and secretly practices homosexuality but denies it."[25]

In addition, these social scientists argue that homosexuals gain their identity through an association with particular locations. The gay bar has been cast as a "social institute in America"[26] and as the primary "source of group solidarity."[27] In addition, the gay bar has been described as the primary place where the "homosexual publicly identifies himself as a homosexual," realizes "that there are many other young men like himself," and becomes aware of "the stigma of public identification for the first time in his life."[28] These writers also identify the streets, rest rooms, parks and public baths as public places for homosexuals.[29]

Furthermore, the sexual acts which homosexuals engage in are described in behavioral, nonemotional—and therefore dehumanizing—terms. Typically these acts are described as "touching, kissing, petting, frictation, stroking the genitalia, mouth-genital contact, and anal intercourse."[30] These acts, it should also be noted, are typically viewed as part of a pattern of "anonymous promiscuity."[31]

Finally, although some claim that "homosexuality is a neurotic disease,"[32] more moderate psychiatrists have posited that many homosexuals are unified by virtue of their recognition that they are "troubled by their homosexuality."[33] Hatterer, for example, used a series of clinical interviews to support this contention.

Such referents have generated relatively precise quantifications of the size of the collective. Hayes, for example, claimed that homosexuals are "America's largest subculture."[34] More precisely Arno Karlen explained that

> of the two hundred million people in the United States, some ten million are or will become exclusive or predominant homosexuals—more than there are Jews or Latin Americans. People with at least a few years' significant homosexual experience may number more than twenty-five million—more than blacks.[35]

Thus, as used by social scientists, the isolation, stereotyping, situational, dehumanizing, and psychological themes are aptly unified, transcended, and entitled by a fantasy type which casts the homosexual as a degenerate. In part or in whole, these themes depict the "homosexual" as degraded from the normal moral standard, debased by a psychopathic tendency, sexually perverse, and showing signs of reversion to an earlier culture stage. Illustrative of the ways in which these themes are employed by social scientists is Hoffman's dramatic explanation of the particular case of David and Tom. David and Tom actually meet, and Hoffman's account of their interaction includes all five themes of degeneracy:

> By the time Tom had finished his martini, he had developed enough courage to walk over to David, to whom he was attracted, and make a conversational opener. Tom began the conversation by asking David about the bar, and David's quite friendly response led him to believe that he might have some chance of getting him to come home to bed with him. Soon David detached himself from his group of friends and began talking with Tom alone. They exchanged some biographical information, although not their last names. Last names are characteristically not mentioned in gay bar conversations because of the wish to preserve a certain degree of anonymity in what is clearly an illicit situation. They told each other what their occupations were, although they did not give the names of the firms for which they worked. Tom told David that he was married and this increased David's attraction to Tom, since he equated heterosexual potency (something he did not possess) with "masculinity," which he, and most homosexuals, consider the single most desirable feature of their partners. While David was not one of those homosexuals who is especially after "straight" males, the prospect of going to

bed with a heterosexual or, at any rate, a bisexual male distinctly appealed to him. . . .

When they got to bed, they continued necking and petting until finally Tom made it clear that he wanted to perform fellatio on David. He indicated his wish by gestures rather than by conversation, i.e., he first fondled David's pelvic area, and finally began to fellate him. This is something Tom had done before, something he especially liked to do. It was, as a matter of fact, with this act in mind that Tom went to the gay bar in the first place. David ejaculated in about 15 or 20 minutes, after which they both lay in bed for a while, and engaged in some light necking. After a few more minutes, David asked Tom if he would screw him, which, although Tom did not especially want to do, he consented to. When this was over, they both lit up cigarettes and lay in bed smoking for a while.

David asked Tom if he wanted to spend the night with him, but Tom said no, he had to go back and sleep with his wife. He told David that he had told his wife he was going out for a few drinks with the boys, and as it was getting to be about 3:00 in the morning, he had better get going. David gave Tom his phone number and Tom said he would call him, although he never did.[36]

Beyond the particular themes which control such a description, the overall vision unifying the themes presumes that a typical or average gay scenario exists. Published research findings fail to establish this presumption, and existing evidence suggests that multiple life-styles—different in kind—constitute the gay community. In the most comprehensive study done to date, Alan P. Bell and Martin S. Weinberg[37] found it necessary to use the word homosexual in its plural form to refer to the sexual preferences they examined. In their view, the word homosexual, in its singular form, ignored the statistical validity of the diverse social groupings they identified. Thus, the notion of a typical homosexual or homosexual practice is a social scientific fantasy, not only in Bormann's sense of the term, but literally as well.

Fantasy #2: Mainstreaming the Homosexual

As a social strategy, mainstreaming is an accommodating tactic designed to eliminate a sect orientation and the concomitant special treatments associated with such an orientation. The recent attempt to mainstream the physically handicapped, for example, has involved adjustments in social attitudes, employment environments, and even in physical architecture. Yet, mainstreaming also presumes that an identifiable norm exists and that variations from this norm are differences in degree, not kind. Thus, a typical dictionary definition describes mainstreaming as a process of adjusting to a prevailing current or direction of activity or influence.

As a controlling perspective for examining homosexuality, a mainstreaming research strategy entails a perception, definition, and description of the homosexual quite different from that governing the homosexual as degenerate fantasy. Though not explicitly advocating a social policy of mainstreaming the homosexual, a massive body of published social scientific research is unified by this mainstreaming perspective. The mainstreaming fantasy clusters into three themes which suggest that the homosexual can be considered part of the mainstream of America. First, the fantasy particularly requires that homosexual behavior itself be drastically reconceived so that its distinctiveness, dehumanizing image, and frequency would no longer be perceived as threatening behavior. Second, the fantasy requires an alternative conception of the social reality of homosexuals; if they are to be mainstreamed, homosexuals can no longer be viewed as a unified and isolated subculture. Third, and finally, if homosexuals are to be mainstreamed, the psychological pathology associated with the group has to be eliminated. In fact, three themes are played out to satisfy the requirements of the mainstreaming fantasy.

The first theme of the mainstreaming fantasy offers an alternative conception of homosexual behavior itself. Rather than view homosexual behavior as a discrete kind of behavior, the entire issue of sexual preference is cast as a relative issue with variation only in the degree of homosexuality or heterosexuality which may exist in particular individuals. Pomeroy, and virtually all of the research sanctioned by the Kinsey Institute, employs a heterosexual-homosexual continuum to describe sexual preference. Pomeroy argues for the continuum in these terms:

> In cultures that have no serious social sanctions against homosexual relations, males do not tend to develop an exclusive pattern of homosexuality, but, instead, combine homosexual and heterosexual activity. In our own culture a dichotomy is made between the two types of behavior, and often people are forced into deciding whether they are "homosexual" or "heterosexual." I recall a twenty-four-year-old single male patient of mine who announced that he was a homosexual. Inquiry revealed that he had had four overt homosexual experiences between the ages of fourteen and nineteen, and that he was slightly aroused by thinking about and seeing males. He also had dated many girls, had had intercourse with several of them, and was very much aroused by thinking of them and seeing them.[38]

Given this perspective, Pomeroy and his associates have made repeated use of their Likert-type scale that classifies individuals from 0 (exclusively heterosexual) to 6 (exclusively homosexual).[39] Such a continuum implies that individuals differ in their sexual preference only in degree. However, the mainstreaming fantasy is even more clearly revealed in Pomeroy's observation that "if we could break down this irrational concept of a dichotomy between heterosexuality and homosexuality, we might understand better how to help patients change in the direction of heterosexuality if that is their desire."[40]

Other social scientists have also sought to posit a conception of homosexual behavior that would close the gap between homosexuals and heterosexuals. Homosexuality, in this fantasy, is no longer described solely in behavioral terms. The Sex Information and Education Council of the U.S. (SIECUS) has noted, for example, that homosexuality includes "emotional involving sexual attraction, between individuals—male or female—of the same sex."[41] Similarly, others have argued that even the exclusive homosexual is not engaged in homosexual acts as frequently as might be suspected. Karlen argued, for example, that exclusive homosexuals engage in overt sexual relations with someone of the same sex only one hour and forty-five minutes per week.[42] Moreover, others have reported that 15 to 20 percent of those identifying themselves as homosexual have never engaged in an overtly sexual act with someone of their own sex.[43] In addition, SIECUS has concluded that 85 percent of exclusive homosexuals are "unrecognizable," i.e., possess no "effeminate characteristics."[44]

Embedded in these research claims is an alternative conception of homosexual behavior, its distinctiveness, its image, and the frequency of its occurrence. The threatening dimensions of homosexuality are minimized by such research findings, which imply that the homosexual is much closer to the mainstream of sexual practices than had previously been realized.

Not only is the mainstreaming fantasy sustained by positing an alternative conception of homosexual behavior; these social scientists also offer a different view of the social reality of homosexuals, who are no longer viewed as a unified and isolated community. As *The Wolfenden Report* argued some twenty years ago and as the National Institute of Mental Health has more recently put it, homosexuals are distributed randomly across all socioeconomic, cultural, intellectual, political, geographic,and professional groupings.[45] In a similar vein, Hayes argued that a large number of homosexuals refuse to "refer to [their] subculture life" and "may eschew gay terminology."[46] Likewise, in a more vivid study, Humphrey demonstrated that one quarter of those homosexuals engaging in impersonal and anonymous sex acts espouse some of the most violent and demeaning public attacks on homosexuals.[47] Such findings suggest that homosexuals, as a class, ought not be considered social in the sense that homosexuality involves "allies or confederates" or "pleasant companionships with one's friends or associates."[48] Ultimately, this theme suggests that homosexuals are not always part of a velvet underground, but may in fact find heterosexual interactions essential.

Finally, the mainstreaming fantasy gains credibility insofar as the psychological pathology associated with homosexuality is eliminated. In this regard, studies carried out by Evelyn Hooker function as compelling evidence for those endorsing the mainstreaming fantasy. Hooker demonstrated that experienced clinical psychiatrists were unable to distinguish randomly selected homosexuals from randomly selected heterosexuals when provided with complete test results from all known psychodiagnostic measures.[49]

The social vision implied by the mainstreaming fantasy differs remarkably from the vision created by the homosexual as degenerate fantasy. The mainstreaming fantasy is a more humane vision that may reduce the discrimination and social tension gay males and lesbians face as well as reinvigorate the liberal mystique that all have equal access to full participation in the public domain. At the same time, the fantasy may create false expectations for those anxious parents and friends who would change the orientation of gay males and lesbians. Moreover, for gay males and lesbians, the mainstreaming fantasy is counterproductive to those explorations designed to isolate, define, and develop a gay identity and a gay community. In addition, the mainstreaming fantasy indirectly supports the Anita Bryant stance, which rationalizes a hatred of homosexuality while professing a love for the homosexual. Much as the mainstreaming fantasy attempts to separate the homosexual from exclusive and intensive homosexual behavior, Bryant distinguishes the sin of homosexuality (a target to be destroyed) from the "homosexual" sinner (a group to be "saved" despite themselves).[50]

A Paradoxical Rhetorical Vision

If these two fantasies are viewed as mutually dependent and defining dimensions by the social scientists, the rhetorical vision is paradoxical.[51] One fantasy implies that homosexuals possess an observable identity (degeneracy), while the second fantasy suggests that homosexuals, as a collective, possess no universally shared characteristics. It is possible, of course, to argue that the two fantasies are temporally discrete and therefore nonparadoxical because the two fantasies, it might be reasoned, do not simultaneously define same-sex relationships. Certainly, Fantasy #1 appeared in the literature more frequently in the 1950s and 1960s, and Fantasy #2 more usually characterizes research published during the 1970s. However, the temporal distinction can be overemphasized, for both fantasies are distributed across the three decades, and in the public domain—as opinion polls repeatedly indicate[52]—Fantasy #1 remains the more powerful of the two. Moreover, both fantasies can be found in the *same* research reports. Hoffman, for example, argued that every homosexual is unique but, nevertheless, proceeded to provide archetypal examples (David and Tom). Similarly, while claiming that homosexuality is a meaningless social concept, the National Institute of Mental Health simultaneously argued that homosexuals (as well as their families and friends) share common attitudes, beliefs, and reactions about homosexuality.[53]

A distinct impression emerges that the rhetorical vision of social scientists, in this matter, is paradoxical. The concept of homosexuality seems to startle and confuse social scientists as much as it does those outside that scholarly community. The social scientists themselves may have likewise sensed dissatisfaction with the two fantasies, for a third fantasy seems to be emerging. Although it is difficult to determine whether this vision will gain sufficient support from other social scientists to warrant identifying it as a socially shared fantasy among members of the social scientific community, the 1980s may be dominated by the kind of research recently released by the Kinsey Institute[54] and by William Masters and Virginia Johnson.[55] Though the two studies differ radically in method, both possess common assumptions which could provide the foundation for a third fantasy. Both teams of researchers deal with homosexuals who identify themselves as gay and as part of a gay community, both teams attempt to make comparisons between different kinds of subgroups or life-styles reflected in each culture, both teams attempt to treat each culture as independent and viable, and both teams explore the possibility that the homosexual culture may provide helpful feedback to those dealing with social and sexual difficulties within the heterosexual class. The ultimate vision implied by such an approach suggests that social scientists, if this vision attains the status of a socially shared fantasy, may begin to produce research which demonstrates that heterosexuals and homosexuals are distinct but extremely compatible cultural systems. I have tentatively entitled this vision the "Cultural Compatibility Fantasy."

Even with the addition of this third fantasy, however, the paradoxical nature of social scientific research will remain, for all three fantasies, in major part, stem from the use of a particular word and the referents for that word. Social scientists have reacted to the word homosexuality and to its behavioral referent, sexual acts between members of the same sex. Quantitatively, the word homosexual (and its concomitant referent) specifies an extremely small part of the life experiences of those persons preferring same-sex relations; by Karlen's estimate, homosexual acts constitute but 1 percent of the behavior of those classified as exclusively homosexual. Moreover, 15 percent of those who identify themselves as homosexuals have never had any kind of sexual release with another person of the same sex.[56] Qualitatively, and probably because the word homosexual is technically a biological and medical term, the more profound social and cultural self-definitions of that act and the responses to that act by others are not directly specified by the word homosexual.

For example, insofar as a homosexual act is perceived as a stigma, perhaps Erving Goffman's emphasis is a more valuable point of departure for the researcher. Goffman argues that the stigma of a sexual act may go far beyond the province of the act itself, and it is the stigma itself which becomes the " 'master status determining trait' that lies at the heart of a person's public and inner identity."[57] The issue is *not* that the study of same-sex stigmas would exhaust the study of homosexuality. A shift of emphasis is being recommended. Rather than focus on a particular biological act as an operational definition for a research design, I propose that the diverse kinds of self and other responses to the biological act constitute the research base for investigation. Thus, I suggest that the study of self and other definitions and responses to those definitions—in all of their complex forms—are the proper objects of research, particularly for the communication and rhetorical scholar.

As an alternative to the current attention given to the word homosexual and its referent, I would suggest that the word gay and its referents are more likely to produce insightful understandings regarding the social and cultural meanings of same-sex relationships. In this context, the word gay specifies a more complex as well as a different kind of human action than the sphere of actions identified by the word homosexual.

The word homosexual draws attention primarily to an overt biological and sexual release that gains its specificity because the release occurs between two members of the same sex. With this release as a central definitional base for research, the consequential social behaviors and responses to those behaviors are examined predominantly as extended by-products of the sexual and biological release. The word homosexual thus places its focus on an explicit sexual act and then on its coincidental behavior.

In contrast, the word gay is a meaning-centered, social, and multidimensional concept. The word gay identifies those who have adopted a particular *world view* or perspective of reality which is *self-imposed* and a *self-defined* determinant of the attitudes, beliefs, actions, and even the vocabulary affecting human interactions. Thus, the word gay specifies a kind of *consciousness* controlling personal identities, social predispositions, and anticipatory orientations. Multiple and dependent factors define and unify this gay consciousness and the gay community that shares this world view.

Particularly, the word gay emphasizes a *preference* for same-sex relationships in the sense that by act, fact, or principle, same-sex relations are given advantage over opposite-sex relations. Likewise, the word gay refers to an *affectional* preference in that same-sex relations are mental or emotional inclinations involving loving, tender, and caring responses toward members of the same sex.

Moreover, the word gay includes a recognition of and concern for the existence of *diverse gay life-styles* which involves a deference for the self-conceptions of each of those life-styles as defined by different gay subgroupings as well as the kinds of heterosexual responses to these diverse gay life-styles. These diverse gay life-styles are a unifying force within the gay community, for the existence of such diversity functions as an important interest variable as well as a set of potential options when change is required in personal life. Moreover, these diverse life-styles are unified by a common preference for same-sex relations.

In addition, these related preferences exist in a heterosexual world, and, given current popular attitudes toward same-sex relations, the word gay is also associated with the activities of the gay liberation movement; the word thus carries the connotations of a *positive self-image* involving a sense of *pride* and *power* in a potential or actual *confrontational* context if or when others reject or deny the interpersonal significance of same-sex relations.

The word gay also, of course, refers to the preference for a potential or ongoing *sexual* relationship with those of the same sex. This sexual preference exists, however, in the context of the other dimensions specified above.

The word gay is thus a summative or constitutional concept. It is multidimensional in the sense that a worldview, self-conception, group membership, life-style, and affectional and sexual preferences—as well as one's sense of pride and power—are adopted in an actual, implied, or potentially confrontational context. It is a dynamic concept in the sense that all of its social references are mutually dependent. It is a selective concept in the sense that not all homosexuals (those engaging physically or psychologically in same-sex releases) satisfy the self and group identity requirements specified by the word gay. Likewise, the word gay includes those who may not have engaged in any overt same-sex release. Ultimately, the study of gay relationships is identified by the self-statements and concomitant attitudes, beliefs, and actions of those preferring same-sex affectional relationships.

For the rhetorical or communication researcher, then, the word gay specifies a set of dimensions that are more likely to draw a researcher's attention to different kinds of symbol-using norms and to the different responses to those norms. As Karlen aptly put it, "There has been very little thought given to homosexual behavior as a communication system, and careful study in this direction would probably lead to a better understanding of various homosexual roles and the 'scripts' for those roles."[58]

Conclusion

Social scientists have published massive quantities of analyses cast as definitional and descriptive of same-sex relationships. Viewing these findings and analyses as persuasive messages that create a social conception of same-sex relations, I have used Bormann's method of fantasy theme analysis to identify the major content and stylistic themes within these social scientific discourses. Two major recurring fantasies permeate the rhetoric of social scientists: the homosexual as degenerate and mainstreaming the homosexual. These fantasy types are paradoxical, for one implies that homosexuals possess an identifiable identity (degeneracy) while the other suggests that homosexuals, as a collective, possess no universally shared characteristics. As an alternative to the social scientists' attention to the word homosexual and its referents, I propose that the word gay and its referents are more likely to generate insightful understandings of the social and cultural meanings of same-sex relations.

Chapter 16

Media Reaction to the 1979 Gay March on Washington

Jeffrey Nelson

In June 1969 hundreds of gay persons fought back against police who were harassing them and other patrons of a well-known gay bar in New York. Stonewall, as the occurrence came to be called because this was the name of the bar, emerged as the rallying point in the 1970s for many gay men and lesbians attempting to establish their full rights as American citizens.

Ten years after the New York episode, on October 14, 1979, with Stonewall as well as countless other instances of discrimination and harassment on their minds, tens of thousands of persons marched on Washington to demand equal opportunity for gays throughout the United States.[1] Specifically, the group made the following requests of the Washington establishment:

1. Pass a comprehensive lesbian/gay rights bill in Congress.
2. Issue a presidential executive order banning discrimination based on sexual orientation in the Federal Government, the military and federally-contracted private employment.
3. Repeal all anti-lesbian/gay laws.
4. End discrimination in lesbian mother or gay father custody cases.
5. Protect lesbian and gay youth from any laws which are used to discriminate against, oppress and/or harass them in their homes, schools, jobs and social environments.[2]

Since the only way most Americans could learn of the march was through the mass media, it seems useful to gain a better understanding of media reaction to this October event. Leading gay figures have rarely shown pleasure with press and broadcasting coverage of gay activities, claiming that such coverage has been too scanty and generally biased against their movement. Activist David Goodstein echoed the thoughts of many of his cohorts when he wrote: "Straight journalists seem to hear only what they want to hear, that which is familiar. Media leaders fail to take gay people and our concerns seriously enough to hear what we are saying."[3] But Goodstein and others in the movement seem acutely aware of their dependence on the media if they hope to bring their message to the American populus and, in the long run, effect social change.[4]

Before delving into an analysis of the media coverage of the Washington march, one should know in some detail the motives and objectives of those involved in this march. Social relations expert Kenneth Burke has formulated a "pentad" for understanding the motivations of human beings that includes the Act (what takes place), Scene (when or where it is done), Agent (who does it), Agency (how it is done), and Purpose (why).[5] The pentad represents a simple, clear model for comprehending the motives and objectives of the persons who organized the October 14 activities.

The first pentadic term, the Act, in this case consisted of calling attention to the nationwide gay rights movement, while the Scene involved a nation's people very doubtful about granting equal legal rights to gays, as well as a President and Congress also timid in this regard.[6]

The Agent comprised many thousands of marchers from the entire United States and ten foreign countries. Some of the contingents included religious, social service, and political organizations; parents and friends of gays; a youth division; college groups; neighborhood associations; and business groups.[7] Organizing the entire event were a number of gay activists from various parts of the United States.[8]

The Agency involved a march down Pennsylvania Avenue and through the governmental district of Washington, culminating in a rally on the mall near the Washington Monument. The purpose of the march was to urge the President and the Congress to enact legislation guaranteeing the civil rights of gays.

While the pentadic description above offers a basic understanding of the essential elements of the march, other related elements should be considered as well. One factor, the Co-agents, as Burke calls them, played an important role. Co-agents are allies of the Agent and help the Agent accomplish the purpose.[9] The importance of Co-agents to the Washington march was indicated by the prominent spot in the official program listing organizations that supported the October 14 activities.[10]

Understandably, the march organizers were also desirous of getting wide support from the gay community throughout the nation; a unified effort would result in the strongest showing. However, this hoped-for support was not forthcoming, at least not to the extent that organizers had wished. The original organizing committee had to be dissolved, for instance, because of internal struggles.[11] And many gays simply could not get enthused about the march, since they did not feel particularly threatened or maligned by the establishment.[12]

Some gay leaders expressed concern about the march leadership, who they claimed represented more leftist views of gay activism than the mainstream homosexual community. Others feared that the affair would bring out a preponderance of the more exotic gays, such as drag queens, chain-and-leather types in their distinctive "uniforms," and others with whom the straight community could not easily identify.[13]

Moreover, gay leaders in the host city responded half-heartedly to the march idea. They have an excellent relationship with the local Washington political establishment and, for the most part, seem to have a good life in the nation's capital; they have made much progress over the past several years using their own methods. Thus, they did not become as involved with October 14 as they could have been because of their disagreement with the timing and organization of the march.[14] "It should have been a clue to a lot of people that the national and local organizations did not give immediate endorsement," stated Bob Davis, former head of the Washington Gay Activist Alliance, which endorsed the march with reservations.[15]

In short, the march organizers did not have as many enthusiastic Co-agents as would have been ideal to put forth the strongest effort. This is not to deny the fact that the march had considerable backing; it is to say that the situation could have been better.

In addition to an Agent and a Co-agent, Burke notes, in certain cases there may be a Counter-agent. A Counter-agent is the enemy of the Agent and attempts to keep the Agent from accomplishing the goal.[16] The Washington march certainly had no dearth of Counter-agents; witness the overturn of gay rights ordinances by the voters in Dade County, Florida, St. Paul, Minnesota, and other communities.

A coalition of fundamentalist church ministers and conservative Christian lobbying groups arranged to stage a news conference and prayer session in the Rayburn House Office Building during the march, to protest the gay movement. Included in the assemblage of about seventy-five persons was well-known television evangelist Jerry Falwell. Also present was the Rev. Richard Zone, executive director of the activist religious group Christian Voice, who said he had asked approximately 40,000 ministers across the country to urge their parishioners to sign a petition asking President Carter "to resist efforts to legitimize homosexuality by giving special consideration under law to those who practice such acts."[17] The coalition was supported by Rep. Larry McDonald (D.-GA), who had introduced a House resolution in July calling for the lawmakers to go on record opposing "special consideration or protective status under the law" for gays.[18] And Anita Bryant sent a telegram announcing that she would pray "for those misguided individuals marching in Washington today who seek to flaunt their immoral lifestyle."[19]

Another component of Burke's pentad that merits closer analysis is the Purpose. While the march organizers were indeed trying to get gay rights legislation approved by the Washington establishment, it seems that they had a broader objective as well: to gain more complete acceptance of the gay community by citizens throughout the nation. Thus, while the immediate audience addressed was the nation's political leaders, just as important to be reached were residents of the entire country. The march leaders were using one audience—the Washington establishment—to provide a focus through which the other audience—all citizens of the United States—could be addressed. This rhetorical device of appealing to two groups simultaneously can truly be an effective method of promoting civil rights for minorities.[20]

With an understanding of Burke's pentad as it relates to the Washington march, then, the thoughts and actions of the participants are clearer, giving one a more complete comprehension of the October 14 events.

Before analyzing the media coverage of the march, one should appreciate the responsibilities of the media in reporting the news. Virtually all journalists agree that the objective of the press in a free society is to offer full public disclosure. The press is "the intelligent apparatus of those in whom ultimate authority is supposed to reside—the people."[21] It operates on the theory that the full and free flow of information is necessary to any kind of social and political freedom.[22] In short, the press should objectively tell the American people what they need to know to maintain their free society.

Since the media do not have infinite space or time, they cannot report every event that might be of interest to the nation's citizens. But they should report the major happenings on the American scene. And when many thousands of persons march down Pennsylvania Avenue, calling for equal rights and opportunity for a significant minority of the nation's populus—a minority as high as 10 percent according to some expert estimates—that happening would seem to be a major one.

However, it was not as significant an occurrence as it might have been. As already noted, a number of gay leaders offered only lukewarm endorsement, if any. While march leaders hoped for a crowd of 100,000, it is doubtful the number of participants equaled this figure. Estimates ranged from 25,000 to 75,000.[23]

With these points in mind one can understand more fully the coverage or lack of it given the march by television, radio, newsmagazines, and newspapers.

Television, the primary source of news for most Americans, gave the march a good deal of attention. As a matter of fact, all three major networks reported on the Washington activities in their newscasts that day, October 14. And there were few, if any, complaints from gay leaders concerning the objectivity displayed by these networks. Millions of Americans throughout the nation received information on the march activities, and this information seems to have been relayed in a serious and positive manner. Nevertheless, there were complaints from gays that the networks did not allot enough time to the march coverage. The fact that the reports lasted no longer than a minute or two was hardly applauded in certain gay quarters.[24]

While Sunday is not a popular time for listening to radio for most Americans, this medium does reach millions of persons throughout the day. Since there are literally thousands of radio stations throughout the nation, and their logs do not list all news stories given, it would be near impossible to ascertain the coverage offered the October 14 march by each station. Yet it is known that wire services did carry reports of the march, so news material was available to the stations that wished to broadcast it.[25] And at least one radio network, NBC, had its own reporter and technician on the scene and carried live spots on its 2 P.M. and 4 P.M. News on the Hour programs. Further, other NBC radio reports were probably aired on Sunday and/or Monday as well.[26] Gay leaders, possibly forgetting the importance of radio as a medium of communication for many Americans—even on a Sunday—made little note of this medium's coverage of the Washington march.

It is easy to sum up the reporting by national newsmagazines—*nil*! None even mentioned the march, a situation that not surprisingly drew criticism from some gay leaders.[27] Due to the plentiful coverage given gay matters recently, especially in *Time* and *Newsweek,* it does not seem probable that the editors purposely snubbed the march.[28] The most likely explanation is that the editors simply did not deem the October 14 activities sufficiently newsworthy.

The newspaper, to which many millions look every day for current information, is not limited by time, as television and radio are; nor is it greatly limited by space, as newsmagazines are—since they publish only once a week. Editors of daily newspapers can pretty much tell what they want to tell—in capsule form or in great detail—depending on their perceptions of the event.

The newspaper represents a medium generally kept intact for researchers to study, whether one day later or twenty-five years hence. Networks and individual stations keep logs of daily programming but in most cases do not keep tapes of these programs. Yet, indirectly, the newspaper sheds light on the broadcast world, for many conglomerates that control newspapers also control broadcast stations, and it would be folly to think that a publisher and/or owner would give the staff free rein over the organization's activities without concern for the employer's personal beliefs and feelings.

To analyze newspaper coverage of the march five publications were selected, representing different regions of the country as well as varied political and sociological attitudes: two liberal newspapers, the Washington *Post* and *The New York Times;* two middle-of-the-roaders, the Los Angeles *Times* and the Cleveland *Plain Dealer;* and the conservative Chicago *Tribune.*[29] The owners of each of these newspapers also control at least two broadcast stations and in most cases more.[30]

Newspaper editions for the weekend encompassing the march were analyzed—from Friday, October 12, through Monday, October 15. On Monday each publication carried an article describing the activities; thus, each paper did indeed give the march some attention.

The papers providing the least publicity on Monday were the *Tribune* and the Los Angeles *Times.* The *Tribune* printed a 65-line story on an inside page of the first section, with a bold-faced headline at the top of the page. Moreover, it was the only news story at the top, making it easy to see. The space devoted to the article covered approximately 8 percent of the page.[31]

The Los Angeles *Times* gave the march 66-line coverage, also on an inside page of the first section. The *Times* printed a bold-faced headline for the story and placed the article near the top of the page. Again the report occupied about 8 percent of the page.[32]

The New York Times likewise printed its coverage on an inside page of the first section. Although the article appeared on the bottom half of the page, it covered 82 lines, had a bold-faced headline, and was accompanied by a photograph of the marchers coming down Pennsylvania Avenue. The story covered 16 percent of the page.[33]

The Cleveland *Plain Dealer* was much more generous than the three previously discussed papers. It offered front-page coverage, with a large photograph of the marchers, and the article carried over to another page in the *Plain Dealer*'s first section. The entire piece included 120 lines of text; it took up 24 percent of the front page and 10 percent of the inside page.[34]

The Washington *Post* also saw fit to give the march front-page coverage. The article, with a large photograph of the marchers, was continued inside, where two more large photographs accompanied the text. The whole article included 183 lines of text, and covered 17 percent of page one and 35 percent of the inside page.[35]

While the *Tribune* opted to give coverage only on Monday, October 15, the other four newspapers offered additional reports that weekend. For instance, on Friday, October 12, the Los Angeles *Times* printed a 20-line article on the march; and on Sunday, October 14, *The New York Times* published a 34-line report.[36]

The *Plain Dealer* published an additional 48-line story on Friday, then on Sunday, on the front page of its U.S. and World section, printed a major report, carrying over to an inside page for a total of 158 lines.[37]

The Washington *Post,* representing the host city for the march, offered the most coverage of the October 14 affair, publishing a story each day of the weekend. On Friday there was a 112-line story; on Saturday, an important 256-line feature article, starting on the first page of the Metro section and continuing inside. The latter article was accompanied by three photographs. And on Sunday the *Post* ran an additional 36-line story.[38]

Just because a newspaper published reports of the event does not mean it offered these reports in an objective, unbiased manner. Yet a study of the news editions listed above indicates that the accounts were open and fair. Typical of the reporting was this beginning to the October 15 Chicago *Tribune* article: "An estimated 50,000 persons, bearing banners from nearly every state in the union, marched through the nation's capital Sunday, demanding civil rights protection for homosexuals."[39] In the twelve newspaper articles studied, no direct attacks or even negative innuendos were made concerning the Washington march.

Objectivity seems also to have been used in the broadcasting media. Even though gay leaders did not get as much air time as they would have liked, they had no complaints about the manner in which the reports on the march were handled; in fact, there was even some praise for the broadcasting industry's role in reporting the event.[40]

A matter that did arouse some concern in the gay community was the publicity given the Counter-agent of the marchers, the conservative Christian group who prayed and held a press conference on Capitol Hill to show their opposition to the march. While no complaints were directed to the broadcasting media in this regard, there was displeasure registered concerning the amount of coverage given the Christian group in the newspaper.[41] It seems important to determine how much space, proportionate to the march itself, the newspapers did provide the Counter-agents.

The *Tribune* devoted just 3 percent of the space to the fundamentalists, while the Los Angeles *Times,* in its two pieces, gave the group 17 percent of the coverage. *The New York Times* showed a 10 percent share. The *Plain Dealer,* in its three articles, gave the Counter-agent only 4 percent of the space. The Washington *Post,* the publication that covered the march in greatest detail, showed a 9 percent level. In all five newspapers only one headline even mentioned the conservative Christian group, and none of the photographs published related to this group's activities.[42]

Journalists gave scant attention to the fundamentalist gathering; moreover, they certainly did not try to favor it over the gays. This objectivity in reporting on the Counter-agent's activities is exemplified by the Los Angeles *Times*' opening statement relating to the matter: "Nearby (the march) a coalition of conservative ministers branded the homosexuals as sinners and urged them to repent. They held a news conference and prayer session in a congressional office building to protest the march."[43] Throughout the reporting, on both sides of the fence, fairness seems to have been the rule.

If fairness was indeed the norm in the media reports on the October 14 activities, and the march did get the publicity that has been noted, one might question the complaints aired by gays about the news coverage. Proponents of a special interest are going to be biased toward this interest and thus can hardly be expected to maintain objectivity; protests about the amount and quality of news coverage are common in this regard.[44] Besides, in this particular case, the persons complaining about the coverage do not seem to have made a significant effort to expose themselves to a wide range of the media.[45]

All this is not to dismiss the grievances registered by gays in regard to television, newsmagazines, and newspapers. On the contrary, these protests at the very least cause newspersons to think again about the amount and manner of coverage they gave the Washington march.

Gay leaders, however, must look to themselves too. As noted earlier, the march leadership did not have the backing of its own community—in size or in strength—that could have made the October 14 activities even more significant and worthy of greater news coverage. But this was just the first national gay effort for a single event; the next time the organizers will have experience behind them.

Finally, not only gay leaders but the rank and file as well must make their views known to the media if they hope to obtain full coverage of future gay-related events. Goodstein addressed the issue directly to each individual:

> When the straight media ignore gay people, we hope you'll raise hell with them. . . . The only way journalists will learn, is by constant, unrelenting pressure on them to open their eyes and ears. It is our responsibility to keep after them until they notice who we are.[46]

With the media, then, gays clearly do have opportunities to influence their destiny; whether they take advantage of these opportunities probably will determine to a great extent the progress of the gay movement over the next decade.

Chapter 17

Educational Responsibilities to Gay Male and Lesbian Students

Joseph A. DeVito

Some years ago teachers and writers recognized that not all students and readers were white: some were black, some were Oriental, some were Chicano. More recently they recognized that not everyone was male; there were women sitting in their classes and reading their books. Now it needs to be recognized that not all students and readers are heterosexuals: some are gay, some are lesbian.[1]

I do not mention blacks and women to imply that the cases are identical; in fact, they are quite different. Blacks and women, for example, are not told they are sick and degenerate because they are black or because they are women. Gay men and lesbians are told—by peers, by the media, by teachers, and by textbook authors—that they are sick because they are homosexual. Blacks and women are not thrown out of their families (condemned by their parents and abandoned by their children) because they are black or because they are women; gay men and lesbians often are.[2] Instead, I mention the case of blacks and women to emphasize that discrimination against the homosexual is a human rights issue, just as it is when the discrimination is focused against blacks or women or, in fact, any group—the Puerto Ricans in New York, the Mexicans in the Southwest, the aged, the blind; to emphasize that prejudice in any form is destructive to both sides and to society in general; to emphasize that discrimination —despite its deep-seated roots—can be combated and in time reduced, or maybe even eliminated.

In many ways the educational responsibilities to gay and lesbian students must logically begin with administrators. Administrators have the responsibility for providing an atmosphere in which gay and lesbian teachers, counselors, deans, and the like are permitted and encouraged to function as gays and lesbians.[3] In this, an administrator's responsibility is no less than it is in regard to women and blacks.

This responsibility toward gays and lesbians is at once easier and more difficult to comply with than the responsibility toward other minority groups. Whereas administrators in many instances have to locate and recruit women and blacks, there is—you can be sure—a pretty fair sampling of gay men and lesbians already on campus, and the difficult problems of quotas and of what constitutes affirmative action do not have to be dealt with—at least not as a priority. Instead, the task is to provide an atmosphere that is conducive to gay and lesbian teachers functioning as gay men and lesbians, an atmosphere that would be supportive of their coming out of the closet should they wish to. This responsibility will not be easy to fulfill. The social pressures from uninformed and/or homophobic parents, alumni, students, and the community-at-large are not easy to face.[4] But no prejudice is easy to deal with, and confronting bigotry appears the only appropriate strategy. Academicians have the obligation to expose untruths and injustices wherever found. When these are found in schools, departments, and classrooms, it becomes even more important to confront and expose such prejudice directly and immediately.

Gay men and lesbian students need role models just like women and blacks do—or in fact like anyone does. Because teachers are among the most effective role models, administrators and the college community as a whole need to make special efforts to provide such models. Further, these role models should be representative of the gay and lesbian community as a whole and should be open and out of the closet. Otherwise, their function as role models will be severely restricted. This is not to say that closet gays and lesbians cannot function as effective role models; in many cases they can and do. Some gay and lesbian students are able to identify gay and lesbian teachers and may seek them out for both personal and professional guidance. Yet, role models that are more clearly and generally identifiable as gays and lesbians, with a gay and lesbian life-style, also need to be provided, for the benefit of the gay and lesbian students and as a rebuttal to the negative stereotypes so long ingrained in hetero- and homosexuals.

No administrator would be able to hold his or her job for very long if the benefits for blacks were not equal to those for whites, if the benefits for women were not equal to those for men. But the gay teacher is denied the benefits he or she would receive if straight. For example, health insurance is denied to the gay teacher's mate, and transportation expenses for relocating are denied to a lover but are normally paid for a husband or wife. Similarly, the heterosexual's mate is provided with free or reduced tuition at the college or university. The homosexual's mate is denied such benefits. The children of a homosexual faculty member's mate are denied the benefits that would be granted to the children of a heterosexual faculty member's husband or wife. This is true regardless of how long or how happy the respective relationships are. A one-year heterosexual marriage entitles the husband or wife to these various benefits; a twenty-year homosexual union entitles the mate to nothing.

Such differences must not be allowed to be trivialized by those who rigidly hold on to and enforce such distinctions and differences. Consider the implications, for example, if a black teacher's husband or wife was not covered by the health insurance plan, if the teacher's contract explicitly stated that only white couples were entitled to relocation allowances, if only white mates and children of white marriages were entitled to reduced or free tuition. Recognize that such practices are discriminatory and clearly say—as in *Animal Farm*—we are all equal, but heterosexuals are more equal than others. If gay and lesbian teachers are forced to function in second class—and come to be grateful for being allowed to teach in the first place—then we have something akin to slavery. Thus, an administrator's task is not only to find and hire gay and lesbian teachers, but to secure for them total equality and an atmosphere that is supportive and accepting. Such an atmosphere proves beneficial not only to gay and lesbian teachers, but also to students and to society.

The concern of teachers and writers should be two-fold. First, they should be concerned with the rights of gays and lesbians who are their students and readers. A teacher may teach a class that is all male or all female, or that is all white or all black or all Chicano. But she or he will probably never teach a class that is all straight. Second, teachers and writers should be concerned with the education of all their students—gay and straight—regarding such issues as the stereotypes of the gay and the lesbian that exist in the minds of students and readers which are far removed from reality and which are damaging to self-actualization and to meaningful interaction and communication. Clearly, these stereotypes (the maladjustment, the creativity, the inability to engage in permanent relationships, the artistic sense, the undependability, the preoccupation with sex, the sensitivity), exist not only in the minds of the heterosexual students, but also in the minds of the homosexual students.[5] Such stereotypes prevent both meaningful intrapersonal communication in the gay and lesbian and meaningful interpersonal communication, whether gay-to-gay or gay-and-straight. Teachers function partially to help students self-actualize their potential. If teachers fail to do this, then largely they have failed their responsibility as educators.

These concerns may be approached through three major goals. These goals (actually responsibilities) are considered in relation to gay and lesbian students-readers but are really basic rights, applicable to all persons. I stress the case of gays and lesbians, because it is this group that is currently being denied these rights.

First, I think the teacher has a responsibility to present a case for and promote equal human rights for all persons. Much as the teacher has an obligation not to denigrate women or blacks or Chicanos, the teacher also has an obligation not to denigrate gays and lesbians. But the responsibility goes beyond the avoidance of the negative to the clear affirmation that equal human rights is not some abstract irrelevance, but that it clearly and specifically applies to gays and lesbians as well as to any and all other groups. It involves a recognition, an acceptance, and an active affirmation of equality not only for the individual specific student, but equality also for gays and lesbians as a group and for the gay and lesbian life-style.

Second, the teacher has a responsibility to assist students to develop a positive self-concept about their basic, unchanging, and unchangeable identities. This means that the teacher has the responsibility to encourage women to have a more positive self-image about their "womanness" and to encourage blacks to have a more positive self-image about their "blackness." It is similarly the responsibility of the teacher to encourage gays and lesbians to have a more positive self-image about their "gayness" and their "lesbianness"; to see, for example, that homosexuality is not a deficiency or a maladjustment, that it is instead a positive and legitimate life-style, an approach to a loving and fulfilling life—no better or worse than but fully equal to heterosexuality. This is an extremely difficult but crucial task, since the self-concept of gays and lesbians—to a greater extent than that of any other group—is consistently attacked, not only by Anita Bryant and similar types, but often by well-intentioned though ignorant parents, relatives, and friends.[6]

Most gays and lesbians in college—and the situation seems even more difficult for high school and elementary school students—are going through troublesome times, and despite the fact that great advances have been made during the last ten years, we still live in a negative, repressive, homophobic atmosphere where the student is made to believe that he or she is sick, degenerate, in need of religious saving and psychiatric help, and a disappointment to his or her parents, friends, and church.[7] It is the teacher's responsibility (although not the teacher's alone) to provide a positive, supportive atmosphere where the student feels he or she may excel, lead a happy and productive life, and be gay or lesbian.

Third, the teacher has a responsibility to promote mutual understanding and effective communication among students. If such effective communication is to take place, it is essential that nongay students come to understand and accept the equality of gay and lesbian students, and the gay life-style as a legitimate alternative to the heterosexual life-style.[8] There must be an assumption of equality if there is to be effective and mutually beneficial communication. This does not mean heterosexual students should see homosexuality as an alternative life-style for themselves. Rather, it means they should appreciate that the gay and lesbian life-style may serve as an effective and equally legitimate alternative for others.

For some, these responsibilities will prove difficult to acknowledge.

Consider how hard it would have been to accept these same propositions about blacks 100 years ago—or even 50 years ago—not to mention that a large segment of the population will still not accept them. With propositions of this nature there are levels of acceptance rather than simple acceptance-or-rejection. These three propositions might best be viewed as ultimate objectives rather than as immediate goals that can be internalized tomorrow. They are difficult to accept for homosexuals as well as for heterosexuals. Both homosexuals and heterosexuals have grown up in essentially the same environment and have been taught essentially the same values and beliefs. Therefore, it should not be surprising to find that many homosexuals cannot accept (viscerally) their own equality with heterosexuals. I'm sure, however, that in the not-too-distant future these propositions will seem mild at best.

Specific Guidelines for the Educator

Increased awareness and concern for gay and lesbian students-readers need to be translated into actual practice in order to have any significant effect on the students, on the academic experience, and on the community as a whole. Here I sketch, in a preliminary way, some of the guidelines that might be useful.

Recognition of gay and lesbian existence. Perhaps the first guideline for educators is to recognize emotionally as well as intellectually, in behavior as well as in thought, gay and lesbian existence. Depending on the method in which the data are collected and on the definition as to what constitutes a gay or a lesbian, statistics seem to range from 4 to 25 percent. The obstacles involved in securing accurate statistics on such an issue should be obvious, and it is likely the statistics that are available probably reflect a much smaller percentage than actually exists.[9] But whether there are only 4 percent, 25 percent, or a great deal more (or less) should not matter in terms of recognizing that there is a sizable minority of persons who do not fit into the majority culture's model of heterosexuality.

It should be recognized further that not only do gays and lesbians exist, but they have a history. This history includes the murder of homosexuals by the majority culture—by burning, by stoning, by hanging—imprisonment; castration; expulsion from school, job, church, family, and armed forces; commitment to insane asylums; and general ostracism.[10] But this history also records the contributions made by homosexuals to art, music, science, literature, and in fact, to any and all areas of knowledge.[11] For example, it would be impossible to write the history of communication and rhetoric without including the important contributions of homosexuals; from Plato and Socrates, through Francis Bacon, to contemporary researchers and writers, the contributions have been undeniable.

Those who would argue that the ideas, insights, and contributions of these theorists can be appreciated apart from their homosexuality are denying the seminal role the homosexuality of these persons played in their lives. No idea exists apart from the experiences of the individual; no idea exists apart from the context in which it is given birth. Those experiences and that context are homosexual. Their homosexuality was an integral part of their day-to-day lives, of their total emotional and intellectual existence. No one hides his or her private life for ten, twenty, thirty, or forty years without this hiding, this fear of discovery and rejection of peers and family, manifesting itself in each and every aspect of the person's life. To deny that an individual's homosexuality is significant is, in many instances, an attempt to deny the legitimacy and the equality of this homosexuality.[12]

But most important, the gays and lesbians that teachers and writers should be concerned with most are in their classrooms.[13] If even the most conservative statistics are used, in every classroom there is at least one gay or lesbian student. In all likelihood there are several—even many. If a textbook is used by 50,000 students, the number of gays and lesbians reading it number in the thousands, regardless of how one computes their number.[14]

Once teachers and writers recognize that gays and lesbians do in fact exist (and that existence will invariably become more visible over the next several years), they need to recognize that there are such things as gay and lesbian behaviors, and that these behaviors are different in essential respects from heterosexual behaviors—a difference to which researchers need to direct energies to identify and describe.

The same is true for gay and lesbian relationships and for the gay and lesbian life-style. Too often the heterosexual community assumes and teaches (and, unfortunately, part of the gay community has learned) that it is the heterosexual relationship and the heterosexual life-style that everyone is to model. Thus, such issues as fidelity, male bonding, female bonding, sexuality, permanent relationships, sex-role distinctions, family, marriage, division of labor on the basis of sex, and the like are heterosexual concepts or are defined from a heterosexual perspective and are not necessarily applicable to gays and lesbians. If writers and teachers are at all concerned with relational communication, it should be clearly recognized that, as a field, they are building a model that is heterosexual and that is, in many ways, inappropriate and inapplicable to the gay male and lesbian.

Avoidance of stereotypes. Special care needs to be taken to avoid stereotyping gays and lesbians. Not all gay males are effeminate and not all lesbians are masculine; in fact, Masters and Johnson have reported that there is no correlation between gayness and effeminacy in men and between lesbianism and masculinity in women.[15] These stereotypes do not exist only in the popular mind; unfortunately, they have been internalized by many gays and lesbians as well as by heterosexuals. One consequence of this is that many gays and lesbians cannot identify with their gay and lesbian community because they have internalized these negative stereotypes and resent being associated with them.

If the sexual behaviors of gays and lesbians were plotted, the result would be the familiar bell-shaped curve that would be similar in many respects to that of heterosexual men and women. The curves would differ in their measures of central tendency on some variables, but it would be the great degree of overlapping of the two curves that would prove most illuminating and most surprising to those unfamiliar with such issues.

Gays and lesbians are not maladjusted.[16] Needless to say, some have psychological problems, but these problems do not result from their homosexuality, but rather from society's responses to the homosexual and lesbian. This distinction, I think, underlies the American Psychiatric Association's "non-sickness" position and should be obvious to anyone who has lived in a homophobic society. Let me make this more specific. The unhappiness, the guilt, the shame that the gay male and lesbian feel are not the result of their homosexuality, but of society's reaction to this homosexuality. A large and powerful part of that reaction is made up of the attitudes and behaviors of teachers—from elementary through high school and into college and graduate school—and writers who reinforce these negative attitudes and perpetuate these stereotypes.

Avoidance of the heterosexual presumption. Besides avoiding homosexual stereotypes, teachers and writers need to avoid the heterosexual presumption. There is clearly a presumption of whiteness, maleness, and heterosexuality in our culture and more specifically in education and in literature. The hypothetical individual is a white heterosexual male. Perhaps the best evidence of this presumption is that when the individual in question does not fit into this model, special linguistic tags are felt to be necessary; for example, we say, the black engineer, the woman doctor, the gay teacher, the lesbian reporter.

In avoiding this presumption a few facts need to be recognized. For example, not all relationships are heterosexual. Some relationships are homosexual. Marriage is not the only state to which one should aspire. It is not the only state that persons over thirty have to enter or should enter. The single state and the homosexual union are alternatives; they are not substitutes for those who could not enter into heterosexual unions. They are equally valid alternatives.

The sexist nature of language has been documented in a number of works written in the seventies.[17] In this work it has been amply demonstrated that there is indeed a presumption of maleness and that language as used does in fact discriminate against women. But it also discriminated against gays and lesbians. In addition to language being sexist, it is also heterosexist. Just as the hypothetical individual is always male, the hypothetical couple is always heterosexual, always male-and-female. Two persons who love each other are invariably portrayed as male and female unless the love is qualified a hundred times as nonsexual. But gender combinations do not have to be "he and she." They may be "she and she" and "he and he"; "woman and woman" is as acceptable a gender combination as any other.

Similarly, relational terms often discriminate against gays and lesbians. Words like marriage, husband, and wife are applicable only to heterosexual unions. Two men who have been together for twenty years are not related as husband and wife; they are not married. In gay parlance they are lovers, but as popularly used and understood, this word is too general and does not include the years of commitment, the permanency of the relationship, and a host of other dimensions that are included in both the denotative and connotative meanings of the word marriage.

This presumption of heterosexuality is further supported by the acceptability and sanctioning of the homophobic response. In a classroom normally devoted to an expression of liberal philosophies, the gay and lesbian cause in general is seen as somehow not fitting into the appropriate mold and is consequently fair game for abusive criticism. In this, the classroom is, unfortunately, no different from the television talk show that seeks to put homosexuality on exhibit, or from the situational comedy show where humor is extracted from someone's real life pain. The implicit argument is that since homosexuality is wrong (morally and legally), it is permissible to denigrate gays and lesbians and to even deny gays and lesbians certain rights. And this, of course, is the very argument that has been used throughout history and is today being used to support such discriminatory practices as entrapment, denial of housing accommodations, and denial of job opportunities and promotions, seen most obviously in the legal exclusion of gays and lesbians from teaching, from the military, from police and fire departments, and from the clergy.

When these discriminatory and exclusionary tactics are applied in the classroom—as they often are—they are even more reprehensible when it is realized that the gays and lesbians in the classroom—teachers as well as students—are often prevented from defending themselves and their fellow members for fear of reprisals. Thus, for example, one teacher might hesitate to support the rights of a teacher who may be gay for fear that this will brand the first a gay or lesbian and hence an undesirable. The Briggs Amendment and similar proposals in various states would make it illegal for a homosexual to teach and for anyone to support the right of a homosexual to teach. So not only will such legislation prevent homosexuals from teaching, but it will also prevent anything from being done to help them. It is not surprising that the Briggs Amendment was defeated in California. It is surprising and scary that thousands actively supported the amendment and that its equivalent is currently on the books in Oklahoma.

Recognition of the influence of affectional preference on communication. As persons interested particularly in the study of communication, writers and teachers need to acknowledge that there are many ways in which affectional preference seems to influence communication processes and outcomes. A few of the relationships that seem worthy of study and research are discussed below. All are offered in the nature of hypotheses.

A. Self-considerations. It should be evident that in a society where gays and lesbians are regarded as degenerate and maladjusted that their self-concept will differ from their heterosexual counterparts. Insofar as self-concept influences communication, gay and lesbian communications will differ from heterosexual communications. Self-disclosure is perhaps the most interesting area, and has only recently been touched on by writers who have addressed the issue from the point of view of their own coming out of the closet. Merle Miller's *On Being Different* is one of the best examples.[18] But the homosexual's self-disclosure as a communication process is going to be very different from the heterosexual's self-disclosures; related variables such as trust, friendship, and love will also differ.

B. Language. The most obvious variable and the one which even the unobservant can observe is that of language.[19] Each subculture has its own sublanguage that functions as a means for group identification and for the exclusion of nonmembers. At the same time, the sublanguage of the group gives an excellent indication of what is and what is not important to the subculture, to its values, and to its attitudes. But perhaps the most important aspect is that the sublanguage often gives clues to what the subculture members think of themselves. When the gay lexicon includes such high-frequency words as fag, dyke, queen, auntie, and fag hag, it becomes obvious there is a great deal of internal and internalized discrimination. To argue (as some have done) that it is permissible and even healthy for group members to use derogatory terms in reference to themselves—on the theory that it is healthy to laugh at oneself—seems absurd and appears only to solidify in their own minds the negative attitudes and stereotypes of the majority culture. The connotative meaning systems for these terms—among gays and among straights—will be similar, to my mind, and in that similarity will be found evidence for the negative effect of such terms.

C. Message formulation and encoding. Much as we receive what is useful to us or what we need, we also operate our message formulation and encoding system on similar principles. Because of such principles as immanent reference (we are always talking about ourselves and our immediate environment), determinism (all messages are motivated), and recurrence (we repeat those messages that are particularly important and meaningful to us), the messages formulated by gays and lesbians and by straights will invariably be different. Much as our messages are influenced by our gender (or perhaps by the differential learning of the sexes), they are also influenced by our affectional preference.

D. Message perception and decoding. Numerous studies have determined that we attend to messages that serve our needs, whether these be needs to reduce dissonance, to gain ego gratification, or to fill informational voids. Persons with different affectional preferences will obviously focus on different message elements.

E. Contextual differences. To say that much of gay and lesbian, and straight communication occurs in different contexts is obvious to many and seems totally incorrect to others. Suffice it to say that communication which is of a uniquely gay and lesbian nature occurs often in contexts that are almost unknown to the straight community. The discos, for example, are significantly different. The gay bars and the singles bars that are the nearest equivalent are likewise very different. But I am really thinking of the gay contexts for which the straight world does not have equivalents, or at least not in most places; the baths are perhaps the clearest example. That the context influences the messages is obvious; what needs to be discovered is how this influence is exerted, what influence it has on the participants, and in what ways it influences interpersonal interactions.

F. Subcultural difference. There are so many obvious but nontrivial subcultural differences that it would be impossible to catalog them all. That many gays operate on a different clock is perhaps the clearest example of subcultural differences. The gay male or lesbian who has lived the life of a heterosexual and enters the gay world at middle age will surely experience culture shock, if only for the difference in time treatments. Actually, this differential time treatment is more accurately a subcultural variation within the homosexual subculture.

There are also important differences in ethical standards. Many would have us believe that the gay and lesbian community operates without ethics, and from an outsider's point of view this is not an unreasonable assumption to make. But it is not an absence of ethical standards that governs gay and lesbian behaviors, but rather different ethical standards. Concepts such as fidelity, cheating, premarital sex, dating, friendship, love, and so many others are often given different definitions.

G. Field of experience. The field of experience of gays and lesbians on the one hand, and of straights on the other differ greatly. It should be no surprise to find that when there is no commonality, there is no communication. Without some overlapping in our fields of experience we cannot communicate with any degree of effectiveness. Empathy, supportiveness, friendship, and so many other variables will be influenced by the overlapping or non-overlapping of the fields of experience. And this is why it is so important for gays, lesbians, and straights who are friends to talk about their respective affectional preferences and each to educate the others. In this way there will be a sharing of the field of experience, and meaningful communication may begin.

H. Relational development and deterioration. Gay and lesbian relationships develop and deteriorate differently than straight relationships. Little is known about heterosexual relationships; even less is known about homosexual relationships. But the differences between them are perhaps the most interesting. For example, the role of sex in the development of a relationship—whether gay, lesbian, or straight—will normally be very different. Similarly, the deterioration of straight relationships, to their eventual dissolution and termination, is commonly delayed or even prevented because of the difficulties of divorce, child custody, alimony, parental and societal pressures, religious beliefs, and the like. Gay and lesbian relationships, however, probably terminate at a much earlier point in time because these retarding factors are not present. And this has given many the idea that gay and lesbian relationships are short-lived. In one sense they are. But where there is a gay or lesbian relationship, it is usually a happy and mutually productive one. I am not sure that the same could be said of heterosexual relationships.[20]

There are many actions administrators, teachers, writers, and researchers can take to ensure that gay and lesbian students are accorded equal rights and that the interplay between affectional preference and communication is understood. The few suggestions and assumptions made here are not intended to be in any way definitive; rather, they are in the nature of preliminary thoughts that have yet to be worked out in detail.

Part V

Gay Liberation as a Rhetorical Movement

Chapter 18

Consciousness-raising Among Gay Males

James W. Chesebro, John F. Cragan, and Patricia McCullough

Little attention has been given to the small-group process employed by radical revolutionaries. Rhetorically, political radicals and revolutionaries are characterized by their "rhetoric of confrontation."[1] Yet it is the small-group process which precedes confrontations that produces the new perceptions, evaluative standards, and commitments to concrete political actions controlling the confrontations.[2] This study examines the small-group process of the radical revolutionary called *consciousness-raising*.

Because consciousness-raising has been widely discussed and employed by radical revolutionaries,[3] an initial working definition of the process can be offered. Consciousness-raising is a personal, face-to-face interaction which appears to create new psychological orientations for those involved in the process. Participants develop new group identities often forming "new minorities" which may focus upon sociocultural divisions such as sex, age, sexual preference, education, wealth, power, or prestige.[4] As a result, members often perceive other group members as "sisters" and "brothers" of a new "cultural family" and "community."[5] However, the personal face-to-face interaction technique is selected because it is consistent with the radical revolutionary's belief that shared personal experience should generate political theory and action.[6] As a political interaction, the primary effort of the small group is to determine the nature and causes of the group's "oppression" and to provide the foundation for "revolutionary acts to eliminate oppression."[7] Therefore, consciousness-raising sessions often create new political values. The radical revolutionary claims to have been converted to socialism, humanism, participatory democracy, existentialism, and community identity, and to have rejected the traditional values of capitalism, materialism, representative democracy, rationalism, and self-reliance.[8] From the perspective of the radical revolutionary, consciousness-raising is the process employed to create many of these new value commitments.[9] After consciousness-raising sessions, members may often feel "a profound and reflective alienation of the spirit from a system cancerous with racism, exploitation, and its own aggressive expansion."[10]

The characteristics and the impact of consciousness-raising make this process an appropriate small-group technique for scholarly examination. Moreover, consciousness-raising has been described as a distinct form of small-group interaction by members of the "movement," and the assertion itself is intellectually stimulating even if an examination does not verify the claim.[11]

Purpose and Design

The primary purpose of this study is to identify the aggregate or central symbols which characterize the different stages in consciousness-raising. Because consciousness-raising is a relatively new phenomenon, first employed in 1966–67, pre-established constructs, such as role, decision-making, leadership, and temporal-topical theories, were not employed in this study. Instead, we chose to describe the behavior and apparent intentions of those in the sessions. Accordingly, our objective was to capture and preserve meanings and values within the groups studied,[12] offering only those interpretations that would enable outsiders to detect the functional stages through which group members passed while raising their level of consciousness.

Three consciousness-raising sessions formed the basis of this study. The sessions were held approximately every two weeks, with sessions ranging in length from an hour and three quarters to two and a half hours. One member of the research team participated in all three sessions as a participant-observer.[13] The other two researchers did not participate in any of the sessions.

There were six, five, and four subjects at each of the three respective consciousness-raising sessions. Different subjects were used in each of the sessions. All subjects identified themselves as revolutionaries, voicing a profound sense of alienation from the established social system. Thirteen of the fifteen subjects had been directly involved in confrontations with tactical police squads in at least one major city, and all were active and militant members of gay liberation in Minneapolis and in other cities throughout the country. Moreover, most of the subjects were "veteran" consciousness-raising participants. Thirteen of the fifteen subjects had participated in at least two consciousness-raising sessions before, and some of these subjects had been involved in more than fifty such sessions. Subjects were told that they would be in a consciousness-raising session, but no definition of consciousness-raising was offered and none of the subjects requested a definition. After the sessions, subjects generally agreed that a consciousness-raising process had occurred. One subject pointedly remarked, "I really like consciousness-raising like this because it doesn't involve the therapy and confrontations found in other kinds of sessions." The researchers believe that the sessions studied were in fact consciousness-raising because each session followed the description and fulfilled the expectations found in radical revolutionary discussions of this process.[14]

All sessions were tape recorded. Subjects were told in advance that the sessions would be taped, but the microphone was concealed and was not mentioned during the actual recording. After the taping of one session, subjects felt that use of the tape could be "counter-revolutionary" because group members would be numbered, codified, and dehumanized and that the sessions ought to remain private. The tension resulting from this feeling on the part of the subjects was considerably reduced because one of the researchers was a member of gay liberation. Researchers interested in the area of consciousness-raising, however, should be aware of the difficulties which may result from tape recording group sessions.

Two strategies are available for determining the function of observed communicative behavior. The investigators can ground inferences in immediate projective data, or they can infer the function of behavior based on their own intuition and existing evidence.[15] Employing the latter strategy, the three researchers listened to the tapes separately and independently identified the stages through which the consciousness-raising sessions passed. All three researchers identified the same stages, with only minor exceptions regarding the precise point at which each stage began and ended. There was substantial agreement on the apparent purpose, functions, and rhetorical characteristics of each stage. The same stages were found in all three sessions.

It should be noted that the researchers varied in their prior knowledge of the consciousness-raising process and of the objectives and issues of the gay liberation movement. One researcher had participated in consciousness-raising sessions several times prior to this study and was an active member of gay liberation. A second researcher was acquainted with consciousness-raising through the literature of women's liberation and was considered a "close friend" and "highly regarded guest" in the gay community. The third researcher was unaware of the nature of consciousness-raising and was not well known by gay liberation members.

Stages in Consciousness-raising

The consciousness-raising process was found to consist of four stages. These stages were identified on the basis of a synthetic description of the group sessions; i.e., "themes" which were topically and temporally similar or related provided the basis for identification of the four stages. The functional and rhetorical characteristics of each stage of the process are described here.

Stage One: Self-realization of a New Identity

As is the case with most small groups, primary tension existed during this warm-up stage.[16] There were long periods of silence and brief and abrupt discussions of assorted topics. As the social tension subsided, this stage exhibited definite functional and rhetorical characteristics.

Functional characteristics. All three groups initially sought to establish the "credentials" of the group members by seeking out the behavioral patterns and identity of each member. As members of a gay liberation consciousness-raising session, members provided "evidence" that they were homosexuals. This was accomplished by relating personal experience, and by dress, mannerisms, and language choices. As the credentialing process continued, each member also suggested how his behavioral patterns constituted a cultural and life-style commitment to a gay subculture. The function of this interaction ultimately seemed structured to determine the degree to which each member perceived homosexuality as an integral part of his self-identity.

The second functional characteristic of this stage was that the participants sought to gain group acknowledgment of oppression against the life-style. Descriptions of past experiences and various discussions of towns, airports, bars, TV shows, and people were persistently shaped by accounts of discrimination against individual group members. A typical interaction was:

MEMBER A: I was in Duluth once. It has *one* gay bar!
MEMBER B: Ya, small towns do that.
MEMBER C: Sick!
THE GROUP: Ya.—Right.—Uh huh.

The third functional characteristic was a sharing of the public rhetoric of the national gay liberation movement—a group process of recognizing that oppression and liberation are national issues. National political actions were freely interpreted and supported. For example:

MEMBER A: Have you seen the recent issue of *Gay?*
MEMBER B: Fidelifacts is the latest—G.L.F. [Gay Liberation Front of New York] is picketing them.
MEMBER C: Why?
MEMBER B: For $12.50 they will tell an employer if you are gay.
MEMBER C: Oh my God!
MEMBER A: They shouldn't just picket the place—they should burn it.

Rhetorical characteristics. Stage One was also characterized by unique sets of language choices. Fantasy themes, originally identified by Robert Bales[17] and recast as a rhetorical concept by Ernest Bormann,[18] were virtually unique to this first stage for all three groups. While many personal fantasies did not chain out, many others provided a drama in which heroes and villains for the gay movement were clearly present and strongly agreed upon by group members. In one session, for example, a fantasy chained out from a reference to David Reuben's book[19]:

MEMBER A: I was waiting in a gas station all alone for five minutes.
MEMBER B: Reuben says that's plenty of time—three or four minutes. *(laughter)*
MEMBER C: How does Reuben know? *(laughter)* He thinks all fat people are homosexuals or very small people who like food. *(laughter)*
MEMBER A: Reuben says some of the world's greatest chefs are faggots. *(loud laughter)*
MEMBER C: Gore Vidal, in reviewing Reuben's book, did note that Reuben himself is portly. *(laughter)*

In this fantasy, the stereotyped homosexual (the effeminate, sex-driven male) is viewed as oppressive to the group members and is defined as an imposed image created by the larger society represented by Reuben.

Although a fantasy may fulfill several functions for a group,[20] fantasies employed toward the end of Stage One began to produce a polarization between "we" (a reference to the entire, national gay community) versus "they" (the entire straight society). Excerpts from such a fantasy are presented below. This fantasy dealt with the image of the homosexual on television and continued for nearly five minutes:

MEMBER A: They had a take off on that Aqua Velva commercial in "Dynamite Chicken"—you know that underground movie. This guy—this character comes out and says: "I want to be an Aqua Velva man." Then the director says: "Do it with some balls!" Then the actor says: "Props! Props!"
MEMBER B: Cool!
MEMBER C: Did you see the latest "Love American Style"? It has a man at work who keeps getting letters signed "Ducky-Poo"—he starts comparing handwriting and then the boss *(laughter)* comes out and says: "You're doing a fine job." And then he says: "I thought you were going to say, for a second, that I wasn't doing enough!" *(laughter)*
MEMBER D: That's "Love American Style"! *(laughter)*
MEMBER B: The other night on the Carol Burnett Show, Gay-Gay comes on stage and Annette Fabre said: "Where have you been?" And he says: "Oh, I was just out cruising through the neighborhood."

MEMBER C: Wow! No doubt about it!
MEMBER D: We're going the route of the blacks—gradually we are being worked into "Uncle Tom roles."
MEMBER A: That is an Uncle Tom role—that old thing, you know. "Every man you see turns you on"—and all that shit.
MEMBER D: I would really like to see a show that has an obviously gay person snubbing the ugly straights.
MEMBER B: Ya—put them down.

While fantasy themes were a dominant rhetorical characteristic of Stage One, the interactions were also very open and noncombative, with little if any disagreement among group members. For all three groups, the tone of the conversation was light and friendly during this stage. Stage One was predominately past-oriented, and members functioned as individuals. However, as the sessions moved into Stage Two, the orientation of the participants shifted to the present, and group solidarity began to build.

Stage Two: Group Identity Through Polarization

Functional characteristics. As the groups moved into the second stage of the consciousness-raising process, they began to build group solidarity by securing a group consensus that the gay community was a distinct subculture of the larger society, accordingly linking the immediate group to the broader national liberation movement. The division created between the gay community and the larger society is reflected in the following interaction.

MEMBER A: Don't invite people to the house just because they are straight—yet be open to the fact that there are people you get along with who are straight—just don't think about the fact that they are straight.
MEMBER B: I really wonder, you know, if that's possible. You're aware of that fact that they are straight at a social level. I do think we invite them because they are straight—that's clearly a very real thing at least.
MEMBER C: I'm not sure if we're talking about a problem or a solution, but at this point, it's difficult to have a social relationship with straights that is honest and open.
MEMBER B: Ya, for too fucking long now, that's what we've tried to do. But it's time we find out who we are, what we are, what our range of life is. It's time we pulled together and find out what it is to be gay.
THE GROUP: Ya.—Right.

This initial division subsequently allowed the groups to identify an "enemy." While enemies could be detected in the fantasy themes of Stage One, during the second stage the enemy was more explicitly identified in the "here and now." The groups persistently denounced heterosexuals as "sexists."[21] The following exchange is typical of interactions in all groups:

MEMBER A: Those ugly straights are forcing their values on us.

MEMBER B: That's sexism—all the rights, privileges, and power are based upon having the "right" sexual preference and looking and acting straight.

The third functional characteristic of this stage was a discussion of oppression within the gay community; some of the oppressed were also viewed as oppressors. For example, the Chicago gay liberation group had apparently rejected certain occupations, such as hairdressers, for gay people. One group interpreted this policy as a case in which the oppressed had become the oppressor. Such topics set the scene for a more extensive discussion in the next stage of the unique identity of gay people.

Rhetorical characteristics. Stage Two was present-oriented with few attempts at fantasizing. The frequently used we-they division began to take on a new meaning, with "we" referring not just to the specific members of the consciousness-raising sessions but to the entire gay liberation movement, while "they" referred to the entire straight world. Correspondingly, there was a reduction in words like homosexual and faggot, and an increase in words like gay, brothers, sisters, and gay community. Likewise, the tone and mood of the groups changed during this stage. While in the first stage the groups often laughed about the oppressive dimensions of the larger society, in the second stage the tone and mood grew more serious and a great deal of overt hostility and aggression toward heterosexuals was present. Tension and hostility was seldom directed at other group members. Thus, the second stage produced polarization between the straight and gay worlds. It was a very somber discussion of the here and now. It allowed the participants to move to an examination of the unique features of gay life with the feeling that their life-style is obstructed by an oppressive society.

Stage Three: New Values for the Groups

The general purpose of this stage was to free the gay world from heterosexual values and in the process to determine what new values should regulate the gay world. We have often been tempted to identify this stage as the "creation of a new vision."

Functional characteristics. Four functional characteristics were observed in this stage. First, particular values of the straight or establishment world were identified by the group members. Second, these values were identified as factors which condition or control the gay world. Third, these values were attacked as being irrelevant to the gay world. Fourth, new values for the gay world were proposed.

The most common pattern for the discussions of these issues was to present a value of the straight world, assess its effect on gay people, and then determine what the new value should be. For example:

MEMBER A: Most of our literature, novels and so forth link happiness, love and romance to heterosexuality. The thing is that these things are almost hidden and become standards we don't even think about.

MEMBER B: Gay people are only aware that these standards do not apply to us—but we do not know what new standards to apply.

MEMBER C: People are going to come out with new ideas that work for us and help us. We've got to start with respect as the basis, not predetermined ways of acting with someone else.

In another group, marriage was identified as an institution which represses some straight and all gay people, because society has conditioned its youth to marry and have children. Such a standard, the group concluded, denied the value of pleasure of and for itself and also created a form of self-hate in gay people because the standard could not be met. The new vision, reasoned the group, should not value a relationship for its length of duration. Instead, the standard for evaluating a relationship should be the ability to create and rotate roles and behavior based upon the nature of the people involved, not upon the dictates of society.

The particular value discussed in each group seemed random and dependent upon the unique combination of people in a given session, but each group found the discussion of some value appropriate at this stage. It was also observed that each of these value topics stressed the uniqueness of gay experiences and the need for further exploration of what those experiences are and ought to be.

Rhetorical characteristics. Contrast and comparison were the major rhetorical forms employed during Stage Three. The contrast was exclusively between homosexual and heterosexual relationships. The dialogues were predominantly future-oriented with an occasional attempt to fantasize, but the image of the "ideal" life-style as a whole seemed unclear. Hostility toward straights had been present in Stage Two; but in this stage it was intensified, and the anger or rage was directed toward the whole value structure of the larger society rather than toward any particular individual or policy-making institution. The tone among the members of the groups was cooperative, few arguments developed, and little or no competitive interaction took place among the group members.

Stage Four: Relating to Other Revolutionary Groups

Functioning as a test of the revolutionary openness of gay liberation, group members sought to determine if gay people were oppressing other oppressed groups. From a larger movement perspective, this stage was apparently intended to insure that there is constant, cultural revolution within the movement, and it also appeared to be an effort to remove all forms of oppression from within and from without. Accordingly, the groups sought to identify other kinds of subcultures which might potentially become viable political forces and part of the larger revolutionary movement.

Functional characteristics. In general, the groups tended to (1) identify a common principle or value held by most people, both gay and straight; (2) determine the ways in which this principle oppressed a particular group of people; (3) determine if this group could validly be called a "minority group"; (4) assess the kind of oppression such a minority faced, how such a minority might be liberated, and what function such a minority might perform within the larger revolutionary movement; and (5) determine the impact such a group might have on gay liberation.

Although each group discussed a different minority group (the bisexual, the aged, and the sadomasochists), the discussion of the aged provides a good example of the type of interaction which took place.

MEMBER A: A lot of gay people—straights for that matter—are really hung-up on being young, being with young people, and staying young as long as possible.

MEMBER B: Yes, it is especially bad when you see someone trying to live out a life that has passed.

MEMBER C: In *Gay Sunshine,* they call the whole hang-up *youthism,* and they call it a philosophy.

MEMBER B: You see it everywhere. Beauty contests run on it—every woman is 17 or 18. It's as if no one over 30 were beautiful.

MEMBER C: It's the old people who are really put down by it.

As the group interaction evolved, the validity of the aged as a minority group was assessed.

MEMBER A: I did work in geriatrics. They experience a reversal back to childhood. You wouldn't believe what goes on in those nursing homes.

MEMBER B: Maybe it's not senility—I mean senility might not be a regression to childhood but a becoming of being.

MEMBER A: No, not in most of these cases. Most of them have a mental thing—you know, senility.

MEMBER B: No! I mean a characteristic of being old may be a dropping of previous norms and we all wind up calling it senility—a negative term—so we don't have to deal with it. *(All members are interrupting each other—voices are loud and excited.)*

MEMBER A: No, because they are—*(interruptions)*—I'm just trying to define this—these people were in a special home because they were incapacitated—you know lack of blood and so on—their rational process had declined. *(Members A and B interrupt each other.)*

MEMBER C: Hey—don't oppress each other. *(Members calm down somewhat.)*

MEMBER B: Let me suggest a thought! Growing old is a process of and by itself. Senility might be defined by itself without a comparison to other life periods, even if it is biologically caused.

MEMBER A: Except the tragedy is when they do something like wet their beds, they react horribly to it. They start to cry because they are ashamed.

MEMBER B: However, with liberation, they would look at bedwetting as a fact of life—something that is part of being old—and perhaps work out a thing that would reduce shame. They need to redefine their life-styles.

Similar patterns of interaction developed on the topics of bisexuality and sadomasochism in the other two groups.

Rhetorical characteristics. The cooperative and nonargumentative atmosphere that prevailed in earlier stages disappeared. Group members became irritated with each other, interrupted each other, and insisted that their viewpoints be adopted. In two of the consciousness-raising sessions, the tension grew so strong that the topics were dropped and the group analyzed the members' hostility toward each other. Members then became apologetic and the groups moved back toward unity. For example, after a heated discussion of the nature of sadomasochistic relationships, two members had the following exchange.

MEMBER A: I'm not arguing—I'm not trying to define different life-styles—I'm talking about the individuals themselves. *(Several members attempt to speak.)*

MEMBER B: But you're not talking about them—it's not a death relationship for the people in the relationship—it's pain as pleasure.

MEMBER A: I'm talking about the people involved! They carry it to the extreme! A logical extension of what they are doing is death for them.

MEMBER B: No! You are the one carrying it to its logical extreme. They don't go that far. *(Long pause. The group is silent and very tense.)*

MEMBER A: I know—I really got strong there—I'm sorry.

During this stage, the members no longer spoke in terms of we-they but returned to the use of "I" and "you" found in Stage One. The other minority groups under discussion were referred to impersonally with words like "it" or "the group." Stage Four, then, stressed the members' tolerance of other life-styles, and the tension was broken only when the participants recognized that they were oppressing each other. Such recognitions generally forecasted the end of the sessions. This stage brought members to the fringes of their own oppressive attitudes, thus allowing them to reach new levels of consciousness during the sessions.

STAGES IN CONSCIOUSNESS-RAISING

I. Stage One: Self-realization of a New Identity
- A. Functional Characteristics
  1. Establishing credentials.
     - a. Reference to a behavioral-biological identity.
     - b. Identification of a behavioral-biological identity as a basis for a life-style or cultural identity—the emergence of a "new" personal identity.
  2. Acknowledgment of oppression against this life-style.
  3. Recognition of liberation as a national issue.
- B. Rhetorical Characteristics
  1. Chained-out fantasy themes.
  2. "I"–"you" reference among group members.
  3. Open and noncombative atmosphere.
  4. Time or temporal reference: past tense.

II. Stage Two: Group Identity Through Polarization
- A. Functional Characteristics
  1. Securing group consensus that there is a culturally divided world.
  2. Identification of the "enemy."
  3. Identification of oppression from within the subculture.
- B. Rhetorical Characteristics
  1. Generalized we–they reference between the movement and the larger society.
  2. Tension and hostility toward the external enemy.
  3. Somber, social atmosphere among immediate group members.
  4. Emergence of the cultural family; frequent use of terms such as "brothers," "sisters," and "community."
  5. Time or temporal reference: present tense.

III. Stage Three: Establishing New Values for the Group
- A. Functional Characteristics
  1. Identification of "establishment" values.
  2. Recognition that "establishment" values have conditioned the subculture.
  3. Rejection of "establishment" values.
  4. Determination of new values for the subculture.
- B. Rhetorical Characteristics
  1. Contrast and comparison.
  2. Cooperative, noncompetitive verbal interaction among group members.
  3. Increased hostility toward the entire value structure of the external enemy.

4. Time or temporal reference: future tense.

IV. Stage Four: Relating to Other Revolutionary Groups
   A. Functional Characteristics
      1. Identification of a common principle held by most people.
      2. Recognition that the principle oppresses another group.
      3. Determination of whether this group is a valid "minority group."
      4. Assessment of the kind of oppression faced by and the function to be served by this minority group within the larger revolutionary movement.
      5. Determination of the potential impact of this minority group upon the immediate group.
   B. Rhetorical Characteristics
      1. A return to the I–you relationship in the immediate group.
      2. Impersonal references to the new "minority group" considered.
      3. Competitive, argumentative atmosphere among group members, with a move toward cooperation toward the end of the stage.
      4. Recognition of oppression against one another within the immediate group, resulting in a reduction of hostility.

Implications

This study has generated implications for several areas, including (1) the reliability of the data reported here, (2) previously reported small-group research, (3) small-group methodology, (4) our understanding of the rhetoric of confrontation, and (5) future studies of consciousness-raising.

1. The consciousness-raising stages identified here appear generally reliable and generalizable to other revolutionary groups employing this process. The stages described here are consistent with those identified by Kearon,[22] Tanner,[23] O'Connor,[24] and Allen,[25] as well as with previous descriptions of consciousness-raising in larger gay liberation groups.[26]

2. While readily apparent similarities exist between consciousness-raising and other kinds of small-group processes, the data compiled here suggest that consciousness-raising may function as a unique small-group technique. In contrast to encounter groups which tend to emphasize an individual's social adjustment in the present,[27] consciousness-raising appears to emphasize a community identity designed to create a political orientation necessary for future changes in the larger society. The stages of small group evolution identified by Bormann,[28] Bales and Strodtback,[29] Tuckman,[30] Zaleznick and Moment,[31] and others[32] support such an observation, but the writings of these authors also suggest that traditional small-group techniques and training may be only a prerequisite to effective participation in consciousness-raising.

3. This study also suggests that participant observation is a method which might be employed to examine small-group processes, especially

when other methods of observation are inappropriate. Participant observation is used extensively in anthropology and sociology;[33] and Bruyn has argued that if observational factors such as time, place, circumstances, language, intimacy, and consensus are varied, participant observation functions as a valid research design.[34] In this study, these factors did vary among the three observers, and their independent examinations of the data resulted in the identification of the same stages in all sessions studied.

4. This study suggests that consciousness-raising may function as a useful mechanism for understanding rhetorical confrontations between the militant and members of the established social system. Some examinations of militant action, such as the *Report of the President's Commission on Campus Unrest,* express interest in the origins of the "pure idealism,"[35] "free existential act of commitment,"[36] and commitment to "participatory democracy"[37] found within the protest movement. Insofar as consciousness-raising precedes confrontations and focuses directly on the formation of new goals and values, an explication of consciousness-raising interactions may partially explain rhetorical confrontation themselves.

5. While this study was designed as an exploratory study with synthesis as its major logical approach, a host of analytical examinations of consciousness-raising would now seem appropriate.

Conclusion

Although the rhetoric of confrontation has received a great deal of attention, the small-group process used by radical revolutionaries to achieve the level of consciousness necessary to engage in rhetorical confrontation has not been extensively examined in the discipline of speech-communication. The present study focused on and attempted to capture the frame of reference of those involved in this process. The expressed personal-social motives of those involved in the sessions were used to identify the functional and rhetorical characteristics of four stages in consciousness-raising. In moving through a four-stage process, participants created a new identity for themselves (Stage One), perceived themselves as pitted against agents of the establishment (Stage Two), denied establishment values and advocated newly created ones (Stage Three), and finally agreed to support the liberation efforts of unrecognized oppressed groups, hence broadening the revolution (Stage Four).

Chapter 19

From "Commies" and "Queers" to "Gay Is Good"

James Darsey

In the early morning hours of June 28, 1969, New York City police made what was supposed to be a routine raid of a gay bar on Christopher Street, in Greenwich Village. Instead of the usual passivity, fear, and resignation, however, police encountered angry patrons who threw rocks and bottles while chanting "Gay Power," and the first gay riot in history erupted into three nights of violence. This event became known as the Stonewall Rebellion.[1] Later that year *Time* magazine published a cover story entitled "The Homosexual: Newly Visible, Newly Understood," the first such national publicity to be received by gays.[2] America was rudely awakened to the fact that an invisible minority of "ten to twenty-five million people, about as large as blacks and twice as large as Jews,"[3] was about to step out of obscurity and into the limelight, where it could flex its muscle.

Surely, however, gay people did not suddenly spring onto the stage as a full-grown social movement in 1969. Where did they come from, and where had they been for all those years? Stonewall represented more than just angry gay people protesting the closing of a bar; it represented evidence that gay people had managed to create a conception of themselves and their rights that was antithetical to—in fact inimical to—the views held by the surrounding society.[4] The transformation of gays from "the boys in the band" to the gay liberation front poses interesting problems for the student of rhetoric and social movements. This study, then, is a study of changing consciousness both as it is reflected in and motivated by discourse—not discourse alone, but a situational discourse always shaped by its interaction with the social milieu, a milieu that the discourse has, in part, helped to shape. In this respect the focus of and impetus for this study take direction from Stephen Lucas' study of the rhetoric of the American revolution:

> Too often analysts fail to come to grips with the intrinsically kinetic nature of movement rhetoric. A social or political movement is not a material object that exists only in a given place and at a given time, but is a progression of human behavior which takes place across time and which must be understood in temporal as well as in spatial terms. Neither a movement nor its discourse is static—both are dynamic, fluid, and mutable. My point is not that the discourse of a movement unfolds chronologically; this has long been acknowledged at a theoretical level. Nor is my contention that movements proceed through various stages and that these stages are accompanied by permutations in rhetoric; this too has long been recognized. The temporal progression of discourse is not as vital to understanding the rhetoric of movements as is the cumulative metamorphosis of discourse in response to emerging exigencies.[5]

Of interest here is the evolving consensus as it is reflected in discourse and as it shapes new exigencies.[6] Although only the discourse emanating from homophile presses is examined in this essay, the fact that argumentation demands consensus as a point of departure as surely as it seeks a revised consensus as a destination[7] makes it possible to assert that, to the extent the argumentation is functional within the context of many messages representing both sides of an issue over time (as is the case in this study), the consensus represents a functionally valid view of a collectively held reality at a given point in time. I can only persuade you if I argue from premises you accept. In producing a single message I may be mistaken in my assumptions of what you will accept, but if you can argue back, if the situation is interactive as is the case with social movements, then I can correct my assumptions, and over a series of messages, my messages will reflect basic premises that constitute legitimated knowledge for both of us. It is a change in this collectively held reality that is being sought here.

A Note on Method

The procedure used in choosing the messages analyzed here is described in detail in an earlier study.[8] The method is designed to facilitate analysis of an entire movement by first isolating distinct rhetorical eras and then sampling a representative body of discourse within each era. After the sample is chosen the unit of analysis is the "value-appeal." Following the suggestion of a number of students of social movements, I have defined social conflict as ultimately a conflict of values; thus it is reasonable that the rhetoric produced by social movements would be a value-oriented rhetoric.[9] Value appeals have been operationally defined by using a system of coding developed by psychologist Ralph White in the 1940s

> to provide a method by which any kind of verbal data—e.g., propaganda and public-opinion materials, as well as autobiographies, clinical interviews, and

other devices of personality study—can be described quantitatively with a maximum of relevance to the underlying emotional dynamics, and to bring out the all-pervasive character of the value-system of our own culture.[10]

After the sample of discourse is reduced to a quantified series of value-appeals, points of consensus at any given time can be identified by applying Toulmin's analysis of argumentation and determining whether a given appeal represents a claim (disputed statement—attempt to create revised consensus) or whether it represents data or warrant (undisputed statements—represent current state of consensus).[11]

To make discussion manageable I have concentrated on only the most characteristic, most prominent values coded for each of the five coded phases.[12] For this reason only the five most frequently used appeals for each phase are examined. In all but one phase the five most frequently used value-appeals accounted for a majority of all the appeals used. In Phase II the five most frequently used appeals still represented 45.5 percent of all appeals. The top five appeals for each period and their cumulative percentage of occurrence in each period are presented as Table 8. When the appeals were coded and tabulated, it was possible to represent each appeal in discussion with a hypothetical example suggesting how the appeal was used, or with typical examples from the discourse. It was also possible to understand the argumentative structure of the appeal, using Toulmin's designations of claim, data, and warrant.

The Rhetoric of the American Homophile Movement

Available evidence indicates there have been forms of homosexual activity in all cultures. Arno Karlen dates homosexual practices in the eastern Mediterranean to "centuries or even millennia before the Greeks."[13] Plato wrote of homosexual relationships in various works; and the authors of the Bible were well aware of such practices, as illustrated particularly in Genesis and Leviticus, and in Paul's epistle to the Romans. Homosexuality has at various times and places been celebrated, tolerated, and castigated, but it has always been.

From the beginning, homosexuality was viewed in America vis-à-vis the Judeo-Christian tradition—homosexuality is a *moral* failing that warrants severe punishment in the *legal* sphere. As early as 1566, Jonathan Katz finds a documentation of an execution in Florida on charges related to sodomy.[14] Katz documents other early instances of homosexual practices in the developing colonies. One case of particular interest was the law reform effort of Virginia, begun in 1776. Typical of his liberal, humanitarian stance, Thomas Jefferson was among those to propose that punishment for the crimes of rape, sodomy, and bestiality be changed from death to mere castration.[15]

Table 8

TOP FIVE VALUE-APPEALS FOR EACH PERIOD OF GAY RHETORIC*

Phase Rank	I	II	III	IV	V
1	Obedience (Ob)	Justice (J)	Justice (J)	Justice (J)	Justice (J)
2	Likeness (Li)	Tolerance (T)	Truth (Tr)	Unity (U)	Safety (S)
3	Adjustment (Ad)	Truth (Tr)	Determination (D)	Achievement (A)	Unity (U)
4	Tolerance (T)	Unity/ Naturalness (Na)	Tolerance (T)	Self-regard (Sf)	Achievement (A)
5	Unity (U)	Knowledge (K)	Knowledge (K)	Tolerance/ Recognition (T/R)	Adjustment (Ad)
	54%	45.5%	68.1%	57.1%	61.3%

*The bottom figure represents the percentage of total appeals accounted for by the top five appeals in each phase. Ties are included.

Given the severity of their plight it is surprising that homosexuals remained so quiet for so long. Most theories of social movements that find the origins of movements in conditions of oppression or deprivation are confounded when faced with the behavior of homosexuals in America. Sociologist Edward Sagarin has noted this problem:

> No group so large in number (although size is a matter of dispute), so completely stigmatized, and placed into so disadvantaged a position remained so long unorganized in this organizational society. When one recalls that these deviants never wanted for educated and intellectual adherents, it is all the more puzzling that no homophile organization appeared in America until after the Second World War.[16]

There were in fact early homophile organizations in America, but these were apparently no more than local social gathering places maintaining an elusive existence on the outer fringes of society.[17] One attempt to organize homosexuals in a political way, in 1924, was quickly squelched.[18] Although there had been a full-blown homosexual rights movement in Europe prior to World War II, students of this movement conclude that the powers that be were singularly successful in preventing the importation of the movement into the United States.[19] As Sagarin suggests, it has only been since the end of World War II that there has been a sustained homophile rights movement of any magnitude in America.

The social climate in America following World War II was fraught with confusion and change. One American history text describes the atmosphere:

> American Society underwent a rapid transformation in the years after World War II. Rising incomes, greater mobility, new opportunities for education, growing urbanization, revolutions in science and technology, new freedom in literature and the movies, and the demand by lower economic groups, especially blacks, for full political, social, and economic rights, all created confusion and conflict and tested the strength of the country's social fabric.[20]

The increased mobility and the growing urbanization created an atmosphere of anonymity; neighbor no longer knew what neighbor was up to, and further, neighbor was likely to be too preoccupied to worry much about it. World War II had demonstrated the vast power of nuclear weaponry, and the resulting fear of annihilation created an atmosphere in which people lived for the moment, leaving neighbors to do what they pleased. Such attitudes resulted in an increased tolerance for those who were "mentally disturbed" and a reevaluation of sexual mores.[21]

Against this background it seems only natural that in 1938 a group of women students at Indiana University petitioned the university to inaugurate a course in marriage. A biologist on the faculty, Alfred Kinsey, was involved in this movement. What most impressed Kinsey as he became involved in this effort was the paucity of reliable information available on human sexual behavior.[22] Ten years after the petition effort, Kinsey and his associates published the first study under the auspices of the Institute for Sex Research, *Sexual Behavior in the Human Male.* Sagarin describes its publication:

> In 1948, there burst forth on the country a veritable sexual "atom bomb." Dropped from the solemn halls of a scholarly enclave in a small Indiana town, this bomb, or the radiation from its explosion, affected almost every home in America in a few brief months. Attitudes toward sex would never be the same again.[23]

As the first printing of 20,000 copies was quickly exhausted and the book made the list of best-sellers,[24] the country was most astounded, not by the incidence of masturbation or of pre- and extramarital sex, but by the figures on homosexual behavior among males.[25] In fact, the figures on homosexual behavior reached proportions that amazed even Kinsey and his colleagues.[26]

The figures were no less astonishing to homosexual society than they were to heterosexual society, but for homosexuals they contained a clear mandate—organize! "If millions of men were homosexual, then would there not be a handful, a score, or a hundred who would be equipped to lead a social movement? Would such a movement not gain wide support among these leaderless people, and would it not be one difficult to suppress?"[27] According to the accounts of Sagarin and Katz, homophile organizations sprouted all over the country like fungi after a summer rain.[28] Some of the organizations in existence today and the movement as a whole can trace direct lineage from these early organizations.

The rhetorical component of early homophile organizations was extremely limited. Most organizations were primarily interested in providing social activities for members, protecting them from the law, reconciling their religious beliefs with the homosexuality, and convincing them they were not "sick" simply because they were homosexual. Much of the early discourse was in the form of lectures given to various groups by outsiders, usually doctors and lawyers. Most of this discourse lacked a vehicle for its dissemination and preservation; very few homophile groups were in the publishing business until the mid-1950s. *One* magazine began publishing in 1953, and *The Mattachine Review* was inaugurated in 1955.

Even more important than the limited scope of publishing to the character of early homophile discourse was the movement's lack of focus. Kinsey had helped homosexuals to discover themselves; now the question was what to do with this discovery. The answers to this question would only begin to evolve and crystallize as the newly founded movement faced its first menace—Joseph McCarthy and company.

Phase I: Joseph McCarthy and the Creation of a Devil

During the time when homophile organizations were just getting underway, the federal government, under the leadership of senators Joseph McCarthy (R.—Wis.), Kenneth Wherry (R.—Neb.), and Lister Hill (D.—Ala.), was attempting to purge its ranks of "sexual perverts" on the belief they constituted security risks. On March 1, 1950 *The New York Times* reported the findings of a Senate investigating committee that, since 1947, ninety-one persons had resigned State Department jobs while under investigation as security risks. It was the expressed opinion of State Department witness John Peurifoy that "most of these were homosexuals."[29]

On December 15, 1950 the Senate Committee on Expenditures in the Executive Departments issued a report entitled "Employment of Homosexuals and Other Sex Perverts in Government"[30] that, among other things, documented 4,954 cases concerning "perverts" in federal jobs (4,380 in the military services and 574 in civilian capacities) which had been processed since January 1, 1947. This report became a major document of the homosexual witch-hunt that ran concurrently with the better-remembered McCarthy "red scare." Thanks to the McCarthy hysteria, the movement had a devil, an oppressor; it was McCarthy who gave the movement direction and ideological purpose. The impact of McCarthyism is clear in the value-appeals made by movement presses during this time.

Obedience. The primary value-appeal of this first true discursive era for the homophile movement was obedience. The most typical use of such appeals stressed that homosexuals were obedient to society's laws, customs, and mores in every way but sexual preference:

> The organization is definitely not seeking to destroy any of society's existing institutions, laws, or mores.[31]

> The Mattachine Society advocates no illegal activities whatever.[32]

At one point, a Mattachine publication even claimed a common goal with society of "reducing the high incidence of sex variance in future generations."[33] Along these same lines, under the fire of McCarthyism, homophile groups were also eager to discredit any rumored connections with communism.[34]

Likeness or conformity. The obedience appeal was generally connected to a likeness or conformity appeal. The resulting argument was, in essence, "See, we (homosexuals) obey all the same laws (almost) and support all the same institutions that you (straight society) do. Therefore, we are just like you."

There was a subtle side to this argument aimed at stereotypes. If homosexuals are just like heterosexuals in all ways except sexual preference, then there is as much diversity among homosexuals as there is among heterosexuals; i.e., for every lisping, limp-wristed homosexual hairdresser, there is a homosexual lawyer who enjoys white-water canoe racing on weekends:

> Deviates are found in all vocations from ballet dancers to rugged athletes, from the brawniest laborer to the tenderest invalid, from the subnormal to the genius. He (we will assume the "she") certainly has no monopoly on the arts, nor does refinement of nature indicate his sexual bent.[35]

At this point in time little research had yet been done on homosexuals, their demographics, or their sexual habits. There was consequently minimal data to support such highly assertive claims.

By combining the obedience and conformity appeals, gay people were laying the groundwork for a claim that they deserve tolerance and justice from the straight community. These latter claims were implicit in the early rhetoric (for anyone who cared to extrapolate somewhat), but they were probably not functional as claims for any but members of the homosexual community.

Adjustment. Early homophile leaders were also concerned with convincing both homosexuals and heterosexuals that homosexuality per se was not an illness: "Homosexuality is not a sickness unless one accepts the prejudice of society, if one considers the pretended normality of others as the unique morality, even at the expense of one's own."[36] One essay used obedience appeals in a unique, negative way to make an overall case for adjustment and the related area of self-regard.[37]

The importance of the "adjustment" claim should be apparent. It is not likely that a successful social movement will result from ranks of members and potential members who feel they are in some way defective. Not only will membership lack sufficient esteem to make demands for reforms that at base they do not feel they really deserve, but society is not apt to acquiesce to a group of "sick" individuals as long as they can effectively be labeled as such.

Tolerance. The problem of mobilization is compounded when the portion of the membership that does not consider itself sick also fails to consider itself oppressed. Many gay people had excellent jobs, successful careers, economic security, no entanglements with the law; the problem of homosexual oppression is an elusive one.[38] Oppression of gay people is not something that is immediately obvious to all heterosexuals or even to all homosexuals. In response to this problem, most of the tolerance appeals in this first period were intended to establish that there was a *lack* of tolerance: "The exclusively homosexual are hounded by law, haunted by prejudice and isolated more than any other single minority."[39]

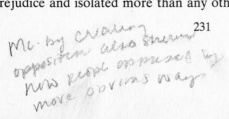

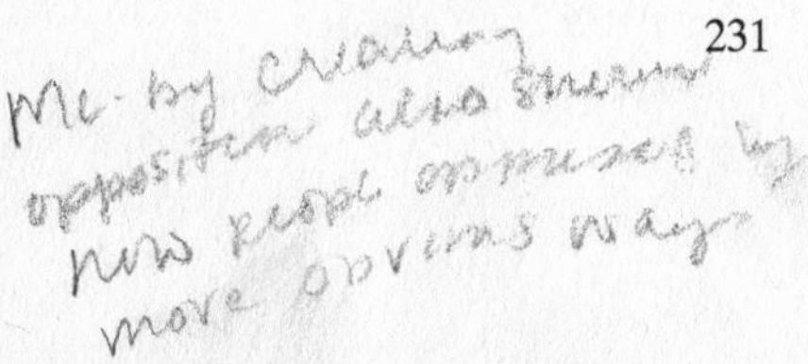

All the appeals considered so far can be seen as "elementary claims"; they are the claims that must be granted before the movement could actually pursue the general goal of a social movement: improving the lot of its membership. Criminals and psychopaths do not campaign for rights. Society incarcerates them. Equally, groups that feel no oppression rarely begin social movements. Social movements arise out of a feeling of relative deprivation.[40]

Unity. The logical conclusion that arises from the acceptance of these "elementary claims" is organization. Acceptance of the appeals presented by the movement in this earliest period legitimizes the need for the movement. What directions the movement will take, however, are still matters for debate. As an indication of this debate, the last major appeal in Phase I is a unity appeal. Most of the appeals to unity in this period were statements demonstrating a lack of unity in the movement, the need for the absent unity being implicit in the appeals. "What can a society accomplish if half of it feels its object is to convince the world we're just like everyone else and the other half feels homosexuals are variants in the full sense of the term and have every right to be?"[41] The unity appeals became especially prominent with a threatened schism in Mattachine and the formation of the sometimes rival One, Inc.

These five claims derived from the primary value-appeals in Table 8, then, profile the major rhetorical concerns of Phase I.[42] Most important for our purposes, it may be argued that these five claims reflect the state of social knowledge concerning homosexuality which existed in the United States from 1950 to 1955. Arguments posed by homophile groups arose out of a need to undermine the legitimacy of certain notions held by society-at-large; thus the claims made by homophile groups (e.g., that homosexuality is not a sickness) may be viewed as antithetical to the mainstream of social knowledge at this time. At the same time the data and warrants used in homophile discourse are within the mainstream of social knowledge. As claims become data and warrants they indicate changes in social knowledge; i.e., a new consensus is achieved that legitimizes that which was formerly illegitimate. The progression becomes evident only as we look at the change in claims across phases.

McCarthyism is, historically, the second major event in the life of the young movement. Ironically, McCarthyism was beneficial to the homophile organizations in that it provided the movement with a cause, but it was undoubtedly also successful in keeping many potential members "in their closets." In 1954 the Senate censured McCarthy;[43] the public apparently had caught a glimpse of insanity in his single-minded campaign, and his reign of terror came crashing down around him.

Phase II: The Beginning of the Long Journey Toward Legal Reform

The dissolution of McCarthyism in itself would probably have ushered in a new era for homosexuals. Not only did 1954 and 1955 signal the decline of an oppressive force, but they also marked the feeble beginning of a liberating force. In 1955 the American Law Institute proposed a model penal code that removed homosexual behavior among consenting adults from the jurisdiction of criminal law.[44] This was followed by a similar recommendation in Great Britain, in 1957, in what was popularly known as the Wolfenden Report.

Although nothing concrete was done with these recommendations on either side of the Atlantic for several years, the announcements had a great impact on shaping the tactics of the homophile movement. Such decisions gave a glimmer of hope that gains could be made in the area of legal reform, and were undoubtedly responsible for a shift from the concentration of movement activities on questions of the nature and origins of homosexuality (about which most of them could do little anyway) to questions of legal rights. The impact of these decisions was increased by the fact the modern black rights movement was mounting a major assault on discrimination through legal reform with the decision of the U.S. Supreme Court in the case of Brown v. the Board of Education, in 1954.

Justice. Given this environment in the mid-1950s, it should come as no surprise that the dominant appeal of this second discursive era was justice, which remains the overwhelming concern expressed in movement discourse from this point on. For homosexuals, most of this concern was (and is) legal rather than, say, moral. Homophile presses have continued to exhibit a strong awareness of legal decisions concerning homosexuals.

Legal questions are of special importance to homosexuals. Prior to 1961, homosexual sex was illegal in every state in the union. Although vaguely worded sodomy statutes technically outlaw heterosexual behavior that falls within their province, they have been used almost exclusively against homosexuals.[45] It is true that simply the state of being a homosexual is not illegal, but few people are willing to identify themselves as such without reason, i.e., homosexual contacts. The result is, as Edwin Schur has sagaciously noted, "Crime laws, by definition, create criminals."[46]

Tolerance. In this second discursive period, justice and tolerance were usually linked in the discourse. Most appeals to justice and tolerance dealt forthrightly with issues of the law. Most of the combined justice-tolerance appeals concentrated on the lack of favorable conditions for homosexuals:

> These reflections on homosexuality seem to have some value. They ought, in any case, to help us to realize that, far from being justified, the hostility that we meet makes little sense, however much it may claim to do do so.[47]

> There is no sense to persecuting a large minority group for one harried man's meaningless violence [written in response to the scandal following the Stephen Nash murders].[48]

Truthfulness. Often, injustice and intolerance are perpetuated by the kind of misinformation that surrounds a particular minority group. Thus, it should not be surprising that homophile presses began acknowledging and fighting some of the misconceptions commonly held about homosexuals in this early period of the movement's development:

> Frequently a community becomes inflamed by a particularly brutal sex murder of the psychopathic variety. Police, press, and the general public tend to panic and make wildly irrational attempts to root out all sex deviates from the community—on the preposterous assumption (encouraged by unethical scare headlines) that every sexually unorthodox person is a potential sex murderer, that homosexuality is synonymous with sex psychopathy.[49]

Homosexuals put forth these arguments in the hope they would justify claims that homosexuals were deserving of tolerance and justice. Eventually, with some segment of the population, this might prove to be true, but at least during this phase, such assertions apparently acted more as claim than as warrant.

Unity. Unity was a major concern of the movement in Phase II also. In this early stage of development the movement was occupied with building its strength. Unity appeals in the second phase differed from those presented earlier in that they were growth-oriented, while those in Phase I constituted a holding action. During the McCarthy era the movement was mostly interested in establishing the unified front necessary for survival. After the threats of the early 50s had passed, more members could be persuaded to emerge from their closets: "Thus it is that each and every reader of this magazine should frequently ask himself, what am I doing to help the homosexual cause? [sic] Everyone needs to be inquiring into ways of continued and increased support."[50]

A related appeal worth mentioning here is generosity, although it does not rank as a major appeal. During this early stage of getting its feet on the ground, the movement was interested in support—not only the support that numbers bring, but economic support as well. It is only during this second period that any generosity appeals have been recorded:

> Yet the safest and most passive contribution any homosexual can make is in giving money. Money means that new research can be made, reports written,

newer arguments set forth for everyone to sharpen his wits on, ministers interviewed, lawyers consulted, encouragement made to the faint-hearted, answers to the disturbed, angered and distressed.[51]

Naturalness. Ranked the same as appeals to unity during this period were appeals to nature. In absolute terms, nature appeals in Phase II almost numbered as many as in Phase I. The naturalness of homosexuality was an important issue for the early movement. The claim in these appeals was that homosexuality is natural. We can see that if homosexuality is natural and naturalness is good, then homosexuality is good:

> Would it not rather be nature herself who alone should have the right to lead these individuals toward a proper means of not reproducing their own kind? In a word, would not homosexuality then become a natural means of racial, or familial selection?[52]

> Nature has indicated the way for us, for never are two diatoms or two snowflakes just alike. Nature abhors conformity. Whatever be the sameness-es and the interconnections it is diversity that is natural. Rigid controls are unnatural and, in the long run, self-defeating. Deviation is here to stay. Why not relax and enjoy it?[53]

Knowledge. The final major appeal in Phase II is an appeal for knowledge—knowledge concerning homosexuality. Homosexuals were making many claims about themselves during this period: homosexuals were not child-molesters; homosexuals were not automatically psycho-paths; homosexuality was natural. Most of these claims were still presented assertively; firm data did not attend their issuance.

Homosexuals were, and continue to be, interested in research on homosexuality. In the sample from Phase II, nowhere is this better expressed than in the article "The Homosexual: One Idea as to What Makes Him," wherein members of the homosexual community were encouraged to participate in a cytological experiment.[54]

Phase III: Quiet Strength and Independence

In 1961 lawmakers in the State of Illinois became the first legislative body in the United States or in Britain to incorporate the reforms suggested by the American Law Institute or the English Committee on Homosexual Offenses and Prostitution (the Wolfenden Committee). In that year Illinois revised its entire penal code by virtually adopting the American Law Institute's model in toto. In this context the measures on homosexuality aroused little public debate, but they provided a great precedent for the movement.[55]

In many respects the Illinois decision was a harbinger of the spirit of the sixties; many gains were quiet but substantial. This same year, 1961, also saw the Democrats regain control of the White House. The Kennedy years were encouraging ones for groups interested in human rights: 1960 brought the first black sit-in in Greensboro, North Carolina, followed by many such events in the years to come; in 1961, a convention of Students for a Democratic Society approved the Port Huron Statement, affirming a set of essential ideals for a developing world; in 1963 Martin Luther King, Jr. spoke to more than 200,000 persons gathered in Washington, DC, in one of the nation's largest demonstrations. For the time these other organizations and causes were to occupy center stage. Homophile groups were chiefly to use the hospitable climate of the sixties to solidify and fortify. Most of the concerns were extensions of those raised previously.

Justice. In Phase III the top-ranked rhetorical concern was again justice. However, justice appeals in this period differed from those in the previous period in their affirmative stance. Given the example of the burgeoning black rights movement, the homophile movement began to show less concern for demonstrating that there was a lack of justice for homosexuals and more concern for asserting their right to it:

> So-called security investigations based on homosexual implications can go no farther than we permit. Americans understanding the honorable traditions of our democratic heritage will prove their patriotism by exposing and crushing every sneaky, undercover resort to unconstitutional procedures, whatever its source.[56]

> The time for justice has now come. No force can hold it back. It is right—in the eyes of man and God—that it should come.[57]

This new, affirmative stance was also reflected in the large numbers of determination-cum-justice appeals found during this period. These hybrid appeals are discussed below in looking at determination, which was ranked for Phase III.

Truthfulness. In Phase II, truthfulness again became a major concern for the movement. More scientific, psychological, and sociological research had been done by this time, and homosexuals reflected an awareness of this growing body of knowledge. As more diverse, often opposing scientific views surfaced on various aspects of homosexuality, homosexuals tended to be less dependent on authorities in shaping self-view. The emphasis of the argument in the third phase shifted from "Let's help science find the truth about us" to an attitude that homosexuals as homosexuals were the authorities and the final arbiters of scientific opinion. Homosexuals did not divorce themselves from science. Science was needed to lend respectability to claims made by homophiles, but with the proliferation of opinions there were more from which to choose. In Phase III, homosexuals showed a greater willingness than before to stand in judgment of what was true and what was not:

> The *Hollywood Citizen-News* has printed another slanderous and vicious attack on homosexuals.[58]

> Of all the lies assiduously cultivated by our enemies, the most damaging one is that we are child-molesters. Parents are justly terrified and furious over the prospect of their children being sexually molested. Probably the greatest part of their hatred of homosexuals can be attributed to this fear. The *Citizen-News* article, naturally, ties us once again to such heinous activity. We have never met a homosexual, who knows he is a homosexual and is active as one, who has the slightest interest in children sexually.[59]

> Many books have been written in scientific double-talk to prove homosexuals are sick, disturbed, and perverted. Some of them have sold very well. Some have been accepted as fact by many people who should know better.[60]

Determination. This assertive, affirmative stance was also evidenced in a newfound emphasis on determination. Given the black rights movement as an example, determination was presented as a means to an end; determination was the way to justice and tolerance. One article contrasting the favorable political climate toward homosexuals in San Francisco with the unfavorable climate toward homosexuals in Los Angeles makes clear the idea that San Francisco homosexuals had worked for what they had; it had not, and would not, come easily.[61]

Tolerance. In abstract terms, tolerance and justice remained the only expressed ultimate goals of the movement during Phase III. Homosexuals had not yet abandoned the feeling that it was necessary to demonstrate the existence of intolerance. "The very idea that homosexuals are deserving of first-class citizenship inspires many prominent liberals to a manifestation of the George Wallace syndrome. The homophile movement seems to provide the dividing line where real liberals are separated from the phony liberals."[62] Blacks had created a mood for justice and a mood of militance, but homosexuals were caught in the crossfire. The rhetoric of human rights had created an impression that no one deserving was really oppressed any more, but homosexuals were still not a legitimate minority in most eyes. Many of the excerpts quoted in other contexts above demonstrate a perceived lack of tolerance for the homosexual community by society-at-large.

All was not resignation, however. As with the justice appeals, many of the tolerance appeals were linked with appeals to determination:

> As it always has, *One* depends upon its readers, upon you, to help it in its program of making homosexuals and their way of life understandable and

acceptable to the heterosexual majority. To act upon this imperative will take courage. But until this courage is found, *One* is going to be hampered by reaching only those readers who least need to be persuaded and educated.[63]

Knowledge. Like appeals to truthfulness, appeals to knowledge changed tenor during Phase III. There were still many statements concerning the lack of reliable knowledge on the subject of homosexuality, but as with truthfulness, there was also a great conviction that homosexuals were their own best authorities. Instead of merely searching for knowledge, homosexuals felt a need to take what they knew to larger audiences, as illustrated in the tolerance and determination appeal above.

Phase IV: Stonewall and Aggressive Self-identity

After twenty years of organized efforts, homophile groups could indeed claim gains for their members, but homosexuals were still largely the invisible minority. Even the sixties, which were such tumultuous times for other groups, were relatively quiet for homophile liberation. Although there was growth and activity, these were not the years for monumental decisions or dramatic confrontations for the homophile movement.

On June 28, 1969 all that changed. The *Mattachine Midwest Newsletter* describes the events of this night:

> When the New York Police entered and closed the Stonewall Club during the early morning hours of June 28 a year ago, it must have at first seemed like a rerun of a segment of that old, worn-out Official Harassment Story. But this time things were different; the evicted patrons didn't follow the usual script. Instead, throwing rocks and bottles and chanting "Gay Power," they reacted against years of harassment with an explosion of pent-up, angry frustration. This—history's first gay riot—and the demonstrations which followed it marked the first time that large numbers of gay people stood up against repression. For this reason the Stonewall riot is regarded as the birth of the Gay Liberation Movement.[64]

The Stonewall rebellion, as it has come to be known, became Bastille Day for gay liberationists. In creating gay liberation it was almost as though a new movement had been invented. In tone it resembled the difference between Martin Luther King, Jr. and Malcolm X. In fact, the experiences of Mattachine Midwest, in Chicago, seem to indicate that the new branch of the movement appealed to an almost completely new membership.[65]

It was this new "gay liberation" component of the movement that became visible. Many Americans—even many gay Americans—came to know gay liberation as *the* movement, often believing there were no activities on behalf of homosexual rights before 1969. The older groups.

represented by the Mattachine societies, had been involved with gaining respectability and with the assimilation of members into society. According to John Waite Bowers and Donovan J. Ochs' definitions, the early groups expressed a vertical deviance.[66] On the one hand, their desire to stay within the value structure of the status quo made them uncontroversial, and consequently, they often went unnoticed. Gay liberation, on the other hand, was a laterally deviant arm of the movement.[67] Gay liberationists painted a lavender line down the center of Christopher Street in New York City (the location of the Stonewall Inn), burned real wooden closets at a rally in Chicago, paraded huge phallic symbols as floats, and popularized a form of guerrilla theater known as radical drag, in which men dress as women with no attempt to disguise the fact that they are males. On a deeper level these groups also began to reject societal values they found self-condemnatory: the sanctity of the family unit, the superiority of heterosexuality, and the taboo on promiscuity. These are the things from which controversies are made; these are the things that attract attention. The appeals of this period reflect a newfound militance and an assertive, sometimes uncompromising tone.

Justice. Justice continued to be the main concern of homophile discourse, but gay people—as they were now calling themselves as a measure of self-definition[68]—were no longer begging the straight community for rights. Many of the justice appeals indicated that gays were fighting battles in the courts and legislatures.[69]

A subtle reflection of new confidence and militance was the movement's use of sarcasm. The homophile movement had matured to the point where movement leaders could now see themselves as superior to many of their oppressors, and derisive comments followed. A prime example is an editorial entitled "How About Us Shorties?"

> And just to prove that the silly season is really upon us, along comes Texas. If sex law reform proposed in that state goes through, it will still be illegal for a guy to fuck another guy, but every lonely cowpoke will be able to legally screw his horse (Texans are all tall, besides being long).
>
> Since reading this report, we have been trying to fathom the reasons behind the peculiar Texas proposals, but we can only guess. They must have something to do with the history of the West and the great importance of the horse during that era when a man's most valuable possession was his horse. His horse was not only the pioneer cowboy's means of transportation but often his only companionship for many a saddlesore day. It is natural that the Texas legislators might hesitate before breaking this bond that is hundreds of years old.
>
> But we should also like to point out respectfully that next to the horse, the lonely cowpoke's only companions were usually other lonely cowpokes and that certain bonds grew between them during the long days and chilly nights. This, too, is a part of our history and our heritage and should not be

lightly dismissed by the great state of Texas, which has, even today, some of the friendliest cowboys in the West.

And so, Texas, be mindful of your history. After all, what can a short Texan do with a horse?[70]

Saul Alinsky notes the significance of such rhetorical maturation. Alinsky's fifth rule of power tactics is, "Ridicule is man's most potent weapon."[71]

Unity. Unity appeals gained prominence again in Phase IV. This resurgence resulted from the splintering of the movement after Stonewall. The Mattachine societies, SIR, and One, Inc. had been unchallenged, moderate-progressive vanguards of the movement through the sixties. The post-Stonewall period saw the proliferation of younger, more radical groups like the Gay Liberation Front and the Gay Activists Alliance. Occasionally, these groups exhibited open animosity toward one another. The movement was deeply concerned with its ability to survive division. This is especially well illustrated in a piece titled "Conference Stresses Unity," published by the Mattachine Society of New York.[72]

Achievement. The proverbial carrot on a stick is a useful motivator, especially during times of organizational stress. If members can see gains, evidence that the organizations in the movement are accomplishing, then drive and a sense of purpose can be maintained. Organizations at this time were eager to demonstrate they were effective, had made achievements, and had something to offer the gay community.

> New York City agreed in Federal Court, in a case started out of the MSNY office, that it would no longer discriminate against homosexuals in employment; drag queens picketed *A Patriot for Me;* plainclothes cops (at MSNY's urging) were removed from subway toilets; and homosexuals found political voices.[73]

Self-regard. Self-regard, which was not in evidence as a rhetorical appeal during Phase III, resurfaced in Phase IV to become a matter of major importance. In absolute terms the magnitude of concern with self-regard expressed in Phase IV had been absent for an entire decade. This revival took two distinct levels: professional and popular.

On the professional level, gays were battling the American Psychiatric Association (APA) because of its automatic classification of homosexuality as a psychopathology. An editorial in *Gay* congratulates a Gay Liberation Front chapter for breaking up an APA meeting where papers on aversion therapy for homosexuals were being presented.[74] Most of these confrontations and questions related to the psychiatric establishment were considered under appeals to adjustment, however.

In the popular arena, gays were reshaping their identity in the wake of Stonewall. Just as blacks in the previous decade had chosen to reject the label of "Negro" for that of black, gays were seeking to define themselves on their own terms.[75] Although many earlier issues (such as the psychopathology argument) had not been completely resolved, the homophile movement, with its redefinition, sought to lessen their integrity as issues. Franklin Kameny's slogan, coined during the Stonewall riots, sums up the issue best: "Gay is good."

Tolerance. By the end of the fourth phase tolerance was the only value appeal to claim a major status in every period of homophile discourse to 1972. Tolerance appeals failed to change much during the first four periods. In Phase IV there was still a strong emphasis on demonstrating a lack of tolerance, but along with achievement, examples of increased tolerance were used to bait movement members.[76] Tolerance was a particularly dangerous appeal for the homophile movement. If evidence of intolerance could not be kept before movement members, the movement would lose its momentum. However, if no progress was being made over the years, the membership could become discouraged.

Recognition. In 1969 *Time* magazine published the first nationally circulated cover story on the gay subculture titled "The Homosexual: Newly Visible, Newly Understood."[77] This same year the *Chicago Sun Times* magazine published a special section called "The Homosexuals: A Newly Visible Minority."[78] Recognition, in and of itself, became a goal for the movement.[79] With overtones of achievement the movement presses eagerly for reported acknowledgments of the gay subculture from politicians, in the popular press, in the movies, and in television.

Aggression. Perhaps as vital a sign of the times as any of the major appeals was the comparatively large number of aggression appeals during this phase. Although not ranked in the top five appeals for Phase IV, aggression was a popular rhetorical technique. More important, it was the period following the Stonewall rebellion, which was the only phase to exhibit more than an incidental appeal to aggression.

Phase V: Uncertain Maturity and the Decline of Radicalism

In the spring of 1970 four students were shot and killed by national guardsmen in an antiwar protest at Kent State University. This incident, along with the death of a student at the University of Wisconsin at Madison when a bomb exploded in Sterling Hall, began to dampen the spirit of protest that had characterized the 1960s. Many protesting groups, particularly blacks, had been neutralized by partial incorporation or co-optation.

Radicalism lingered perhaps a bit longer in the gay movement than it did in other movements, primarily because gays had gotten off to a late start. But by 1973 even the gays had begun to settle down to the lackluster but important tasks of working through established channels for specific goals and programs. In 1973 the United States made its withdrawal from Vietnam virtually complete, signaling the end of an era; America was tired of the screaming. Of more direct concern to gays than Vietnam was the fact that six states had joined Illinois in repealing restrictions on sexual relations among consenting adults in the period from 1970 to 1973 (three of the six did so in 1973).[80] This was also the year one of the movement's long-standing opponents, the APA, changed the classification of homosexuality per se as a psychopatholgy in the *Diagnostic and Statistical Manual II*.[81] With the threat of its most prominent devils diminished for the time, the movement began a quiet offensive, working on bits and pieces of the total program laid out in those idealistic 60s, when all things seemed possible. The most serious threat faced by the movement during this period was not external, but internal: how to maintain the lagging support of members.

Justice. The final rhetorical period covered in this study was characterized by specifics. Justice was no longer merely justice, but justice in tax laws,[82] in military opportunities,[83] and in law enforcement.[84] There were still ill-defined cries for "justice," but discourse during this period, for the most part, proposed specific action for specific ills. Homosexuals had gained a problem-program orientation that marks a mature movement.

Safety. Safety became a very real issue for the movement in Phase V. Like other radical-fringe groups, gay groups were horrified to learn that FBI surveillance techniques had been used against them. The presence of wholesale government record-keeping was seen as a direct threat to many members of gay groups who wanted their association with the cause to remain anonymous:

> If any group in the United States is likely to suffer from this "chilling" effect, it is the gay community, much of which remains closeted (or "underground") and fears exposure of its sexual orientation. Joe or Susy Smith, teaching at a junior high school in Salem, North Carolina, are going to be far less likely to go to a gay rights meeting if they think their names are going to end up on some government file as suspected homosexuals.[85]

Unity. Safety was not the only concern for the homophile movement during the post-1973 period. Problems of unity continued to plague the movement. Innumerable organizations sprouted and wilted, and in the process, every imaginable political bent and ideological orientation was represented. At a time when the movement lacked direction, all this superfluous action was just so much wheel-spinning. The movement was again faced with the necessity of trying to reconstruct a unified front.[86] One response to the problem was the creation of coalitions that provided the necessary unity, while allowing for the seemingly uncontrollable diversity.[87]

Achievement. With morale at an ebb, the movement continued to stress achievement appeals. Many organizations celebrated landmarks during this period, all of which afforded ample opportunity to assess progress.[88] These appeals were particularly important as a holding action while the movement sought new direction.

Adjustment. Not since the movement's earliest days had questions of adjustment been a major concern. In 1973 the debate came to the fore again, with the announced intention of the APA to reconsider its official view on homosexuality as a psychopathology:

> The psychiatrists and so-called psychotherapists, more than any other organized group in America, have been the most persistent enemies of the homosexual community. Their names are legion: Bergler, Bieber, Ellis, Hatterer, Socarides, and Cappon. Some of these men have crusaded actively to make life for homosexually inclined people as difficult as possible. Charles Socarides, for example, once recommended a "national treatment center" to which all homosexuals would be sent. He was frequently a witness for the U.S. Government in cases wherein the government wished to fire a known homosexual employee. Socarides would drop in on the trial and testify that the "homosexual condition is psychopathic." Such a dear sweet man. A healer. We note with interest that he will be among those arguing for the status quo at the APA meeting in Honolulu.[89]

In 1973 homosexuals were no longer willing to consider that their mental health was an issue to be resolved. In 1973 the APA was seen as retaining a repressive label for homosexuals when homosexuals had decided themselves that it was unfair and untrue.

The Quiet Years Before Anita

One of the chief reasons there was little forward motion immediately following 1973 was that "forward" was a difficult place to find. As John Murphy details, the oppression suffered by homosexuals is an ambiguous, often elusive thing that does not lend itself to easy analysis.[90] One reaction homosexuals had to this uncertain state of affairs was consciousness-raising. If we understand the function of consciousness-raising as a search for that which is not immediately apparent, then it is logical that it should have been employed by the homophile movement at this point in time.[91] Consciousness-raising was employed by the homophile movement to make tangible the nature of its devils at a time when these devils were subtle and elusive, and in doing so, the movement was given new direction.

This climate of ambiguity was destined to change in 1977, when Dade County, Florida, attempted to pass an ordinance outlawing discrimination against gay persons in housing, employment, and public accommodations. This action generated the first countermovement by antigay activists to gain national attention. Led by the gospel-singing queen of the orange groves, Anita Bryant, this group succeeded in defeating the proposed referendum and, drunk with its own success, proceeded to take its cause nationwide, and the devil was made real again. This study, however, stops short of analyzing the rhetorical aftermath of Anita Bryant's "children's crusade." At the time the original study from which this essay is extracted was written, the post-Anita era was too young to hazard generalizations about its eventual complexion. Now there are other, detailed studies available of the discourse of this period.[92] I believe the homophile movement is still in this era. Yet it is possible to suggest of its character that the discourse exhibits a certain homogeneity determined by the situation; that many old issues are being revived, because a broader audience is finding them for the first time; that even though old issues are being revived, they are not being argued in the same way they were before—the evolution of the discourse itself has so altered the situation that it is doubtful that the old consciousness will ever return—progress may be halting and slow, but it is not Sisyphean.

The Overall Argumentative Picture

The picture is not altogether clear, which is due in large part, no doubt, to the rhetorical complexity of social movements. The discourse analyzed in this study had three distinct audiences that it reached with varying degrees of success: (1) homosexuals committed to the movement, and their sympathizers; (2) homosexuals not committed to the movement; and (3) the heterosexual majority. Because these audiences exhibit varying degrees of commitment to gay rights, it is expected that argumentative components would not function uniformly for all receivers.

For example, in Phase I those committed to the movement were probably willing to accept the claim that homosexuals suffer from intolerance and discrimination as data for an as-yet unexpressed claim that such conditions need to be changed. The thrust of the claim is not in that direction, however, at least not as it is expressed in the discourse analyzed here. At this point in time the statement is a functional claim because its primary focus is on the uncommitted audiences. Energy is not wasted in having data questioned by the uncommitted or in stalling the progress of the vanguards of the movement while bringing up the argumentative rear, because the claim as it is presented in Phase I carries within it an implicit claim that conditions need to be rectified.

To further cloud the picture we must realize that the change in argumentative function is not unidirectional. Certain premises may be allowed to slip by because they have been suppressed, they have not been recognized, they are relatively unimportant at a given time, or the arguments that can be built from them have not been recognized by the opposition. Any number of explanations is possible. Like the Israeli-Arab conflict, however, conquest of a territory is precarious, and claims believed to have been granted may be called into question again. For instance, homosexuals are seen as operating on the presumption that it is accepted that they are not child-molesters, psychopaths, etc. In both cases, the issue has been treated implicitly. We have recently seen this issue explicated, however, by Anita Bryant's Save Our Children campaign in Dade County, Florida, where a two-to-one majority rejected the validity of the homosexuals' claim. For both these reasons—audience and the two-way flow of argument—trends in argumentation traced through such devices as Toulminian diagrams cannot be expected to be clear, self-explanatory pictures, but the complexity required of the explanation may be seen as an accurate indicator of the complexity of the argumentative process.

When any claim assumes new consensus as data or warrant, it is not to be expected that this new consensus will be universal. Even today—although the black rights movement would be quite correct in assuming consensus with society on the fact that blacks are, as a race, biologically equal to whites—the Arthur Jensens of this world are willing to argue for the biological inferiority of blacks. Arthur Jensen is an extreme example of a claim that is still being contested but not in a significant way. Jensen's group is so far behind the mainstream of social knowledge that it is unlikely the black rights movement would have to pay Jensen's following much rhetorical attention. The homophile movement, however, is a much younger movement. It can be seen in the newfound national interest that almost all the homophile movement's most elementary claims remain arguable in a very real sense.

Any movement must be prepared to deal with its "rear flank" to whatever extent it remains within shooting distance, to whatever extent it remains a vocal and formidable rhetorical force within the view and consideration of the mainstream of social knowledge. Research indicates there are two gross divisions of the ways in which reactionary and conservative forces may be handled by a social movement. First, when a statement has changed function (e.g., has moved from claim to data), it may remain explicit in future argumentation, and can be treated as claim for conservative audiences. That the statement is still in full view, where all feel secure that it is open to scrutiny, is important. The second response to an evolution of function is to suppress the argumentative component, to treat it implicitly. This implicit treatment appears to have two disparate functions: (1) It is used for very controversial issues that the movement needs to have accepted but which are not likely to be conceded. The movement seemingly employs the logic of "out of sight, out of mind."[93] (2) It is used for less controversial issues that can be expected to function enthematically when left unstated.

More obvious than any other trend in the evolving argumentation is a tendency toward increased complexity over time. As the movement builds a history, not only does it assume more and more common ground with society-at-large (i.e., it is able to offer more support for its claims in the form of data and warrants), but the variety of the relationships appears to increase. Over time it seems that a movement may not only expect to establish additional data-warrant consensus, but that consensus may be based on history, concession, or saturation; it may be implicit or explicit; and it is never universal. The complexity is heightened by the realization that as the movement becomes larger and more visible over time, it also both becomes more, diverse sources of discourse (organizations) and reaches more, diverse audiences.

Despite the tremendous complexity involved in the discourse of a social movement over a quarter century, what is clear from this analysis is that people in the United States, by and large, now hold different beliefs about homosexuality than they did twenty-five years ago; that is, the area of knowledge on which there is widespread consensus has changed. In 1950 homosexuals were *claiming* they were not sick; in 1973 they were *asserting* it; in 1950 homosexuals were attempting to establish that they were victims of discrimination; in 1973 they were asking for specific reforms to mitigate discrimination; in 1955 homosexuals were dangerous; in 1973 homophile presses had buried this as a dead issue. In the final analysis the arguments indicate that Americans now "know" different things about homosexuality than they "knew" in 1950; consensus on what is true has changed. This rhetorical conclusion is substantiated by sociological evidence. In 1969 a Harris poll revealed that 63 percent of Americans considered homosexuality harmful to the American way of life.[94] Yet, in 1977 Yankelovich, Skelley, and White reported that 56 percent of those polled "said they would vote for legislation guaranteeing the civil rights of homosexuals."[95] More recently, a *Time* cover story proclaimed that while gay people "still encounter suspicion and hostility and occasionally violence, and their campaign to live openly and freely is still far from won . . . they are gaining a degree of acceptance and even sympathy from heterosexuals, many of whom are still unsure how to deal with them, that neither straights nor gays would have thought possible just the day before yesterday."[96] This is certainly a far cry from Joseph McCarthy.

The gains made by homophile groups in the period studied may not seem earthshaking; these groups have not made tremendous advances and those that have been made are precarious. However, when one realizes that the gains which have been made are largely changes in consciousness, the progress seems miraculous. And it is the inevitable conclusion that the gains shown here have resulted from the creation of a new rhetorical myth, for nothing in the objective world has changed that could account for these altered views: the nature of homosexuality has not changed since prehistory; drastic changes in law have not led opinion here, for laws remained essentially unchanged from their Judeo-Christian heritage until 1973 (and they are only beginning to accommodate a new knowledge of homosexuality). Nor can scientific-psychological opinion claim credit for altering the public view; oppression has persisted despite the enlightened theories of people like Magnus Hinschfield and Sigmund Freud, and has actually been aided in recent times by the likes of Irving Bieber and Charles Socarides. It is through the discourse of the homophile movement that a new "people" appears to have been created,[97] new beliefs legitimized, new consensus achieved. "Gay is good" is not the result of a search for knowledge; it is the creation of knowledge through the evolution of discourse.

Chapter 20

Troy Perry: Gay Advocate

David J. Robinson

Twelve persons gathered at a house in Huntington Park, California, on October 6, 1968, for the first service of what was to become Metropolitan Community Church (MCC). The service was conducted by a Pentecostal minister, the Rev. Troy Perry, returning after several years to a role he had not played since he had been removed from his Church of God pastorate because he was homosexual. Of the twelve, nine were already known to the minister and three were strangers, attracted by an advertisement in a gay newspaper.[1]

A year later those attending Sunday services at MCC filled the 800-seat theater in which they met, and on November 16, 1969, Troy Perry held his first outdoor, daylight gay liberation march and rally, which attracted, by my count, nearly two hundred persons.

By 1979 the Universal Fellowship of Metropolitan Community Churches was a denomination, numbering 121 meeting groups (chartered churches, missions, and study groups) in thirty-one states and seven nations.[2] And when Perry, as moderator of the Universal Fellowship, spoke at a national gay liberation rally in Washington on October 14, 1979, he faced a crowd that was announced from the platform to include 250,000.[3]

Although Perry has not done it alone, he has undoubtedly been responsible for an important current in the stream of gay emergence. The history of MCC is roughly contemporary with that of the emergence, which first gained national prominence in the Stonewall riots during the summer of 1969. The growth of the church through its first decade was undoubtedly facilitated by the relatively liberal social climate of the 1970s, but the church also contributed to the movement and to this social climate, and both the legal status and the generally perceived social status of homosexual Americans have been profoundly improved.

Some of Perry's success as a leader in the movement can be attributed to the rhetorical strategies of his presentations immediately before and during these rallies, specifically at the November 9 and 16, 1969, Sunday services of MCC; at the Los Angeles rally of November 16, 1969; at the "free concert" held in the Sylvan Theatre in Washington on the evening of October 13, 1979; and at the Washington Monument rally held the following day. I and my wife were observers/participants at each of these events. Our two small children also attended the 1969 rally, much to the surprise of some onlookers and participants. On each occasion a tape recorder captured Perry's speeches and transcriptions of these events became the basis of a dissertation.[4] While such an approach can yield only specific data, and while another speaker in the same circumstances, using Perry's own words, might experience sharply different results, the study of a successful speaker yields inferences that may contribute to the development of a gay rhetoric.

Gays are not the only stigmatized minority that seeks to emerge from the closet into the daylight of respectability; similar feelings are shared by ex-convicts, discharged mental patients, and recovered alcoholics. Homosexuals are no more likely—or able—to change what they are than are these other people to change what they have been; thus gay rhetoric is a rhetoric of stigma.[5]

Occasions and Settings

In 1969 the California penal code still identified specific sexual acts (oral and anal copulation) as felonies per se, without reference to the gender(s) or marital status of the participants. Apparently, the laws were never enforced against heterosexuals. The felony status of the offenses made it an extremely grave matter for a homosexual to be charged with committing such an act. At best, a person so charged could usually hope only for a reduction of the charge to a misdemeanor such as loitering (cruising) or solicitation (asking). Conviction on even these reduced charges meant mandatory lifetime registration as a sex offender, together with the revocation of any public license the convict might hold, whether it be a barber's license or a teacher's certificate. An ad hoc group called the Committee for Homosexual Law Reform was created to press for legislative relief. Perry was a member of this committee, as were several prominent heterosexual clergymen. The committee laid plans for a rally to be held on the steps of Los Angeles' California State Building. Perry was to be both master of ceremonies and principal speaker.

Never before had a rally like this taken place in Los Angeles, at least not in the daylight. There was no reservoir of experience to aid the committee in planning for the public response to such a demonstration. Accordingly, on two successive Sundays Perry made the forthcoming rally the focal point of his sermons and his pastoral remarks, in an attempt to recruit participants.

The rally itself was essentially uneventful. The demonstrators gathered at Los Angeles' Old Plaza, formed a narrow procession, and walked quietly on the sidewalk (no parade permit had been obtained) the few blocks to the civic center and the state building. The rally was held on the First Street steps of the building, opposite the Los Angeles *Times* building. A few folding chairs had been set up at the top of the broad stairs, together with a public address system. As master of ceremonies, Perry, who had led the march, introduced a rather lengthy succession of speakers. When it came his turn to speak he stepped back to be introduced by his secretary.

By contrast, the 1979 march in Washington was approached rather fearlessly by its organizers, most of whom were lesbian activists. The Sylvan Theatre, site of the "free concert," is an outdoor amphitheater in the park adjacent to the Washington Monument. Although there are no seats for the audience, which traditionally spreads blankets on the grass, the stage has theatrical lighting and sound-amplification capabilities. Attendance at the concert was estimated at 10,000. Gay comedienne Robin Tyler served as both producer and mistress of ceremonies. The concert consisted of individual appearances by gay nightclub entertainers, recording artists, and personalities, including Perry. Also appearing were a gay men's chorus and an all-gay marching band, both from Los Angeles. The night was chilly, the grass was wet from recent rains, and most of the entertainers and personalities were careful to keep their performances and speeches brief.

The next day the marchers stepped off at noon from their forming grounds on the mall below the Capitol and proceeded along Pennsylvania and Constitution avenues, around the Ellipse, stopping at the rally site, west of the Washington Monument. A temporary stage had been erected that was equipped with a powerful public address system. The format was typical of such events and included a series of entertainers and speakers. Because the crowd was unexpectedly large, the march took a longer time to complete than had been anticipated. Although the start of the rally was delayed approximately an hour, marchers continued to pour into the grounds for another half-hour after it had begun. Once again, Perry was introduced by Robin Tyler.

The Audiences

When people gather to declare that their closets are now open (whatever the nature of these closets), a certain paradox ensues. The message of liberated emergence is directed at the general public, but the general public is seldom there to hear it. When Martin Luther King, Jr. spoke of his dream in 1963, his large audience probably included few militant segregationists and not many neutrals. Although the MCC congregation includes some heterosexuals, the majority of those attending MCC services are gay. It was a Sunday afternoon when Perry led his marchers through downtown Los Angeles, and the streets were all but deserted. A week earlier Perry had assured his congregation that this would be the case. Ten years later thousands of banners, placards, and posters were displayed along the line of the Washington march; only a handful urged the marchers to repent. Most of the spectators were actually supporters. The general public wasn't there, because it usually learns of such rhetorical outpourings only after the fact and only second-hand. While speakers at such events occasionally address the outside world, it is recognized by those present that they speak only in a form of apostrophe.

In 1969 the challenge of attracting and rallying a gay audience was particularly difficult—a least for the first time. Unlike blacks, whose principal stigma is visible, most gays are reasonably capable of disguising their minority status. Any visible commitment to the movement is a form of coming out, an unnecessary and potentially embarrassing display of a status that the heterosexuals who stand in judgment (outsiders who stand in judgment always seem to be heterosexual) may view as criminality, as a moral shortcoming, as mental illness, or as a combination of these. Whereas a Martin Luther King must persuade potential followers that they have rights, that their rights are being infringed on, and that they should do something about it, the gay liberation advocate must additionally—before even getting to the real business at hand—persuade followers to reveal, more or less publicly, what they have been anxious to hide. This suggests that the speechmaking which takes place in pre-rally sessions is at least as important as that which takes place during the rally.

If proof of such reticence to be seen were necessary, it was quite apparent in the Los Angeles march. As the procession of rallyists made its way along the sidewalk on the west side of the street, another procession of sorts paralleled its movement on the east side. The second group, numbering about twenty, did not march in formation, but drifted casually along the boulevard, carefully avoiding eye contact with the marchers and with one another. When the crowd formed for the rally, most of the "second procession" remained across the street; a few circled the block repeatedly, presumably so they would not be identified with the rally. I recognized several of the bystanders as regular attendees at MCC.

Timidity was not the only force disposing Perry's followers to nonattendance at the rally. Within the gay majority of MCC were those who wanted the church to be devoted exclusively to religious causes, and before another year had passed Perry faced a special meeting of the church, called to challenge his policy of public demonstrations. Perry won the vote of confidence taken at this meeting by an overwhelming margin,[6] but the minority voices had been heard. Perry had heard them before. During the MCC service on November 16, 1969, he observed:

> People have said, "Reverend Perry, we love you. You're our pastor. But we don't think you ought to be out marching or holding rallies of this sort," and I appreciate that concern. But I feel like when MCC was started a long time ago, this church was going to be different. It would be awfully easy for me to sit back and draw my salary each month, and preach to you once on Sunday, and counsel with you in my home, and attend meetings. But I feel like I have to do more. I feel like—some of you, I know, can't make the stands, and I don't—I don't argue with you. I say "God bless you." I know. I have teachers in this church; I have people with security clearances; I have people who are executives of companies, and it's just impossible for them to face the T.V. cameras. And I respect you for that. I do expect you to pray for your pastor, though. I feel like there are some things I must do. I'll promise you this, though: I'll never bring a reproach on this church. I will only do those things that are right, aboveboard, and out in the open.

In the decade between the two rallies the nature of the gay audience changed somewhat. In 1979 the free concert—the meeting intended to stir up enthusiasm for the rally—was held outdoors, in public view, and Perry spoke with confidence when he assured a noisy, delighted audience that

> next year on Gay Pride Sunday we're going to have a National Come Out Day when we come out to everyone all over this country. If we haven't come out to our parents, we're going to come out to them. And when we finish coming out to our brothers and our sisters, then we're going to come out, if we need to, to our employers. Then we're going to pick up the telephone and call four people at random [applause and laughter] in the cities we live in. We're going to say, "guess who this is." We're not going to be invisible any more!

The Speaker

Troy Perry is a Pentecostal preacher from the South. It is unlikely anyone hearing him for the first time would miss this fact. Born in Tallahassee in 1940, educated in the public schools of Florida and Alabama, he retains the sound of his homeland. His postsecondary education in a Bible college near Chicago did not impair his southern sound. The voice is tenor in range, with more than a hint of southern nasality, and has a tendency to hoarseness. Within the confines of most churches he hardly needs the assistance of a microphone; he shouts, and his voice often fails him toward the end of a lengthy speech. Impromptu station-platform rallies on the trip from Los Angeles to Washington had all but robbed him of his voice at the 1979 rally.

More noticeable than his accent or vocal shortcomings is his difficulty with conventional American English. Occasionally, he becomes ensnarled in verbiage:

> Finally the subject came up about what happens if some hoodlums come in and jump on the crowd, and finally another fellow said, "Well, the real test will come when Reverend Perry's leading this march, if we all step back if there's somebody jumps on there, beating him up, if we all sit down and don't do anything."[7]

> We learned immediately that we had a lot of friends on board when Robin [Tyler] and I were getting in our compartment and all at once someone came up, and they discovered that there were these homosexual males and lesbians on this train, and this one man spoke up to this porter and he told him, he said, "We want to be in another area. We want to be in a place where we won't be bothered." And the porter spoke up and said, "Listen Mary, if you don't like our train, get off of it."[8]

Perry does not always shout. When speaking before a small group or in a television studio for one of his innumerable interviews or talk-show appearances, the voice becomes more modulated, the articulation more precise, the grammar less awkward, but he never seems to be entirely comfortable with the cadences of General American.

Perry's idiosyncrasies of speech tend to give him the image of a poorly educated Southern preacher. However, repeated exposures to his preaching suggest that Perry's country-boy image is not entirely accidental. Although he has only a Bible-college background, he is surrounded by well-educated colleagues; he cannot escape their help and direction.

MCC is not the first gay church; the Church of the Beloved Disciple, in New York, is older. According to gay journalist Jim Kepner, there have been a number of short-lived attempts to develop such organizations, but these churches have typically been liturgical in their emphasis, have had "a surplus of archbishops and a shortage of members," in short, have been exercises in "ecclesiastical high drag."[9]

By contrast, Perry's approach to preaching is similar to that of thousands of Fundamentalist or Pentecostal preachers throughout the Bible Belt. It is in the style of the full-gospel radio broadcasts that grace the Southern airways on a Sunday afternoon. It is inelegant and rather inefficient. But in spite of or perhaps because of his stylistic character, Americans can perceive Troy Perry as sincere. At first, Perry's success seemed paradoxical, particularly in Hollywood, with its traditional image of homosexual hairdressers, interior decorators, and dancers. But just as most homosexuals originally came from heterosexual households, many of the sophisticates of Hollywood originally came from rural mid-America. If they want to, they can relate to him.

Persuasive Appeals

Perry's rhetorical approach is rooted in his understanding of homosexuality and homosexuals. Because he is gay, it is not surprising that women do not constitute a major part of this understanding. To be sure, he consistently refers to his "gay brothers and sisters," he is publicly respectful of lesbians, and MCC has a substantial number of female clergy and staff members. But the illustrations he develops and the personifications of gays in which he indulges (for instance, the "listen, Mary" story quoted above) characteristically depict males. Further, he apparently holds a rather traditional view of homosexual males as effeminate, ineffectual, and silly. In the pulpit he occasionally lapses into that brittle, cutting conversational mode that some gays resentfully call "bar talk." In bar talk the humor is essentially self-denigrating; gays are usually the objects of their own jokes. But many gay males engage in it; it is their language. Paradoxically, Perry himself does not impress the observer as being effeminate, ineffectual, or silly himself. He does not need to speak bar talk.

But if he insults gays by seeing them as silly, he redeems himself by picturing them also as being subject to normal human motivations and as having great latent effectual power. In Perry's view, the heterosexual world typically sees gay males in much the same way but does not suspect (or underestimates) the latent power. Perry delights at the spectacle of heterosexuals plunged into consternation by the discovery that gays are not afraid of straights and are willing to cause embarrassment and to challenge their persecutors directly. God does not discriminate against gays either, but holds them to be at least the equals of straights. The paradoxical characteristics of Perry's rhetorical stance are examined more closely below, through detailed description of his speechmaking.

November 1969

Troy Perry's approach to speechmaking is a surprise only if one can be surprised by conventionality. If his style and delivery are those of a Southern full-gospel preacher, his invention, as a whole, confirms the impression.

The Sunday services that I attended at MCC commenced with a song service conducted by the minister of music. The sound was more resonant than heard in most churches, because about nine out of ten singers were male. No distinctively homosexual symbolism was visible. The shape of a cross was projected in strong light on the theater's dark curtain. A small cloth-draped altar positioned in front of the stage held communion chalices, a plate of wafers, candlesticks, and a massive silver cross. Perry wore a black cassock, white surplice, and black liturgical stole. A large silver cross hung from his neck.

I knew that I was not starting another Pentecostal church. I was starting a church that would be truly ecumenical. I had asked the religious backgrounds of those first twelve. They were Catholic, Episcopal, and various Protestant sects. I fervently sought to serve a really broad spectrum of our population. It would have to be a church that most could understandably and easily identify with, and accept it as not being unusual or odd. It seemed to me that it should be traditional, almost like those they attended in childhood, or not too different from that. . . .

At the start I wanted everyone to relate to me as their pastor. Some had trouble doing this because I wasn't wearing a Roman collar, or wearing robes. I talked to those from the more informal sects about this, and they said, "Well, it's not going to bother us. You're still going to be Troy, and no matter what you wear, that's not going to change your preaching." Some said, "As long as it doesn't change your preaching style, or your message, we're for it." So I went out and bought full pulpit attire to help some of my flock relate better. It did help, and it's never hurt anybody. The important thing is that they feel the spirit of the Lord. What I wear doesn't stop them.[10]

An indication Perry correctly assessed his audience's needs might be seen in the tendency of many in the congregation to join the choir in singing choral responses, "amens," and the like, since they had been active in church choirs before and had memorized the harmonies of standard choral music.

As Perry lunged to the pulpit he shouted, "If you love the Lord this morning, will you say 'Amen!' " The congregation responded instantly and vigorously. Perry carried a small pack of file cards, apparently prepared by ushers and greeters, and announced visitors by name. He is a practitioner of the "How many of you here are originally from Ohio?" method of conducting church services, and would interrupt a stream of discourse to ask, "Wonder if someone would like to say something for the Lord right quick." The testimony always came forth quickly. Aimee Semple McPherson used the same techniques during the 1920s.[11]

Nearly all the sights and sounds of the MCC service are conventional and homelike to the observer, if that observer has had experience in Christian churches in America. Perry remains true to his original dedication to the gospel. *Newsweek* misstated the nature of MCC in titling a 1970 article "The Homosexual Church."[12] The *Los Angeles Times* came closer to the truth when it referred to MCC as a "Church for Homosexuals."[13]

In the November 9, 1969 service, Perry introduced a typical "gays are silly" theme.

We do want you to remember they're having the brunch today, if you purchased tickets. I saw them today and I couldn't believe—they had silverware and chandeliers—they're making the Parsonage look like the Ritz. And somehow that neighborhood—I don't know.

In the same service Perry gave an excellent example of "heterosexual consternation." At the time MCC was attempting to purchase a church building in Los Angeles that was being sold by its congregation. Perry reported to MCC that the negotiations had not been successful. The governing body of the other church had not even been willing to talk with them. MCC negotiators had been able to establish dialogue only by offering to bring the MCC congregation to attend services with the other church, then inviting the press to witness the unusual display of tolerance. "Well, when their church group heard this, why of course they decided to talk to us right then and there."

The sermon on November 9 was clearly intended to allay the fears of Perry's followers as they uneasily contemplated the following week's rally. It commenced with an entertaining narrative of several boyhood experiences in which he had been afraid; then a narrative of a meeting held the previous week, in which the rally planners had expressed their fears of violence and even of being recognized. Perry told the congregation about some of the placards being prepared for the rally: "The Lord Is My Shepherd, and He Knows I'm Gay" (which Perry later adopted as the title of his autobiography) and "I'm Not Afraid Any More" (which became the motif of the sermon). Then he related two religious stories: the story of Nehemiah (whom Perry incorrectly identified by another name), who spoke for Israel in telling an oppressing government that Israel was no longer afraid, and who subsequently helped expel the oppressors, and a tear-jerking story of Foursquare missionaries dying unafraid at the hands of Chinese Communists:

> The mother cried out and she says, "Quick, quick," she says, "shoot me—I'm not afraid any more," she says, "I'm willing. I'm looking to my God, who is the author and finisher of my fate."
>
> Saints, let me tell you, don't be afraid any more. Stand on your feet and know that God is God and you're His child.

And the prayer followed:

> We're thankful, O Lord, because we're not afraid any more. We know if we have perfect love in you, we don't have to be afraid any more. . . . When the enemy stands at the door, we won't be afraid because we know you are holding us in your hands.

And to the audience:

> If you're not afraid any more, would you say "Amen"?

They said it.

Further evidence of Perry's image of homosexuals as having normal, conventional motive-susceptibilities was found in the conclusion of the November 9 service, in the form of a singularly ecumenical communion service in which the communicants came forward to form a line across the front of the auditorium (approximately where an altar rail would be in a conventional Christian church). The clergy moved along the line, placing a wafer on the tongue of each communicant and letting each sip from the chalice. Following communion, an adult and an infant were baptized. Although there were numerous baptisms at MCC during the period of the study, few involved infants. Perry also performed marriage ceremonies that, except for the gender of the participants, would not readily be distinguished from other Protestant weddings.

Perry was not afraid to come to grips with the less religious aspects of the gay life-style. The MCC choir rehearsed on Sunday morning, "so if you don't do missionary work too late on Saturday nights . . ." The rest of the sentence is lost in general laughter. To Perry, salvation is a matter of faith and repentance, even for homosexuals.

The themes of gay silliness, susceptibility to conventional persuasion, and latent power emerge repeatedly in Perry's speechmaking. After making his rather eloquent "I feel like I have to do more" statement on November 16, he gently teased the males in his congregation: "So get out those false mustaches, those dark glasses and come down. We'll see you down that way. God bless you." Later he referred to the difficulties the deacons were having as they attempted to carry out a traditional visitation campaign, concluding with a request that members give their church "your *real* names and addresses!"

The heterosexual consternation theme also emerged on November 16 at MCC. This time it was in a story that (if it was intended to be believed literally) had a functionary of the Los Angeles Park Department, which owned the property at the Old Plaza on which the march was to assemble, dropping the telephone when she learned what kind of people were seeking a use permit. But the story turned somewhat bitter as Perry reported he had been asked to call back the next day, which turned out to be Saturday, when the department was closed, and the telephone rang unanswered. They never obtained the permit, so the actual formation took place on the sidewalk in front of the Old Plaza Church, an ancient Spanish mission that currently served a Chicano Catholic parish. Perry later stated that some of the (presumably heterosexual) parishioners were puzzled by the sight of a young man in liturgical garb assembling and leading a large band of rather unconventional-looking people. Another instance of consternation.[14]

If one had expected brilliant oratory at the Los Angeles rally, Perry's remarks would have been a disappointment. He delivered a totally conventional rally speech. But for its specific references, an unsuspecting bystander might have mistaken the speech for something from the women's movement or an antiwar rally. A few sentence fragments from the transcription tell the story adequately:

> They said it couldn't be done . . . they won't let people see their faces . . . you've made a liar out of some people . . . we're not afraid any more . . . I've prayed to my God and I have the assurance some things are going to happen . . . we've walked a bit, now let's run a while . . . let's keep going . . . look around and be proud . . . you have twenty million brothers and sisters . . . our day is coming . . . write your congressman . . . tell him you're a citizen . . . can you say "Amen"?

October 1979

In Washington, Perry spoke only briefly. When he appeared at the free concert, 10,000 persons struggled painfully to their feet to give him a standing ovation. He still wears a clerical collar, his black hair is streaked with gray, and he is thirty-nine. The church is successful. The movement recognizes Troy Perry as a founding father.

The delivery has not changed significantly. The language is still awkward, and the Southern accent still pronounced. He remains a Pentecostal preacher, as he was ordained.

He tells several stories about the train ride from Los Angeles to Washington. He used to threaten to send President Carter and Miss Lillian back to Plains, Georgia, unless. . . . The cadences of his speech are reminiscent of other speeches that have been heard on the mall:

> We're going back to Mississippi, we're going back to Alabama, we're going back to Utah, we're going back to Nevada. We're going back to the states that haven't changed their laws and say, "We're never, ever going away again. We're here to stay, and we're going to have our rights, too, just like everybody else."

Facing the mammoth crowd on Sunday afternoon, Perry the preacher reminded his audience that Anita Bryant claimed to have talked with God. But twelve MCC churches have been "arsoned and burned to the ground." This time the apostrophe is not to the whole heterosexual world: "People who claim the name of God! Shame on you, you hypocrites! Let me tell you now, you don't know God. You couldn't possibly know God!"

This speech was just another in a long series of rally speeches. But Troy Perry is Troy Perry, and he closed humorously, calling attention again to gay foibles and heterosexual consternation: "They didn't know what to do when they saw demonstrators throwing Molotov cocktails and running away in their Gucci shoes. . . . They may talk about limp wrists in America, but these are the strongest wrists in the world!"

If Troy Perry really owns any rhetorical magic, it would seem to consist of a combination of genuine Christian ministerial zeal, a good sense of conventional civil rights advocacy, and a usefully accurate understanding of the rhetorical susceptibilities of many gay men. Although he displays less understanding of lesbians, he knows what he has to do to keep their support, and he does it. Overall, he holds a gently humorous view of the frailties of homosexuals, yet he is aware of the latent strength that underlies their self-denigrating bar talk. But perhaps his greatest rhetorical asset is his recognition of the straight world's inability to deal with the combination of Molotov cocktails and Gucci shoes.

Chapter 21

Lesbianfeminist Rhetoric as a Social Movement

Vicki Nogle

When I first publicly examined the impact of lesbianfeminist rhetoric in 1979,[1] the "impact" of lesbianfeminist rhetoric was an organizing technique, which allowed me to cover a lot of ground in a short amount of time. I touched the "impact" on the lesbianfeminist social movement evolving, on the unique rhetorical situations exemplified in the rhetoric, on the strategies operating in response to those situations, and finally, on the "impact" of lesbianfeminist rhetoric on the lives of wimmin involved/absorbed in this rhetoric. I want to address these same issues in this essay; but I want to do so from the perspective of a movement study. Not only because I *believe* that a lesbianfeminist movement is in progress (a position I have but recently become comfortable with), not only because it provides another way of coming to terms with what is happening in the rhetoric, but also because such a perspective provides a framework for discussing the unique characteristics of this movement that provide insight and greater understanding of social movements in general.

The Representative Anecdote of the Lesbianfeminist Movement

Leland Griffin's discussion of the "inception period of a movement" provides a point of departure. He notes that "movements begin when some pivotal individual or group—suffering attitudes of alienation in a given social system, and drawn (consciously or unconsciously) by the impious dream of a mythic order—enacts, gives voice to, a *No.*"[2] Griffin argues that a movement's initial "no" (which he calls a "representative anecdote" for purposes of analysis) serves both to announce a stand, "a standing together; an *understanding*,"[3] and to "embody, implicitly or explicitly, the key terms and equations of the movement." These terms and equations "identify *what equals what, what opposes what, what follows what.*"[4]

The article "The Woman-Identified Woman," by Radicalesbians, functioned as the initial "no" for the lesbianfeminist movement. The article first appeared in *Notes from the Third Year,* in 1971. In analyzing a social movement, hindsight is the only means available for determining which document functioned as the initial "no" for the movement. My position that "The Woman-Identified Woman" functioned as the "representative anecdote" for the lesbianfeminist movement is supported two ways—by tracing direct references to this article in lesbianfeminist rhetoric, and by tracing the "understanding" embodied in this article through lesbianfeminist rhetoric.

"The Woman-Identified Woman" has been reprinted three times in its entirety. It is included in two anthologies, *Out of the Closets: Voices of Gay Liberation* and *Radical Feminism.*[5] Copies of it are available from KNOW, Inc., located in Pittsburgh.[6] The adjectives with which the rhetoric of lesbianism and/or feminism describe this article point to its influence in the years since it was first published. Sidney Abbott and Barbara Love describe it as "the important Radicalesbian position paper."[7] Del Martin and Phyllis Lyon include it as one of the " 'classics' of the underground" on the subject of lesbianism as a political statement.[8] *The New Woman's Survival Sourcebook* terms it a "revolutionary tract."[9] Jane Rule uses the phrase "by now much-quoted" to describe this document.[10] And finally, Jeanne Córdova calls it "that now famous radical lesbian document."[11]

Numerous citations within current literature alone are not enough to establish "The Woman-Identified Woman" as the representative anecdote for the lesbianfeminist movement. That this document embodies the "understanding," the key terms and equations, and the "mythic order" of the lesbianfeminst movement supports its role in the inception of this movement. Woman-identified woman is a central term in lesbianfeminist rhetoric, and has come to symbolize wimmin's primary commitment to ourselves as wimmin.

The appearance of woman-identified woman in lesbianfeminist rhetoric takes numerous forms. Rita Mae Brown has explored the practical application of lesbianfeminist theory in wimmin's lives. In her article "Living with Other Women" she discusses "women-identified collectives" as a means of implementing the lesbianfeminist movement's "mythic order":

> The women who wrote "Woman-Identified Woman" and the women who have come to understand it are in a transition period. Those of us who believe in this concept must begin to build collectives where women are committed to other women on all levels—emotional, physical, economic and political. Monogamy can be cast aside, no one will "belong" to another.

> Instead of being shut off from each other in overpriced cubicles we can be together, sharing the shitwork as well as the highs. Together we can go through the pain and liberation of curing the diseases we have all contracted in the world of male dominance, imperialism and death. Women-identified collectives are nothing less than the next step towards a Women's Revolution.[12]

Charlotte Bunch, after explaining the "woman-identified woman," turns to the political implications of lesbianfeminist theory:

> Woman-identified Lesbianism is, then, more than a sexual preference, it is a political choice. It is political because relationships between men and women are essentially political, they involve power and dominance. Since the lesbian rejects that relationship and chooses women, she defies the established political system.[13]

From a political perspective, Bunch articulates the lesbianfeminist's "understanding"of the necessity of working within her own movement:

> Lesbians must form our own political movement in order to grow. Changes which will have more than token effects on our lives will be led by woman-identified Lesbians who understand the nature of our oppression and are therefore in a position to end it.[14]

Some lesbianfeminists have even expanded their "understanding" into a realm that, at first glance, looks like it's *outside* the lesbianfeminist movement. Córdova illustrates this movement in her self-definition:

> I now define myself as a lesbian separatist. I define myself as a lesbian, rather than lesbian-feminist, in the sense and with the belief that lesbianism is the state of total woman-identification, in the sense that lesbianism is the complete realization of sisterhood among women, in the sense that lesbianism is the bonding principle between women.[15]

Even though she switches from lesbianfeminist to lesbian separatist, the key term woman-identification forms the basis of her self-definition.

In these instances woman-identified woman becomes the key term. To show that in this movement, as in all social movements, key terms and equations undergo change as they become internalized by the movement's members is a complex process. Key terms provide us guideposts in recognizing rhetoric that belongs to a movement. The danger lies in allowing them to act as blinders, and refusing to see the expansion of the key terms as they reappear in the movement's rhetoric. If we fail to see the expansion, we lose a sense of what's happening within a movement as it interacts with its countermovements and/or as its members interact with one another.

I perceive the lesbianfeminist movement to be in a bonding stage. Its vision was embodied in "The Woman-Identified Woman," published in 1971. Since then a bonding process has been occurring, as its members internalize the understanding of this movment and put their input back into the movement. This process propels the movement in enacting its mythic order through its rhetoric. Before discussing its content and its manifestations in lesbianfeminist rhetoric, I want to summarize the social forces operating that culminated in this document, and that simultaneously gave birth to the lesbianfeminist movement.

The Social Context of the Lesbianfeminist Movement

The lesbianfeminist movement is a unique social movement in that it emerged out of two social movements already in progress in the early seventies: the women's liberation movement and the gay liberation movement. While it is impossible to pinpoint the exact moment the movement began, Rita Mae Brown has described its inception:

> The early movement (referring to the Women's Liberation Movement) blatantly discriminated against the lesbian, in some cases expelling women who were lesbians. A few women refused to be repulsed. At the same time other old gay women ("old" not referring to age but to political awareness) helped found and shape the Gay Liberation Movement. As the lesbians in Women's Liberation became increasingly dissatisfied over their treatment at the hands of heterosexual women, the lesbians in Gay Liberation became dissatisfied with their treatment at the hands of homosexual men. These women came together and tried to define what had been their lives and what their lives were now becoming due to some heavy changes in consciousness. Their effort became the paper "The Woman-Identified Woman."[16]

An awareness of the social forces coming together from which the lesbianfeminist movement emerged is essential to understanding the rhetoric propelling this movement. For the situation in the early seventies was a coming together of two *mutually exclusive* social movements; neither one of which, alone, could address satisfactorily the oppression inherent in the lesbianfeminist's social reality.

The women's liberation movement focused on the oppression the lesbianfeminist encountered by being a "woman in a man's world." Its rhetoric identified the sexism operating in the dominant, patriarchal social order. The mythic order embodied in the rhetoric was a vision in which wimmin were *incorporated* into the dominant social order, as equal participants. The rhetoric manifests this vision by demanding for wimmin equal access to educational opportunities, equal pay, and equal responsibilities in the home (childrearing and domestic chores). Disappointingly for the lesbianfeminist, the mythic order of the women's liberation movement continued to envision a woman's primary relationship as being with a man. For the lesbianfeminist, whose primary relationships are with *wimmin,* this integral part of the women's liberation vision does not account for a vital part of her social reality, loving other wimmin.

The gay liberation movement's vision centered around a reality the women's liberation movement excluded—wimmin's primary relationships with other wimmin. Its rhetoric identified the homophobia operating in the dominant, heterosexist social order. Its mythic order embodied a vision that would *expand* the dominant social order to include homosexuality. It envisioned an expanded social order in which men could relate sexually to men, and wimmin to wimmin, *within* the hierarchical structure of the dominant social order. Since this view sought a horizontal expansion of the dominant social order, the lesbianfeminist could not buy into the mythic order of this movement. For while it would sanction her loving other wimmin, it would maintain her second-class citizen status as a womyn, thus continuing to deny her full participation in society.

Birth in the coming together of two mutually exclusive social movements has had ramifications on the form and direction of the lesbianfeminist movement. The movement exists in a dialectical relationship between the women's liberation movement and the gay liberation movement. It is at once a part of, and separate from, each. It is not enough to state that the lesbianfeminist movement overlaps the women's liberation movement in its struggle against sexism, and overlaps the gay liberation movement in its struggle against homophobia. The relationship is more complex. Where there is identification, there is division, and the lesbianfeminist movement continually defines itself in terms of what each of these two mutually exclusive movements is not, as well as the characteristics shared with each. Failure to maintain this dialectical relationship with the women's liberation movement and the gay liberation movement would be absorption of the lesbianfeminist movement into one of them. Lesbianfeminist rhetoric manifests this dialectical relationship.

Social Order in "Woman-Identified Woman"

The inception of the lesbianfeminist movement with its document, "The Woman-Identified Woman," embodies not only a resounding "no" to the dominant social order, but to the mythic orders contained within the women's liberation movement and the gay liberation movement as well. The understanding embodied in this document begins with naming their alienation from the dominant social order: "It should first be understood that lesbianism, like male homosexuality, is a category of behavior possible only in a *sexist society* characterized by *rigid sex roles and dominated by male supremacy*" (emphasis added).[17] Shortly thereafter the article discusses homosexuality specifically:

> Homosexuality is a by-product of a particular way of setting up roles (or approved patterns of behavior) on the basis of sex; as such it is an inauthentic (not consonant with "reality") category. *In a society in which men do not oppress women,* and sexual expression is allowed to follow feelings, the categories of homosexuality and heterosexuality would disappear.[18]

These two excerpts are formed in the dialectical relationship operating between the lesbianfeminist movement and the gay liberation movement. That the category "homosexuality" emerges from rigid sex roles set up on the basis of sex by the dominant social order reveals an identification with the gay liberation movement. For both movements share the alienation of homosexuality as a category of behavior designating a failure to function within the prescribed roles of heterosexuality. Yet notice the mythic order identified immediately following the statement of shared alienations: "In a society in which men do not oppress women . . ." Implicit in this vision is the realization that for the lesbianfeminist, it is not enough that "sexual expression is allowed to follow feelings" (the mythic order embodied in gay liberation rhetoric, what I termed the horizontal expansion of the dominant social order). The vision must also include an end to male control. These two elements, comprising identification and division with the gay liberation movement, constitute the mythic order of the lesbianfeminist movement.

That there is not complete identification with gay liberation is reinforced explicitly in the next paragraph of the article. It begins, "But lesbianism is also different from male homosexuality, and serves a different function in society."[19] Later in the paragraph homosexuality is subsumed as an indication of the contempt of the dominant, patriarchal social order for wimmin: "The grudging admiration felt for the tomboy, and queasiness felt around a sissy boy *point to the same thing:* The contempt in which women—or those who play a female role—are held" (emphasis added).[20] The lesbianfeminist rejects the mythic order of the gay liberation movement not because it is inaccurate—the oppression she experiences from being placed in the homosexual category is valid enough—but because the mythic order is incomplete. It does not address her oppression being a womyn in a patriarchal social order.

The dialectical relationship between the lesbianfeminist movement and the women's liberation movement is at once more obvious and more complex. Lesbianfeminist rhetoric manifests the dialectical relationship between these two movements against the backdrop of the dominant patriarchal social order. Interwoven in "The Woman-Identified Woman" is the uncovering of two rhetorical strategies of the dominant patriarchy: using the sexual category "lesbian" to oppress wimmin in maintaining the "female" sexual/social role, and using the sexual category "lesbian" to thwart the women's liberation movement. The article continues by explaining the long tradition of using the label lesbian to control wimmin who were perceived as too independent:

> For in this sexist society, for a woman to be independent means she *can't be* a woman—she must be a dyke. That in itself should tell us where women are at. It says as clearly as can be said: women and person are contradictory terms. For a lesbian is not considered a "real woman." And yet, in popular thinking, there is really only one essential difference between a lesbian and other women; that of sexual orientation—which is to say, when you strip off all the packaging, you must finally realize that the essence of being a "woman" is to get fucked by men.[21]

Having revealed the heterosexual core of the female role, the article then reveals the pervasiveness of control when the patriarchal social order uses the label lesbian to keep wimmin in their place:

> Affixing the label lesbian not only to a woman who aspires to be a person, but also to any situation of real love, real solidarity, real primacy among women, is a primary form of devisiveness among women: it is the condition which keeps women within the confines of the feminine role, and it is the debunking/scare term that keeps women from forming any primary attachments, groups, or associations among ourselves.[22]

The equations contained in these last two excerpts are important in ascertaining "what equals what, what opposes what, what follows what" within the lesbianfeminist movement. The key equation in the lesbian-feminist analysis is the relationship between "woman" and "person." To be a woman in the patriarchal social order means one cannot be an autonomous person, because a woman is defined by her relationship to a man, whatever form the prescribed relationship: girlfriend, wife, mistress, even prostitute. Any straying from the female role, with its implied dependency on a man, i.e., any show of independence as a person, makes a womyn vulnerable to the label lesbian, whether or not she relates sexually to wimmin.

This key equation of the dominant social order—"woman" and "person" are mutually exclusive—marks the dialectical relationship between the lesbianfeminist movement and the women's liberation movement. "The Woman-Identified Woman" reveals the patriarchy's use as a strategy of the label lesbian within the women's liberation movement to keep wimmin within the female role even as they struggle for equality:

> As long as the label "dyke" can be used to frighten a woman into a less militant stand, keep her separate from her sisters, keep her from giving primacy to anything other than men and family—then to that extent she is

> controlled by the male culture. Until women see in each other the *possibility* of a primal commitment which includes sexual love, they will be denying themselves the love and value they readily accord to men, thus affirming their second-class status (emphasis added).[23]

I emphasized "possibility" in the above excerpt because it points to a common misconception about the lesbianfeminist movement, both within the women's liberation movement and the dominant culture: That we want all wimmim to relate sexually to wimmin. The issue is much broader than one's sexuality. In relating to the woman and person analysis, the mythic order of the lesbianfeminist movement embodies a vision of wimmin no longer defining themselves *in terms of men.* This vision opens the possibility of a womyn developing herself as an autonomous person by relating primarily to other wimmin. Until that possibility exists, as long as the essence of their identity is wound up in their relationship to men, wimmin cannot be full participants in society.

The second strategy the lesbianfeminist rhetoric seeks to reveal, the dominant patriarchal social order using the sexual category lesbian to thwart the women's liberation movement, is evident in the lesbianfeminist analysis of this movement:

> As long as male acceptability is primary—both to individual women and to the movement as a whole—the term lesbian will be used effectively against women. Insofar as *women want only more privileges within the system,* they do not want to antagonize male power. They instead seek acceptability for women's liberation, and the most crucial aspect of that acceptability is to deny lesbianism—i.e., to deny any fundamental challenge to the basis of the female.[24]

For the lesbianfeminist there cannot be complete identification with the women's liberation movement not merely because it denies her sexuality, but because of the *implications* of that denial. Denying lesbianism *maintains* the dominant social order's definition of a woman in terms of her relationship to men and thus denies her full autonomy as a person. The identification the lesbianfeminist feels with the women's liberation movement in its struggle for equal participation in the social order is perceived as inadequate as long as this basis of the female role remains unchallenged.

The complexity of the dialectical relationship between the lesbianfeminist movement and the women's liberation movement is further manifested in the women's liberation movement's attempt to come to terms with the issue of lesbianism:

> It should also be said that some younger, more radical women have honestly begun to discuss lesbianism, but so far it has been primarily as a sexual "alternative" to men. This, however, is still giving primacy to men, both

because the idea of relating more completely to women occurs as a negative reaction to men, and because the lesbian relationship is being characterized simply by sex, which is divisive and sexist.[25]

From the lesbianfeminist's perspective, the women's liberation movement has thus far failed to see the broader issue beyond one's sexuality—that the heterosexual core of the female role continues to deny wimmin complete autonomy, because it continues to define a woman in terms of someone else, men, and not in terms of herself as a person.

The mythic order of the lesbianfeminist movement is not that all wimmin relate sexually to wimmin, but

> that women begin disengaging [themselves] from male-defined response patterns. In the privacy of our own psyches, we must cut those cords to the core. For *irrespective* of where our love and sexual energies flow, if we are male-identified in our heads, we cannot realize our autonomy as human beings (emphasis added).[26]

The vision embodied in this movement involves a new sense of self for wimmin, not a mere change in one's sexual activity. For the lesbianfeminist movement, the *means* by which wimmin cease to develop their sense of self from men, through men, and by men, lies with themselves, as wimmin:

> Only women can give to each other a new sense of self. That identity we have to develop with reference to ourselves, and not in relation to men. This consciousness is the revolutionary force from which all else will follow, for ours is an organic revolution.[27]

This is the vision carried through lesbianfeminist rhetoric.

Countermovements

I have presented a lengthy analysis of the article "The Woman-Identified Woman" in order to trace the unique emergence of the lesbianfeminist movement out of two mutually exclusive social movements already in progress. I have tried to show the complex dialectical relationships operating between the lesbianfeminist movement, and the gay and women's liberation movements. These dialectical relationships are important not only in understanding how the lesbianfeminist movement emerged, but also in understanding the development of a countermovement, necessary to any social movement. Griffin states: "The development of a countermovement is vital: for '*it is the bad side that produces the movement which makes history, by providing* a struggle.' "[28] Has a countermovement developed for the lesbianfeminist movement? If so, who comprises it? If not, can it be termed a movement?

The lesbianfeminist movement can add new insights into our understanding of a countermovement. My analysis of the lesbianfeminist movement leads me to the conclusion that we must broaden our conceptualization to include the possibility of a movement moving through several countermovements before it encounters the "one which makes history in the process of enacting its social order," for this is what I see happening within the lesbianfeminist movement.

The gay liberation movement and the women's liberation movement are functioning as countermovements for the lesbianfeminist movement. From the lesbianfeminist perspective, each of these movements still "speaks for the state of Corruption,"[29] the dominant social order, in their effort to change this order. It is shortsighted to conclude that lesbianfeminist rhetoric is an attempt to expand either movement. My analysis of "The Woman-Identified Woman" makes it clear that the lesbianfeminist vision cannot be incorporated into either movement without a total restructuring of it, in essence, a killing of the movement.

Griffin discusses this stage of the lesbianfeminist movement:

> Its second strategy—since attitudes are but beginnings, mere "incipient acts"—is to provoke action. It is a strategy designed to move the converted —through "piety, fear, and the like emotions"—to rise up and cry *No* to the counter-movement (thereby saying *Yes* to the movement).[30]

The lesbianfeminist movement is engaged in a struggle to get its members to say "no" to both the gay and the women's liberation movements, thereby affirming their realization (in the act of saying "no") that only within the boundary of the lesbianfeminist movement can the "state of Corruption," the current patriarchal social order, be eliminated.

Again, the complexity of the lesbianfeminist movement becomes apparent. For clearly, within the gay and the women's liberation movements there is some "no"-saying to the dominant social order. The lesbianfeminist movement, with its dialectical relationships to these two movements, is dealing *indirectly* with the countermovement the dominant social order is developing around both movements. Getting its members to say "no" to the gay and the women's liberation movements will not suddenly create a countermovement from the dominant social order. Such a countermovement has been developing indirectly for the lesbianfeminist movement all along. Getting its members to say "no" to the two movements from which it emerged *will* shift the focus of the struggle from the quasi-cures for the ills perpetuated by the dominant social order to a more direct confrontation with the dominant social order in the struggle to eliminate it.

The lesbianfeminist movement will be doomed if it does not succeed in its second strategy. Failing to win its current struggle with its two countermovements will cost it members for one of two reasons: either its members will buy into one of the countermovements—totally, or its members will attempt to split their time and energies *between* the two mutually exclusive movements. The former will lead members to leave the lesbianfeminist movement. The latter will sap the lesbianfeminist movement's strength by leading members to reject that *only* in this movement can wimmin eliminate the dominant patriarchal social order, with its sexism and homophobia, and only in the realization of the lesbianfeminist vision can wimmin emerge as autonomous human beings.

The struggle with the women's liberation movement will prove the most difficult for the lesbianfeminist movement. For many wimmin, this movement provided their first consciousness of their status within the dominant patriarchal order. It is painful to recognize its boundaries and to realize you have moved beyond them. There is the feeling of wanting to take the movement with you, to incorporate it into the lesbianfeminist movement. This feeling is evident in "The Woman-Identified Woman" in the beginning of the last paragraph of this document: "It is the primacy of women relating to women, of women creating a new consciousness of and with each other, which is at the heart of women's liberation, and the basis for the cultural revolution."[31] But the distinction is clear; the lesbianfeminist movement views itself as the heart of wimmin liberating themselves but not as the heart of the women's liberation movement. And while lesbianfeminist rhetoric reaches out to all wimmin for members, it will say "no" to the women's liberation movement as long as this movement maintains the dominant patriarchy's social/sexual female, no matter how "liberated" she becomes.

Awareness of the Relationship Between Language and Power in the Lesbianfeminist Movement

In addition to its unique emergence, I have observed one additional characteristic of the movement that I want to discuss: its awareness of the means by which social orders are created, maintained, and destroyed. This awareness is evident in the lesbianfeminist's analysis of the dominant patriarchal social order's use of the label lesbian to maintain female roles. But the synonymous relationship between control of language and control in a social order has been articulated directly in lesbianfeminist rhetoric. Charlotte Bunch, for example, voices the connection in her analysis of name-calling: "Labels are not just name-calling. Behind each label is the implicit threat of social, economic, or physical reprisal—the denial of life-supporting systems or even life itself if you step too far out of line."[32] Julia Stanley specifies some specific control strategies the dominant patriarchal social order uses against wimmin:

Within the patriarchy, language is used to deceive, to coerce, to protect those who hold power. Wimmin can't allow the boys to continue to control English (or any other language). We must make English our own, in our way, to serve *our* purposes.[33]

One of the fundamental functions of language is self-definition. Stanley explains:

Naming ourselves; naming our lives; naming our actions. Without language, I am nameless, I am invisible, I am silent. If I refuse language, I refuse myself. Through my language, I define myself to myself: I can "see" myself. My language always goes before me, illuminating my actions; through my language, I create myself, for myself, and for other wimmin.[34]

In the struggle to define ourselves, lesbianfeminists approach language as a double-edged sword—necessary if we are to carve out a language valid to our life experiences, and yet always aware that we begin with the only language available to us. Mary Daly refers to "the contaminated words of our patriarchal false heritage . . . [terms that] are all polluted with patriarchal associations, [and which] function not only as means of expression, but also as mind pollutants."[35] Lesbianfeminists are aware that the words we use to define ourselves may alienate us from other wimmin through the patriarchal meaning of words.

The words lesbian and dyke are illustrative of wimmin evolving their own meanings for words that have been used against them in the past. J.R. Roberts recounts an experience where the old, patriarchal definition of dyke and the new, womyn-based definition of dyke collided:

Although I don't ever recall having used the word *dyke* in the old pejorative sense, I do remember when I first began using *dyke* in a liberated sense. It was late 1973; I had just "come out" via the Lesbian/Feminist Movement. During a conversation with an older Lesbian friend who had come out years earlier without the aid of a movement, I referred to the two of us as *dykes*. Her reaction was equivalent to "Hey, wait a minute! Watch yer mouth!", as if I had uttered some terrible obscenity. She then proceeded to enlighten me as to the older, negative meaning. But, I said, I don't see it that way at all. To me *dyke* is positive; it means a strong, independent Lesbian who can take care of herself. As I continued with the movement, *dyke* took on even stronger political implications than "activist." It signified woman-identified culture, identity, pride and strength—women, alone and together, who lived consciously and deliberately autonomous lives, no longer seeking definitions or approvals according to male values. Soon my older friend also began identifying positively with the word *dyke*.[36]

Transformations like the one described above propel the lesbianfeminist movement as wimmin move beyond patriarchal associations into creating their own meaning, their own social reality, themselves as wimmin.

Part VI

Gay Rights and the Political Campaigns

Chapter 22

Gay Civil Rights and the Roots of Oppression

Sally Miller Gearhart

"No, we don't have any of them on our staff. After all, we work with young people here." "Who cares what they do in bed? They do their work, they're okay with me." "Sure we have some, but they keep a low profile. And anyway, they look very masculine." "I don't want to talk about aberrations. We aren't equipped to help them here." "I've worked with them and I get along fine with them." "We accept all people. There's no bigotry here, even on that subject." "I've never met one, but I'm sure I'd know if I did." "There aren't so many of them. I don't understand all the uproar."

These are the attitudes found among administrators, speaking either formally or informally, about homosexual persons. Implicit in this range are the standard misconceptions, i.e., that homosexuals are all male, stereotypical in behavior, sick, few in number, child-molesters, self-isolating, and are to be defined exclusively by their genital activity.

This essay is the effort of an open lesbian academician (and past administrator) to (1) review the status of gay people's civil rights, showing how these rights have been fought for legislatively, out of what context the U.S. Supreme Court will probably address the question, and what fundamental constitutional issue is actually at stake; (2) suggest that the deeper roots of gay oppression lie in the oppression of women; and (3) explore briefly the role of administrators in the quest for gay rights. As this effort proceeds, I hope myths and stereotypes will begin to fade.

Estimates of the size of the committed homosexual population in this country range from 10 million to 40 million (5 percent to 20 percent), an elusive figure simply because the overwhelming majority of homosexuals do not (and for good reason) affirm this fact in public. Moreover, as Alfred Kinsey's research has shown, same-gender sex acts and "urges" involve a much broader spectrum (among men, 50 percent of the population).[1] In the words of the Rev. Tom Maurer, of the University of Minnesota's Program in Human Sexuality, "If the citizens of the United States were to turn overnight from white or black or brown to shades of *green* according to the amount of sexual experience they have had with members of the same sex, we would all be in for quite a surprise tomorrow morning."[2] Clearly, gay persons are a sizeable minority of U.S. citizenry.

There is nothing in the Constitution nor any national statute that makes homosexuals criminals—or homosexual acts criminal acts. However, there have been, at one time, statutes in every state legislating against specific sexual acts: oral and anal intercourse. For these crimes in those states it has been homosexuals—and among homosexuals, exclusively homosexual men—who have been harassed or arrested, while a vast heterosexual population exercising this same creativity in its intimate communication has not even been aware it is engaging in criminal acts. Walter Barnett, author of *Sexual Freedom and the Constitution,*[3] observes that if the laws against human sexual expression which have been in effect for so many years in California were enforced without bias (that is, not just exclusively in the arrest of gay men), then 98 percent of the state's population would be behind bars. The other 2 percent, he maintains, simply have no imagination.

It is necessary to note here that even gay men are not usually arrested for the sexual acts themselves, but rather for "solicitation in a public place to engage in lewd or dissolute conduct." In California, 85 percent of the bookings of gay men takes place under Section 647(a) of the state penal code, which does not restrict the acts, but the asking of someone to commit these acts. With the January 1976 law change it is now legal in California to indulge in "lewd and dissolute acts" but still illegal to solicit to do so. A number of states passing decriminalization statutes find themselves facing this paradox.

Not only do these state laws make homosexuals (and heterosexuals) into criminals, they have been the basis of the denial of the gay person's civil rights. Until 1961, when Illinois instituted its sex law reform decriminalizing oral and anal intercourse, homosexuals were "unapprehended felons" in every state. (Many heterosexuals were, too, of course.) This gave employers ample excuse for firing gay persons or for not hiring them in the first place; landlords and realtors, banks and insurance companies could refuse housing, financial help, or coverage if clients were suspected of being homosexual. Homosexuality's criminal status drove a whole society further into hiding, generating and perpetuating myths and stereotypes about homosexuals that robbed them of dignity and humanity, to say nothing of their equal rights.

Thanks to some long overdue research on the nature of human sexuality, to some giant strides in law reform in other countries, and to the energy and insights of the women's liberation movement and gay liberation, some consciousness has been raised. By 1975 eight states (Colorado, Connecticut, Delaware, Hawaii, Illinois, Ohio, Oregon, North Dakota) and the District of Columbia had decriminalized the sex acts in question, between consenting adults. Momentum has gathered, and in 1975 alone five states joined the list (Arkansas, California, Maine, New Mexico, Washington). The number of states decriminalizing homosexuality has sharply increased since 1975. Further, a number of cities have passed antidiscrimination ordinances for gay people such as Ann Arbor, Berkeley, Columbus, Detroit, East Lansing, Ithaca, Minneapolis, Palo Alto, San Francisco, Seattle. In March of 1975 Rep. Bella Abzug (D.-NY) introduced legislation to amend the 1964 Civil Rights Act by adding "affectional or sexual preference" to race, religion, and sex as areas of proscription against discrimination. She was backed by the sentiment of a host of national professional organizations that have made policy statements in support of nondiscrimination against homosexuals. A similarly worded bill has been introduced in every session of Congress since 1975.

The battle is also being waged throughout the judicial system, with the testing in courts of the legal sanctions against homosexuality. The Supreme Court, when it finally rules in the case of a gay person, will probably do so on the basis of the Fourteenth Amendment (guaranteeing equal treatment for all citizens) and on the basis of the right to privacy. A person has the right to privacy unless she or he is doing something so threatening to the government that the government is compelled to intervene.

There is nothing in the First Amendment—territory of so many civil rights contests—that directly addresses the matter of privacy. However, when decisions have come down from the high court regarding an individual's right to privacy, the justification has found its ground either (1) in the presumption that privacy is "implicit in the concept of ordered liberty" as guaranteed by the Constitution and thus needs no specific constitutional reference, or (2) in the specification of certain "zones of privacy" in the Constitution, notably the zones of speech (stated in the First Amendment) and of association (implicit in the First Amendment).

Several precedent-setting decisions on the part of the high court have already paved the way for what many gay groups believe will be a ruling for a homosexual person's rights to privacy. *Griswold vs. Connecticut* established any married couple's right under guarantees of privacy to use whatever birth control they wished.[4] In 1969, *Stanley vs. Georgia,* the court ruled that any single citizen had certain rights of privacy, in this case the right of private consumption of a pornography collection.[5] In 1972 *Eisenstadt vs. Baird* established (by precedent of *Griswold* and *Stanley*) that the right of use of birth control had nothing to do with marital status, that unwed persons could use whatever birth control they chose in the privacy of their own bedroom.[6]

It seems only a matter of time before, for instance, a gay Texan or South

Carolinian rides the appellate route up to the nine justices in Washington. The argument is that if two unmarried consenting adults are allowed the privacy of the bedroom, then by the equal protection clause of the Fourteenth Amendment, so a gay citizen will be.

This, then, is the expected judicial route of gay rights. Ironically, this expected route fails to address the real legal basis of gay oppression, for the fundamental violation of the gay person's rights is not in the violation of freedom of speech or in the violation of rights of assembly or association; it is not even in the violation of privacy as "implicit in the concept of ordered liberty." Although it will never be argued from this posture, the violation of the gay person's constitutional rights lies in that very tricky and most volatile part of the First Amendment which would separate church and state. Our legal system, based on British common law, derives from the Magna Carta, a document that draws its precepts and its language out of the Bible and from Judeo-Christian teaching. Sanctions against human sexuality and particularly homosexuality have ridden the patriarchal path from the Bible right into state laws.

But it is not just laws derived from the Judeo-Christian tradition that legislate against gay people; the deeper oppressor is the Judeo-Christian mind-set or value system that is so deeply entrenched in every citizen of the Western world—even in atheists and agnostics. The oppressive function resides in the legislator's *head,* in the judge's *head,* in the psychological marriage of what is *legal* to what is *godly.*

In state after state gay groups have challenged legislators; in state after state the pattern has been the same. First, the legislator explains that he or she votes against decriminalization because homosexuality is sick. The gay group then offers the assurance of the American Psychiatric Association, the ultimate source in the nomenclature of mental illness, which in December 1973, after a long struggle, changed homosexuality from the category of psychiatric disorder to the healthy category of variant.

Confronted with this, the legislator flees to the myths, and if this move were not so tragic it might provide high comedy. In a number of ways—not the least of which is the assumption that homosexuals are exclusively males—the legislator reveals the appalling depths of his or her ignorance: Homosexuals seduce children; they aren't "real men"—invariably revealing that by their "girlish motions" and "the way they talk"; and they are all hairdressers, interior decorators, or ballet dancers. Gay groups present data showing that 97 percent of child molestations are committed by heterosexual men and occur within a family context (fathers, brothers, uncles, stepfathers, grandfathers).[7] They introduce the legislator to homosexual Sgt. Leonard Matlovich who has served three tours of duty in Vietnam, has earned a Bronze Star and a Purple Heart, has an impeccable military record, and in addition to these "proofs" of manhood, has a voice as deep as any male legislator. They then dare him or her to decriminalize homosexuality so the thousands of other "real men" in the military can reveal their true identity. They point to the fact that there in electoral politics with him are avowed homosexual people, for example, Elaine Noble of Massachusetts and Allan Spear of Minnesota (plus hundreds more "in the closet" of whom they know many personally). They remind the legislators that far from being restricted to jobs like hairdressing, homosexuals are represented in every profession, that unbeknownst to them they brush against homosexuals every day.

At this point the legislator offers up a last—and most formidable—protest: "It's a sin." With this, any pretense of separation of church and state vanishes. (Variations are "an abomination unto the Lord," "sodomy," "unnatural," "blasphemous," "not in the order of nature or of creation," and "perverse.") If the legislator is really threatened, he or she thumps the Bible, as in Sacramento, and shouts predictions of hell and damnation against sex law change. If the legislator's successful, a state like Kansas will change its laws to allow oral and anal intercourse but only between members of the opposite sex; homosexuals are still criminals.

In trying to confront the "godly" mind-set itself, gay groups present the legislator with the twelve references in the Bible to homosexuality, and show how highly respected biblical scholars have proved each of them to be a misinterpretation or a mistranslation.[8] These groups refer to the recent public statements in support of gay rights made by a number of mainline Christian denominations, one of which has ordained an openly gay minister. They offer the testimony of the ecumenical National Council of Churches, whose governing board (1975) adopted a resolution supporting nondiscrimination on the basis of affectional preference, claiming the violation of gay civil rights to be immoral. They present the overwhelming evidence of practice itself, the Kinsey reports, Johnson and Masters, the reality that reproduction is not the only objective of sexual expression, that it has not been so for thousands of years—the double standard of sexual behavior standing in stark testimony to that—and that love and affection in something besides the missionary position are part of most sexual expression in the United States.

Resistance on the part of the legislator even to listen to all this evidence, all these arguments, suggests that below the "godly" mind-set there may be yet another, more fundamental motive for the oppression of gay people. Exploration of this motive requires a departure from the arena of rights or constitutionality and a venture into the more speculative realm of theory and analysis.

While it is true that all oppressed groups are victims of the same mind-set, it is also true that gay people and women share a special aspect of struggle. Sex-role socialization and, in "civilized" nations, the tyranny of its partner institution—the nuclear family—are the mechanisms by which both women and gay people are kept in places useful or, at most, tolerable to the dominant culture. Thus the limitations placed on gays and on women are qualitatively different from those placed on other minorities.

To address the question of sex roles is to address not the most immediate, but probably the deepest of human concerns; it is to reach the resting place of Western culture's most profound attitudes and fears, a place deeper even than the Judeo-Christian value system and, in the eyes of many, the very bedrock of this religious tradition itself. One voice from the deep place articulates the reality as the fear on the part of every self-respecting civilized *man* that he will be like a *woman.* But that only partially states the case. Another voice more accurately names the deep reality: woman-hatred, *institutionalized misogyny.*

Institutionalized misogyny is not the hatred of individual men for individual women, not the hatred of individual men for women in general; if these are facts of existence, then they must be identified and dealt with by individual men. Institutionalized misogyny is that social phenomenon which is expressed by women as well as by men and which is nearly as devastating to men as it is to women. It is manifested in two self-perpetuating myths: the myth of the half-person and the myth of male superiority. The myth of the half-person begins when at the birth of the perfectly healthy and potentially whole human child—bisexual, and psychologically androgynous—the genitalia are identified. At that moment every institution in the system goes into high gear to guarantee two things: (1) that both girl and boy children will ultimately be exclusively heterosexual, thus limiting their natural potential; (2) these institutions relentlessly insist that a female child will have *only* certain qualities like intuitiveness, emotionality, and nurturance. She cannot have rationality, aggressiveness, and adventurousness, because these characteristics are exclusive to a male child. Someday these two half-persons will miraculously come together in that sanctified union called heterosexual marriage, and through it will create of their halfnesses one whole person. Millions of Americans every year testify to the illusory nature of the myth; it simply doesn't work. Yet, until recently, the myth has prevailed unchallenged. A man continues to believe he does not have to be emotional because his wife *is* his emotion *for* him. The wife continues to think she doesn't have to be strong because her husband *is* her strength *for* her. And there they are, neurotically dependent on each other for their very life, and victims of the death-clutch syndrome, in which one partner, in either piggyback or full frontal attack, leaps on the other all teeth and fingernails and screams those immoral and immortal words, "I can't live without you!"

The other myth, the myth of male superiority, is a little more obvious. By its light, even the best of women know themselves to be inferior to even the worst of men. The myth of male superiority puts *values* on the qualities attached to women, and these values are always just a little less than those attached to men's qualities. It is noble to be nurturing but better to be adventurous; cute to be subjective but more acceptable to be objective; very quaint to be intuitive but better to be rational.

Through the perpetuation of these myths, society's misogyny becomes increasingly the norm, apparent not only in sexist jokes but in every woman's second-rate social and economic status, her obliteration from history, her media image, her own depleted self-image, the way she laughs, the clothes she wears, the thoughts she thinks—or fails to think, the way she walks—or fails to walk, the words she says—or fails to say, the jobs she has—or fails to have, the jobs she wants—or fails to want. Of that societal disdain each woman has drunk so deeply that a hatred of herself as woman poisons her every thought and action; she becomes her own worst enemy, believing she doesn't want to do self-fulfilling things because she believes she can't do them, and believing she can't do them because she's been so deeply programmed to believe she shouldn't do them. With that societal disdain she has sprinkled her separate prison of isolation and has secured herself from all others; further, this societal disdain of women has steadily fed the fires of competitiveness and corporate capitalism until only now does a woman realize the extent of her complicity and that of other women in the whole planet's pell-mell race to annihilation.

To the extent that the gay man does what only women are supposed to do—love men—and to the extent that he allows himself to touch something more than just the masculine side of himself—his feminine—to that extent, the gay man receives his share of society's misogyny. In fact, to the extent that *any* man refuses to remain a half-person, to the extent that he celebrates his capacity for wholeness within himself, to that extent any man can feel the effects of woman-hatred.

The lesbian—the philogynist, the lover of women—is the antidote to society's woman-hatred. She has somewhere along the way said "no" to the sex role that society has prepared for her. She has said "yes" to her own capacity to be more than what society calls feminine. She has rejected the myth of the half-person, embracing instead the potentiality of her wholeness: her intellect and her energy as well as her nurturance and relational capacity. She has rejected the myth of male superiority, throwing off self-hatred/woman-hatred, and daring to love other women, daring to love herself, a woman. The lesbian is the very *embodiment*—the extreme, the superlative—of women's struggle against sex roles. In the face of ten thousand years of misogyny, the lesbian is the incarnation of the movement among women to love themselves again, to love other women again.

Not all women will discover their lesbianism; nor is it the political line of women's liberation that they must do so. It is true that, however they express it, increasing numbers of women are discovering their philogyny. Moreover, the evidence is accumulating, and lesbians the world over can testify that when two persons of such tremendous sexual and emotional capacity as two women are thrown together in a loving sexual circumstance, the earth does seem to have a tendency to move off its axis. Still, a distinction must be made between sexual experimentation and self-identification as a lesbian. A number of women are "trying sex" with other women these days; that's clearly not lesbianism. Contrarily, a number of women who have identified themselves as lesbians for years have never experienced a sexual relationship with another woman. The lesbian is a woman whose "primary erotic, psychological, emotional and social interest is in a member of her own sex, even though that interest may not be overtly expressed."[9] She cannot be defined by her sexual expression alone any more than the gay man can be defined solely by his sexual expression. Lesbianism is a life-style, a mind-set, a body of experience, and when it's tempered in the fires of feminism, it is the most formidable political posture that can confront the dominant culture. Any woman who with real political consciousness is moving toward her own self-love, moving toward overcoming her isolation from other women is moving toward the lesbian life-style; if she's really woman-loving, and professionally and financially able to do so, she won't mind being called a lesbian; in fact, she will be glad to call herself by that term whether or not she has ever experienced what the patriarchy would define as the sine qua non of lesbianism, i.e., a sexual relationship with another woman.

Neither the women's movement nor its partner, gay liberation, is going to be satisfied with equal rights within the system. This is far too superficial. Women, gay people, and it is hoped, all men, are not going to be satisfied until societal misogyny is a bleak part of human history, until the economic system and the value system underlying it—itself built on woman-hatred—are overturned and re-created.

Philogyny, that political ideology of which the conscious lesbian is the embodiment, requires an affirmation that no one of us has to be a half-person, that there's no such thing as superiority—male or female—only difference. It requires of women that they be whole persons, claiming aggressiveness and intellect as well as subjectivity and caring; it requires of men that they find and love the woman in themselves so that they don't have to keep conquering the woman outside themselves. Until sex-role socialization is a thing of the past, until both women and men stand forth strong and self-loving in their wholeness-unto-themselves, authentic relationships and real communication across sex lines are at least unlikely and, as experience more and more frequently indicates, probably impossible.

It is significant that administrators even in the academe—highly touted bastion of liberalism—are still in overwhelming majority not only Anglo, but male. Recently, women's voices have been loud and clear in their demands on administrators, on the system. But in the light of a growing consciousness of gay oppression—connected to women's oppression but still very different—what could administrators be expected to do?

An ideal but almost fatuous solution might echo the World War II legend of the Danes who all wore the Star of David with the Jews so that the whole populace—and thus no one—was indicted. Administrators could all come out as homosexual. By a broad definition like male bonding (which excludes women) it would be no lie. The notion is fatuous only because society has made too great the difference between gay and straight. Yet the underlying desire is to be taken seriously: that administrators by some declaration of commonality claim unto themselves all the sin-and-sickness labeling heaped on the homosexual and by that act render meaningless the oppressive societal attitude. The effect of such an act might be miraculous: millions of closeted faculty, students, and staff would sigh in relief; blackmailers would have the wind whipped from their sails; incredibly, an atmosphere of directness and honesty might creep into the hallowed halls; the college campus might gingerly begin to reclaim its abdicated role as vanguard in creative ideas, leader in humanistic reform. Slowly the reality of same-sex relationships (and their health and beauty) might become an assumption of language as well as of attitude: drama teachers, for instance, would make as much a point of mentioning the heterosexuality of an author as they do of one's homosexuality; social science instructors would refer to partners instead of man and wife; education teachers would talk of heterosexual teenage attachments as frequently as of homosexual ones; health centers would cease the heterosexual assumption implicit in, "What kind of birth control do you use?" And faculty social functions would invite always "a special one" or "a friend" instead of "your husband" or "your wife."

But such an identification of administrator with the homosexual would presume too much. It would presume that administrators want to stop oppressing gay people. It would presume that administrators are enough in communication with one another even on one campus to make such a move effective. Most of all it would presume that administrators are self-aware enough, morally responsible enough, courageous enough, and unpressured enough by their own investment in the hierarchy to lay on the line their own images, their own "manliness," and in many cases, their own jobs. Nothing more quickly exposes the lie of liberalism and the sickness of the system than the easy and rationalized dismissals of just such a suggestion of personal risk. Gay people understand very well both the terror and the pressure of the administrators in their refusal to entertain such a risk; but this understanding does not go far in relieving the pain of gay oppression.

Nor is the issue only personal, for what is at stake in this challenge of the administrator to identify with the homosexual is the sanctity of sex-role socialization and thus the whole societal superstructure of power relations that is fashioned on this institution. For the academe or any part of it to claim homosexuality would be for the academe or that part of it in a sense to deny its own identity; the psychological connection is clear: "gay" equals "womanlike" equals "soft," "easy," and "without discipline or rational substance." The great tradition of higher learning would have to examine itself honestly and undergo a total transformation of values—a transformation, many gay and women's groups believe, that would humanize and make whole for the first time in history the experience of education.

To speak more realistically, the most administrators can be expected to do is to initiate some self-protecting moves that will at least create an atmosphere of greater tolerance for and acceptance of gay people. In this vein individual administrators can make policy statements supportive of gay civil rights and further can urge the support of such statements on the part of all those she or he works with. Such statements hurt no one and could help many.

In the case of a professional organization such as the Association for Communication Administration (ACA) or the Speech Communication Association (SCA)—where administrators wield considerable influence—policy statements could have incredible impact on such legislation as the Abzug Amendment to the Civil Rights Act. What is vital here is not so much the adoption of such a resolution—although from the gay perspective this would be the primary concern—but the discussion and debate that would surround a professional body's proposal of a resolution on gay rights, whatever the outcome of the free discussion. The body would at least be assured of its own vitality, the exercise of advocacy, and some practice in its own discipline; at least the consciousness of the association and of the public would be raised. For teachers of speech communication such debate might reactivate some sense of professional meaning, of personal excitement, and of social responsibility reflective of the rhetorical tradition long associated with these qualities.

If a professional association such as the ACA or the SCA cannot muster the concern necessary to bring such resolutions to the floor, then it may well be true that in our determination to become refined critics, in our eagerness to behave like respectable social scientists—objective, neutral—we have lost our age-old commitment to free expression and public responsibility. Herman Cohen, in addressing the Western Speech Communication Association, regrets

> that we have chosen not to comment on the communicative climate of our country; that we have chosen not to comment on possible restraints which have been placed on our freedom to communicate; that we have chosen not to comment on public issues or public figures which have implications for free and open communication.[10]

His address was a plea for the professional attention of speech communication practitioners to the present climate of communication and to the issues being called forth or repressed by that climate.

The question of gay rights would be only one of many that should elicit the concern of such a professional organization. Yet to that portion of the population restricted in its freedom by laws, by a mind-set, by a deeply entrenched attitude toward women and that-which-is-womanlike, the concern of a professional organization is important. To a gay group there seems no agency more historically or morally equipped to hear its voice, to evaluate the issues, to air the implications, and if change is decided on, to urge that necessary change than is that professional group whose expertise is communication and whose traditional concern has been the freedom of public discourse.

Chapter 23

Referendum Campaigns vs. Gay Rights

Jan Carl Park

In a recent article on Christian fundamentalism in the United States, a 1979 Gallup poll was cited that estimated there were approximately 55 million born-again Christians, "comprising nearly one in four Americans."[1] Paul Gebhard, director of the Sex Research Institute at Indiana University, recently estimated that there are approximately 20 million gay men and lesbians comprising the homosexual community of the United States.[2] Both groups have experienced phenomenal growth in their numbers in the past decade, but not until recently have these two groups welded their latent political power into voting coalitions in opposition to each other. Recent political clashes between these two groups have, on the part of gay rights advocates and fundamentalist Christians alike, encouraged the formation of organized advocacy agencies. Perhaps the best example of this clash can be seen in local city and county referendum campaigns designed to repeal gay rights ordinances passed by county and city commissioners.

This essay focuses on the use of the referendum process to adjudicate the rights of gay minorities by providing a definition of petition or issue-oriented referenda. It provides an overview of the history of referenda usage in the United States, illustrating the frequency of application, rhetorical importance of referenda campaigns, and significance with regard to repealing gay rights legislation, and concludes with observations made by the National Gay Task Force's *Laguna Conference Report on Initiative and Referenda Campaigns* of the losses and gains in gay rights referenda campaigns.

Gay rights ordinances were designed to protect homosexual minorities against discrimination in housing, employment, and use of public accommodations. It is through the use of the petition referendum, however, that Christian coalitions have brought to public vote the rights of gay minorities. Prior to the Dade County Referendum (Miami, 1977) sexual preference legislation—or gay rights legislation as it has come to be called—received favorable support in forty American cities and towns.[3] Inspired by Anita Bryant's successful Miami campaign, New Right groups have succeeded through the use of referenda to overturn sexual preference legislation in four cities and counties: Dade County, Florida (Miami, 1977); St. Paul, Minnesota; Wichita, Kansas; and Eugene, Oregon. In other cities, the gay rights referenda continue to emerge. Clearly, the major legislative obstacle for the advancement of gay rights ordinances in the United States today is the employment of the petition referendum.

A referendum is

> a procedure brought about when petitions signed by the requisite number of voters require that a legislative enactment be submitted to a popular vote. The filing of petitions within a given period of time—usually 90 days—suspends the application of the law or postpones the date when the law should go into effect. If approved by the electorate, the law continues on the statute book, as adopted by the legislative body, but if disapproved it is as if it had never been passed.[4]

Three types of referenda exist in the United States: the petition referendum, where "citizens may petition for a referendum—usually with the intention of repealing existing legislation"; the legislative referendum, where "the Legislature may voluntarily submit laws to the electorate for their approval"; and the constitutional referendum, in which the state constitution may require "certain questions to be submitted to the people, often debt authorizations."[5] The first type of referenda, the petition referenda, are the principle source of current gay rights campaigns.

The referendum in the United States as a "mechanism for translating public wishes into public policy" has been a common form of "direct democracy" in action.[6] Howard Hamilton, an authority on the history of referenda in the United States, surveyed the use of local (city and county) referenda and concluded that the national volume of local referenda was "ten to fifteen thousand annually."[7] Hamilton's survey indicated that the "national average of state wide referenda" was "70 in odd years and 300 in even years."[8] The volume and frequency of referenda campaigns therefore indicate a phenomenal expression of community concern on numerous issues confronting cities, counties, and states.

Stanley Scott and Harriet Nathan, in a study of issue-oriented referenda, discuss how referenda campaigns shape voting opinion and attitudes: "Opinion molding in referenda campaigns tends to be accomplished not through debate on the merits of the issue, but by emotional appeals and scare tactics, catch phrases, and slogans that oversimplify complicated problems."[9] Few realize the large degree of voting power held by organized interest groups of community voters: powers that in the past denied basic rights to many minorities and today determine social issues as widely divergent as restricting the use of alcohol on Sundays to abortion rights.

The idea that people should participate directly in the legislative process through the use of the referenda is a comparatively recent development in the United States; however, its history dates back to the Swiss cantons, which had established "direct legislation" as early as 1874.[10] Lockard observed that in the nineteenth century "the Jacksonian era, democratization of parties, the long ballot, and the spoils system were further developments of popular participation in government."[11] Winston Crouch provides the following thumbnail sketch of the birth and growth of referenda use in American cities:

> In 1897 the Nebraska legislature passed a general enabling statute permitting municipal electors in that state to use the initiative and the petition referendum to legislate on municipal problems. The following year two California cities, San Francisco and Vallejo, established direct legislation procedure through their freeholder charters. After Des Moines drew attention to the commission plan of city government in 1907, a large number of states adopted initiative and referendum for use within commission-governed cities.[12]

Today every state permits the use of the initiative and/or referendum devices in certain classes of cities, with the petition referendum having the widest acceptance.[13]

The rapid acceptance of direct legislation devices in the United States resulted from dissatisfaction with state legislatures and boss-ridden city councils of the late nineteenth- and early twentieth-century governments.[14]

> The move to enlarge the public's role and to diminish that of the elected officials was thus not only consonant with a respected tenet of American political thinking, it was a practical matter of "fighting the crooks." Since elected officials could not be trusted, the reasoning ran, alternative ways to achieve legislation and countermand undesired legislative acts should be provided.[15]

The petition referendum served as a "psychological outlet for early twentieth-century voters who were appalled by the nineteenth-century revelations of the muckrakers and who were deeply mistrustful of the inefficient and often venal state and local legislative bodies of that day."[16] Scott and Nathan, in their overview of the history of referenda, contend that the "reform of one generation can become the governmental roadblock of the next."[17] If the Civil Rights Act of 1964 were not passed, the liberation of blacks from racial discrimination in housing, employment, and public accommodations would still be in the hands of voters and sympathetic local governments who passed fair housing ordinances. The freedoms that black minorities enjoy today would be subject to the success or failure of referenda campaigns. Gay activists argue that only national legislation, similar to the Civil Rights Act of 1964, will free gay minorities from the threat of recision campaigns structured around petition referenda.

The implications of the use of petition referenda to rescind gay rights legislation are significant when one considers that this type of referenda "runs the risk of being decided by special interest pressure, by slogans and by spurious issues unrelated to the facts, or by simple neglect when many or even most registered voters do not participate."[18] Anti–gay-rights forces have come to see the petition referendum as a way to "bypass the irredeemably liberal officials" and "institute the conservative legislation the people long for."[19] In a comprehensive study of referenda from 1945 to 1976, Austin Ranney, past president of the American Political Science Association and current Resident Scholar at the American Enterprise Institute, made the following observations concerning the liberal-conservative nature of referenda outcomes:

> Liberal positions on economic questions (right to work and taxation laws) generally won, conservative positions on social issues (death penalty, abortion, and racial discrimination) won, while the environmentalists broke even with the advocates of economic growth on nuclear power issues. This pattern is consistent with the widely held view that American voters are predominantly liberal on economic questions and conservative on social issues.[20]

Past studies of fair housing referenda campaigns show conservative coalitions consistently voting down antidiscrimination ordinances for black minorities prior to the 1964 Civil Rights Act. These findings support Ranney's observations and predict referenda victories for anti–gay-rights advocates, victories that will continue to motivate the use of the referenda by the New Right as a political tool.

However, gay rights advocates have achieved victories in the two most recent referenda campaigns, in Seattle and in the State of California. Campaigners will be the first to admit the unique nature of these two campaigns in comparison to the four previous losses, and caution against overconfidence. Jeanne Córdova, reporting in the *Seattle Gay News,* observed: "The goddess smiled on California when she gave them John Briggs, and Seattle gays were twice blessed by having Dennis Falk and David Estes lead the campaign against them. Gays would not have chosen three men more remarkable for their lack of credibility, obvious fascism, and political stupidity, if they had been clairvoyant."[21]

Charles Kneupper concluded that "despite the successful campaigns in Seattle and in California in 1978, the preceeding and substantial rejections of pro-gay campaigns make it evident that no clear or overwhelming consensus exists for gay rights."[22] Kneupper observes, "It would be a mistake to generalize nationally on the basis of the Proposition 6 campaign. It would be best to say that a defeat was averted by the rejection of Proposition 6, but little was gained in positive protection of the civil rights of gays or to provide redress of individual acts of discrimination."[23] Whether continued losses occur over gay rights campaigns or victories such as Seattle and California are repeated, it is clear that "the gay liberation movement has reached a pinnacle in moving gay concerns from the realm of personal and moral discussion to public and political debate."[24]

Gay men and lesbians are the victors of each and every campaign struggle. No matter how bitter the taste of defeat is at the conclusion of the campaign, "failure could be seen as a form of victory in terms of overall movement development," concluded the National Gay Task Force's *Laguna Conference Report on Initiative and Referenda Campaigns.*[25] Kneupper contends that the campaigns "destigmatized gays,"[26] and the task force report concludes "the public was legitimately bombarded with information about homosexuality to which they had rarely had access. . . . It is certain that many non-gay citizens in all of the campaign cities learned more about the issues of homosexuality than ever before."[27] Destigmatization and education of the public about gay men and lesbians is indeed a major victory, but the power of the referendum process to repeal sexual preference legislation will continue to cloud gay rights advances. Only with national legislation or an executive order will gay men and lesbians be freed from having their life-styles placed before public approval in the form of a referendum vote.

Chapter 24

Ideologies in Two Gay Rights Controversies

Barry Brummett

On the seventh of June 1977 voters in Florida's Dade County, which includes Miami, overwhelmingly repealed an ordinance forbidding discrimination against homosexuals in housing and employment. Massachusetts legislator Elaine Noble said, "If the Dade County battle is won by Anita Bryant's proponents, it will not be long before they turn up in key states . . . trying to do similar things."[1] On April 25, 1978, voters in St. Paul, Minnesota, repealed that city's gay rights ordinance.[2] Subsequent repeals of similar ordinances in Wichita and in Eugene, Oregon indicate that gay rights is a major national controversy.

Understanding the rhetoric for and against gay rights is difficult because the arguments seem to have no common theme. In both Miami and St. Paul, "the origin of this movement is puzzling."[3] Many issues surfaced in the rhetoric of both sides: human rights, morality, minority protection, children, education, majority rule, and decency. This essay argues that the rhetoric of each side *is* unified and consistent despite a bewildering multitude of themes. By examining the implications of pro and anti gay rights arguments, I hope to show one way of understanding that rhetoric.

This essay focuses on the rhetorical appeals of both sides in the Miami and St. Paul campaigns because they were the first repeal attempts in the two largest cities, as of this writing.

The gay rights arguments concern three intertwined issues: (1) What does it mean to be sexual? In deciding how to deal with different kinds of sexuality in society, the public needs to know what sexuality is, how it is acquired, and how it relates to other aspects of life. (2) What does it mean to be political? The public needs to know how to handle differences and strangeness in society and how to devise standards for joint political behavior.

In arguing what it means to be sexual and political, each side addresses a more basic issue. Each side is best understood by its respective answers to a third issue: (3) What does it mean to be human? The vision each side holds of what it means to be human is the core of an *ideology*[4] that generates each side's answer to issues 1 and 2, as well as immediate issues like education and majority rule.

This study is justified in three ways. First, this rhetoric is a textbook example of how a ratio within Kenneth Burke's pentad may be used in critical inquiry to reveal and explain ideologies. As noted above, the discipline of communication is increasingly interested in the study of ideologies. Ideologies motivate and guide political rhetoric and give it purpose. This essay may serve as a paradigm for analyzing ideologies *rhetorically* and may thus contribute to our discipline's knowledge of what an ideology is and how it functions. Second, the two ideologies studied in this essay are central to the rhetoric of some other controversies. Although my focus is the gay rights dispute, I shall briefly mention how the ideologies involved inform the rhetorics of a few other conflicts. Therefore, the essay will contribute to our understanding of issues beyond gay rights. Finally, the subject has intrinsic interest. As noted above, gay rights has received national attention and has been a local issue all across the country. Some critical insights into its many themes may help to illuminate a major national controversy.

Before reconstructing the symbolic unity of each side's rhetoric, I shall briefly turn to Burkean theory for a conceptual framework.

Ideology and the Pentad

Kenneth Burke argues that any situation may be understood by describing it through the five terms of scene, act, agent, agency, and purpose.[5] In a public controversy, people will try to define the problem and change audience perceptions of the world by placing responsibility for the way things are with one or more of those five terms.[6] Indeed, a controversy may be defined in Burkean terms as a situation in which disorientation and confusion exist. Rhetoric is called on to clarify and define the situation by orienting issues to one or more terms of the pentad. Imagine two speakers addressing the exigency of a sharp increase in the cancer rate. One speaker may argue that we face disaster because we have violated God's plan. Such a speaker defines the situation in terms of *purpose.* Another speaker will define the situation in terms of *scene* by orienting the rhetorical situation to careless pollution of the environment with carcinogens. Featuring one kind of term or ratio between terms over another creates different definitions of a situation.

Burke argues that people characteristically do not define one situation with scene, another situation with agency, another with act, etc. Rather, the *disposition* to define most things in life with one term or ratio serves as the core of an ideology for most people.[7] Life makes sense for most of us as we repeatedly explain experience to ourselves and others with one term or ratio. A system of values and beliefs forms around that core as people apply the controlling term or ratio to particular issues. Therefore, the terms or ratios of the pentad are *motives* for people to make choices and take actions in controversies. People are motivated to respond to arguments in the gay rights controversy within a set of specific issues.

Because rhetoric that addresses many different issues may flow from one orientation, seemingly disparate issues may be symbolically related by way of their controlling term. One group's rhetoric on school desegregation may be consistent with another group's rhetoric on nuclear disarmament because both rhetorics define their situations in terms of a shared conception of *agents*. One group may accept or reject rhetoric addressing disarmament because that rhetoric's controlling term is consistent or inconsistent with the group's existing definition of terms in desegregation.

The two sides in the gay rights dispute are anchored in two opposing ideologies. These ideologies feature the same two terms, yet they are diametrically opposed. In answering question 3, "What does it mean to be human?" each side stresses a *ratio between act and agent:* the world is the way it is, and people are what they are and do what they do, because of the relationship between people and their actions. But supporters of gay rights feature the *agent:* people are what they are and must be dealt with on their own grounds. *Acts are derivative* from agents, people do what they do because of the kinds of people they find themselves to be. Opponents of gay rights argue just the opposite. A person is what he or she is through his/her *actions* or the actions of others. People are essentially malleable. Therefore, actions are primary and *agents are derivative.*

These two ideologies may inform the rhetoric of a number of issues: urban reclamation, farm price supports, detente. This chapter traces those two ideologies as they are manifested in issues 1 and 2—What does it mean to be sexual and political?—and further into particular issues of minority protection, morality, etc. Agent ideology or act ideology unifies the rhetoric for or against gay rights. Definitions of politics and sexuality are inherent in specific issues: competing versions of the agent-act ratio are most clearly seen by examining these particular problems. In the rest of the essay, first in pro gay rights rhetoric and then in anti rhetoric,[8] I shall trace the rhetorical expression of act ideology or agent ideology in three issues: (1) standards for sex and politics: rights vs. morals, (2) living with political and sexual difference: minority protection vs. majority rule, (3) political and sexual education: bringing out vs. putting in.

The Pro Gay Rights Argument

Standards for Sex and Politics: Rights

An ideology dominated by the agent demands that people be taken on their own terms. An agent should not be held accountable because he/she happens to be black, Jewish, or gay. For "black, Jewish, or gay" are all *conditions of being* an agent. Therefore, Pro rhetoric strongly relies on the ultimate term of rights, since rights adhere to agents. We speak of human rights. Indeed, it is difficult to refer to rights and not mean that some person has that right. One has the right to do acts, but a *person* possesses that right. An implication of arguing for "rights" is that acts are derivative from an agent. If the agent did not have the right to act, the act would not rightfully take place.

When Pros sound the theme of *rights,* they often do not specify the right to engage in a particular *act.* Pros stress the right *to be* gay and to be protected in that state of being from discrimination. Slogans in Dade County mocked Anita Bryant's orange juice commercials: "A day without human rights is like a day without sunshine."[9] Arthur Bell stridently proclaimed that "the real fight is between thinking people of all colors and sexual persuasions and irrational, ill-informed women and men who refuse to understand that the issue is one of civil rights, not recruitment, pollution, or corruption."[10] Vice President Arlie Scott of the National Organization of Women held that "the real issue is not gays teaching children but equal rights for all minorities."[11]

Pros specifically opposed their standard of rights to the Antis' standard of morality: "It, therefore, is not a morality issue."[12] Ora Lee Patterson of the St. Paul Human Rights Commission put it most clearly: "This is not a moral issue. It's a human-rights issue."[13] As we shall see later, morality is a term that features acts. In rejecting moral standards for sex and politics, Pros denied that the issue was one of acts. As gay activist Robert Kunst argues, "The ordinance has nothing to do with sex acts whatsoever."[14]

Pros argued that approval of the agent's right *to be* gay ought to be separate from approval of his/her acts, since the agent is primary and acts are secondary. Bishop Herbert Chilstrom of the Lutheran Church in America separated issues of act and agent in arguing, "We are not dealing with the question of homosexuality, but the basic civil rights of some people who are homosexuals."[15] Mayor George Latimer of St. Paul attributed the ordinance's repeal to the fact that "we just were not able to convey to people who abhor the practice of homosexuality that they should set those feelings aside when it comes to granting them civil rights."[16] A statement by the St. Paul Citizens for Human Rights argued that "the issue is not whether the people of St. Paul approve of homosexuality. The issue is whether the people who happen to be gay should have the same basic rights afforded other St. Paul citizens."[17] The St. Paul *Post Dispatch* editorialized that the ordinance "does not signify approval of homosexual behavior"[18] or actions; rather, it guarantees rights to agents. And the Rev. Dale Anderson urged support of the ordinance by voters "regardless of how they may or may not view human sexuality."[19]

The argument that gays have no choice over their condition is the clearest indication that Pros emphasize agent over act. As Catholic Archbishop John Roach put it, "Some persons find themselves to be homosexual."[20] The condition of being that kind of agent comes first: nothing gays have *done* causes them to be gay. As Miami gay activist John Campbell put it, "Why in the world would anyone choose the anguish, heartbreak and discrimination of being gay?"[21] Or in the words of a St. Paul citizen, "Nature plays a trick on certain people and makes them homosexual."[22] Gays do what they do because of the kind of people they are. But they are not that kind of people because of anything they have done.

Living with Political and Sexual Difference: Minority Protection

Whether one emphasizes acts or agents affects how one lives with difference. Pro rhetoric assumes that differences in the body politic stem from unchosen states of being rather than from divisive acts. Given that assumption the wisest course is to accept the fact of difference and adjust policy to the agents involved. An important theme in Pro rhetoric compares the plight of gays with other, more "established" minorities: blacks, Jews, Native Americans, etc. Pros thus argue that gays "find themselves" in that condition, as do blacks, and must be accepted on those terms.

Pros typically argued, "Perhaps if we just replaced the word 'gay' with Jew or Latin or black. . . ."[23] One gay rights activist declared that "Miami is our Selma."[24] Minnesota Pros asked, "Who is next on the St. Paul citizens' list? Jews? Blacks?"[25] "If you can rationalize withholding one group's rights, how much harder can it be to rationalize denying or repealing the rights of others?"[26] At one rally, Minnesota State Sen. Allan Spear "equated the fight to the right-wing attack against the rights of poor women, affirmative action and Indian tribal rights."[27]

A focus on the agent lies behind a growing interest in ethnic identity. One finds that one is black, Czech, or Jewish. Ethnicity is a condition of being a person. Because an agent ideology holds that the world exists as the individual perceives it, that the human mind and character is the primary shaper of reality, a stress on agents is relativistic. Such a focus requires a pluralistic, decentralized society, and it features tolerance rather than control. Agent ideology can also accommodate the exceptional individual. Special people, like different social groups, need to be tolerated or celebrated.

Political and Sexual Education: Bringing Out

Education is a central issue in the gay rights controversy. But it means very different things given an agent or act ideology. Pros de-emphasize the creative power of education. They believe that a person's essential character is given. Education is an act that develops the potential which is already in agents, a potential which cannot be implanted by action. Education brings out of students their best possibilities.

Rosalynn M. Carroll, black chairwoman of the St. Paul School Board, stated the Pro view of education most clearly when she denied that gay teachers could make children gay: "That's the same as telling me that if a white person teaches a black child, all those beautiful black children would miraculously turn white."[28] A person's sexual orientation is a condition of being, just as much as is one's race, and education cannot change that orientation. "The Human Rights Ordinance does not make other people gay," argue the Pros, because people are already gay or heterosexual.[29] In denying that gays could teach a child to be gay, the Minneapolis *Star* editorialized that "homosexuality begins at an early age, before a child enters school."[30] Some Pros denied that education was an issue at all: "The issue is not whether gay teachers will be teaching our children."[31]

The Pro position on education is similar to an agent focus in other controversies. The growing emphasis on bilingual, culturally sensitive education is a part of the rhetorical ideology that features agents. Such education does not stress giving children information which they must learn. Instead, it deals with children as they see the world. A child who does not speak English well or is not from mainstream culture is educated on his/her own terms; his/her potential is developed. A focus on agents pervades the "human potential" movement. Esalen, EST, and other "pop" psychologies seek to develop the potential of the "whole" person. They urge acceptance of the individual on his/her own terms and reject changing the person radically to what he/she is not. These issues are the rhetorical cousins of Pro arguments. To the extent that mainstream America is suspicious of minorities, of bilingual and culturally sensitive education, of the human potential movement, then Pro rhetoric may be rejected because of its rhetorical family connections as well as for its own content.

The Anti Gay Rights Arguments

Standards for Sex and Politics: Morals

Opponents of gay rights legislation define a person's sexual or political character by his/her acts. A person is gay because he/she *does* something; perhaps he cooks, or she smokes a pipe. A key ultimate term in Anti arguments is morals. Morality is a concept which attaches itself primarily to *acts.* We speak of "immoral acts." When we refer to agents as immoral we justify ourselves by naming some act which the person does which makes him/her immoral. If the act is repented, the person's standing will usually change back to "moral." An immoral agent is created by immoral acts. An act ideology assumes that agents are responsible for who they are, that people make themselves through their actions. An act-centered rhetoric therefore will say much about what people should and should not *do.*

Thus one finds the term moral in Anti arguments. In an article by Michael Novak of only two ten-inch columns, we find the word moral or some form of it eleven times.[32] In a half page single column article by the St. Paul Citizens Alert for Morality, one finds "moral" or "immoral" ten times.[33] Bob Green, who at this time was Anita Bryant's husband, congratulated St. Paul citizens on "the stand you're taking against the immoral forces that are contributing to the breakdown of this country."[34]

The link between morality and act is clear in the wording of much Anti rhetoric. Gayness is usually referred to as an "act," a "life-style," or "behavior," rather than as a condition of being: "The homosexual act is just the beginning of the depravity."[35] Nobody put it more clearly than Anita Bryant: "I don't think a homosexual is a homosexual until he commits the act."[36] A St. Paul citizen complained that "those who practice perverted acts are trying to force us to accept their immorality," and in his three-paragraph letter the words act or action appeared six times.[37] Other Antis complain that gays "want the ordinance to give moral sanction, legal protection for their unnatural acts."[38] Novak links morality and action, declaring that "many believe that homosexuality represents a deficient form of emotional and moral life," and refers to "homosexual acts."[39] George F. Will fears for the loss of "old moral moorings" because of the "homosexual subculture, based on brief, barren assignations."[40] The wording is important, for this immorality is *based on* actions rather than resulting in them. Note the link between acts and morality in Anita Bryant's statement, "Homosexuals should not ask for a special-privilege ordinance to give community sanction to an act that God says is immoral."[41]

In stressing actions, the Antis often specifically deny that rights are an issue. A St. Paul student argues that "gay rights have nothing at all to do with human or civil rights"; rather, "the gay rights issue is a question of morality—it is just that simple."[42] Anita Bryant agrees in arguing that "it's not a political issue. It's a moral one."[43] And again, "It is not a civil rights issue because anyone could be defined as a legitimate minority."[44] Mike Thompson agrees: "There is no human right, no civil right to corrupt children."[45] Antis argue that rights can be surrendered by acts, and they claim that gays have done so. The St. Paul Citizens Alert for Morality argue that "if a person is discovered in a crime and apprehended, he no longer has full, unrestricted rights like a moral person. Because of his act of immorality, he now has restricted rights."[46] A St. Paul citizen argued: "I would be enraged if a moral person had any of his access to the five basic human privileges, or rights, restricted. However, an immoral person by his own actions restricts his access to basic human rights."[47]

Anti speakers separate agents and acts by arguing that they "love the sinner but hate the sin."[48] St. Paul Antis claimed they "did not hate anyone."[49] Evangelist Jack Wyrtzen says "I want you to know we don't hate homosexuals. We hate homosexuality. We love homosexuals, we love lesbians."[50] By hating the act but not the agent, Antis make the act primary. If the agent were primary and Antis hated the act, they must hate the causative agent as well.

Anti rhetoric judges agents by their sexual and political acts. Sexually, agents' actions may make them "sinners." Politically, agents' actions may make them "criminals." Anti rhetoric argues that to be sexual or political is to engage in actions that may save or damn the agent.

A sin is an act, and committing sin defines the agent as a sinner. Anita Bryant's position is clear: "The Bible clearly says homosexuality is an abomination."[51] In both Miami[52] and St. Paul,[53] Antis called for an "army of saints" to combat the sin of homosexuality. Evangelist Jack Wyrtzen, who has never owned a pet, moralistically asserts that "homosexuality is a sin so rotten, so low, so dirty that even cats and dogs don't practice it."[54] One caller on a Miami radio call-in show argued that "homosexuality is an abomination. I don't know where it says it in the Bible, but I feel it in my heart. I feel Jesus Christ said it." Another observed that "Jesus Christ wasn't gay. There were no gay bars in his time. Jesus don't go to no gay bar."[55]

If gayness is an act of sin, then it can be repented. To be truly repentable, gayness must be freely chosen. Anti rhetoric features *choice* as a component of sexuality. George Will, for instance, bases much of his argument on this supposition: "To the extent that homosexuality is, in some sense, a 'choice' of character, as many homosexuals insist."[56] Novak, referring to "gay alliances," remarks that "homosexuality . . . is a fully moral choice."[57] Bryant protege Mike Thompson also claims "these guys have a choice."[58]

If sexuality is based on chosen acts, then some acts can justify a person sexually. The character of the agent is derived from acts which protect him/her like a talisman. Reporters approaching Anita Bryant, for instance, are asked if they are married.[59] Marriage is an act by which the agent can establish his/her sexual character. Once married there are other acts which reinforce a good agent. Schoolteacher Inez Wilcox energetically declared, "I don't know what the Bible says about gay people, but I do know that Jesus said go out and have children. I believe in the word of God so I went out and had ten. Could a gay couple follow the word of God like that?"[60]

The political corollary of sin is crime. Anti rhetoric argues that the act of sexuality is subject to legal standards. Such a definition of sexuality could only result from an act focus. One cannot be criminal for a condition of being. Anita Bryant equates homosexuality with murder,[61] and argues that it should be considered a felony.[62] A group called the National American Party for Manhood distributed fliers backing capital punishment for homosexuals.[63] One St. Paul citizen said "I'm against homosexuals. The Old Testament says they will be stoned to death."[64] And a Miami sticker advocates the punishment, "Kill a Queer for Christ."[65]

The violence expected from gays is an interesting indication of their alleged criminality. Bryant's former husband expects her to die at the hands of "some militant homosexual."[66] Bryant herself is shocked at "the viciousness or vindictiveness of the homosexual community."[67] The Rev. Jerry Falwell claims that "so-called gay folks would just as soon kill you as look at you."[68] A St. Paul citizen warns that "extending the hand of tolerance to the gays, San Francisco has found, ends with their hands at your throat."[69]

Living with Political and Sexual Difference: Majority Rule

Pro rhetoric stresses the importance of tolerating difference and perpetuating a pluralistic society. Anti rhetoric stresses majority rule and the importance of voting. I shall argue that such an argument is consistent with an ideology of action.

Antis argue that majority rule creates properly moral standards for society. Therefore, society should be molded by decisions rendered through majority voting. Differences should give way to moral standards dictated by the majority. A revealing statement in a political ad argues, "Yes, the majority can still determine the difference between right and wrong."[70] The ambiguity of "determine" is important: it can mean discern or fiat, or both. Other Anti rhetoric complains, "A small group of gay activists and their friends pushed through the amendment over the objections of a much larger majority of citizens."[71] Bob Green congratulates St. Paulites on the same theme: "You see, you've awakened a sleeping giant. The vast majority of the American people is coming awake and taking a stand."[72] And elsewhere, he argues, "The heartbeat of this country is turning conservative, and one day we'll see the heartbeat break through. The majority is no longer apathetic."[73]

In celebrating the resurgence of the majority, Antis find a convenient target; the expert, the powerbroker, the individual in charge. Such a target is especially appropriate since the ordinances in question were passed by powerful city or county legislative bodies after lobbying by special interest groups. Bob Green is therefore moved to complain, "We're being run in this country by a small group of very active people."[74] Other Antis agree: "A small group of militants has been dictating to the majority in the United States."[75] Sometimes that small group is described as "experts," know-italls who claim scientific evidence in support of gay rights: "Is there anyone who will claim things are not getting even worse? Of course there is. Some 'expert,' somewhere, will." But these experts are suspect: "You can dig up an expert to take any side of any controversial issue." And the result of expert opinion: "No room for the people in a democracy anymore."[76]

A majority vote against gay rights is often defined in Anti rhetoric as a "message" sent to the rest of the nation. St. Paul Councilwoman Rosalie Butler argues, "I think the people of St. Paul gave a very positive message: that they will support candidates who stand up for decency and morality."[77] Just before the St. Paul election a political ad promised, "Tomorrow, you will be able to show the nation that parents are important: that the family unit is sound."[78] And shortly after the election, a St. Paul citizen hoped that the vote would become a message: "I hope that the vote to repeal the Gay Rights amendment to the St. Paul ordinance (and the Miami vote) tells members of legislative bodies something concerning how the people, those whom they are to represent, feel about this matter."[79]

When Pros describe the ideal body politic as one that protects minorities and individuals, that argument is clearly consistent with an agent focus. But does the Anti rhetoric of majority rule, voting, denigration of experts, and "sending a message" express an act ideology?

The values of voting and majority rule are closely connected, since votes determine majorities. But voting is an act rather than a state of being. People go to the polls to assert themselves, and by their actions things happen. The corporate agent of the United States is derived from that act, we are what we make of ourselves at the polls. An act ideology defines correct sex and politics through voting. The majority really does *determine* the difference between right and wrong. In such a view of the body politic there can be no room for the expert. For an expert is a highly trained *agent,* distinguished for what he/she knows rather than for what he/she does. The act of voting is the active transmission of a message, and that is why majority vote as message is featured in act-dominated Anti rhetoric.

"Send them a message" suggests a political relative, the rhetoric of George Wallace. "Send them a message" was the slogan of his Presidential campaigns. The act focus as manifested in majority rule, voting, etc., is also akin to the pioneer myth in this country. Nameless individuals, the faceless masses, came to these shores to make a new land. They made new people of themselves as well. A person was what he/she made of him/herself through acts. Whether born a serf or aristocrat, that made little difference on the Oregon Trail. What counted was what one could *do.* And so the importance of actions in defining who one is has been an enduring American value.

Political and Sexual Education: Putting In

Pro rhetoric stresses the role of education in developing the potential that already exists in agents: education draws possibilities out of people. Anti rhetoric stresses the role of education as an active process of putting information into agents: education is an act that molds pliable agents. Anti rhetoric features the active role of gays in educating children.

Anita Bryant voices the typical argument: "Since homosexuals cannot reproduce, they must freshen their ranks with our children. . . . They will use money, drugs, alcohol, any means to get what they want."[80] Mayor Latimer of St. Paul felt that the defeat of that city's ordinance was due to this concern: "What if he (a gay) is teaching my children?"[81] Many Antis became involved through fear for their children: "When I started this, I was just one mother, trying to help her children," as Anita Bryant said.[82] In St. Paul, the Citizens Alert for Morality merely "want to keep perverted and immoral people from close contact with their children."[83]

Recruitment is a persistent theme, with Mike Thompson charging that "recruit they will. In our schools, by foster children, by becoming adoptive parents."[84] Bob Green charged that gays "do much of their recruiting among children."[85] A St. Paul citizen envisioned "subtle" appeals by gay teachers to the "trusting innocents" in their charge and claimed that "gay teachers in high schools can be counted on to happily deliver 'enlightening' presentations on sex."[86]

Why are children focused on so intently by Anti rhetoric, and what does that reveal about the role of education? A child is innocent and malleable. He/she may be made into a particular kind of agent through certain actions. Children are demi-agents, neither sexually nor politically complete. Antis fear that their children will be recruited by gays. They believe that sexual character can be molded by acts of recruitment. Therefore, what a child is taught in school is far more important than the child's character on entering school.

The idea of education as an act that molds agents has currency in the wider political scene. A resurgence of the "three Rs," of traditional education in which information is put into agents to make them better people, is consistent with a focus on action. Antis' suspicion of a pluralistic society may also lead to a distrust of difference in education. Thus, children may be made to learn Standard English no matter what their culture or condition upon entering school. Because of the power of educational action, learning standard truths is supposed to mold agents to the norms determined by majority rule.

Conclusion

In this essay I have tried to present the arguments for and against gay rights in Miami and St. Paul as consistent and unified. Each side is informed by powerful, unifying ideologies that feature either agents or acts. One's ascription of causative, defining power in the world will be different depending on an agent or act ideology. That ideology will determine one's position on what it means to be human, political, and sexual.

Edwin Black argues that rhetoric offers to its audience a view of who they are.[87] Implicit in every argument is the statement, "A certain kind of person likes this argument; agree to the propositions of this rhetoric, and you will be just such a person." Within the scope of this chapter I am unable to argue whether an individual consenting to Pro or to Anti rhetoric is "better" or more ethical. But let the reader consider the implications of either camp: tolerance, pluralism, relativism, and a willingness to celebrate difference—or—moralism, tyranny of the majority, and an eagerness to impose norms. The choice is not merely which ordinances we will have, but what kind of people we will be.

Appendix 2: Abbreviations

aMM.................Interview a with Ross Robertson and Mike de Ryter
BB.....................Bill Birch
BCs o/c.............Back channels opening and closing
bM.....................Interview b with Bill Birch
Butting INT.....Butting in Interruption
c.........................Back channel closing
cM.....................Interview c with Sam Neill
DEC Q...............Declarative Questions
DISJ Q...............Disjunctive Question
dM.....................Interview d with Ian McPherson
eFM..................Interview e with Karen Guilliland and Philip Rushmer
F.........................Female
fFF.....................Interview f with Moira Ransom and Shona Solomon
FO.....................Fran O'Sullivan
gF......................Interview g with Sandra Toone
hF......................Interview h with Fran O'Sullivan
HYPO Q............Hypothetical Question
IM......................Ian McPherson
INT....................Interruption
KG.....................Karen Guilliland
M.......................Male
MB.....................Maggie Barry
MD....................Mike de Ryter
MLT...................Mean length of turn
MR.....................Moira Ransom
o.........................Back channel opening
POLAR Q..........Polar Question
PR.......................Philip Rushmer
Q.........................Question
re........................Restatement of specified question type
RR......................Ross Robertson
s.........................second(s)
s/t.......................seconds per turn
Silent INT........Silent Interruption
SN......................Sam Neill
SS.......................Shona Solomon
SSS+.................Smooth Speaker Switch Paused
ST.......................Sandra Toone
t..........................turn(s)
TAG Q..............Tag Question, Face Attack
TCI.....................Turn Competitive Incoming
w.........................word(s)
w/s.....................words per second
w/t.....................words per turn
WH Qs..............WH-Question
+.........................positive affect
=.........................neutral affect
–.........................negative affect
Σ.........................summation of

Chapter 25

Religious Fundamentalism and the Democratic Process

Ronald D. Fischli

The 1960s and 1970s in the United States have marked an era replete with social and political movements. Never in our history has the meaning of civil rights and morality been scrutinized from such a sweeping variety of viewpoints. Images transmitted via television screens linger as testimonial to nearly two decades of activism by increasingly numerous and diverse groups expressing grievances: Martin Luther King, Jr., delivering his "I Have a Dream" speech on the steps of the Lincoln Memorial, four students dying at Kent State, clenched fists raised at the Olympic Games in affirmation of Black Power, feminists continuing their struggle to assure passage of the Equal Rights Amendment, active oldsters rejecting mandatory retirement laws. Such events serve as continual reminders that political and social activism remains alive and well in the American body politic.

In recent years one movement in particular has gained public attention both because of the inroads it has made and because of the countermovement those inroads ignited. The action and reaction imbued the word gay with a new, indeed predominant, meaning and rendered singer Anita Bryant a saint or a demagogue, depending on one's point of view. I speak, of course, of the controversy generated by the opposition mounted by Bryant's Save Our Children organization[1] against the Gay Liberation Alliance (GLA) predominantly during 1977 and 1978. The volatility and divisiveness that marked the confrontation between the GLA and Save Our Children have largely prevented a careful consideration of Bryant's position. What follows is an explication of the motivations implicit in her position,* an analysis of the rhetorical strategies she employed, and an

*It should be noted that late in 1980 Anita Bryant shifted her position somewhat, saying in an interview in *Ladies' Home Journal* (Dec. 1980), "As for gays, the

evaluation of her rhetorical stance. Evidence for the study has been drawn primarily from Bryant's book *The Anita Bryant Story,* subtitled *The Survival of Our Nation's Families and the Threat of Militant Homosexuality.* Bryant herself has affirmed the book as the fullest expression of "our side of the story, the truth as to what really happened in Dade County, why I stood."[2]

Political and social gains by gay activists during recent years have made the time ripe for the eruption of a countermovement such as that led by Bryant. The GLA has awakened society to the pervasiveness of homosexuality by encouraging homosexuals to come out of the closet and to reject guilt feelings about their sexual proclivities—a conversion capsulized in the slogan "Gay is great!" Homosexuality no longer appears on the American Psychiatric Association's list of mental disorders, has been removed from criminal status in eighteen states, and has been ruled invalid as a consideration in employment practices by a number of institutions, including the U.S. Civil Service Commission and several large corporations. Nowhere have gay inroads penetrated further than in San Francisco, where, *Newsweek* magazine reports, 28 per cent of the voters are homosexuals.[3] In San Francisco, sexual acts between consenting adults are legal, laws prevent the public schools and businesses transacting with the city from discriminating against homosexuals, and the school system's family-life curriculum includes material reflecting homosexual life-styles.

Similar inroads seemed imminent in another part of the country when an ordinance prohibiting discrimination against homosexuals in housing, public accommodations, and employment was introduced before the Metro Commission of Dade County, Florida, with passage virtually assured. And such would have been the case, were it not for one resident of Miami, Dade County's principal city. To the gays' appeals for "more," Anita Bryant cried, "Enough!" Events began building toward a confrontation during the first week of January 1977, when Bryant learned that the nine-member Dade County Metro Commission would vote on the ordinance, an amendment to chapter 11A of the Dade County Code, on January 18. As it related to education, the ordinance, if passed, would apply only to Dade County's private schools, since its public schools fall under state jurisdiction. It was on this fact in particular that Bryant, an avowed born-again Baptist, focused her objections, although she unequivocally condemned homosexual acts as immoral. Said Bryant, "The thought of known homosexuals teaching my children especially in a religious school bothered me" (p. 14).[4]

At the Metro Commission hearing concerning the ordinance, each side

---

church needs to be more loving, unconditionally, and willing to see these people as human beings, to minister to them and try to understand. . . . I'm more inclined to say live and let live, just don't flaunt it or try to legalize it."

presented its case. The position of the Dade County Coalition for the Humanistic Rights of Gays, led by Jack Campbell, the owner of a chain of gay bath-houses, essentially asserted as a "right" laws protecting persons openly pursuing homosexual life-styles from reprisals in housing, education, and employment. The antigay forces, with Bryant as their unofficial leader, presented statements claiming the ordinance would condone un-Christian acts, grant special privileges to homosexuals, and allow homosexuals to serve as role models for children. Despite the objections by the Bryant forces, the commission passed the measure by a five-to-three vote (one commission member was absent). That vote became a catalyst for Bryant and her sympathizers, and soon Save Our Children, Inc., with Bryant as its president, was born. The Save Our Children organization petitioned more than 66,000 signatures (a minimum of 10,000 were required) to achieve one of two goals: (1) to cause the commission to reverse its decision or (2) to bring the issue before the voters by means of a referendum. The commission chose the latter course. On June 7, after a heated campaign, Dade County citizens voted 202,319 to 89,562 for repeal of the ordinance.

The campaign and subsequent defeat of the ordinance further exacerbated progay reaction. Extensive media coverage of the events leading to the referendum had extended the controversy nationwide. As proof of the relevance of the controversy to the nation as a whole, Bryant pointed out that a Gay Rights Bill (HR 2998) introduced in Congress by Rep. Edward Koch of New York would amend the 1964 Civil Rights Act to outlaw discrimination on the basis of "affectional or sexual preference." The battle lines were squarely drawn. Save Our Children, with Anita Bryant as its unrivaled flag figure had become a national countermovement to the Gay Liberation Alliance. Soon after the referendum in Dade County, Bryant began touring the country as part of the Revive America Crusades. Directed by evangelist Cecil Todd, the crusade championed "Bible morality" and numbered among its priorities the reversal of the Supreme Court decision regarding prayer in the public schools; "cleaner and more wholesome" television programs; opposition to "child molesting, smut, and pornographic books and movies"; and support for Bryant's "campaign to protect America's children from being recruited by militant homosexuals to their lifestyle."[5]

Anita Bryant's stance has drawn indignant opposition from some circles equaled only by the adoring support from others. The National Gay Task Force declared,

> Bryant is really the perfect opponent. Her national prominence (through her commercials for the Florida Citrus Growers) insures national news coverage for developments in the Dade County struggle, while the feebleness of her arguments and the embarrassing backwardness of her stance both makes her

> attacks easier to counteract and tends to generate "liberal" backlash in our favor. Her "Save Our Children" campaign vividly demonstrates just why gay rights laws are needed—in order to protect our people against the sort of ignorant, irrational, unjustifiable prejudice typified by Anita Bryant.[6]

Reflecting the opposing viewpoint, a grass-roots supporter of Bryant wrote:

> Anita . . . has a vast amount of courage. Standing up for what she believes is right, she impressively remains steadfast in her moral beliefs. Her morals to me symbolize rationality, godliness, sensibility and quality. Anita, though constantly endangered, due to her moral convictions, remains one of the most well-known and most respected women in our great country of America.[7]

Such attitudinal polarization has been the most obvious result of Bryant's stand against homosexuality. Opponents tend to view her as a threat to moral enlightenment, while supporters rally behind her as a defender against moral degeneration. This polarization has been accompanied by and productive of various ironies and irrational acts. The Dade County ordinance that sparked the entire controversy was introduced by Ruth Shack, the wife of Anita Bryant's agent, Dick Shack. The coincidental selection of the name "Hurricane Anita" (the names are selected years in advance) by the National Hurricane Center provided tempting material for jokes by Bryant's opposition. The Gay Liberation Alliance encouraged consumer boycotts of products of the Florida Citrus Commission, for which Bryant has advertised orange juice since 1968. The attempted boycott proved ineffectual, if not counterproductive. The Bryant forces claimed sales rose 25 percent. The GLA also pressured the Singer Sewing Machine Company to cancel a planned talk show that Bryant would have hosted.[8] Perhaps the most blatant act against Bryant occurred at a news conference in Des Moines, Iowa, when a male homosexual threw a banana cream pie into her face. Such ironies and strategies, of course, evade and distort the issue instead of confronting and illuminating it. They spring from the frustrations emerging, as Parke Burgess has observed, when a culture loses the sense of unanimity grounded in a singular moral system and falls into the disharmony spawned by conflicting moral codes —fundamentalist Christianity and humanistic liberalism in the case in question. Burgess notes:

> When times are out of joint . . . society loses its sure anchor of shared values reflected and promoted by symbolic action. Normally pragmatic adjustments of institutional strategies give way to moralistic confrontation regarding values themselves; communication breakdowns then reflect and promote the

emergence of competing systems of moral demand. Subsequently, rhetorical strategies promoting unified, effective action in behalf of one system of moral demand are dramatically confronted by strategies equally justified by other systems, and so long as rhetorical unity within competing rhetorics obtains without compromise discussion on the public stage is doomed to conflict and ineffectiveness. Having lost the ultimate appeal to an overarching system of moral demands, the rhetoric of society virtually reverses its unique and essential role: heightening identification within groups only sharpens division between them.[9]

At base level, Bryant's stand against gay activists (she chooses to call them "militant homosexuals") represents nothing new. Her arguments adhere to a philosophy generally characterized as religious fundamentalism. Certain general assumptions of fundamentalist reasoning, however, merit illumination at this point, for they inform Bryant's more specific refutation of homosexual life-styles. Writing in 1927, W.B. Riley, then the president of the World's Christian Fundamentals Association, articulated these thoughts concerning religious fundamentalism and its implications:

> Fundamentalism is forever the antithesis of modernist critical theology. It is made up of another and an opposing school. Modernism submits all Scripture to the judgment of man. According to its method he may reject any portion of the Book as uninspired, unprofitable, and even undesirable, and accept another portion as from God because its sentences suit him, or its teachings inspire him. Fundamentalism, on the contrary, makes the Bible "the supreme and final authority in faith and life." Its teachings determine every question upon which they have spoken with some degree of fullness, and its mandates are only disregarded by the unbelieving, the materialistic and the immoral. Fundamentalists hold that the world is illumined and the Church is instructed and even science itself is confirmed, when true, and condemned when false, by the clear teachings of the open Book, while Liberalism, as *The Nation* once said, "pretends to preach the higher criticism by interpreting the sacred writings as esoteric fables."[10]

Two major ideas underlie Riley's reasoning: (1) the scriptures as the divinely inspired and inviolable word of God and (2) the consequent viability of strict interpretation of the Bible as a code for living. These two essential assumptions also undergird Bryant's stand against homosexuality. As scriptural evidence for her rhetorical stance, she quotes a number of passages, including 1 Corinthians 6:9-10 and Leviticus 20:13. The passage from Corinthians reads, "Know ye not that the unrighteous shall not inherit the kingdom of God? Be not deceived: neither fornicators, nor idolators, nor adulterers, nor effeminate, nor abusers of themselves with mankind,/Nor thieves, nor covetous, nor drunkards, nor revilers, nor extortioners, shall inherit the Kingdom of God." Leviticus 20:13 warns, "If a man also lie with mankind, as he lieth with a woman, both of them have committed an abomination: they shall surely be put to death; their blood shall be upon them." Perhaps because of the Bible's emphasis on male homosexuality, Bryant's discussions in *The Anita Bryant Story* focus more strongly on male than on female homosexuality, but clearly she condemns lesbian relationships on the same basis.

The dichotomy drawn by W.B. Riley between religious fundamentalism and modernism, or liberalism, also warrants discussion in relation to the Save Our Children campaign. Riley's arguments reveal a distrust of scientific rationalism and humanistic sentiments that conflict with the message of the scriptures. On the basis of such a distrust, Bryant rejects recent efforts by gays and gay sympathizers to present homosexual relationships as alternate life-styles. The surfacing of homosexuals in American society she sees as a "classic case of liberal reform by stealth" (p. 74). Homosexuality, insists Bryant, can be viewed only as God defines it, a sinful abomination. Bryant's struggle to bar admitted homosexuals from teaching in the nation's schools recalls an earlier confrontation between fundamentalist and liberal thought—the "Monkey Trial" conducted in Tennessee in 1925. In that trial the issue in question concerned whether John Scopes, a Tennessee schoolteacher, should be allowed to teach Darwin's theory of evolution. Joining the defense, liberal thinker Clarence Darrow squared off against fundamentalist William Jennings Bryan to attack the intellectual weaknesses in the latter's thinking. Bryan clung steadfastly to the supremacy of religious faith over rationalism. Whether the debate between the Gay Liberation Alliance and the Anita Bryant forces will prove as memorable as the Scopes trial remains to be seen, but the similarities in the two incidents suggest that the fundamentalist-modernist dichotomy is a long-standing one in the nation's traditions.

As it functions in the political arena, Anita Bryant's fundamentalist stance against legal protection for admitted homosexuals exemplifies what historian Richard Hofstadter has termed "paranoid style." According to Hofstadter, the "central image" of paranoid style "is that of a vast and sinister conspiracy set in motion to undermine and destroy a way of life."[11] Additionally, Hofstadter argues that paranoid style insists that the conspiracy must be defeated not through "the usual methods of political give-and-take, but an all-out crusade."[12] Since paranoid style comprehends "a conflict between absolute good and absolute evil," it demands from its audience not "a willingness to compromise" but "the will to fight things out to the finish."[13] Hofstadter characterizes the conspiratorial "enemy" as "a perfect model of malice, a kind of amoral superman: sinister, ubiquitous, powerful, cruel, sensual, luxury-loving. . . . Very often the enemy is held to possess some especially effective source of power: he controls the press; he directs the public mind through 'managed news'; he has unlimited funds; he has a new secret for influencing the mind . . . ; he has a special technique for seduction . . . ; he is gaining a stranglehold on the educational system."[14] As succeeding paragraphs illustrate, the absolutist, militant, and conspiratorial dimensions of paranoid style suffuse Bryant's rhetorical arguments against homosexuality.

Bryant's rhetoric comprehends a world of absolute rights and wrongs. Hers is a world of blacks and whites, admitting of no grays, where heroes and heroines must maintain unceasing vigilance against evil. Her militance is justifiable because it is "right"; the gay activists' militance is condemnable because it is "wrong." Bryant's certainty of the validity of her stance inheres in her shocked reaction to the Metro Commission's vote in favor of the gay rights ordinance: "I was visibly stunned. . . . I couldn't believe it. I was devastated. I sat there, and I heard the result of the vote, and I thought. *This is a free country, and if we present our case and we're right and if it's proven, then we should win it*" (p. 26). The stance grows out of a pristine view of life: "God says there are some things that are evil and some things that are good. That's simple enough for even a child to understand. Certain things are right; other things are wrong. But they are right or wrong because God says so. We are right when we do God's will; we are wrong when we do not" (pp. 37-38). The purgative impulse in Bryant's militant rhetorical posture emanates from these statements: "Even if my livelihood is stripped away from me, I will not be moved. I'd rather have the love of God and be making this a better place to live for my children and other children" (p. 27).

The stylistic choices evident in Bryant's rhetoric reinforce her absolutist reasoning. Military metaphors suggestive of a pitched battle permeate her rhetoric. As Bryant characterizes the situation, Dade County became a "testing ground" (p. 22) where "battle lines were drawn" (p. 21) between militant gays and Bryant sympathizers. The "housewives and mothers, religious and civic leaders" opposing the "militant homosexual . . . activists" were "foot soldiers" who "had neither marshaled our defenses . . . nor developed a strategy" (p. 21) but who "stood strong in our defense against . . . encroaching moral decay in America" (p. 27) and who "had to march out of our living rooms and fight for the repeal of this ordinance" (p. 28). The defeat of the ordinance constituted a "victory" (p. 125) for the Bryant forces. Bryant's description of the two sides in the conflict reinforces the triumphant tone by suggesting that the economic underdog has prevailed morally. Against the gay's national effort to solicit financial contributions, Bryant sets her side's "grateful" acceptance of "unsolicited" funds (p. 86): "The Lord honored our faith and answered by sending the money from God's people. For the most part, the money came in small amounts. It was a grass-roots response, mirroring the concern of the citizens of our land. In contrast, the homosexuals received mostly large amounts from 'gay' bars, businesses, and from the sale of obscene anti-Anita Bryant T-shirts" (p. 48).

Having essentially assumed from biblical evidence that God's way, via

Anita Bryant, equals the right way, Bryant proceeds to the conclusion that any differing points of view concerning homosexuality are either ill-intentioned or misguided, thus are either consciously or unwittingly part of a larger conspiracy. She claims that expressions of dissent by such notables as Rod McKuen, Liv Ullman, Paul Williams, Jaye P. Morgan, Jane Fonda, Martha Raye, Shirley MacLaine, Phyllis Diller, Ed Asner, Peter Lawford, and Johnny Carson constitute examples of a "show-biz conspiracy to ridicule and discredit me" (p. 36). She objects to religious viewpoints differing from her own as "revisionist interpretations" (p. 108). The media, too, draws Bryant's indignance, despite her own documentation of her use of it to make her views heard through newspaper stories and advertising and through appearances on such shows as *The PTL Club, The 700 Club,* Jerry Falwell's *Old Time Gospel Hour,* the *Phil Donahue Show,* and *Who's Who.* She contends that "those who, like the militant homosexuals, laugh in the face of sin . . . are the offenders; we, the morally concerned citizens, are the defenders. This has been reversed by the media largely through the efforts of the militant-homosexual community which knows how to get to the decision-making media people and to our representatives in government both local and federal" (p. 37). Bryant and her sympathizers have also presented arguments against feminist groups. She documents arguments claiming that "women's-liberation programs—many of them fostered by women with lesbian tendencies—have weakened family ties . . ." (p. 53). Also, at a Revive America rally, Cecil Todd spoke out against the recent "marriage" of gay rights and the women's coalition at the National Women's Conference.[15] He was referring to the conference's endorsement of laws prohibiting discrimination against homosexuals. The endorsement occurred in Houston, Texas, in November 1977.

Because of her intimate psychological alignment with what she considers to be absolute truth, Bryant reacts to attacks on her beliefs as attacks on her personally, as attempts to discredit her by flying in the face of ultimate realities. In contrast, she views her opposition to homosexuals as stemming not from any personal vendetta against gays but from a repugnance for the homosexual act: "We are not against homosexuals, but we are against the act" (p. 42). Homosexuality, she insists, is a "spiritual problem" (p. 91). Bryant reaches this conclusion despite her own admission that "even the majority of medical scientists are not in total agreement" (p. 110) concerning the nature and causes of homosexuality. For Bryant, this fact presents no contradiction, for God's pronouncement must supersede man's: "The reason is not difficult to understand—you cannot pinpoint sin under a microscope or isolate it in some lab" (p. 110). Extending the idea that homosexuality is a sin leads Bryant to the conclusion that it can be cured spiritually (again, despite scientific opinions to the contrary). To Bryant, though homosexuality constitutes "a bondage almost unequaled in the spiritual world" (p. 107), "God has provided all the help, hope, and love a person needs to overcome his or her sin problems" (p. 31). These conclusions transform Bryant's stance into an act of "love for . . . homosexuals" (p. 45) and lead her to assert that she longs "to reach out and help the homosexual" (p. 97), to guide him to the redemption described in 1 Corinthians 6:11: "And such [homosexuals and other transgressors] were some of you: but ye are sanctified, but ye are justified in the name of the Lord Jesus, and by the Spirit of our God."

One other major argument encompassed by Bryant's rhetoric warrants particular attention. That argument grows out of her strategy of linking the homosexual issue to child molestation and recruitment. To her conviction that the Bible condemns homosexuality as a sin, Bryant adds the contentions that (1) "public approval of admitted homosexual teachers could encourage more homosexuality by inducing pupils into looking upon it as an acceptable life-style" and (2) "a particularly deviant-minded [homosexual] teacher could sexually molest children" (p. 114). Bryant's logic concerning recruitment runs thus: "Homosexuals cannot reproduce [homosexuals]—so they must recruit. And to freshen their ranks, they must recruit the youth of America" (p. 62). A pamphlet published by the Save Our Children organization for use in the campaign in Dade County carried local and national newspaper headlines relating homosexual and pornographic exploitation of children by such persons as teachers and scoutmasters. Further, the pamphlet emphasized recruitment as the overriding issue in the campaign. A portion of the pamphlet read:

> The ordinance is not needed . . .
> It endangers our children . . .
> It is a dangerous precedent . . .
> It threatens your home . . .
> It attacks free enterprise . . .
> It debases religion . . .
> It is a peril to the nation . . .
>
> Any of these reasons is enough.
>
> But the overwhelming reason is that Metro's pro-homosexual ordinance is an open invitation to recruit our children! Vote FOR children's rights. Vote FOR repeal. (p. 89)

The strategy of linking child exploitation to the homosexual issue is a devious one. Not only has scientific research failed to support Bryant's inferential leap that homosexuals lead children astray, but biblical doctrine —her sole basis for her rhetorical stance—fails to support such a claim. This strategy might well serve, through the unjustifiable arousal of fear, to sway persons possessing ambivalent or uneasy feelings about homosexuality to reject moves by the gay community for societal sanctions. The strategy seeks to negatively color one phenomenon, homosexuality, which seems to some a borderline moral issue, by attaching it to another, child molestation, which is generally abhorrent. Bryant herself testifies to the power of this strategy: "No doubt our emphasis on scriptural references citing homosexuality as a sin helped to swing votes. That, and the work of our hard-core foot soldiers—God's people. But we also know that many tolerant, broadminded citizens voted for repeal because they felt uneasy at the prospect of an avowed homosexual becoming a role model for their children" (p. 126).

Beyond the issue of child exploitation, Anita Bryant's rhetorical position discloses a more general logical discrepancy. Bryant's world view assumes a societal structure where fundamentalist Christianity reigns supreme, a society instrinsically bound to ethical principles based on a strict interpretation of the scriptures. That the United States possesses a long-standing and on-going Judeo-Christian tradition defies argument. That Christian values impact on the nation's cultural dialogue seems obvious. But to impose on society in general a world view that peremptorily writes off as evil and destructive any viewpoints contradicting literal biblical doctrines threatens the machinery of democracy by disrupting the countervailing forces at play among American society's various religious and secular impulses.

Whether or not society as a whole ultimately accepts or rejects them, antifundamentalist sentiments deserve access to the marketplace of ideas. By unequivocally dismissing homosexuality as evil, Bryant invites society to ignore the one thing that homosexuality unarguably is—a fact of life. Her rhetorical strategies seek to stir in all of society a sense of guilt for permitting the "sin" of homosexuality to surface. Such a position belies the American tradition of tolerance implicit in the First Amendment to the Constitution: "Congress shall make no law respecting an establishment of religion, or prohibiting the free exercise thereof; or abridging the freedom of speech, or of the press; or the right of the people peaceably to assemble, and to petition the government for a redress of grievances." This amendment essentially guarantees separation of church and state and insists that communicative channels remain open to the expression of a broad range of secular and religious ideas.

At this point, I must take issue with a statement made by State Representative Tom Collier of Arkansas and quoted in *The Anita Bryant Story:* "When God's law and the country's laws conflict, God's law should be supreme" (p. 96). Within the sanctity of Anita Bryant's religious ideals, God's law (or rather, God's law as interpreted by Bryant) may indeed reign supreme. That is her constitutional right. But within the arena encompassing the totality of American culture, neither Judeo-Christian nor sectarian sentiments command inherent moral supremacy. The conflict between Bryant's fundamentalist stance and that of gay activists is not, as Bryant interprets it, a confrontation between good and evil but rather a collision of two differentially based value structures. Both positions are "moral" in a sense—Bryant arguing for the invocation of literal Christian doctrine, the GLA calling for legal protection of homosexuals from a humanistic viewpoint.[16] To reject societal acceptance of homosexuality as a valid alternate life-style, as does Bryant, solely on a fundamentalist basis is not enough. Viewed from the democratic standpoint, Bryant's rhetorical stance waxes no better, albeit no worse, per se than that of the gay activist. The following paragraph from an article by Edwin Black effectively articulates the relationship between the democratic process and absolutist philosophies such as Bryant's:

> Quite clearly we have had raging in the West at least since the Reformation a febrile combat of ideologies, each tending to generate its own idiom of discourse, each tending to have decisive effects on the psychological character of its adherents. While in ages past men living in the tribal warmth of the *polis* had the essential nature of the world determined for them in their communal heritage of mythopoesis, and they were able then to assess the probity of utterance by reference to its mimetic relationship to the stable reality that undergirded their consciousness, there is now but the rending of change and the clamor of competing fictions. The elegant trope of Heraclitus has become the delirium of politics. Thus is philosophy democratized.[17]

In the ongoing confrontation between gay activists and the Bryant forces, one major question still hangs in the balance: What status will homosexuality assume in American society? Viable answers to that question will not come as a result of absolutist reasoning that unrealistically seeks to squelch or eliminate homosexuality. Nor will they come as a result of irrational pie-in-the-face reprisals enacted in the name of civil rights. Effective solutions will result only from reasoned and flexible dialogue among both homosexuals and heterosexuals cognizant of the need for both self-expression and self-criticism in the democratic process. In her book Anita Bryant asserts that God has given America a "space to repent" (p. 30). That is, she believes that the "normal majority" (p. 125) of Americans have slipped into sinful ways through their tacit acceptance of such "evils" as homosexuality. According to Bryant, God has granted the normal majority a limited time to cure this "social epidemic" (p. 42) in order to perpetuate America's greatness, manifestly implicit in its Christian character. From the democratic viewpoint, however, it might well be said that what America has been given, by virtue of the Constitution, is a "space to ponder." Within that space lies the possibility for assessment and reassessment, definition and redefinition, in the face of a continually evolving social order. In contrast to Bryant's view, the space-to-ponder rationale pictures America as a powerful but not omnipotent society, no more manifestly destined than any other, including fundamentalist Christianity as one—but only one—moral force among a myriad of philosophical outlooks.

Notes

Introduction

1.Connie DeBoer, "The Polls: Attitudes Toward Homosexuality," *The Public Opinion Quarterly,* Vol. 42 (Summer 1978), p. 276.

2. See "The American Freshmen: National Norms for Fall," published by the American Council on Education and the University of California at Los Angeles.

3. "Homosexuals in America," *The Gallup Opinion Index,* October 1977, Report No. 147, p. 13.

4. Isadore Rubin, *Homosexuality* (New York: SIECUS Publications Office, 1967), p. 7.

5. State of Minnesota Human Rights Commission Task Force on Homosexuality, *The Isolation, Sex Life, Discrimination, and Liberation of the Homosexual* (St. Paul, MN: State of Minnesota Human Rights Commission, 1971), p. 1.

6. James W. Chesebro, "Paradoxical Views of Homosexuality in the Rhetoric of Social Scientists: A Fantasy Theme Analysis," *Quarterly Journal of Speech,* Vol. 66 (April 1980).

7. Alan P. Bell and Martin S. Weinberg, *Homosexualities: A Study of Diversity Among Men and Women* (New York: Simon & Schuster, 1978).

8. National Institute of Mental Health, *Final Report of the Task Force on Homosexuality* (Washington, DC: National Institute of Mental Health, October 10, 1969), p. 4.

9. Ibid.

10. Rubin, *Homosexuality,* op. cit., p. 8.

11. Sandra Lipsitz Bem, "Androgyny vs. the Tight Little Lives of Fluffy Women and Chesty Men," *Psychology Today,* Vol. 9 (September 1975), p. 58. For a discussion of the reliability and validity of Bem's measure, see Paul Siegel, "Androgyny, Sex-role Rigidity, and Homophobia," chapter 12 in this book.

12. A host of studies have employed a design similar to the one described here. For an example of one such study, see Rodney G. Karr, "Homosexual Labeling and the Male Role," chapter 1 in this book.

13. P.H. Hoch and J. Zubin, *Psychosexual Development in Health and Disease* (New York: Grune & Stratton, 1949).

14. Wardell B. Pomeroy, "Homosexuality," in *The Same Sex: An Appraisal of Homosexuality* (New York: Pilgrim Press, 1969), p. 4.

15. Arno Karlen, *Sexuality and Homosexuality: A New View* (New York: W.W. Norton, 1971), p. 519.

16. James W. Chesebro, John F. Cragan, and Patricia McCullough, "Consciousness-raising Among Gay Males," chapter 18 in this book; and Joseph J. Hayes, "Gayspeak," chapter 4 in this book.

17. Joshua Dressler, "Study of Law Student Attitudes Regarding the Rights of Gay People to Be Teachers," *Journal of Homosexuality,* Vol. 4 (Summer 1979), pp. 315–40.

18. David E. Newton, "Representations of Homosexuality in Health Science Textbooks," *Journal of Homosexuality,* Vol. 4 (Spring 1979), pp. 247–54.

19. Stephen F. Morin, "Heterosexual Bias in Psychological Research on Lesbianism and Male Homosexuality," *American Psychologist,* Vol. 32 (August 1977), pp. 629–37.

20. Thomas K. Fitzgerald, "A Critique of Anthropological Research on Homosexuality," *Journal of Homosexuality,* Vol. 2 (Summer 1977), pp. 385–98.

Chapter 1 Homosexual Labeling and the Male Role

1. K.G. Shaver, *An Introduction to Attribution Processes* (Cambridge, MA: Winthrop, 1975).
2. G.K. Lehne, "Homophobia Among Men," in D. David and R. Brannon, eds., *The Forty-nine Percent Majority: The Male Sex Role* (Reading, MA: Addison-Wesley, 1976).
3. A.P. MacDonald, "The Importance of Sex-role to Gay Liberation," *Homosexual Counseling Journal,* Vol. 1 (1974), pp. 169–80; A.P. MacDonald and R.G. Games, "Some Characteristics of Those Who Hold Positive and Negative Attitudes Toward Homosexuals," *Journal of Homosexuality,* Vol. 1 (1974), pp. 9–28; A.P. MacDonald et al., "Attitudes Toward Homosexuality: Preservation of Sex Morality or the Double Standard," *Journal of Consulting and Clinical Psychology,* Vol. 40 (1973), p. 161.
4. I.K. Broverman et al., "Sex-role Stereotypes and Clinical Judgments of Mental Health," *Journal of Consulting and Clinical Psychology,* Vol. 34 (1970), pp. 1–7.
5. A. Farina, "Stigmas: Potent Behavior Molders," *Behavior Today,* Vol. 2 (1972).
6. K.T. Smith, "Homophobia: A Tentative Personality Profile," *Psychological Reports,* Vol. 29 (1971), pp. 1091–94.
7. MacDonald and Games, "Some Characteristics of Those Who Hold Positive and Negative Attitudes Toward Homosexuals," op. cit.
8. A. Bandura, "Vicarious Processes: A Case of No-trial Learning," in L. Berkowitz, ed., *Advances in Experimental Social Psychology,* Vol. 2 (New York: Academic Press, 1965).
9. F.H. Kanfer, "Vicarious Human Reinforcement: A Glimpse into the Black Box," in L. Krasner and L.P. Ulman, eds., *Research in Behavior Modification* (New York: Holt, Rinehart & Winston, 1965).

Chapter 2 Coming Out as a Communicative Process

1. See George Weinberg, *Society and the Healthy Homosexual* (New York: St. Martin's Press, 1972), p. 121.
2. Max Black, ed., *The Morality of Scholarship* (Ithaca, NY: Cornell University Press, 1967), p. vii.
3. Northrup Frye, "The Knowledge of Good and Evil," in ibid., pp. 1–28.
4. Mike Silverstein, "An Open Letter to Tennessee Williams," in Karla Jay and Allen Young, eds., *Out of the Closets: Voices of Gay Liberation* (New York: Pyramid, 1974), pp. 69–72.
5. Erving Goffman, *Stigma: Notes on the Management of Spoiled Identity* (Englewood Cliffs, NJ: Prentice-Hall, 1963).
6. Peter Fisher, *The Gay Mystique* (New York: Stein & Day, 1973), p. 23.
7. Martha Shelley, "Gay Is Good," in Jay and Young, eds., *Out of the Closets,* op. cit., p. 23.

8. Merle Miller, *On Being Different: What It Means to Be a Homosexual* (New York: Random House, 1971), p. 6.
9. E. Levitt and A. Klassen, "Public Attitudes Toward Homosexuality: Part of the 1970 National Survey by the Institute for Sex Research," *Journal of Homosexuality,* Vol. 1 (1974), pp. 29–43.
10. S. Lubeck and V. Bengston, "Tolerance for Deviance: Generational Contrasts and Continuities"; paper presented at the American Sociological Association, September 1977.
11. A.P. MacDonald and R.G. Games, "Some Characteristics of Those Who Hold Positive and Negative Attitudes Toward Homosexuals," *Journal of Homosexuality,* Vol. 1 (1974), pp. 9–27.
12. Goffman, *Stigma,* op. cit., p. 87.
13. Ibid., pp. 87–90.
14. A. Bell, "Kings Don't Mean a Thing," *Playboy,* October 1978, pp. 158ff.
15. Evelyn Hooker, "The Homosexual Community," in John H. Gagnon and William Simon, eds., *Sexual Deviance* (New York: Harper & Row, 1967).
16. See D. Altman, *Homosexual: Oppression and Liberation* (New York: Avon Books, 1971).
17. Goffman, *Stigma,* op. cit.
18. Gagnon and Simon, eds., *Sexual Deviance,* op. cit.
19. J.A. Lee, "Going Public: A Study in the Sociology of Homosexual Liberation," *Journal of Homosexuality,* Vol. 3 (1977), pp. 49–78.
20. Altman, *Homosexual: Oppression and Liberation,* op. cit.
21. George A. Kelly, *A Theory of Personality: The Psychology of Personal Constructs* (New York: W.W. Norton, 1963).
22. B.M. Dank, "Coming Out in the Gay World," *Psychiatry,* Vol. 34 (1971), pp. 180–95. Used by permission.
23. K. Plummer, *Sexual Stigma: An Interactionist Perspective* (London: Routledge & Kegan Paul, 1975).
24. Ibid.
25. Goffman, *Stigma,* op. cit., p. 25.
26. See Miller, *On Being Different,* op. cit.; John Murphy, *Homosexual Liberation: A Personal View* (New York: Praeger, 1971); Silverstein, "An Open Letter to Tennessee Williams," op. cit.; and Jay and Young, eds., *Out of the Closets,* op. cit.
27. J.G. Delia, "Constructivism and the Study of Human Communication," *The Quarterly Journal of Speech,* Vol. 63 (1977), pp. 66–83.
28. Kelly, *A Theory of Personality,* op. cit., p. 21.
29. J.C.J. Bonarius, "Research in the Personal Construct Theory of George A. Kelly: Role Construct Repertory Test and Basic Theory," in B.A. Maher, ed., *Progress in Experimental Personality Research* (New York: Academic Press, 1965), II, pp. 1–46.
30. Cited in N. Mihevc, "The Stability of Construct Subsystems in the Political Domain." Unpublished dissertation, University of Illinois, 1974.
31. V.E. Cronen, "Belief Salience and Interpersonal Impression: An Extension of the Constructivist Position," *Communication Quarterly,* Vol. 26, No. 3, 1978, pp. 19–25.
32. Dorothy I. Riddle and Stephen F. Morin, "Removing the Stigma: Data from Individuals," *APA Monitor,* November 1977, pp. 16, 28.
33. J. Gurko and Sally Gearhart, "The Sword and the Vessel Versus the Lake on the Lake: A Lesbian Model of Nonviolent Rhetoric." Paper presented at the Modern Language Association, December 1979.
34. Murphy, *Homosexual Liberation,* op. cit.

35. Martin S. Weinberg and Alan P. Bell, *Homosexuality: An Annotated Bibliography* (New York: Harper & Row, 1972).

36. See James Foratt, "Word Thoughts: Homosexual," in *Come Out!* (New York: Times Change Press, 1970); J. Johnston, *Lesbian Nation: The Feminist Solution* (New York: Simon & Schuster, 1973); J. Kepner, editorial, *One,* 1968, p. 3; M. Lesher, "Choose Four: Lesbian/feminist, Woman, Dyke, Gay, Chick, Homosexual, Lesbian, Amazon, Girl," *Lesbian Connection,* February 12, 1974; Murphy, *Homosexual Liberation,* op. cit.; and Weinberg, *Society and the Healthy Homosexual,* op. cit.

37. Rita Mae Brown, "Take a Lesbian Out to Lunch," in Jay and Young, eds., *Out of the Closets,* op. cit.; Radicalesbians, "The Woman-Identified-Woman," *Notes from the Third Year: Women's Liberation* (New York: Notes from the Second Year, Inc., 1971), p. 81.

38. Radicalesbians, "The Woman-Identified-Woman," op. cit.

39. James Darsey, "Escalation of Agitative Rhetoric: A Case Study of Mattachine Midwest, 1967–1970," a paper presented at the Central States Speech Association convention, April 1977.

40. James F. Darsey, "Catalytic Events and Rhetorical Movements: A Methodological Inquiry," unpublished master's thesis, Purdue University, 1978.

41. Donald Webster Cory [Edward Sagarin], *The Homosexual in America* (1951; reprinted, New York: Arno Press, 1975).

42. Miller, *On Being Different,* op. cit.

43. Carl Wittman, "Refugees from Amerika: A Gay Manifesto," in Joseph A. McCaffrey, ed., *The Homosexual Dialectic* (Englewood Cliffs, NJ: Prentice-Hall, 1972); R.S. Schaffer, "Will You Still Need Me When I'm Sixty-four," in Jay and Young, eds., *Out of the Closets,* op. cit., pp. 278–79.

44. L. Clarke and J. Nichols, *Roommates Can't Always Be Lovers* (New York: St. Martin's Press, 1974).

Chapter 3 Lesbians, Gay Men, and Their "Languages"

1. Robin Lakoff, *Language and Woman's Place* (New York: Harper & Row, 1975). See also Casey Miller and Kate Swift, *Words and Women: New Language in New Times* (New York: Anchor Press, 1977).

2. Stephen O. Murray, "Ritual Insults in the Subcultures of the Oppressed." Paper presented to the annual meeting of the American Sociological Association, 1977.

3. The lexicon of Greek male homosexuality is explored with great care and exactitude in K.J. Dover, *Greek Homosexuality* (Cambridge, MA: Harvard University Press, 1978).

4. See, for instance, A.B. Holder, "The Bote: Description of a Peculiar Sexual Perversion Found Among North American Indians," *New York Medical Journal,* Vol. 50, No. 23 (December 7, 1889), pp. 623–25. Reprinted in Jonathan Katz, *Gay American History* (New York: Thomas Crowell, 1976).

5. George Devereux, "The Case of Sahaykwisa," in Katz, *Gay American History,* op. cit., pp. 304–8.

6. Regina Flannery, "Men's and Women's Speech in Gros Ventre," *International Journal of American Linguistics,* Vol. 12, No. 3 (July 1946), pp. 133–35.

7. An example of this language might be found in the deathbed dialogue between Enkidu and the sun god Shamash in the Sumerian poem *The Epic of Gilgamesh.*

8. Writing in 1891, in his *A Problem in Modern Ethics,* J.A. Symonds observed

that "the accomplished languages of Europe in the nineteenth century supply no terms for this persistent feature of human psychology [homosexuality], without imparting some implication of disgust, disgrace, vituperation." Many of the ideas for the first two sections of this paper came from the admirable and suggestive work of Jeffrey Weeks, *Coming Out: Homosexual Politics in Britain from the Nineteenth Century to the Present* (London: Quartet Books, 1977).

9. Unpublished manuscript.

10. Thomas S. Szasz, *The Manufacture of Madness* (New York: Harper & Row, 1970).

11. Eric Bentley, "The Homosexual Question," *The American Review*, Vol. 26 (1977), pp. 288–303.

12. Kevin J. Burke and Murray S. Edelman, "Sensitivity Groups, Consciousness-Raising Groups and the Gay Liberation Movement." Paper presented at the annual meeting of the American Political Science Association, 1972.

13. " 'Gay' Not Proper," *Alternate Magazine*, Vol. 1, No. 1 (November 1977), p. 7.

14. "Are Lesbians 'Gay'?" *MS.*, Vol. 3, No. 12 (June 1975), pp. 85–86.

15. J. Rogers Conrad, "Homosexuality in the Social Sciences: Definition, Reification and Key Status." Paper presented at the annual meeting of the American Anthropology Association, 1976.

16. Michael Davidson, "Notes on Nomenclature," in *Some Boys* (London: David Bruce and Wabon, 1970), pp. 191–93.

17. Szasz, *The Manufacture of Madness*, op. cit.

18. Charley Shiveley, *Fag Rag*, No. 25 (Summer 1978), p. 2.

19. Thomas Dotton, "Gay Is Straight," *Fag Rag*, No. 20 (Summer 1977), p. 3.

20. Radicalesbians, "The Woman-Identified-Woman," in *Notes from the Third Year: Women's Liberation* (New York: Notes from the Second Year, Inc., 1971).

21. See, for instance, Laud Humphreys, *Tearoom Trade: Impersonal Sex in Public Places* (Chicago: Aldine, 1970).

22. Patricia Nell Warren, *Front Runner* (New York: Bantam Books, 1975).

23. Hal Fischer, *Gay Semiotics: A Photographic Study of Visual Coding Among Homosexual Men* (San Francisco: NSF Press, 1977).

24. Michael Emory, ed., *The Gay Picture Book* (Chicago: Contemporary Books, 1978).

25. Ray Birdwhistell, *Kinesics and Context: Essays on Body Motion* (Philadelphia: University of Pennsylvania Press, 1970).

26. Richard Dyer, ed., "Stereotyping," *Gays and Film* (London: British Film Institute, 1977), pp. 27–39.

27. Rita Mae Brown, "The Good Fairy," *Quest*, Vol. 1, No. 1 (Summer 1974), pp. 58–64.

28. Yvon Thiverge, "Linguistic Oppression and Liberation," *The Body Politic*, Vol. 19 (July/August 1975), p. 25.

29. Julia Penelope has dropped her father's surname. I have mentioned it here, since all her work until 1979 has been published under Julia P. Stanley.

30. "Homosexual Slang," *American Speech*, Vol. 45, No. 1–2 (1970), pp. 45–59.

31. "Lesbian Separation: The Linguistic and Social Sources of Lesbian Politics," in Louie Crew, ed., *The Gay Academic* (Palm Springs, CA: ETC, 1978).

32. "When We Say 'Out of the Closets'," *College English*, Vol. 36, No. 3 (November 1974), pp. 385–91.

33. "Honey, Let's Talk About the Queen's English," *Gai Saber*, Vol. 1, No. 3.

34. Jack Babuscio's thoughtful "The Cinema of Camp" (*Gay Sunshine*, Vol. 35 [Winter 1978], pp. 18–22), along with work he did for *Gay News* and the British Film Institute, is being assembled into an extended examination of *camp*.

35. See Julia Penelope Stanley and Susan Wolf Robbins, "Mother Wit: Tongue

in Cheek," in Karla Jay and Allen Young, eds., *Lavender Culture* (New York: Harcourt, Brace Jovanovich, 1979), pp. 299–307, and Julia Penelope Stanley and Susan Wolf Robbins, "Lesbian Humor," in *Women, a Journal of Liberation,* Vol. 5, No. 1 (1976), pp. 26–29.

Chapter 4 Gayspeak

1. Earlier versions of this essay profited from the helpful criticisms of professors D.W. Hartley, T.P. Klammer, M.R. Schulz, and H.J. Seller, all of California State University, Fullerton, and Prof. T.D. Terrell, of the University of California, Irvine. I wish to thank also the members of the Linguistics section of the Philological Association of the Pacific Coast, to whom I presented an abridged version of this paper in November 1975.

2. No previous study of gay language has attempted this method. Previous efforts are mostly lexicons without any rigorous analysis—Ronald A. Farrell, "The Argot of the Homosexual Subculture," *Anthropological Linguistics,* Vol. 14 (1972), pp. 97–109; Julia P. Stanley, "Homosexual Slang," *American Speech,* Vol. 45, No. 1–2 (1970), pp. 45–59, and "When We Say 'Out of the Closets'," *College English,* Vol. 36, No. 3 (1974), pp. 385–91; Bruce Rodgers, *The Queens' Vernacular: A Gay Lexicon* (San Francisco: Straight Arrow, 1972). Farrell, Rodgers, and Stanley (1970) provide mostly word lists, although Rodgers is quite exhaustive for gay men's language. Stanley (1974) is an excellent presentation of the radical perspective.

3. Although I refer in several places to the language of both gay men and women, I am speaking primarily about gay *men.* My experience in the lesbian community is not sufficient to delineate a special dialect among gay women.

4. The term setting is intended to mean something more than Gumperz' concept of community (John J. Gumperz, "Types of Linguistic Communities," *Anthropological Linguistics,* Vol. 4, No. 1 [1962], pp. 28–40). I am not speaking here so much of a "community of interaction" as I am of a "situated context." A gay liberationist, for instance, might normally belong to a counterculture "speech community" but might still use secret Gayspeak in certain contexts (e.g., in a family "setting"). Whatever his politics or convictions, his language is usually appropriate to a given context.

5. It is most important to emphasize that there are no easily defined boundaries between the three settings singled out. Gays may use special language in certain contexts but never in others. For instance, men who wish to appear "serious" or "masculine" might use radical-activist or neutral language with one set of friends, although they might abandon this role in order to *camp it up* with another set of friends.

6. Penelope Gilliatt, *Sunday, Bloody Sunday* (New York: Bantam Books, 1971), p. 121.

7. The term is taken from Laud Humphreys, *Out of the Closets: The Sociology of Homosexual Liberation* (Englewood Cliffs, NJ: Prentice-Hall, 1972), pp. 74–76.

8. Carol A.B. Warren, *Identity and Community in the Gay World* (NewYork: John Wiley & Sons, 1974), p. 114.

9. These few examples are selected from a much lengthier list in Rodgers, *The Queens' Vernacular,* op. cit., pp. 164–65.

10. Mary Ritchie Key repeats a very common misunderstanding of usage in Gayspeak when she states, "The pronoun *she* is used to designate the female partner" ("Linguistic Behavior of Male and Female," *Linguistics,* No. 88 [August 1972], p. 28). Similar errors have been repeated so often by linguists that this fanciful notion has been accepted as an article of faith.

11. Robin Lakoff feels that labels are the result of real, observable behavior: "It is very seldom the case that a certain form of behavior results from being given a certain name, but rather, names are given on the basis of previously observed behavior." ("Language and Women's Place," *Language in Society,* Vol. 2 [1973], p. 75).

12. The two most famous discussions of camp are Susan Sontag, "Notes on Camp," *Partisan Review,* Vol. 31 (1964), pp. 515–30 and Alan Brien, "Camper's Guide," *New Statesman,* Vol. 23 (1967), pp. 373–74. Neither one is addressed especially to the use of camp in the gay community; such a complex analysis still remains to be done.

13. In addition to Robin Lakoff and Mary Ritchie Key, see Muriel R. Schulz, "The Semantic Derogation of Women," in Barrie Thorne and Nancy Henley, eds., *Language and Sex: Difference and Dominance* (Rowley, MA: Newberry House, 1975).

14. Louella (pseud.), "Hello from Hollywood," *Data-Boy,* January 5, 1972, p. 18.

15. Lakoff, "Language and Women's Place," op. cit., pp. 50–53.

16. Stanley, "When We Say 'Out of the Closets'," op. cit., p. 386.

17. Allen Young, "On Human and Gay Identity: A Liberationist Dilemma," *Gay Sunshine,* Vols. 31–32 (1974), p. 31.

18. D. Cartier, "A Dyke's Manifesto," *The (Lesbian) Tide,* Vol. 2 (1973), p. 19.

19. Lakoff, "Language and Women's Place," op. cit., p. 50.

20. Rita Goldberger, "Rita Right-On: Radical Rhetoric," *The (Lesbian) Tide,* Vol. 2 (1973), p. 7 (emphasis added).

21. Lakoff, "Language and Women's Place," op. cit., p. 45.

22. Among members of the gay liberation movement there is an especial emphasis on desexualizing the term gay: "Being *gay* no longer simply refers to loving one's own sex, but has come to designate a state of political awareness in which one no longer needs the narrowly defined sex-role stereotypes as bases for identity" (Stanley, "When We Say 'Out of the Closets'," op. cit., p. 390). Similarly, James Foratt writes of *homosexual:* "I find the word hard to relate to because it puts me in a category which limits my potential. It also prescribes a whole system of behavior to which I'm supposed to conform which has nothing to do with the reality of my day to day living." ("Word Thoughts: Homosexual," *Come Out!* [New York Times Change, 1970], p. 16). The position paper of the Paris *Front Homosexual d'Action Revolutionnaire* states that "homosexuality doesn't exist. It is only in the minds of those who see themselves as heterosexuals or those who have been persuaded they are gay by the would-be heteros." (Broadside translated by the group, 1972.)

23. Lakoff, "Language and Women's Place," op. cit., p. 50.

24. John Dart, "'Closet Atheists' Urged to Tell Beliefs," *Los Angeles Times,* February 20, 1975, II, p. 12.

Chapter 5 "Gayspeak": A Response

1. On the use of gay studies, see "Proposal for Division of Gay Studies in Language and Literature in Modern Language Association," mimeographed, n.d., n.p.

2. James Darsey, "Escalation of Agitative Rhetoric: A Case Study of Mattachine Midwest, 1967–1970," a paper presented to the Central States Speech Association Convention, April 1977. Cf. James F. Darsey, "Catalytic Events and Rhetorical Movements: A Methodological Inquiry," unpublished master's thesis, Purdue

University, 1978. This study sketches the history of American homophile discourse from 1950 to 1977 but chiefly illustrates a proposed method for the study of rhetorical movements.

3. This essay by Hayes originally appeared in *The Quarterly Journal of Speech,* Vol. 62 (October 1976), pp. 256–66.

4. Ibid., p. 256.

5. Ibid., p. 257.

6. Ibid.

7. Ibid., p. 258.

8. Ibid., pp. 259–60.

9. For example, "The Drag," circa 1927.

10. Hayes, "Gayspeak," op. cit., p. 260.

11. See Mike Silverstein, "An Open Letter to Tennessee Williams," in Karla Jay and Allen Young, eds., *Out of the Closets: Voices of Gay Liberation* (New York: Pyramid, 1972), pp. 69–72.

12. Hayes, "Gayspeak," op. cit., p. 257.

13. Ibid.

14. For example, see Ernest G. Bormann, *Discussion and Group Methods* (New York: Harper & Row, 1969), pp. 149–50.

15. For an explication of the idea of socially created reality, see Peter L. Berger and Thomas Luckman, *The Social Construction of Reality* (Garden City, NY: Anchor Books, 1967).

16. Vito Russo, "Camp," *The Advocate,* May 19, 1976, p. 17.

17. Ibid., pp. 17–18.

18. See Susan Sontag, "Notes on Camp," *Partisan Review,* Vol. 31 (1964), pp. 515–30. This essay is not concerned with camp as a uniquely gay phenomenon.

19. Russo notes: "The relation of camp to gay humor is the same as the relation of guilt to being Jewish. It's by reputation only. And just as there are some guilty Portnoys, there are some campy homosexuals." (Russo, "Camp," op. cit., p. 17.)

20. Ibid., p. 18.

21. Karla Jay, Foreword, in Jay and Young, eds., *Out of the Closets,* op. cit., p. 1.

22. Ibid.

23. Carl Wittman notes this phenomenon and urges greater solidarity. Carl Wittman, "Refugees from Amerika: A Gay Manifesto," reprinted in Joseph A. McCaffrey, ed., *The Homosexual Dialectic* (Englewood Cliffs, NJ: Prentice-Hall, 1972), p. 162.

24. Ibid.

25. Hayes, "Gayspeak," op. cit., p. 261.

26. James Chesebro, "Rhetorical Strategies of the Radical-Revolutionary," *Today's Speech,* Vol. 20 (Winter 1972), pp. 37–44.

27. For an example of an investigation into this setting, see James W. Chesebro, John F. Cragan, and Patricia McCullough, "Consciousness-raising Among Gay Males," which appears as chapter 18 in this book.

28. Darsey, "Escalation of Agitative Rhetoric," op. cit., p. 1. Many studies have been added since this was originally written, although the numbers are still relatively small.

29. Stuart Byron, "The Closet Syndrome," in Jay and Young, eds., *Out of the Closets,* op. cit., p. 58.

30. Hayes, "Gayspeak," op. cit., p. 257.

31. Martin Hoffman, *The Gay World* (New York: Basic Books, 1968), p. 45. Gerald Goldhaber also reports a heavy use of nonverbal cues among gays (Goldhaber, "Gay Talk: Communication Behavior of Male Homosexuals," *Gai Saber,* Vol. 1 [1977], esp. p. 143, Table 10).

32. Personal correspondence.

33. For an understanding of this term, see Mark L. Knapp, *Nonverbal Communication in Human Interaction* (New York: Holt, Rinehart, & Winston, 1972), especially pp. 79–85.

34. Hayes refers to the importance of these roles in the subculture from a linguistic standpoint; see Hayes, "Gayspeak," op. cit., p. 259.

35. Phil Andros, "Sea-Change," reprinted in Stephen Wright, ed., *Different* (New York: Bantam Books, 1974), p. 49. Used by permission of the author.

36. Since the original writing of this essay, at least one book-length study of the nonverbal behavior of homosexuals has been published: Edward W. Delph, *The Silent Community* (Beverly Hills, CA: Sage Publications, 1978).

37. Hayes, "Gayspeak," op. cit., see note 4. Goldhaber also excludes women. Goldhaber, "Gay Talk" op. cit., p. 137.

38. Paraphrased from a conversation between the white queen and Alice in *Through the Looking Glass.*

Chapter 6 Recognition Among Lesbians in Straight Settings

1. My first attempt at research in the lesbian community was a descriptive participant observation study conducted in the spring of 1976. The setting was a lesbian bar, and the focus of the paper that resulted was different types of talk, including what they were and what they accomplished. I now view this first work as an elementary "cookbook" guide to talk in lesbian bars, inasmuch as it provided instances of appropriate talk and situations for its use. As I became involved in ethnomethodology, I continued to examine lesbian talk, and became fascinated with its highly complex indexical nature and the interpretive procedures employed by members of the lesbian speech community. Having completed an ethnomethodological dissertation on lesbian humor, in 1978, I continue to examine the process of being a lesbian from a communicative perspective as one of my primary areas of research. My thanks to Leonard C. Hawes, who asked questions that led me to other questions. "Simple" questions become complex and interesting when regressed a bit.

2. For an overview of deviant hidden minorities, see Erving Goffman, *Stigma: Notes on the Management of Spoiled Identity* (Englewood Cliffs, NJ: Prentice-Hall, 1963).

3. Passing can be defined as those activities one engages in while attempting to be perceived as a member in a speech community in which she or he is not a member.

4. Incorrigible propositions are those instances of shared social knowledge that are not only unquestioned, but also unquestionable by members. For examples and a clear explanation, see Hugh Mehan and Huston Wood, *The Reality of Ethnomethodology* (New York: John Wiley & Sons, 1975).

5. Although communicative work includes all aspects of symbolic interaction, I am primarily interested in talk as it constitutes social reality. See Stanley Deetz, "Words Without Things: Toward a Social Phenomenology of Language," *Quarterly Journal of Speech,* Vol. 59 (February 1976); Donna Jurick, "The Communicative Constitution of Information: Talk and How Talk Works," dissertation, Ohio State University, 1976.

6. Harold Garfinkel, *Studies in Ethnomethodology* (Englewood Cliffs, NJ: Prentice-Hall, 1967), pp. 55–57.

7. A study of this type, even if tightly controlled, would not be useful to the communication researcher or the lesbian. Knowing, for example, that lesbians hold

eye contact for a fraction of a second longer than other women has little or no practical use nor is it terribly insightful.

8. It is interesting that although lesbians can name specific behaviors and features of passing as straight, the cues to their own "real" identity are unnamed and unnameable. Being capable of verbally identifying passing features points to its accomplishment as work and, more importantly, as unnatural work.

9. Joseph J. Hayes, "Gayspeak," *The Quarterly Journal of Speech,* Vol. 62 (October 1976), pp. 256–66.

10. Ibid., p. 257.

11. The word lesbian is not always consciously thought much in the same way individuals mentally acknowledge recognition of objects without mentally naming them each time they are seen. If one had to stop and name each object that came into view, one would have little time to do much else.

12. The word dyke was used for a long time by straights as a derogatory term for lesbians. More specifically, dyke connotes a masculine, truck-driving–type lesbian. Recently, radical lesbians and a growing number of their less radical sisters have been reclaiming the word dyke to use as their own term of pride and strength.

13. Alfred Schutz, in Helmet R. Wagner, ed., *On Phenomenology and Social Relations* (Chicago: University of Chicago Press, 1973), pp. 116–22.

14. Ibid., p. 116.

15. Ibid., p. 117.

16. Ibid., p. 118.

17. The concept of membership categorization device is loosely borrowed from Harvey Sacks. Sacks suggests the construct of membership categorization devices to investigate the meaning relationship between words. For an in-depth discussion of the original use of this construct, see Harvey Sacks, "On the Analyzability of Stories by Children," in John J. Gumperz and Dell Hymes, eds., *Directions in Sociolinguistics* (New York: Holt, Rinehart & Winston, 1972), pp. 332–38.

Chapter 7 Communication Patterns in Established Lesbian Relationships

1. Alfred Kinsey, cited in "How Gay Is Gay?" *Time,* Vol. 113 (1979), pp. 72–76.

2. D. Tanner, *The Lesbian Couple* (Lexington, MA: Lexington Books, 1978).

3. Paul Watzlawick, Janet Beavin, and Don Jackson, *Pragmatics of Human Communication* (New York: W.W. Norton, 1967).

4. F. Millar and E. Rogers, "A Relational Approach to Interpersonal Communication," in G.R. Miller, ed., *Explorations in Interpersonal Communication* (Beverly Hills, CA: Sage Publications, 1976).

5. P. Ericson and L. Rogers, "New Procedures for Analyzing Relational Communication," *Family Process,* Vol. 12 (1973), pp. 245–67.

6. M. Parks, "Toward an Axiomatic Theory of Relational Communication," a paper presented at the International Communication Association convention, April 1975, p. 3.

7. Ericson and Rogers, "New Procedures for Analyzing Relational Communication," op. cit.; F. Millar, III, "A Transactional Analysis of Marital Communication Patterns: An Exploratory Study," unpublished Ph.D. dissertation, Michigan State University, 1973; E. Rogers, "Dyadic Systems and Transactional Communication in a Family Context," unpublished Ph.D. dissertation, Michigan State University, 1972; M. Parks et al., "Stochastic Process Analysis of Relational Communication in Marital Dyads," a paper presented at the International Communication Association convention, April 1976.

8. Watzlawick, Beavin, and Jackson, *Pragmatics of Human Communication,* op. cit.

9. W. Lederer and D. Jackson, *The Mirages of Marriage* (New York: W.W. Norton, 1968.

10. Parks et al., "Stochastic Process Analysis of Relational Communication in Marital Dyads," op. cit.

11. W. Richmond, *The Adolescent Girl* (New York: Macmillan, 1925); F.S. Caprio, *Female Homosexuality* (New York: Grove Press, 1954); D. Ward and G. Kassebaum, "Homosexuality: A Mode of Adaptation in a Prison for Women," *Social Problems,* Vol. 12 (1964), pp. 168–70; R. Giallombardo, "Social Roles in the Prison for Women," *Social Problems,* Vol. 13 (1966), p. 270; M. Jensen, "Role Differentiation in Female Homosexual Quasi-marital Unions," *Journal of Marriage and the Family,* 1974, pp. 360–67; and D. Cory, "Homosexuality," in A. Ellis and A. Abarbanel, eds., *The Encyclopedia of Sexual Behavior* (New York: Hawthorn Books, 1961).

12. D. Martin and P. Lyon, *Lesbian/woman* (New York: Glide Publication, 1972).

13. A. Oberstone and H. Sukoneck, "Psychological Adjustment and Life Style of Single Lesbians and Single Heterosexual Women," *Psychology of Women,* Vol. 1 (1976), pp. 172–88.

14. D. Rosen, *Lesbianism: A Study of Female Homosexuality* (Springfield, IL: Charles C. Thomas, 1974).

15. H. Gough and A. Heilbrun, *The Adjective Check List Manual* (Palo Alto, CA: Consulting Psychologists Press, 1965).

16. A. Heilbrun and N. Thompson, "Sex-role Identity and Male and Female Homosexuality," *Sex Roles,* Vol. 3 (1977), pp. 65–79.

17. J. DeLora and C. Warren, *Understanding Sexual Interaction* (Boston: Houghton Mifflin, 1977).

18. J. Chafetz et al., "A Study of Homosexual Women," *Social Work,* Vol. 36 (1974), pp. 714–23.

19. Martin and Lyon, *Lesbian/woman,* op. cit.; Oberstone and Sukoneck, "Psychological Adjustment and Life Style," op. cit.; Rosen, *Lesbianism,* op. cit.; Heilbrun and Thompson, "Sex-role Identity," op. cit.; DeLora and Warren, *Understanding Sexual Interaction,* op. cit.; B. Ponse, "Secrecy in the Lesbian World," in C. Warren, ed., *Sexuality: Encounters, Identities, and Relationships,* Urban Life Special Issue (Beverly Hills, CA: Sage Publications, 1976); S. Lessard, "Gay Is Good for Us All," *Washington Monthly,* Vol. 2 (December 1970), pp. 39–49; C. Warren, "Women Among Men: Females in the Male Homosexual Community," *Archives of Sexual Behavior,* Vol. 5 (1976), pp. 157–69; and Chafetz et al., "A Study of Homosexual Women," op. cit.

20. Pairs were contacted in three ways: first, "pyramiding" (Oberstone and Sukoneck, "Psychological Adjustment and Life Style," op. cit.) was employed. This consisted of making an initial contact in a gay community and meeting other lesbians through the initial contact. Second, personal acquaintances in the lesbian community were contacted. Finally, subjects were randomly selected from a list of couples willing to participate in this particular study. The list of pairs was obtained from the presidents of "Mentoris" and "Dinah."

21. Both topics were pretested and found to be conducive to sustained discussion and unlikely to produce revelation of subjects' identities. While the topics could not be considered "typical" conversational issues, the neutrality of the topics and their previous use by other researchers deemed them acceptable for this study.

22. Ericson and Rogers, "New Procedures for Analyzing Relational Communication," op. cit.

23. Additionally, in this coding scheme, an assertion was any completed referential statement that wasn't a talk-over. Questions were those messages other than a talk-over that took an interrogative grammatical form. Talk-overs referred to the way in which a speaker came into the dialogue, i.e., any distinguishable verbal intervention emitted while another was talking. Noncompletes were those utterances that were initiated but were not expressed in a complete format.

24. Ericson and Rogers, "New Procedures for Analyzing Relational Communication," op. cit.

25. Before testing the hypotheses, tests for order, rational control, and stationarity were run. The test for first order was to determine if the observed transition matrix was capable of predicting a message based on the immediate prior message. The Chi-square test was significant (X^2 = 13.33, *df* = 4, *p* .05). The test for relational control was to further test the structure of the matrix. Messages for each column were divided by three in order to determine the expected number of messages for the three cells in each column. The Chi-square test was significant (X^2 = 85.80, *df* = 4, *p* .05). This test for stationarity determined whether the matrix of transition probabilities was constant. In this study the first three minutes of all taped discussions were compared to the last three minutes of all taped discussions by use of a Chi-square test. The null hypothesis was $T = T_1$, where T equaled the first three minutes and T_1 represented the last three minutes of all discussions. The Chi-square test indicated no significant difference between the first three minutes and the last three minutes of the taped discussions (X^2 = 3.799, *df* = 6, *p* .05).

26. To test H_1 a Markov chain analysis of the main study data was conducted. This analysis produced a first-order 3 × 3 matrix. The number of messages that constituted the values was 620. A Chi-square test of the matrix indicated that a significant portion of the messages was transitory (X^2 = 93.3, *df* = 1, *p* .05).

27. Parks, "Toward an Axiomatic Theory of Relational Communication," op. cit.

28. Richmond, *The Adolescent Girl,* op. cit.; Caprio, *Female Homosexuality,* op. cit.; Ward and Kassebaum, "Homosexuality," op. cit.; Jensen, "Role Differentiation," op. cit.

29. Martin and Lyon, *Lesbian/woman,* op. cit.; Oberstone and Sukoneck, "Psychological Adjustment and Life Style," op. cit.; and DeLora and Warren, *Understanding Sexual Interaction,* op. cit.

30. For H_2, a Chi-square test of the transitory cells of the matrix also demonstrated that a significant portion of these matters constituted neutralized symmetry (X^2 = 35.31, *df* = 1, *p* .05).

31. To test H_3, a 9 × 3 matrix was produced for the second-order Markov chain. Cells that contained two one-across messages were considered transitory. Again, a Chi-square test indicated that a significant portion of second-order messages was transitory (X^2 = 170.87, *df* = 1, *p* .05).

32. To test H_4, a Chi-square test was conducted on the transitory cells of the 9 × 3 matrix. Again, two one-across messages per cell was the criterion for transitory, with three one-across messages constituting neutralized symmetry. Results showed that a significant portion of messages within the transitory cells was neutralized symmetry (X^2 = 35.14, *df* = 1, *p* .05).

Chapter 8 Gay Masculinity in the Gay Disco

1. Arthur Schlesinger, Jr., "The Crisis of American Masculinity," in Louis E. Glorfeld, Tom E. Kakonis, and James C. Wilcox, eds., *Language, Rhetoric and Idea* (Columbus, OH: Charles E. Merrill, 1967), p. 303.

2. Ibid.

3. Reported in Connie DeBoer, "The Polls: Attitudes Toward Homosexuality," *The Public Opinion Quarterly,* Vol. 42 (Summer 1978), p. 276.

4. See "The American Freshmen: National Norms for Fall," published by the American Council on Education and the University of California at Los Angeles.

5. Reported in "Homosexuals in America," *The Gallup Opinion Index,* October 1977, Report No. 147, p. 13.

6. Quoted in Arno Karlen, *Sexuality and Homosexuality: A New View* (New York: W.W. Norton, 1971), p. 528. For a more extended discussion of Goffman's conception of homosexuality, see Erving Goffman, *Stigma: Notes on the Management of Spoiled Identity* (Englewood Cliffs, NJ: Prentice-Hall, 1963), particularly footnote #7, pp. 143–44. Goffman's conception, at this point, is consistent with our conception of the type of homosexual interactions that occurs in the gay disco.

7. Alan P. Bell and Martin S. Weinberg, *Homosexualities: A Study of Diversity Among Men and Women* (New York: Simon & Schuster, 1978), p. 438, table 21.6.

8. For an extended discussion of the meaning of the word gay in contrast to the word homosexual, see James W. Chesebro, "Views of Homosexuality Among Social Scientists," chapter 15 in this book. At this point it is sufficient to note that the word homosexual was first coined in 1869 by a doctor named Benkert, writing under the pseudonym of Kertbeny. He coined the word from the Greek *homos,* meaning same. Exactly one hundred years later, in June of 1969, the word was forcefully rejected by the gay liberation movement. However, the notion or concept of *homosexuality* was first employed by a "homosexual" in the first serious work devoted exclusively to same-sex relations, in 1862, by Karl Heinrich Ulrichs, who first wrote under the pseudonym of Numa Numantius and then under his own name. Ulrichs employed the German term *urning,* derived from Plato's *Symposium,* where it was said that "those dedicated to the goddess Urania feel themselves drawn exclusively to males." Ulrichs created the word urning to avoid using the words sodomite and pederast, which had previously been employed to deal with same-sex relations. An individual was defined solely by the type of sexual act they initiated when the terms sodomite and pederast were employed. Ulrichs' effort was to initiate a concept that referred to the sense of community identification an individual might feel. Accordingly, the term urning was designed only to specify an individual's preference for same-sex relations regardless of if or how that preference was executed—if at all. Prior to Ulrichs' decision to coin the word urning, no word existed that specified an individual's same-sex preference. Moreover, Ulrichs coined the word in an effort to eliminate what he believed was the brutal injustice dealt same-sex relations. Same-sex relations, Ulrichs felt, were as meaningful, natural, and nonpathological as heterosexuality. Ulrichs ultimately engaged in a campaign for full legal rights for homosexuals, including the right to legally marry. For additional considerations regarding these historical notes, see Karlen, *Sexuality and Homosexuality,* op. cit., especially pp. 186–87.

9. George Weinberg, *Society and the Healthy Homosexual* (New York: St. Martin's Press, 1972).

10. Stephen F. Morin and S.J. Schultz, "The Gay Movement and the Rights of Children," *Journal of Social Issues,* Vol. 34 (Spring 1978), pp. 137–48.

11. Carmen De Monteflores and Stephen J. Schultz, "Coming Out: Similarities and Differences for Lesbians and Gay Men," *Journal of Social Issues,* Vol. 34 (Summer 1978), pp. 59–72, especially pp. 60–61.

12. Bruce Werner, "Guilt," *Blueboy,* Vol. 20 (May 1978), p. 63. Used by permission.

13. Alan E. Gross, "The Male Role and Heterosexual Behavior," *Journal of Social Issues,* Vol. 34 (Winter 1978), pp. 87–107.

14. Robert A. Lewis, "Emotional Intimacy Among Men," *Journal of Social Issues,* Vol. 34 (Winter 1978), p. 108.

15. Nick Benton, *Sexism, Racism and White Faggots in Sodomist Amerika* (Berkeley, CA: The Effeminist, n.d.), p. 11.

16. Bell and Weinberg, *Homosexualities,* op. cit., p. 86.

17. See Edwin O. Smigel and Rita Seiden, "The Decline and Fall of the Double Standard," *The Annals of the American Academy of Political and Social Science,* Vol. 376 (March 1968), p. 17.

18. See James W. Chesebro, John F. Cragan, and Patricia McCullough, "The Small Group Technique of the Radical Revolutionary: A Synthetic Study of Consciousness Raising," *Speech Monographs,* Vol. 40 (June 1973), pp. 136–46; and Joseph J. Hayes, "Gayspeak," *Quarterly Journal of Speech,* Vol. 62 (October 1976), pp. 256–66.

19. We are not the first to note that the rhetorical figure of paradox permeates the life-style of gay males; see Ralph W. Weltge, "The Paradox of Man and Woman," in Ralph W. Weltge, ed., *The Same Sex* (New York: Pilgrim Press, 1969), pp. 55–66; and Paul Watzlawick, Janet Helmick Beavin, and Don Jackson, *Pragmatics of Human Communication* (New York: W.W. Norton, 1967), p. 200. In the context of the gay disco, by *paradoxical world view,* we mean: "A paradoxical world view is created, mediated, and controlled by a symbol, (1) functioning as a selective principle of interpretation, orientation, perspective, or point-of-view that (2) establishes a relationship between two other opposite or contradictory concepts in such a way that the symbol forces (3) these two opposite concepts to mutually and simultaneously influence the definition of phenomena (4) in multiple and different kinds of situations (5) without eliminating the tension of the opposition." For a context, rationale, and explanation of this definition, direct inquiries to James W. Chesebro, regarding "Paradox and Symbolic Realities: The Rhetorical Criticism of Social Constructions," unpublished manuscript, p. 10.

20. For a convenient sampling of different approaches to ethnographic research, see *Communication Quarterly,* Vol. 25 (Summer 1977), pp. 2–56.

21. For a more extended discussion of this conception of naturalistic research, see Severyn T. Bruyn, *The Human Perspective in Sociology: The Methodology of Participant Observation* (Englewood Cliffs, NJ: Prentice-Hall, 1966).

22. While the concept of everyday communication is seldom treated as a critical concept, we have conceived of the study of everyday communication to be the examination of (1) particular intentions rather than intentionality as an epistemological issue, (2) settings in which agents assume that a single reality exists independent of perception; an intersubjective reality is unconsciously presumed, (3) agents who believe that imperative actions are required rather than dialective exchanges, (4) imminent actions and face-to-face interactions possessing the full scope of all verbal and nonverbal stimuli in which immediate, flexible, continuous, and prereflective symbolic exchanges occur, (5) exchanges in which members of a communication system assume there is a correspondence among their meanings, and (6) agents engaged in continuity in their interactions in terms of geography, time, and social relations. Thus, everyday communication is the study of autobiographical meanings or the pragmatics and self-serving understandings of an inner circle or symbolic enclave in which there is a high degree of dependency, interest, and intimacy. We would not, therefore, perceive formal speeches, academic debates, most written essays, or highly ceremonial occasions typically to be "everyday communication." For more extended discussions of these notions, see Peter L. Berger and Thomas Luckmann, *The Social Construction of Reality: A Treatise in the Sociology of Knowledge* (1966; reprinted Garden City, NY: Anchor

Books, 1967); and Erving Goffman, *The Presentation of Self in Everyday Life* (1959; reprinted Garden City, NY: Doubleday, 1959).

23. For an extended discussion of reactivism in research designs and applications, see Eugene J. Webb et al., *Unobtrusive Measures: Nonreactive Research in the Social Sciences* (Chicago: Rand McNally, 1966).

24. As Webb et al. suggest (ibid.), simple observation occurs whenever the observer has no control over the behavior under investigation and when the researcher-observer assumes a passive, nonintrusive role in the ongoing interactions. This research method typically allows a researcher to gather external physical evidence, observe and record expressive movements, describe physical locations, sample conversations, and measure time/attention durations. The possibility of collecting data unobtrusively while being a physically present but passive observer has been debated; some have claimed that the influence of the simple observer erodes with time, while others claim that observers must also be participants to eliminate this reactive effect; see Webb, et al., pp. 112–41, especially pp. 113–14.

25. The open-ended interview is typically contrasted to the focused questionnaire. Focusing on its intrinsic characteristics, we conceive of the open-ended interview as the use of an interrogative sentence asked of subjects in a natural setting, which is designed to permit spontaneous and unguided responses and which allows subjects to offer any qualifiers, contingencies, or introduce any situational variables they see fit to answer the question. In particular, we assume that open-ended questions are asked of subjects in environments of their own choice and construction, specify a topic area but contain no time/space restrictions, can be qualified by subjects as they wish, and that at least a parasocial relationship exists between the researcher and subjects. For a discussion of the parasocial relationship, see Donald Horton and R. Richard Whol, "Mass Communication and Para-Social Interaction," *Psychiatry,* Vol. 19 (August 1956), pp. 215–29.

26. Our conception of participant-observation is strongly influenced by Bruyn's description of this technique, particularly his experimental categories for verification as an operational definition of the role requirements of the participant-observer; see Bruyn, *The Human Perspective in Sociology,* op. cit., p. 261.

27. For a traditional conception of content analysis, see Ole R. Holsti, *Content Analysis for the Social Sciences and Humanities* (Reading, MA: Addison-Wesley, 1969). In naturalistic research settings and designs, procedures for content analysis are typically altered. Categories generated should reflect the social meanings of those being studied. For a convenient set of verification procedures regarding this content analysis requirement, see Bruyn, *The Human Perspective in Sociology,* op. cit., p. 261.

28. See Webb, et al., *Unobtrusive Measures,* op. cit., pp. 3, 5, 36, 173–74, and 181.

29. Particularly, we have used interviews at the back of various chapters of Karlen's book. In addition, portions of interviews from Hatterer's book shaped our thinking; see Lawrence J. Hatterer, *Changing Homosexuality in the Male: Treatment for Men Troubled by Homosexuality* (New York: McGraw-Hill, 1970).

30. Thomas S. Frentz and Thomas B. Farrell, "Language-Action: A Paradigm for Communication," *Quarterly Journal of Speech,* Vol. 62 (December 1976), pp. 333–49.

31. Ibid., p. 334.

32. The clubs investigated included New York's 12 West, Philadelphia's DCA, Washington, DC's Lost and Found, Houston's The Old Plantation, Los Angeles' Studio One, Minneapolis' Sutton's, and San Francisco's The Rendezvous. Four of these clubs are classified in the Top 20 Hot Spots, a listing of the best discos by *Blueboy* magazine; see "Top 20 Hot Spots," *Blueboy,* Vol. 23 (August 1978), p. 25.

33. Such statistical measures are extremely difficult to obtain in an everchanging and ongoing social environment in an unobtrusive fashion. Typically, we found it useful to isolate a specific area defined by certain geographic limits and then rapidly count the number of males and females within the particular area. Thus, for example, one such check produced a ratio of women to males of 2:25, 1:17, and 3:45.

34. Larry Kramer, *Faggots* (New York: Random House, 1978), p. 6.

35. Clarke Taylor, "Disco Madness," *Blueboy,* Vol. 13 (August/September 1977), p. 32. Used by permission.

36. Erving Goffman, *Interaction Ritual: Essays on Face-to-Face Behavior* (Garden City, NY: Anchor Books, 1967), p. 197.

37. Erving Goffman, *The Presentation of Self in Everyday Life* (Garden City, NY: Anchor Books, 1959).

38. For an example of such reasoning and evidence that supports such a view, see Barbara Westbrook Eakins and R. Gene Eakins, *Sex Differences in Communication* (Boston: Houghton Mifflin, 1978).

39. The foundation for such a view is provided by William H. Masters and Virginia E. Johnson, *Homosexuality in Perspective* (Boston: Little, Brown, 1979), particularly pp. 61–123.

40. This view is "dramatistic" in origin; see, e.g., Kenneth Burke, *A Grammar of Motives and a Rhetoric of Motives* (1945 and 1950; reprinted Cleveland, OH: Meridian/World, 1962).

41. See the definition of paradoxical world view in note #19 above.

42. Andrew Kopkind, "Dressing Up," *The Village Voice,* April 30, 1979, p. 34. Used by permission.

43. James Tyson, "Toward a New Gay Morality or, The Day the Fist-Fucking Stops," *Blueboy,* Vol. 25 (October 1978), p. 19.

44. Patrick Collins, "Where Are We Now?" *Blueboy,* Vol. 25 (October 1978), p. 9.

45. Kopkind, "Dressing Up," op. cit.

46. George B. Leonard, "Why We Need a New Sexuality," *Look,* January 13, 1970, p. 54.

47. Ibid.

48. Morton M. Hunt, *Her Infinite Variety: The American Woman as Lover, Mate, and Rival* (New York: Harper & Row, 1962), p. 65.

49. Reported in William Braden, "Today's GIs Called Different," *Minneapolis Star,* December 16, 1969, p. 8B.

50. For a more detailed discussion of poppers, see Joyce C. Greller, "More Than You Wanted to Know About Amyl Nitrate," *Blueboy,* Vol. 8 (September/October 1976), pp. 67–68 and 71.

51. Gross, "The Male Role and Heterosexual Behavior," op. cit., p. 87.

52. Lewis, "Emotional Intimacy Among Men," op. cit., pp. 108–9.

53. See, e.g., Michael D. Storms, "Attitudes Toward Homosexuality and Femininity in Men," *Journal of Homosexuality,* Vol. 3 (Spring 1978), pp. 257–64.

54. See, e.g., Lewis, "Emotional Intimacy Among Men," op. cit., pp. 110–15, for a more detailed description of these barriers.

55. For a description of such coping devices, see, e.g., ibid., pp. 116–19, and Stephen F. Morin and Ellen M. Garfinkle, "Male Homophobia," chapter 10 in this book.

56. Consider, for example, the ways in which the notion of a paradoxical world view might alter Karlyn Kohrs Campbell's essay, "The Rhetoric of Women's Liberation: An Oxymoron," *Quarterly Journal of Speech,* 59 (February 1973), pp. 74–86.

57. See, e.g., Mark L. Knapp, *Nonverbal Communication in Human Interactions* (2d ed., New York: Holt, Rinehart, & Winston, 1978), pp. 122–23.

58. Classical examples of disengagement include the decision of basically humane individuals to ignore the calls for help of those being attacked in urban centers.

59. Consider, for example, the ways in which the notion of a paradoxical world view might alter Murray Edelman's *Political Language: Words That Succeed and Policies That Fail* (New York: Academic Press, 1977).

60. Eakins and Eakins, *Sex Differences in Communication,* op. cit., p. 6.

Chapter 9 Gay Fantasies in Gay Publications

1. Ernest G. Bormann, "Fantasy and Rhetorical Visions: The Rhetorical Criticism of Social Reality," *The Quarterly Journal of Speech,* Vol. 58 (1972), pp. 396–407.

2. Joseph J. Hayes, "Gayspeak," *The Quarterly Journal of Speech,* Vol. 62 (1976), p. 256 (see chapter 4).

3. The terms gay and gay community used in this essay refer only to gay males. The author recognizes that there is an equally large and important lesbian community. The fictions examined, however, were gay male fictions, and thus the conclusions are limited, in part, to the gay male community.

4. The four issues of *Queens Quarterly (QQ)* published in 1970 comprise the data base for the fantasies of the early 70s. While this was not the only nationally distributed gay publication in 1970, the author considered it the most representative example of the available publications. Additionally, it included more fiction than any other publication. The data base for the fantasies of the late 70s and early 80s was derived from an examination of all issues published during 1979 and 1980 (to date) of *Blueboy, Numbers,* and *Playguy.* While these are not the only contemporary gay publications, they seemed to constitute a sufficiently large sampling.

5. Michael J. Mitchell, "The Talsen Interlude," *QQ,* Vol. 3, No. 3, p. 43.

6. Walter Norric, "Fantasex," *QQ,* Vol. 2, No. 3, p. 6.

7. Rob Arrington, "Larry and the Lieutenant," *QQ,* Vol. 3, No. 3, p. 38.

8. Ibid.

9. Ibid.

10. Mitchell, "The Talsen Interlude," op. cit., p. 43.

11. Ibid.

12. Orlando Paris, "False Glory," *QQ,* Vol. 2, No. 3, p. 11.

13. Ibid.

14. John Goriolan, "The Pumpkin Coach," *QQ,* Vol. 2, No. 2, p. 9.

15. James W. Chesebro, "Communication, Values, and Popular Television Series—A Four Year Assessment," in Horace Newcomb, ed., *Television, the Critical View* (New York: Oxford University Press, 1979), p. 35.

16. Don Teal, *The Gay Militants* (New York: Stein & Day, 1971), p. 1.

17. Ibid., p. 14.

18. *The American Heritage Dictionary of the English Language* (Boston: Houghton Mifflin, 1969), pp. 205 and 1431.

19. Jeff King, "Midnight Sailor," *Numbers,* July 1980, p. 19.

20. John Valentine, "Eli," *Blueboy,* February 1980, p. 85.

21. Marc Feigen Fasteau, *The Male Machine* (New York: McGraw-Hill, 1974) p. 1.

22. Chuck Rush, "Thirst," *Numbers,* June 1980, p. 67.

23. Thom Nickles, "Headway," *Blueboy,* July 1979, p. 82.

24. Frederick A. Raborg, "Michael's Eyes," *Blueboy,* January/February 1979, p. 32.

25. Walter Febick, "Las Palmas," *Blueboy,* July 1979, p. 60.

26. Alan P. Bell and Martin S. Weinberg, *Homosexualities: A Study of Diversity Among Men and Women* (New York: Simon & Schuster, 1978), p. 133.
27. James W. Chesebro, lecture for Communication and Popular Culture, Temple University.
28. Febick, "Las Palmas," op. cit., p. 74.
29. Raborg, "Michael's Eyes," op. cit., p. 32.
30. Richard Michaels, "The Voyeur," *Blueboy,* June 1979, p. 72.
31. Jay Greene, "The Poker Game," *Playguy,* Vol. 3, No. 28, p. 8.
32. Allen Markham, "Cruise of Death," *Numbers,* July 1980, p. 63.
33. Daniel Curzon, "Beer and Rhubarb Pie," *Blueboy,* October 1979, p. 71.
34. Ibid., p. 93.
35. King, "Midnight Sailor," op. cit., p. 19.
36. James W. Chesebro, "Homosexuality as a Communication Variable," in Larry A. Samovar and Richard E. Porter, eds., *Intercultural Communication: A Reader* (3d ed.; Belmont, CA: Wadsworth Publishing Co., 1982).
37. Virginia Kidd, "Happily Ever After and Other Relationship Styles: Advice on Interpersonal Relations in Popular Magazines, 1951–1973," *The Quarterly Journal of Speech,* Vol. 61 (1975), pp. 31–39.

Chapter 10 Male Homophobia

1. G. K. Lehne, "Homophobia Among Men," in D. David and R. Brannon, eds., *The Forty-nine Percent Majority: The Male Sex Role* (New York: Addison-Wesley, 1976); A.P. MacDonald, "The Importance of Sex Role to Gay Liberation," *Homosexual Counseling Journal,* Vol. 1 (1974), pp. 169–80; J.H. Pleck, "Man to Man: Is Brotherhood Possible?" in N. Glazer-Malbin, ed., *Old Family/New Family: Interpersonal Relationships* (New York: Van Nostrand Reinhold, 1975).
2. W. Churchill, *Homosexual Behavior Among Males* (New York: Hawthorn Books, 1967).
3. C. Ford and F. Beach, *Patterns of Sexual Behavior* (New York: Harper & Row, 1953).
4. J. Dunbar, M. Brown, and D. Amoroso, "Some Correlatives of Attitudes Toward Homosexuality," *Journal of Social Psychology,* Vol. 89 (1973), pp. 271–79.
5. M. Brown and D. Amoroso, "Attitudes Toward Homosexuality Among West Indian Male and Female College Students," *Journal of Social Psychology,* Vol. 97 (1975), pp. 163–68; Dunbar, Brown, and Amoroso, "Some Correlatives of Attitudes Toward Homosexuality," op. cit.
6. E. Levitt and A. Klassen, "Public Attitudes Toward Homosexuality," *Journal of Homosexuality,* Vol. 1 (1974), pp. 29–43.
7. Lehne, "Homophobia Among Men," op. cit.
8. Stephen F. Morin, "Heterosexual Bias in Psychological Research on Lesbianism and Male Homosexuality," *American Psychologist,* Vol. 32 (1977), pp. 629–37.
9. Stephen F. Morin, "The Past, Present, and Future of Heterosexism in Psychological Research," a paper presented at the meeting of the American Psychological Association, August 1975.
10. MacDonald, "The Importance of Sex Role," op. cit.; A.P. MacDonald and R. G. Games, "Some Characteristics of Those Who Hold Positive and Negative Attitudes Toward Homosexuals," *Journal of Homosexuality,* Vol. 1 (1974), pp. 9–28; A.P. MacDonald et al., "Attitudes Toward Homosexuality: Preservation of Sex Morality or the Double Standard," *Journal of Consulting and Clinical Psychology,* Vol. 40 (1973), p. 161; Stephen F. Morin and S. Wallace, "Traditional

Values, Sex-role Stereotyping, and Attitudes Toward Homosexuality," a paper presented at the meeting of the Western Psychological Association, April 1976.

11. MacDonald and Games, "Some Characteristics of Those Who Hold Positive and Negative Attitudes Toward Homosexuals," op. cit.

12. Morin and Wallace, "Traditional Values," op. cit.

13. Stephen F. Morin and S. Wallace, "Religiosity, Sexism, and Attitudes Toward Homosexuality," a paper presented at the meeting of the California State Psychological Association, March 1975.

14. Churchill, *Homosexual Behavior Among Males,* op. cit.

15. Lehne, "Homophobia Among Men," op. cit.

16. A.P. MacDonald, "Homophobia: Its Roots and Meanings," *Homosexual Counseling,* Vol. 3 (1976), pp. 23–33.

17. George Weinberg, *Society and the Healthy Homosexual* (New York: St. Martin's Press, 1972).

18. M.E. Lumby, "Homophobia: The Quest for a Valid Scale," *Journal of Homosexuality,* Vol. 1 (1976), pp. 39–47; E.P. May, "Counselors', Psychologists', and Homosexuals' Philosophies of Human Nature and Attitudes Toward Homosexual Behavior," *Homosexual Counseling,* Vol. 1 (1974), pp. 3–25.

19. MacDonald, "The Importance of Sex Role," op. cit,; K. Smith, "Homophobia: A Tentative Personality Profile," *Psychological Reports,* Vol. 29 (1971), pp. 1091–94; Morin and Wallace, "Religiosity, Sexism, and Attitudes Toward Homosexuality," op. cit.

20. R.W. Hood, "Dogmatism and Opinions About Mental Illness," *Psychological Reports,* Vol. 32 (1973), pp. 1283–90.

21. MacDonald, "The Importance of Sex Role," op. cit.

22. Ibid.

23. Smith, "Homophobia: A Tentative Personality Profile," op. cit.

24. D.F. Berry and F. Marks, "Antihomosexual Prejudice as a Function of Attitudes Toward Own Sexuality," *Proceedings of the 77th Annual Convention of the American Psychological Association,* Vol. 4 (1969), pp. 573–74 (summary); Brown and Amoroso, "Attitudes Toward Homosexuality Among West Indian Male and Female College Students," op. cit.; Dunbar, Brown, and Amoroso, "Some Correlatives of Attitudes Toward Homosexuality," op. cit.; J. Dunbar, M. Brown, and S. Vuorinen, "Attitudes Toward Homosexuality Among Brazilian and Canadian College Students," *Journal of Social Psychology,* Vol. 90 (1973), pp. 173–83; Smith, "Homophobia: A Tentative Personality Profile," op. cit.; Morin and Wallace," Religiosity, Sexism, and Attitudes Toward Homosexuality," op. cit.

25. Berry and Marks, "Antihomosexual Prejudice," op. cit.; Dunbar, Brown, and Amoroso, "Some Correlatives of Attitudes Toward Homosexuality," op. cit.

26. Morin and Wallace, "Religiosity, Sexism, and Attitudes Toward Homosexuality," op. cit.

27. N. McConaghy, "Penile Volume Changes to Moving Pictures of Male and Female Nudes in Heterosexual and Homosexual Males," *Behavior Research and Therapy,* Vol. 5 (1967), pp. 43–48.

28. K. Freund et al., "Heterosexual Aversion in Homosexual Males," *British Journal of Psychiatry,* Vol. 122 (1973), pp. 163–69.

29. K. Freund et al., "The Phobic Theory of Male Homosexuality," *Archives of General Psychiatry,* Vol. 31 (1974), pp. 495–99.

30. K. Freund, R. Langevin, and Y. Zajac, "Heterosexual Aversion in Homosexual Males: A Second Experiment," *British Journal of Psychiatry,* Vol. 125 (1974), pp. 177–80.

31. R. Langevin, A. Stanford, and R. Block, "The Effect of Relaxation Instruc-

tions on Erotic Arousal in Homosexual and Heterosexual Males," *Behavior Research and Therapy,* Vol. 6 (1975), pp. 453–58.

32. D. Steffensmeier and R. Steffensmeier, "Sex Differences in Reactions to Homosexuals; Research Continuities and Further Developments," *The Journal of Sex Research,* Vol. 10 (1974), pp. 52–67.

33. J. Millham, C.C. San Miguel, and R. Kellogg, "A Factor Analytic Conceptualization of Attitudes Toward Male and Female Homosexuals," *Journal of Homosexuality,* Vol. 2 (1976), pp. 3–10.

34. A.C. Kinsey, W.B. Pomeroy, and C.E. Martin, *Sexual Behavior in the Human Male* (Philadelphia: W.B. Saunders, 1948).

35. R.I. Evans, "A Conversation with Konrad Lorenz," *Psychology Today,* June 1974, pp. 83–93.

36. Berry and Marks, "Antihomosexual Prejudice," op. cit.

37. Churchill, *Homosexual Behavior Among Males,* op. cit.

38. Brown and Amoroso, "Attitudes Toward Homosexuality Among West Indian Male and Female College Students," op. cit.

39. Smith, "Homophobia: A Tentative Personality Profile," op. cit.

40. Berry and Marks, "Antihomosexual Prejudice," op. cit.

41. George Gallup, "Gallup Poll on Gay Rights: Approval with Reservations," *San Francisco Chronicle,* July 18, 1977, pp. 1:18.

42. George Gallup, "Gallup Poll on the Attitudes Homosexuals Face Today," *San Francisco Chronicle,* July 20, 1977, p. 4.

43. Levitt and Klassen, "Public Attitudes Toward Homosexuality," op. cit.

44. J.P. Alston, "Attitudes Toward Extramarital and Homosexual Relations," *Journal of the Scientific Study of Religion,* Vol. 13 (1974), pp. 479–81.

45. E. Rooney and D. Gibbons, "Social Reactions to Crimes Without Victims," *Social Problems,* Vol. 13 (1966), pp. 400–10.

46. C. Tavris, "Men and Women Report Their Views of Masculinity," *Psychology Today,* January 1977, p. 35.

47. Levitt and Klassen, "Public Attitudes Toward Homosexuality," op. cit.

48. Gallup, "Gallup Poll on the Attitudes Homosexuals Face Today," op. cit.

49. A. Wolfgang and J. Wolfgang, "Exploration of Attitudes via Physical Interpersonal Distance Toward the Obese, Drug Users, Homosexuals, Police and Other Marginal Figures," *Journal of Clinical Psychology,* Vol. 27 (1971), pp. 510–12.

50. Stephen F. Morin, K. Taylor, and S. Kielman, "Gay Is Beautiful at a Distance," a paper presented at the meeting of the American Psychological Association, April 1975.

51. C.C. San Miguel and J. Millham, "The Role of Cognitive and Situational Variables in Aggression Toward Homosexuals," *Journal of Homosexuality,* Vol. 2 (1976), pp. 11–27.

52. Brown and Amoroso, "Attitudes Toward Homosexuality Among West Indian Male and Female College Students," op. cit.; Gallup, "Gallup Poll on the Attitudes Homosexuals Face Today," op. cit.; Millham, San Miguel, and Kellogg, "A Factor Analytic Conceptualization," op. cit.; F.A. Minnigerode, "Attitudes Toward Homosexuality: Feminist Attitudes and Social Conservatism," *Sex Roles,* Vol. 2 (1976), pp. 347–52; R.L. Nutt and W.E. Sedlacek, "Freshman Sexual Attitudes and Behaviors," *Journal of College Student Personnel,* Vol. 15 (1974), pp. 346–51; Steffensmeier and Steffensmeier, "Sex Differences in Reactions to Homosexuals," op. cit.; Morin, Taylor, and Kielman, "Gay Is Beautiful," op. cit.; Morin and Wallace, "Traditional Values," op. cit.

53. Levitt and Klassen, "Public Attitudes Toward Homosexuality," op. cit.;

MacDonald and Games, "Some Characteristics of Those Who Hold Positive and Negative Attitudes Toward Homosexuality," op. cit.; MacDonald et al., "Attitudes Toward Homosexuality," op. cit.; Stephen F. Morin, "Educational Programs as a Means of Changing Attitudes Toward Gay People," *Homosexual Counseling Journal,* Vol. 1 (1974), pp. 160–65; Rooney and Gibbons, "Social Reactions to Crimes," op. cit.; Smith, "Homophobia: A Tentative Personality Profile," op. cit.

54. Levitt and Klassen, "Public Attitudes Toward Homosexuality," op. cit.; Rooney and Gibbons, "Social Reactions to Crimes," op. cit.; Smith, "Homophobia: A Tentative Personality Profile," op. cit.

55. MacDonald and Games, "Some Characteristics of Those Who Hold Positive and Negative Attitudes Toward Homosexuality," op. cit.; MacDonald et al., "Attitudes Toward Homosexuality," op. cit.; Morin, "Educational Programs," op. cit.

56. Millham, San Miguel, and Kellogg, "A Factor Analytic Conceptualization," op. cit.

57. Morin, Taylor, and Kielman, "Gay Is Beautiful," op. cit.

58. Steffensmeier and Steffensmeier, "Sex Differences in Reactions to Homosexuals," op. cit.

59. Brown and Amoroso, "Attitudes Toward Homosexuality Among West Indian Male and Female College Students," op. cit.; Dunbar, Brown, and Amoroso, "Some Correlatives of Attitudes Toward Homosexuality," op. cit.; Dunbar, Brown, and Vuorinen, "Attitudes Toward Homosexuality Among Brazilian and Canadian College Students," op. cit.; MacDonald et al., "Attitudes Toward Homosexuality," op. cit.; MacDonald, "The Importance of Sex Role," op. cit.

60. Minnigerode, "Attitudes Toward Homosexuality: Feminist Attitudes and Social Conservatism," op. cit.

61. J.M. Bardwick, *Psychology of Women: A Study of Biocultural Conflicts* (New York: Harper & Row, 1971); J.M. Bardwick and E. Douvan, "Ambivalence: The Socialization of Women," in V. Gornick and B.K. Moran, eds., *Woman in Sexist Society* (New York: Basic Books, 1971); I.K. Broverman et al., "Sex-role Stereotypes and Clinical Judgments of Mental Health," *Journal of Consulting and Clinical Psychology,* Vol. 34 (1970), pp. 1–7; M. Horner, "The Motive to Avoid Success and Changing Aspirations of College Women," in J.M. Bardwick, ed., *Readings on the Psychology of Women* (New York: Harper & Row, 1972).

62. Steffensmeier and Steffensmeier, "Sex Differences in Reactions to Homosexuals," op. cit.

63. Rodney G. Karr, "Homosexual Labeling and the Male Role," *Journal of Social Issues,* Vol. 34 (1978), pp. 73–83.

64. Ibid.

65. G.J. McDonald, "The Relationship Between Sex-role Stereotypes, Attitudes Toward Women and Male Homosexuality in a Nonclinical Sample of Homosexual Men," a paper presented at the meeting of the Canadian Psychological Association, June 1976.

66. Lumby, "Homophobia: The Quest for a Valid Scale," op. cit.

67. Morin, "Educational Programs," op. cit.

68. Weinberg, *Society and the Healthy Homosexual,* op. cit.

69. Lumby, "Homophobia: The Quest for a Valid Scale," op. cit.

70. Levitt and Klassen, "Public Attitudes Toward Homosexuality," op. cit.

71. D. Clark, "Homosexual Encounter in All-male Groups" in L. Solomon and B. Berzon, eds., *New Perspectives on Encounter Groups* (San Francisco: Jossey-Bass, 1972); J. Keith, "My Own Men's Liberation," in J. Pleck and J. Sawyer, eds., *Men and Masculinity* (Englewood Cliffs, NJ: Prentice-Hall, 1974); Pleck, "Man to Man," op. cit.

72. Stephen F. Morin and R. Alexander, "The Male Sex Role and Gay Male Couples," a paper presented at the meeting of the American Psychological Association, August 1977.

Chapter 11 The Pathogenic Secret

1. Connie DeBoer, "The Polls: Attitudes Toward Homosexuality," *The Public Opinion Quarterly,* Vol. 42 (Summer 1978), p. 276.
2. Gerald M. Phillips and Nancy J. Metzger, *Intimate Communication* (Boston: Allyn and Bacon, 1976), p. 376.
3. Jurgen Ruesch and Gregory Bateson, *Communication: The Social Matrix of Psychiatry* (New York: W.W. Norton, 1968), p. 87.
4. Sidney Jourard, "Self Disclosure: The Scientist's Portal to Man's Soul," in Jean M. Civikly, ed., *Messages: A Reader in Human Communication* (New York: Random House, 1977), p. 163.
5. See H.R. Ellenberger, "The Pathogenic Secret and Its Therapeutics," *Journal of the History of the Behavioral Sciences,* Vol. 2 (1966), pp. 29–42.
6. Carmen deMonteflores and Stephen J. Schultz, "Coming Out: Similarities and Differences for Lesbians and Gay Men," *Journal of Social Issues,* Vol. 34 (1978), p. 65.
7. Clark E. Moustakas, *Loneliness* (Englewood Cliffs, NJ: Prentice-Hall, 1961), p. 41.
8. See G.K. Lehne, "Homophobia Among Men," in D. David and R. Brannon, eds., *The Forty-nine Percent Majority* (New York: Addison-Wesley, 1976).
9. See W. Churchill, *Homosexual Behavior Among Males* (New York: Hawthorn Books, 1967).
10. See George Weinberg, *Society and the Healthy Homosexual* (New York: St. Martin's Press, 1972).
11. Stephen F. Morin and Ellen M. Garfinkle, "Male Homophobia," *Journal of Social Issues,* Vol. 34 (November 1, 1978), p. 30.
12. *The Advocate,* February 21, 1980, p. 7.
13. *The Advocate,* March 6, 1980, p. 10.
14. Ibid.
15. *The Advocate,* January 10, 1980, p. 10.
16. *The Advocate,* December 27, 1979, p. 7.
17. A.P. MacDonald, and R.G. Games, "Some Characteristics of Those Who Hold Positive and Negative Attitudes Toward Homosexuals," *Journal of Homosexuality,* Vol. 1 (1974), p. 34.
18. Martin S. Weinberg and Colin J. Williams, *Male Homosexuals* (New York: Oxford University Press, 1979), p. 152.
19. E. Levitt and A. Klassen, "Public Attitudes Toward Homosexuality," *Journal of Homosexuality,* Vol. 1 (1974), pp. 29–43.
20. Louie Crew, ed., *The Gay Academic* (Palm Springs, CA: ETC Publications, 1978).
21. Joseph Harry and William B. DeVall, *The Social Organization of Gay Males* (New York: Praeger Publishers, 1978), p. 175.
22. *The Advocate,* December 13, 1979, p. 11.
23. Gerard Egan, *Encounter: Group Processes for Interpersonal Growth* (Belmont, CA: Brooks/Cole Publishing Company, 1970), p. 217.
24. See "The American Freshmen: National Norms for Fall, 1979," published by American Council on Education and the University of California at Los Angeles.
25. Ibid.
26. David Kopay and Perry Deane Young, *The David Kopay Story* (New York:

Arbor House, 1977), pp. 197–98. Copyright © 1977 by David Kopay and Perry Deane Young. Used by permission of Arbor House Publishing Company and the authors.

Chapter 12 Androgyny, Sex-role Rigidity, and Homophobia

1. Terri Levy, "Homosexual Labelling: The Lesbian as Perceived by Mental Health Workers," unpublished doctoral dissertation, California School of Professional Psychologists, 1978; William Hensel, "Attributed Sexual Preference and Attitude Similarity of a Social Other as Factors Influencing Interpersonal Attraction: A Social Psychological Investigation of the Homosexual Label," unpublished doctoral dissertation, Ball State University, 1976; Stephen Morin, K. Taylor, and S. Kielman, "Gay Is Beautiful—at a Distance," paper presented at the APA, Chicago, 1975; C. San Miguel and J. Millham, "The Role of Cognitive and Situational Variables in Aggression Toward Homosexuals," *Journal of Homosexuality,* Vol. 2 (1976), pp. 11–27.

2. P. Goldberg, "Are Women Prejudiced Against Women?" *Transaction,* Vol. 5 (April 1968), pp. 28–30; T. Peck, "When Women Evaluate Women, Nothing Succeeds Like Success: The Differential Effects of Status upon Evaluations of Male and Female Professional Ability," *Sex Roles,* Vol. 2 (1978), pp. 205–13.

3. S. Feldman-Summers and S. Kiesler, "Those Who Are Number Two Try Harder: The Effect of Sex on Attribution of Causality," *Journal of Personality and Social Psychology,* Vol. 30 (1974), pp. 846–55.

4. M. Storms, "Attitudes Toward Homosexuality and Femininity in Men," *Journal of Homosexuality,* Vol. 3 (1978), pp. 257–65.

5. San Miguel and Millham, "The Role of Cognitive and Situational Variables," op. cit.

6. P. Goldberg et al., "Another Put-down on Women? Perceived Attractiveness as a Function of Support for the Feminist Movement," *Journal of Personality and Social Psychology,* Vol. 32 (1975), pp. 113–15.

7. M. Jacobson and W. Koch, "Attributed Reasons for Support of the Feminist Movement as a Function of Attractiveness," *Sex Roles,* Vol. 4 (1978), pp. 169–74.

8. A.P. MacDonald, "Identification and Measurement of Multidimensional Attitudes Toward Equality Between the Sexes," *Journal of Homosexuality,* Vol. 1 (1974), pp. 165–82; A.P. MacDonald et al., "Attitudes Toward Homosexuality: Preservation of Sex Morality or the Double Standard?" *Journal of Consulting and Clinical Psychology,* Vol. 40 (1973), p. 161; A.P. MacDonald and R.G. Games, "Some Characteristics of Those Who Hold Positive and Negative Attitudes Toward Homosexuals," *Journal of Homosexuality,* Vol. 1 (1974), pp. 9–27; F. Minnigerode, "Attitudes Toward Homosexuality: Feminist Attitudes and Sexual Conservatism," *Sex Roles,* Vol. 2 (1976), pp. 347–52.

9. Sandra Bem, "The Measurement of Psychological Androgyny," *Journal of Consulting and Clinical Psychology,* Vol. 42 (1974), pp. 155–62.

10. Sandra Bem, "Sex Role Adaptability: One Consequence of Psychological Androgyny," *Journal of Personality and Social Psychology,* Vol. 31 (1975), pp. 634–43.

11. J. Spence, R. Helmreich, and J. Stapp, "Ratings of Self and Peers on Sex Role Attributes and Their Relation to Self-esteem and Conceptions of Masculinity and Femininity," *Journal of Personality and Social Psychology;* J. Morland et al., "Some Psychometric Properties of the Bem Sex-Role Inventory," *Applied Psychological Measurement,* Vol. 2 (1978), pp. 248–56.

12. L. Weinberger and J. Millham, "Attitudinal Homophobia and Support of

Traditional Sex Roles," *Journal of Homosexuality,* Vol. 4 (1979), pp. 237–45; Harris Halpern, "Attitudes Toward Male and Female Homosexuality as Related to Gender, Sex Role Attitudes, and Sex Role Orientation," M.A. thesis, University of Cincinnati, 1979; Minnigerode, "Attitudes Toward Homosexuality," op. cit.

13. George Weinberg, *Society and the Healthy Homosexual* (New York: St. Martin's Press, 1972).

14. Dorothy Riddle, lecture delivered at St. Cloud State University, February 1977.

15. James Millham et al., "A Factor-analytic Conceptualization of Attitudes Toward Male and Female Homosexuals," *Journal of Homosexuality,* Vol. 2 (1976), pp. 3–10.

16. Ibid., p. 9.

17. A.P. MacDonald, "Homophobia: Its Roots and Meanings," *Homosexual Counseling Journal,* Vol. 3 (1976), pp. 23–33.

18. Stephen F. Morin, "The Past, Present, and Future of Heterosexism in Psychological Research," paper presented at the APA Convention, Chicago, August 1975; "Heterosexual Bias in Psychological Research on Lesbianism and Male Homosexuality," *American Psychologist,* Vol. 32 (1977), pp. 629–37.

19. Stephen F. Morin and Ellen Garfinkle, "Male Homophobia," *Journal of Social Issues,* Vol. 34 (1978), pp. 29–47.

20. Levy, "Homosexual Labelling," op. cit.

21. Hensel, "Attributed Sexual Preference and Attitude Similarity," op. cit.

22. A. Wolfgang and J. Wolfgang, "Exploration of Attitudes via Physical Interpersonal Distance Toward the Obese, Drug Users, Homosexuals, Police and Other Marginal Figures," *Journal of Clinical Psychology,* Vol. 27 (1971), pp. 510–12.

23. Morin, Taylor, and Kielman, "Gay Is Beautiful," op. cit.

24. San Miguel and Millham, "The Role of Cognitive and Situational Variables," op. cit.

25. Although San Miguel and Millham's operational definition of aggression (i.e., the amount of money the subject withholds from the confederate) is elegant and intuitively appealing, it does have at least one conceptual flaw. Remember that San Miguel and Millham's subjects are asked to evaluate the performance (as an interviewer) of the confederate, and to decide on the latter's payment *based on that evaluation.* Given the design and instructions, we are not safe to conclude that the motivation behind the withholding of funds was aggression, in any meaningful sense of the word. It is equally reasonable to expect that the subjects generally considered the gay-labeled confederate a poor interviewer. To be sure, this is an instance of antigay prejudice, but it falls far closer to the "devaluation" end of the devaluation-avoidance-aggression continuum. Future research should clear up this muddle by using operationalizations of aggression that are untainted by intermediating evaluation steps. (Good luck with your respective Human Subjects Committees!)

26. MacDonald, "Identification and Measurement of Multidimensional Attitudes," op. cit.

27. K.T. Smith, "Homophobia: A Tentative Personality Profile," *Psychological Reports,* Vol. 29 (1971), pp. 1091–94.

28. J. Dunbar, M. Brown, and D. Amoroso, "Some Correlates of Attitudes Toward Homosexuality," *Journal of Social Psychology,* Vol. 89. (1973), pp. 271–79.

29. Morin and Garfinkle, "Male Homophobia," op. cit.

30. MacDonald and Games, "Some Characteristics of Those Who Hold Positive and Negative Attitudes Toward Homosexuals," op. cit.

31. Millham et al., "A Factor-analytic Conceptualization," op. cit.

32. Alfred Kinsey et al., *Sexual Behavior in the Human Male* (Philadelphia: W.B. Saunders, 1948); Alfred Kinsey et al., *Sexual Behavior in the Human Female* (Philadelphia: W.B. Saunders, 1953); Alan P. Bell and Martin S. Weinberg, *Homosexualities: A Study of Diversity Among Men and Women* (New York: Simon & Schuster, 1978).

33. MacDonald, "Homophobia: Its Roots and Meanings," op. cit.

34. Storms, "Attitudes Toward Homosexuality and Femininity in Men," op. cit.

35. MacDonald and Games, "Some Characteristics of Those Who Hold Positive and Negative Attitudes Toward Homosexuals," op. cit.

36. Morin and Garfinkle, "Male Homophobia," op. cit.

37. The state of masculinity is seen as a relatively fragile one not only from a psychological one, but from a physiological one as well. We know, for example, that all human embryos begin as female. We also know that a tremendously disproportionate ratio of recorded transsexualism involves a move from male to female. For a more thorough treatment of this point, see Warren J. Gadpaille, "Research into the Physiology of Maleness and Femaleness," *Archives of General Psychiatry,* Vol. 26, March 1972, pp. 193–206.

38. Certainly, the sex-role confusion hypothesis is not the only reasonable way to explain the finding that gay males are more threatening to mainstream heterosexual society than are lesbians. At least two alternative explanations are possible: First, we can view the relative indifference of society toward lesbianism as further evidence of the women's traditional second-class status. If the behavior of women in matters of politics, economics, and similar pursuits is discounted, why would their sexual behavior not be similarly viewed with neglect? We do not fear lesbianism because we do not care about it. A second plausible explanation emerges from the casual observation that many heterosexually oriented pornographic films include at least one lesbian lovemaking scene. The implication is that lesbianism is tolerated because lesbian sex necessarily involves female bodies, and is thus of interest to heterosexual males. Perhaps, too, the male expects that the lesbian sex is mere prelude to his own intervention (not at all an uncommon theme in porno flicks).

39. San Miguel and Millham, "The Role of Cognitive and Situational Variables," op. cit.

40. Storms, "Attitudes Toward Homosexuality and Femininity in Men," op. cit.

41. Storms (ibid.) calls this the "delineation" function of the sex-role confusion hypothesis. Consider: The Kinsey statistics are now almost common knowledge. Many Americans are aware that a full 37% of the male sample had had some homosexual experience, and that 4% were exclusively gay throughout their adult lives. How does the male who knows himself to be among the 37% figure delineate between himself and the "typical" homosexual? The sexual inversion myth, which serves to perpetuate the myth that we can spot a queer a mile away, provides a convenient means of separating oneself from "those homosexuals."

42. Bem, "The Measurement of Psychological Androgyny," op. cit.

43. Bem, "Sex Role Adaptability," op. cit.

44. Weinberger and Millham, "Attitudinal Homophobia and Support of Traditional Sex Roles," op. cit.

45. Spence, Helmreich, and Stapp, "Ratings of Self and Peers," op. cit.

46. Morland et al., "Some Psychometric Properties of the Bem Sex-Role Inventory," op. cit.

47. Ibid., p. 256.

48. J. Freedman and Anthony Doob, *Deviancy* (New York: Academic Press, 1968).

49. San Miguel and Millham, "The Role of Cognitive and Situational Variables," op. cit.
50. Storms, "Attitudes Toward Homosexuality and Femininity in Men," op. cit.
51. Sandra Bem, "On the Utility of Alternative Procedures for Assessing Psychological Androgyny," *Journal of Consulting and Clinical Psychology,* Vol. 45 (1977), pp. 196–205.
52. J. Spence and R. Helmreich, "The Attitudes Toward Women Scale: An Objective Instrument to Measure Attitudes Toward the Rights and Roles of Women in Contemporary Society," *JSAS Catalog of Selected Documents in Psychology,* Vol. 2 (1972), pp. 66–67.

Chapter 13 Gay Images on Television

1. E.T. Prothro and L.H. Melikan, "Studies in Stereotype Familiarity and the Kernel of Truth Hypothesis," *Journal of Social Psychology*, Vol. 41 (1955), pp. 3–10.
2. D. Katz and K.W. Braly, "Racial Stereotypes of 100 College Students," *Journal of Abnormal and Social Psychology*, Vol. 28 (1933), pp. 280–90.
3. J.C. Brigham, "Ethnic Stereotypes," *Psychology Bulletin*, Vol. 76 (1971), pp. 15–38.
4. W.E. Vinacke, "Stereotypes as Social Concepts," *Journal of Social Psychology*, Vol. 46 (1957), pp. 229–43.
5. Linda J. Busby, "Sex-role Research on the Mass Media," *Journal of Communication*, Vol. 25 (1975), pp. 107–27.
6. William Raspberry, "Who's the Real Bandito?" *Washington Post*, June 7, 1971, p. A23.
7. *Surgeon General's Scientific Advisory Committee on Television and Social Behavior*, p. 3.
8. Ibid., p. 10.
9. Timothy Myers, "'All in the Family' Impact on Children," *Journal of Broadcasting*, Winter 1976, pp. 24–29.
10. H.T. Himmelweit, A.N. Oppenheim, and P. Vince, *Television and the Child* (London: Oxford University Press, 1958).
11. J.C. Brigham, "Ethnic Stereotypes and Attitudes: A Different Mode of Analysis," *Journal of Personality*, Vol. 41 (June 1973), pp. 206–23.
12. R.M. Williams, *Strangers Next Door* (Englewood Cliffs, NJ: Prentice-Hall, 1964).
13. Bradley Greenberg, "Children's Reactions to T.V. Blacks," *Journalism Quarterly*, Vol. 49 (Spring 1972), pp. 6–19.
14. Busby, "Sex-role Research on the Mass Media," op. cit.
15. George Gallup, "Public Says Homosexuality More Widespread Today," *Daily Pantagraph*, July 18, 1977, p. A4.

Chapter 14 Images of the Gay Male in Contemporary Drama

1. Excerpt from *The Boys in the Band* by Mart Crowley, p. 102. Copyright © 1968 by Mart Crowley. Reprinted by permission of Farrar, Straus and Giroux, Inc.
2. Clive Barnes, *The New York Times*, April 15, 1968.
3. William M. Hoffman, *Gay Plays: The First Collection* (New York: Avon Books, 1979), p. xxvii.
4. Crowley, *The Boys in the Band*, op. cit., p. 99.
5. This essay has not attempted to provide a comprehensive listing of plays with

gay male characters or themes. For a more complete bibliography of plays consult the following: Donald L. Loeffler, *The Homosexual Character in Dramas* (New York: Arno Press, 1975); William Parker, *Homosexuality: A Selective Bibliography* (Metuchen, NJ: Scarecrow Press, 1971); William Parker, *Homosexuality Bibliography: Supplement, 1970–1975* (Metuchen, NJ: Scarecrow Press, 1975); Ian Young, *The Male Homosexual in Literature: A Bibliography* (Metuchen, NJ: Scarecrow Press, 1975); William M. Hoffman, *Gay Plays: The First Collection* (New York: Avon Books, 1979).

Recently The Gay Theatre Alliance has commenced publication of a *Directory of Gay Plays* (New York: Gay Theatre Alliance, 1980).

6. Hoffman, *Gay Plays*, op. cit., p. xiii,

7. Eric Bentley, in Terry Helbing, "Rogues' Gallery," *Christopher Street*, Vol. 2, No. 12 (June 1978), p. 18.

8. George Whitmore, in ibid., p. 19.

9. Hoffman, *Gay Plays*, op. cit., p. ix.

10. Don Shewey, "Theatre: Gays in the Marketplace vs. Gays for Themselves," in Karla Jay and Allen Young, eds., *Lavender Culture* (New York: Jove Publications, 1978), p. 233; and Hoffman, *Gay Plays*, op. cit., pp. xvi–xviii.

11. Hoffman, *Gay Plays*, op. cit., p. xvi.

12. Ibid., p. xxi.

13. Robert Anderson, *Tea and Sympathy*, in *Fifty Best Plays of the American Theatre*, Vol. 4, selected by Clive Barnes, with introductions by John Gassner (New York: Crown Publishers, 1969), p. 152.

14. Shewey, "Theatre: Gays in the Marketplace," op. cit., p. 233. The same article appeared in *Blueboy*, Vols. 20 and 21 (May and June 1978).

15. The Cafe Cino was founded by Joe Cino in 1958, in New York, and began as a bohemian gathering place which evolved into an off-off-Broadway theater encouraging experimental and gay plays by new playwrights.

16. Robert Patrick, *The Haunted Host*, in Ed Berman, ed., *Homosexual Acts: A Volume of Gay Plays* (London: Inter-Action Imprint, 1975), p. 98.

17. Shewey, "Theatre: Gays in the Marketplace," op, cit., p. 235.

18. Allan Pierce, "Homophobia and the Critics," *Christopher Street*, Vol. 2, No. 12 (June 1978), p. 39.

19. Ibid.

20. Ibid., pp. 43–44.

21. Doric Wilson, in Shewey, "Theatre: Gays in the Marketplace," op. cit., p. 241.

22. Felice Picano, "Introduction," in *Two Plays by Doric Wilson* (New York: Sea Horse Press, 1979), p. 9. Used by permission.

23. Robert Chesley, "A Perfect Relationship with Gay Theatre: Playwright Doric Wilson," *The Advocate*, April 5, 1979, p. 33.

24. Doric Wilson, *A Perfect Relationship*, in *Two Plays by Doric Wilson*, op. cit., p. 28. Used by permission.

25. Ibid., quoted at various moments in the play. Used by permission.

26. Picano, "Introduction," in *Two Plays by Doric Wilson*, op. cit., p. 15. Used by permission.

27. Michael Cristofer, *The Shadow Box* (New York: Drama Book Specialists, 1977), pp. 18–19. © copyright 1977 by Michael Cristofer. Excerpted by permission of Drama Book Specialists (Publishers), New York. All rights reserved.

28. Ibid., pp. 22–23.

29. Edwin Wilson, "Holocaust and Homosexuality Suffuse New Play," *The Wall Street Journal*, December 5, 1979, p. 24.

30. Ibid.

Chapter 15 Views of Homosexuality Among Social Scientists

1. James W. Chesebro, John F. Cragan, and Patricia McCullough, "The Small Group Technique of the Radical Revolutionary: A Synthetic Study of Consciousness Raising," *Speech Monographs*, Vol. 40 (1973), pp. 136–46.

2. Joseph J. Hayes, "Gayspeak," *The Quarterly Journal of Speech*, Vol. 62 (1976), pp. 256–66.

3. Virtually all attempts to assess interpersonal, small group, and mass communication have ignored the influence of sexual preference in research designs. Consider, as an illustration, the ways in which the variable of sexual preference could alter James C. McCroskey and Thomas A. McCain's "The Measurement of Interpersonal Attraction," *Speech Monographs*, Vol. 41 (1974), pp. 261–66. In attempting to identify those factors affecting social, task, and physical attractiveness in interpersonal relations, McCroskey and McCain asked 215 undergraduate students to complete a questionnaire for " 'a classmate with whom you are acquainted' " (p. 262). The findings generated by such a research procedure are likely to affect drastically the validity of such a study if the variable of sexual preference is ignored. In responding to one of the "social attraction" statements ("We could never establish a personal friendship with each other.") on a Likert-type scale, for example, a gay male's assessment of another is very likely to be affected by the sexual preference of another regardless of the researchers' attempt to "tap" into only the subjects' traditional conception of sociability. The validity of any findings employing such a questionnaire as well as the validity of the questionnaire itself is suspect when the variable of sexual preference is not directly considered. The point, however, is not that problems exist with the McCroskey and McCain procedure in particular, but that virtually all research designs in speech communication have neglected to assess the ways in which sexual preference have affected the validity of testing procedures, data reported, and conclusions regarding the communication process.

4. Irving J. Rein, *Rudy's Red Wagon: Communication Strategies in Contemporary Society* (Glenview, IL: Scott, Foresman, 1972), pp. 17–28.

5. Werner Heisenberg, "The Representation of Nature in Contemporary Physics," trans. O.T. Benfey, in *The Discontinuous Universe: Selected Writings in Contemporary Consciousness*, ed. Sallie Sears and Georgianna W. Lord (New York: Basic Books, 1972), p. 134.

6. Herbert W. Simons, "Are Scientists Rhetors in Disguise? An Analysis of Discursive Processes Within Scientific Communities," in Eugene E. White, ed., *Rhetoric in Transition: Some Points of Focus* (University Park, PA: Pennsylvania State University Press, 1980).

7. For an overview of Ernest G. Bormann's conception and use of this method, see his several essays: "Fantasy and Rhetorical Vision: The Rhetorical Criticism of Social Reality," *The Quarterly Journal of Speech*, Vol. 58 (1972), pp. 396–407; "The Eagleton Affair: A Fantasy Theme Analysis," *The Quarterly Journal of Speech*, Vol. 59 (1973), pp. 143–59; and "Fetching Good Out of Evil: A Rhetorical Use of Calamity," *The Quarterly Journal of Speech*, Vol. 63 (1977), pp. 130–39. In this analysis I have used Bormann's conceptions of fantasy theme analysis as illustrated in Ernest G. Bormann, Jolene Koester, and Janet Bennett, "Political Cartoons and Salient Rhetorical Fantasies: An Empirical Analysis of the '76 Presidential Campaign," *Communication Monographs*, Vol. 45 (1978), pp. 317–29. See especially note 2 on p. 318.

This method of fantasy theme analysis is applied to a corpus of nineteen studies in this essay. Four criteria were relevant in their selection. First, studies were selected that possessed a social scientific orientation, as determined by two general standards: Each study possessed (1) commonly recognized research norms associated with the social sciences—typified by linguistic rigor (the consistent use of theoretically embedded technical terms as well as constitutive definitions that stipulate rules of correspondence to the real world), observational rigor (mechanical safeguards against human error, verification through replication, and specified rules of measurement), and inferential rigor (methods for reducing reactivism); and (2) commonly recognized theoretical norms associated with the social sciences typified by logical rigor, predictiveness, provocativeness, and manageability (see Herbert W. Simons, " 'Genre-alizing' About Rhetoric: A Scientific Approach," in Karlyn Kohrs Campbell and Kathleen Hall Jamieson eds., *Form and Genre: Shaping Rhetorical Action* (Falls Church, VA: Speech Communication Association, 1978), pp. 34–36). Second, studies were selected that dealt predominantly with those persons or "subjects" who were identified as preferring same-sex relationships. Third, studies were selected that had national distribution, or had authors with a national reputation, or had authors who had received national recognition for their work, or were published or sponsored by a nationally recognized research institution. Fourth, studies were selected that were distributed across the time span of the last twenty-five years, emphasizing the 1960s (eight studies) and the 1970s (seven studies) but not neglecting the 1950s (four studies).

8. Bormann, Koester, and Bennett, "Political Cartoons and Salient Rhetorical Fantasies," op. cit., p. 318, note 2.

9. *Webster's New Collegiate Dictionary* (Springfield, MA: G. & C. Merriam, 1973), p. 298.

10. *Roget's International Thesaurus* (New York: Thomas Y. Crowell, 1946), p. 455.

11. Martin Hoffman, *The Gay World: Male Homosexuality and the Social Creation of Evil* (rpt. 1968; New York: Bantam Books, 1969), p. 12. Used by permission.

12. Ibid., p. 14.

13. Ibid., pp. 22–23.

14. Donald Webster Cory and John P. LeRoy, *The Homosexual and His Society* (New York: Citadel Press, 1963), cover.

15. Michael Leigh, *The Velvet Underground* (New York: MacFadden, [1963]).

16. Hoffman, *The Gay World*, op., cit., cover.

17. Lawrence J. Hatterer. *Changing Homosexuality in the Male: Treatment for Men Troubled by Homosexuality* (New York: McGraw-Hill, 1970), p. 10.

18. Cory and LeRoy, *The Homosexual and His Society*, op. cit., p. 5.

19. Brian Reade, ed., *Sexual Heretics: Male Homosexuality in English Literature from 1850 to 1900* (New York: Coward-McCann, 1970).

20. John Rechy, *The Sexual Outlaw* (New York: Dell, 1977).

21. Wardell B. Pomeroy, "Homosexuality," in Ralph W. Weltge ed., *The Same Sex: An Appraisal of Homosexuality* (New York: Pilgrim Press, 1969), p. 3. Pomeroy's emphasis.

22. Edmund Bergler, *Homosexuality: Disease or Way of Life?* (rpt. 1956; New York: Collier, 1962), p. 13.

23. Hoffman, *The Gay World*, op. cit., pp. 21–22.

24. Cory and LeRoy, *The Homosexual and His Society*, op. cit., p. 4.

25. Hatterer, *Changing Homosexuality in the Male*, op. cit., p. 14.

26. Hoffman, *The Gay World*, op. cit., p. 50; Cory and LeRoy, *The Homosexual and His Society*, op. cit., pp. 105–28.

27. Hoffman, *The Gay World*, op. cit., p. 56.
28. Ibid., pp. 14–15.
29. Ibid., pp. 41–61; Hatterer, *Changing Homosexuality in the Male*, op. cit., p. 12; and Cory and LeRoy, *The Homosexual and His Society*, op. cit., pp. 105–36.
30. Pomeroy, "Homosexuality," op. cit., p. 3.
31. Hoffman, *The Gay World*, op. cit., p. 57.
32. Bergler, *Homosexuality*, op. cit., p. 13.
33. Hatterer, *Changing Homosexuality in the Male*, op. cit., p. 26. See also, pp. 15–26.
34. Hayes, "Gayspeak," op. cit., p. 256.
35. Arno Karlen, *Sexuality and Homosexuality: A New View* (New York: W.W. Norton, 1971), p. 511.
36. Hoffman, *The Gay World*, op. cit., pp. 15–17.
37. Alan P. Bell and Martin S. Weinberg, *Homosexualities: A Study of Diversity Among Men and Women* (New York: Simon & Schuster, 1978).
38. Pomeroy, "Homosexuality," op. cit., p. 6.
39. Ibid., p. 7.
40. Ibid., p. 6.
41. Sex Information and Education Council of the U.S. (SIECUS), *Homosexuality*, Study Guide No. 2, October 1965, p. 5.
42. Karlen, *Sexuality and Homosexuality*, op. cit., p. 525.
43. Task Force on the Human Rights Commission, *The Isolation, Sex Life, Discrimination, and Liberation of the Homosexual* (St. Paul, MN, 1971), p. 48. Also, see note 56 below.
44. SIECUS, *Homosexuality*, op. cit., p. 8.
45. *The Wolfenden Report: Report of the Committee on Homosexual Offenses and Prostitution* (New York: Lancer, 1963), pp. 36–37; and the National Institute of Mental Health, *The Final Report of the Task Force on Homosexuality* (Washington, DC: National Institute of Mental Health, 10 October 1969), p. 3.
46. Hayes, "Gayspeak," op. cit., p. 257.
47. Laud Humphrey, *Tearoom Trade: Impersonal Sex in Public Places* (Chicago: Aldine, 1970).
48. *Webster's New Collegiate Dictionary*, p. 1102.
49. Evelyn Hooker, "The Adjustment of the Male Overt Homosexual," Vol. 21 (1957), pp. 18–31; "Male Homosexuality in the Rorschach," Vol. 22 (1958), pp. 33–54, and "What Is a Criterion?" Vol. 23 (1959), pp. 278–81; all in the *Journal of Projective Techniques*. Also see Pomeroy, "Homosexuality," op, cit., p. 13.
50. See Jan Carl Park, "Anita Bryant: The Rhetoric of Homophobia," paper read at the Speech Communication Association Convention, November 1979.
51. In my unpublished "Paradox and Symbolic Realities: The Rhetorical Criticism of Social Constructions," a paradoxical world view was defined (p. 5) as "a phenomenon created, mediated, and controlled by a symbol, (1) functioning as a selective principle of interpretation, orientation, perspective, or point-of-view, which (2) establishes a relationship between two opposite or contradictory concepts in such a way that the symbol forces (3) these two opposite concepts to mutually and simultaneously influence the definition of phenomena (4) in multiple and different kinds of situations (5) without eliminating the tension of the opposition.
52. See "Homosexuals in America," *Gallup Opinion Index*, October 1977, Report 147.
53. National Institute of Mental Health, *The Final Report*, op. cit., p. 10.
54. Bell and Weinberg, *Homosexualities*, op. cit.
55. William Masters and Virginia Johnson, *Homosexuality in Perspective* (Boston: Little, Brown, 1979).

56. The concept of latent homosexuality is not being used here; this concept has raised several issues and its validity is in question. See e.g., SIECUS, *Homosexuality*, op. cit., p. 6. Rather, the point is most similar to heterosexuals who "know" that they are heterosexual even though they have not had a sexual release with someone of the opposite sex. Also, see notes 42 and 43 above.

57. Quoted in Karlen, *Sexuality and Homosexuality*, op. cit., p. 528. See also Erving Goffman, *Stigma: Notes on the Management of Spoiled Identity* (Englewood Cliffs, NJ: Prentice-Hall, 1963); Goffman has aptly noted, as argued here, that the word homosexuality, as a "medical and legal frame of reference," is "much too broad and heterogeneous a categorization for use here. I refer only to individuals who participate in a special community of understanding wherein members of one's own sex are defined as the most desirable sexual objects, and sociability is energetically organized around the pursuit and entertainment of these objects" (pp. 143–44 in note 7 of Goffman's *Stigma*).

58. Karlen, *Sexuality and Homosexuality*, op. cit., p. 519.

Chapter 16 Media Reaction to the 1979 Gay March on Washington

1. The symbolic importance of Stonewall to gays in the 1970s, especially those involved in the 1979 gay march on Washington, is indicated in Alan Young, "Welcome to the March," and Jim Kepner, "Long, Long Road to Washington," both in *National March on Washington for Lesbian and Gay Rights: Official Souvenir Program* (Washington, DC: March on Washington Committee for Lesbian and Gay Rights, 1979), pp. 1, 11–12; see also *The New York Times*, June 25, 1979, II, 3. Estimates of the crowd size varied widely; this matter is discussed more fully later in the chapter.

2. As listed in *Official Souvenir Program,* op. cit., p. 23.

3. David B. Goodstein, "Opening Space," *Advocate*, Issue 282 (December 13, 1979), p. 5.

4. See ibid.; letter to editor from A. Billy S. Jones, *Advocate*, Issue 285 (February 7, 1980), p. 12; and Kepner, "Long, Long Road to Washington," op. cit., p. 11.

5. Kenneth Burke, *A Grammar of Motives* (Berkeley, CA: University of California Press, 1969).

6. See Doug Ireland, "The New Homophobia: Open Season on Gays," *Nation*, Vol. 229, No. 7 (September 15, 1979), pp. 207–10; also William F. Buckley Jr., "Who Speaks for the Gays?" *National Review*, Vol. 31, No. 17 (April 27, 1979), pp. 578–79.

7. Scott Anderson, "A Monumental March Marks a Big Moment in Gay History," *Advocate*, Issue 281 (November 29, 1979), p. 8.

8. Brandy Moore, "Organizing for Freedom," in *Official Souvenir Program*, op. cit., pp. 30–31.

9. Burke, *A Grammar of Motives*, op. cit., p. 20.

10. *Official Souvenir Program*, op. cit., p. 44.

11. Moore, in ibid., p. 30.

12. Kepner, in ibid., p. 12.

13. Cleveland *Plain Dealer*, October 14, 1979, E1, 3; Washington *Post*, October 12, 1979, C4; Richard Goldstein, "Reasons to Be Cheerful," *Village Voice*, Vol. 24, No. 44 (October 29, 1979), p. 16.

14. Cleveland *Plain Dealer*, October 14, 1979, E1, 3; Washington *Post*, October 12, 1979. C4.

15. Washington *Post*, October 12, 1979, C4.

16. Burke, *A Grammar of Motives*, op. cit., pp. xix–xx.

17. *The New York Times*, October 14, 1979, 46; October 15, 1979, A14; Washington *Post*, October 15, 1979, A20.

18. *The New York Times*, October 14, 1979, 46.

19. Washington *Post*, October 15, 1979, A20.

20. See Richard Fulkerson, "The Public Letter as a Rhetorical Form: Structure, Logic, and Style in King's 'Letter from Birmingham Jail,'" *Quarterly Journal of Speech*, Vol. 65, No. 2 (April 1979), pp. 121–36; while Fulkerson's paper deals with a rhetorical situation in some respects different from the Washington march, the general rhetorical objective is the same: to appeal for the civil rights of a minority; moreover, the basic strategy employed is also parallel: to deliver the message to a relatively small group and use that group as a focus through which a much larger number of people can be addressed.

21. Dale Minor, *The Information War* (New York: Hawthorn, 1970), p. vii.

22. Ibid., p. 9.

23. *The New York Times*, October 15, 1979, A14; Washington *Post*, October 15, 1979, A1, 20; Cleveland *Plain Dealer*, October 15, 1979, A1: Los Angeles *Times*, October 15, 1979, 4; Chicago *Tribune*, October 15, 1979, 9.

24. Anderson, "A Monumental March," op. cit., p. 8; Goodstein, "Opening Space," op. cit., p. 5; interview with Jeff Rhodes, march organizer and participant.

25. See Los Angeles *Times*, October 15, 1979, 4; Chicago *Tribune*, October 15, 1979, 9.

26. Correspondence with James L. Holton, vice president of NBC Radio News, February 1, 1980; other radio networks did not respond to requests for information.

27. See Anderson, "A Monumental March," op. cit., p. 8; Goodstein, "Opening Space," op. cit., p. 5.

28. *Time* and *Newsweek* for 1978–79 together published at least thirteen articles dealing with homosexuality.

29. The accuracy of the sociopolitical labels attached to these newspapers was verified by Howard Novak, head of the Newspaper Division, Cleveland Public Library.

30. *Broadcasting Yearbook 1979* (Washington, DC: Broadcasting Publications, 1979), pp. A51–53.

31. Chicago *Tribune*, October 15, 1979, 9. Unless otherwise noted, all newspapers analyzed have six columns per page; each line represents a single-column line.

32. Los Angeles *Times*, October 15, 1979, p. 4.

33. *The New York Times*, October 15, 1979, A14.

34. Cleveland *Plain Dealer*, October 15, 1979, A1, 9.

35. Washington *Post*, October 15, 1979, A1, 20.

36. Los Angeles *Times*, October 12, 1979, 2; *The New York Times*, October 14, 1979, p. 46 (this article was not published in all editions).

37. Cleveland *Plain Dealer*, October 12, 1979, A4; October 14, 1979, E1, 3.

38. Washington *Post*, October 12, 1979, C4; October 13, 1979, C1, 7; October 14, 1979, B3; the 112 lines in the Friday *Post* report were on a 4-column rather than 6-column page; since the columns were wider than usual, the space devoted to the article was greater than would have been the case if the article had been 112 lines on a 6 column page; actually the story took 17 percent of the page, a substantial proportion.

39. Chicago *Tribune*, October 15, 1979, p. 9.

40. Anderson, "A Monumental March," op. cit., p. 8; Goodstein, "Opening Space," op. cit., p. 5.

41. See letter to editor from William Burr Hunt II, Washington *Post*, October 23, 1979, A16. Evangelist Jerry Falwell and others associated with the Christian group are popular personalities and would be expected to gain publicity for their efforts.

42. From an analysis of all newspaper articles used in this study.

43. Los Angeles *Times*, October 15, 1979, p. 4.

44. For an analysis of the subject, see Sydney W. Head, *Broadcasting in America* (3d ed.; Boston: Houghton Mifflin, 1976), pp. 407–10.

45. Goodstein, "Opening Space," op. cit., p. 5; Anderson, "A Monumental March," op. cit., p. 8; three letters to the editor in the Washington *Post*, October 23, 1979, A16; an interview with Rhodes; also an interview with Dan Kahn, march organizer and participant.

46. Goodstein, "Opening Space," op. cit., p. 5.

Chapter 17 Educational Responsibilities to Gay Male and Lesbian Students

1. For a general overview of homosexuality, see, in addition to those references cited throughout the essay, C.A. Tripp, *The Homosexual Matrix* (New York: McGraw-Hill, 1975) and Martin Hoffman, *The Gay World* (New York: Basic Books, 1968). On the gay student, see J. Lee Lehman, "Gay Students," in Louie Crew, ed., *The Gay Academic* (Palm Springs, CA: ETC Publications, 1978), pp. 57–63, and Barbara Gittings, "Combatting the Lies in the Libraries," in ibid., pp. 107–18.

2. For some idea of the conditions under which gay males live, see Howard Brown, *Familiar Faces, Hidden Lives: The Story of Homosexual Men in America Today* (New York: New American Library, 1976).

3. If anyone doubts that problems confront the gay academic, Louie Crew's essay, "Before Emancipation: Gay Persons as Viewed by Chairpersons in English," in Crew, *The Gay Academic*, op. cit., pp. 3–48 will prove instructive.

4. This concept of homophobia is crucial to an understanding of homosexuality and of homosexual oppression. See George Weinberg, *Society and the Healthy Homosexual* (New York: St. Martin's Press, 1972) and Dennis Altman, *Homosexual Oppression and Liberation* (New York: Outerbridge and Dienstfrey, 1971).

5. On stereotypes, see Tripp, *The Homosexual Matrix*, op. cit., and William Masters and Virginia Johnson, *Homosexuality in Perspective* (Boston: Little, Brown, 1978).

6. See Altman, *Homosexual Oppression and Liberation*, op. cit., for a view of the ways in which gays are oppressed by themselves and by others. For somewhat dated but still useful histories, see, for America, Donald Webster Cory, *The Homosexual in America* (New York: Greenberg, 1957); for Great Britain, H. Montgomery Hyde, *The Love That Dared Not Speak Its Name: A Candid History of Homosexuality in Britain* (Boston: Little, Brown, 1970).

7. That great strides have been made can best be appreciated from recalling that the Stonewall riots occurred at the close of the sixties, on June 28, 1969. And this should be cause for pride. But there have been backlashes; there has been Anita Bryant "saving" children from homosexuals, John Briggs screaming to eliminate gay teachers, and religious leaders of all faiths condemning gays and lesbians to hell. And this should be cause for vigilance. Gains won today may be lost tomorrow. Complacency with the status quo is perhaps the worst possible danger.

8. This issue of communication barriers is covered by Peter Fisher, *The Gay Mystique: The Myth and Reality of Male Homosexuality* (New York: Stein & Day, 1972).

9. On the numbers of homosexuals, see Alfred C. Kinsey, Wardell B. Pomeroy, and Clyde E. Martin, *Sexual Behavior in the Human Male* (Philadelphia: W.B. Saunders, 1948); Alfred C. Kinsey et al., *Sexual Behavior in the Human Female* (Philadelphia: W.B. Saunders, 1953); Masters and Johnson, *Homosexuality in Perspective*, op. cit.

10. For a brief introduction, see Vern and Bonnie Bullough, *Sin, Sickness, and Sanity: A History of Sexual Attitudes* (New York: New American Library, 1977). Louis Crompton, for example, has cogently argued that the word genocide is most appropriate in describing this oppression. "For a remarkable length of time—not less than 1400 years," says Crompton, "homosexual men and women in western society stood under a formal sentence of death, and were, in consequence, systematically killed or mutilated. But there has been no public account of this astonishing crime against humanity, all but unparalleled in its relentless use of sanctified legal traditions, and in its continuance century after century." See Crompton, "Gay Genocide: From Leviticus to Hitler," in Crew, *The Gay Academic*, op. cit., pp. 67–91.

11. A useful source in this connection is Jonathan Katz, ed., *Gay American History: Lesbians and Gay Men in the USA* (New York: Thomas Y. Crowell, 1976). Also see Hans Licht, *Sexual Life in Ancient Greece* (London: Abbey Library, 1932) and Otto Kiefer, *Sexual Life in Ancient Rome* (London: Abbey Library, 1934).

12. On homosexuality as a creative force, see John Murphy, *Homosexual Liberation: A Personal View* (New York: Praeger, 1971).

13. Pertinent to this discussion is Crew, *The Gay Academic*, op. cit.

14. Many leading textbook publishers have prepared guidelines to assist authors and editors in avoiding sexism and in creating positive sexual and racial images. Holt, Rinehart & Winston, Macmillan, McGraw-Hill, Wiley, and Harper & Row, for example, have published relatively extensive guidelines setting forth their position on these issues. Harper & Row, McGraw-Hill, and Wiley concentrate solely on women. Holt, Rinehart & Winston—in the shortest of these guides—in addition to covering women and sexism, also focuses on race, ethnic or national origin, age, religion, and physical condition. Macmillan likewise covers racial and national minorities as well as women and sexism. In none of these publications, however, is the problem of the gay and lesbian addressed. Nowhere is the author or editor advised to or given guidelines in avoiding homosexual and lesbian stereotypes or in creating positive images for the gay and lesbian. But more to the point is that none of these publishers—and I take these five to be a fair and representative sampling—has yet chosen to take a stand on the treatment of the gay and lesbian in educational materials.

15. Masters and Johnson, *Homosexuality in Perspective*, op. cit.

16. See Evelyn Hooker, "The Adjustment of the Male Overt Homosexual," in Hendrik M. Ruitenbeek, ed., *The Problem of Homosexuality in Modern America* (New York: E.P. Dutton, 1963), pp. 141–61, for a classic study on the positive adjustment of homosexuals. For more recent evidence and argument, see Mark Freedman, *Homosexuality and Psychological Functioning* (Belmont, CA: Brooks/Cole, 1971) and "Towards a Gay Psychology," in Crew, *The Gay Academic,* op. cit., pp. 315–26. Contrast these with, for example, one of the most famous studies on the psychological adjustment, or rather maladjustment, of the homosexual conducted by Irving Bieber et al., *Homosexuality: A Psychoanalytic Study* (New York: Basic Books, 1962). In this study—a study that has for years been considered the definitive study of homosexuals and their psychological adjustment—not one real live homosexual was examined. Instead, Bieber and his colleagues studied questionnaires that were administered to 77 psychoanalysts who reported on 106 homosexual patients. From these questionnaires a number of conclusions about

homosexuality were drawn, for example, that homosexuals had close, binding mothers and hostile, detached fathers, and that homosexuals were noncompetitive, clinging children. Also see Weinberg, *Society and the Healthy Homosexual*, op. cit.

17. For a start, see Casey Miller and Kate Swift, *Words and Women: New Language in New Times* (Garden City, NY: Doubleday, 1976); Robin Lakoff, *Language and Woman's Place* (New York: Harper & Row, 1975); and Barbara Westbrook Eakins and R. Gene Eakins, *Sex Differences in Human Communication* (Boston: Houghton Mifflin, 1978).

18. Merle Miller, *On Being Different: What It Means to Be a Homosexual* (New York: Random House, 1971); Karla Jay and Allen Young, eds., *Out of the Closets: Voices of Gay Liberation* (New York: Pyramid, 1974); and Laud Humphreys, *Out of the Closets: The Sociology of Homosexual Liberation* (Englewood Cliffs, NJ: Prentice-Hall, 1972).

19. On language, see Joseph J. Hayes, "Gayspeak," Chapter 4 in this book, and Bruce Rodgers, *The Queen's Vernacular: A Gay Lexicon* (San Francisco: Straight Arrow Books, 1972). For communication in general, see Edward William Delph, *The Silent Community: Public Homosexual Encounters* (Beverly Hills, CA: Sage, 1978).

20. For a discussion of this comparison, see Alan P. Bell and Martin S. Weinberg, *Homosexualities: A Study of Diversity Among Men and Women* (New York: Simon & Schuster, 1978).

Chapter 18 Consciousness-raising Among Gay Males

1. Robert L. Scott and Donald K. Smith argued that the confrontation tactics of the radical revolutionary constitute a distinct rhetoric or genre of discourse. See "The Rhetoric of Confrontation," *The Quarterly Journal of Speech*, Vol. 55 (1969), pp. 1–8.

2. For a discussion of the stages that precede overt political action, see Talcott Parsons, *Theories of Society, Foundations of Modern Sociological Theory* (Glencoe, IL: Free Press, 1961), p. 977.

3. Consciousness-raising was originally conceived by radical feminists of women's liberation. See Lynn O'Connor, "Defining Reality," Pamela Allen, "The Small Group Process," and Liz Bunding, "Problems and Limitations," in *The Small Group* (Berkeley, CA: Women's Liberation Basement, n.d.), pp. 2–18. Also see Carol Hanisch, "The Personal Is Political," Kathie Sarachild, "A Program for Feminist 'Consciousness Raising,' " Irene Peslikis, "False Consciousness," Jennifer Gardner, "Resistances to Consciousness," and Pamela Kearon, "Man-Hating," in *Notes from the Second Year: Women's Liberation, Major Writings of the Radical Feminists* (New York: Radical Feminists, 1970), pp. 76–84, 86; Pamela Kearon, "Power as a Function of a Group," and Carol Williams Payne, "Consciousness Raising: A Dead End?" in *Notes from the Third Year: Women's Liberation* (New York: Notes from the Second Year, Inc., 1971), pp. 99–100, 108–10. Additional information concerning consciousness-raising may be found in Evelyn Leo, "Dependency in Marriage: Oppression in Middle-Class Marriage," Barbara Susan, "About My Consciousness Raising," Betsy Warrior, "Sexual Roles and Their Consequences," in Leslie B. Tanner, ed., *Voices from Women's Liberation* (New York: A Signet Book/New American Library, 1970), pp. 235–54. Also see Robin Morgan, *Sisterhood Is Powerful* (New York: Vintage Books/Random House, 1970), pp. xxiii–xxiv. Notice, too, the "List of 'Consciousness Raising' Films" in *Sisterhood Is Powerful*, pp. 582–83.

Although consciousness-raising has been developed primarily by the women's liberation movement, gay and men's liberation also use this small-group technique. The use of consciousness-raising also appears to be spreading to other revolutionary groups, such as urban guerrillas. See Weather Underground and Bernardine Dohrn, "New Morning—Changing Weather," *Hundred Flowers*, Vol. 1 (January 1971), p. 4; "An Interview with a Weatherman and a Weatherwoman." *Scanlan's*, Vol. 1 (1971), p. 15; "December 1969: Weatherman Goes Underground," ibid.

4. Many writers deal with the different kinds of issues with which a consciousness-raising group may be concerned. For a single example of such a discussion, see Morgan, *Sisterhood Is Powerful*, op. cit., pp. xxiii–xxiv.

5. See Kearon, "Power as a Function of the Group," op. cit., pp. 109–10, for an example of the sense of collective unity, although the concept of "sisterhood" itself reflects the point.

6. Most feminists persistently argue that only shared personal experience justifies political theories and action. For the most vivid descriptions of this perspective, see Hanisch, "The Personal Is Political," op. cit., pp. 76–78; Allen, "The Small Group Process," op. cit., pp. 8–16.

7. For example, see Sarachild, "A Program for Feminist 'Consciousness Raising,'" op. cit., p. 80.

8. See James W. Chesebro, "Rhetorical Strategies of the Radical Revolutionary," *Today's Speech*, Vol. 20 (1972), pp. 38–39.

9. For example, see O'Connor, "Defining Reality," op. cit., pp. 2–7.

10. David Horowitz, "Revolutionary Karma vs. Revolutionary Politics," *Ramparts*, Vol. 9 (1971), p. 27. More generally, other writers discuss this sense of alienation from the system as "rage."

11. Consciousness-raising is often contrasted with sensitivity training in this regard. Sensitivity training is essentially an effort to build an "individual" identity for "social" interactions. See Carl Rogers, *On Encounter Groups* (New York: Harper & Row, 1970), pp. 6–7; Gerald Egan, *Encounter: Group Processes for Interpersonal Growth* (Belmont, CA: Brooks/Cole, 1970), pp. 68–69. Consciousness-raising, as already suggested, is an effort to build a group identity for political interactions. In this regard, O'Connor argues that "the task of the small group is labeled 'consciousness raising' and refers to a long and logical process which leads to a synthesis of the personal consciousness to which the psychoanalysts have given their attention and the political or class consciousness of the marxists" (p. 2). Also, see O'Connor for a discussion of her position that consciousness-raising and group therapy are "very different" (p. 3).

12. For a detailed explanation of how such a research effort is carried out, with extensive discussions of the reliability and validity of this type of design, see Severyn T. Bruyn, *The Human Perspective in Sociology, The Methodology of Participant Observation* (Englewood Cliffs, NJ: Prentice-Hall, 1966).

13. Researchers acting as participant-observers are likely to provide accurate reports of observed events. For discussions of this point, see Florence R. Kluckhorn, "The Participant Observer Technique in Small Communities," *American Journal of Sociology*, Vol. 46 (1940), p. 331; Arthur J. Vidich, "Participant Observation and the Collection and Interpretation of Data," *American Journal of Sociology*, Vol. 60 (1955), p. 354. In addition, Robert W. Friedrichs argues that a participant-observer probably does not alter ongoing processes more than any other type of researcher does. See *A Sociology of Sociology* (New York: The Free Press, 1970), p. 174.

14. See note 3 for a complete itemization of these studies.

15. Leonard C. Hawes, "Development and Application of an Interview Coding System," *Central States Speech Journal*, Vol. 23 (1972), p. 93. The present study

avoided using Bales' category system for the reasons that are outlined by Hawes.

16. See Ernest G. Bormann, *Discussion and Group Methods, Theory and Practice* (New York: Harper & Row, 1969), pp. 167–71.

17. See Robert Bales, *Personality and Interpersonal Behavior* (New York: Holt, Rinehart & Winston, 1970), pp. 136–55.

18. Ernest G. Bormann, "Fantasy and Rhetorical Vision: The Rhetorical Criticism of Social Reality," *The Quarterly Journal of Speech*, Vol. 58 (1972), p. 369–407.

19. David Reuben, *Everything You Always Wanted to Know About Sex But Were Afraid to Ask* (New York: David McKay, 1970).

20. See Bales, *Personality and Interpersonal Behavior*, op. cit., pp. 136–55.

21. "Sexism," as used in this context, is defined in *Philosophy and Objectives* (Minneapolis: FREE/Gay Liberation of Minnesota, n.d.).

22. Kearon, "Power as a Function of the Group," op. cit., pp. 109–10.

23. Tanner, ed., *Voices from Women's Liberation*, op. cit., pp. 253–54.

24. O'Connor, "Defining Reality," op. cit., pp. 2–7.

25. Allen, "The Small Group Process," op. cit., pp. 8–16.

26. See, e.g., James Chesebro, "The First National Gay Lib Convention: One View from Minneapolis" (Minneapolis: FREE/Gay Liberation of Minnesota, November 1970).

27. See note 11 for citations to substantiate this conclusion.

28. Bormann, *Discussion and Group Methods*, op. cit., pp. 113–14.

29. Robert F. Bales and F.L. Strodbeck, "Phases in Group Problem-Solving," *Journal of Abnormal and Social Psychology*, Vol. 46 (1951), pp. 485–95.

30. B.W. Tuckman, "Developmental Sequence in Small Groups," *Psychological Bulletin*, Vol. 19 (1965), pp. 34–40.

31. Abraham Zaleznik and David Moment, *The Dynamics of Interpersonal Behavior* (New York: John Wiley & Sons, 1964).

32. See Bormann's summary of the Minnesota Studies of small-group stages, in *Discussion and Group Methods*, op. cit., p. 282. Commonly recognized T-group stages are (1) forming, (2) storming, (3) norming, and (4) performing.

33. See notes 12 and 13 for discussions of various aspects of the use of participant observation as a research technique.

34. Bruyn, *The Human Perspective in Sociology*, op. cit., pp. 160–270, especially p. 261.

35. *Report of the President's Commission on Campus Unrest* (New York: Avon Books, 1971), p. 62.

36. Ibid., p. 78.

37. Participant democracy is discussed in the *Report of the President's Commission on Campus Unrest*, op. cit. For an additional discussion of this subject, see Students for a Democratic Society, *Port Huron Statement* (New York: Student Department of the League of Industrial Democracy, 1964).

Chapter 19 From "Commies" and "Queers" to "Gay Is Good"

1. Named after the bar that was closed, The Stonewall Inn. The Stonewall rebellion is the event widely recognized as giving birth to the gay liberation movement.

2. *Time*, October 31, 1969, pp. 56–67.

3. Arno Karlen, *Sexuality and Homosexuality* (New York: W.W. Norton, 1971), p. xiii.

4. Results of a 1969 Harris poll reported in the issue of *Time* cited above indicated that 63 percent of Americans considered homosexuals harmful to American life. A 1966 poll commissioned by CBS indicated that 71 percent of Americans viewed homosexuality as an illness. The report concludes: "The findings show that homosexuality is seen as an unquestionably negative phenomenon of our society, strongly rejected as a concept and as a practice, and is to be dealt with punitively when it is discovered." Reported in *Drum*, August 1967, as cited in Martin S. Weinberg and Colin J. Williams, *Male Homosexuals: Their Problems and Adaptations* (New York: Oxford University Press, 1974), p. 20.

5. Stephen E. Lucas, *Portents of Rebellion: Rhetoric and Revolution in Philadelphia, 1765–76* (Philadelphia: Temple University Press, 1976), p. xx and *passim*. For a similar perspective with specific criticism of individual studies of rhetoric and social movements, see James F. Darsey, "Catalytic Events and Rhetorical Movements: A Methodological Inquiry," unpublished M.A. thesis, Purdue University, 1978, esp. pp. 1–13.

6. For an explication of "consensus" in the way we are using it here, see Thomas B. Farrell, "Knowledge, Consensus, and Rhetorical Theory," *Quarterly Journal of Speech*, Vol. 62 (1976), pp. 1–14.

7. Ibid.; Ch. Perelman and L. Olbrechts-Tyteca, *The New Rhetoric*, trans. by John Wilkinson and Purcell Weaver (Notre Dame, IN: Notre Dame University Press, 1969), pp. 14, 65; Stephen Toulmin, *The Uses of Argument* (Cambridge: Cambridge University Press, 1958), p. 97.

8. Darsey, "Catalytic Events and Rhetorical Movements," op. cit., pp. 20–36, 57–77.

9. Rex D. Hopper, "The Revolutionary Process: A Frame of Reference for the Study of Revolutionary Movements," *Social Forces*, Vol. 28 (1950), pp. 270–79. Regarding the value-orientation of social movement discourse, see James W. Chesebro, "Cultures in Conflict—A Generic and Axiological View," *Today's Speech*, Vol. 21 (1973), esp. pp. 17–18. Cf. Edward D. Steele and W. Charles Redding, "The American Value System: Premises for Persuasion," *Western Speech*, Vol. 26 (1962), pp. 83–91; Ralph Eubanks and Virgil Baker, "Toward an Axiology of Rhetoric," in Richard L. Johannesen, ed., *Contemporary Theories of Rhetoric* (New York: Harper & Row, 1971), pp. 340–56; for experimental evidence of this point, see Robert L. Heath, "Variability in Value System Priorities as Decision-making Adaptation to Situational Differences," *Communication Monographs,* Vol. 43 (1976), p. 329.

10. Ralph K. White, *Value-Analysis: The Nature and Use of the Method* (Glen Gardiner, NJ: Libertarian Press, 1951), p. 1.

11. Toulmin, *The Uses of Argument*, op. cit., pp. 94–107. On the use of Toulmin in discourse analysis, see Roderick P. Hart, "On Applying Toulmin: The Analysis of Practical Discourse," in G.P. Mohrmann, Charles J. Stewart, and Donovan J. Ochs, eds., *Explorations in Rhetorical Criticism* (University Park, PA: Pennsylvania State University Press, 1973), pp. 75–95.

12. The reliability of the value-analysis of this study was calculated for both intercoder and intracoder levels. Intracoder reliability yields a Spearmar Rank Order Coefficient of .95, while intercoder reliability for three coders yielded a Kendall Coefficient of concordance of .925.

13. Arno Karlen, *Sexuality and Homosexuality* (New York: W.W. Norton, 1971), p. 6.

14. Jonathan Katz, *Gay American History* (New York: Thomas Y. Crowell, 1976), pp. 14–16.

15. Ibid., pp. 23–24.

16. Edward Sagarin, *Odd Man In* (Chicago: Quadrangle, 1969), p. 79.

17. Katz, *Gay American History*, op. cit., pp. 366–71 and passim.

18. Ibid., pp. 385–93; Edward Sagarin, *Structure and Ideology in an Association of Deviants*, unpublished doctoral dissertation, New York University, 1966, pp. 36–38.

19. See John Lauritsen and David Thorstad, *The Early Homosexual Rights Movement (1864–1935)* (New York: Times Change Press, 1974).

20. Norman A. Graebner, Gilbert C. Fite, and Philip L. White, *A History of the American People* (New York: McGraw-Hill, 1970), p. 1246.

21. Sagarin, *Structure and Ideology*, op. cit., pp. 48–51.

22. "Institute for Sex Research, Indiana University," brochure (Indiana University Publications, 1970), n.p.

23. Sagarin, *Odd Man In*, op. cit., pp. 82–83.

24. "Institute for Sex Research, Indiana University," op. cit.

25. Sagarin, *Odd Man In*, op. cit., p. 83.

26. Alfred C. Kinsey, Wardell B. Pomeroy, and Clyde E. Martin, *Sexual Behavior in the Human Male* (Philadelphia: W.B. Saunders, 1948), p. 625.

27. Sagarin, *Odd Man In*, op. cit., p. 83.

28. Ibid.; Katz, *Gay American History*, op. cit., passim.

29. *The New York Times*, March 1, 1950, pp. 2, 8.

30. U.S. Congress, Senate, Committee on Expenditures in the Executive Departments, Employment of Homosexuals and Other Sex Perverts in Government; Interim Report Submitted to the Committee on Expenditures in the Executive Departments by Its Subcommittee on Investigations Pursuant to S. Res. 280, 81st Congress, 2d Session, 15 December 1950, Sen. Doc, 241; reprinted in part in Edward Sagarin (pseud. Donald Webster Cory), *The Homosexual in America* (1951, rpt. New York: Arno, 1975), pp. 270–77.

31. "The Mattachine Program," *San Francisco Mattachine Newsletter*, June 25, 1954, n.p.

32. Ibid.

33. Ibid.

34. Ibid.

35. Jeff Winters, "Homosexuals Are Not People," *One*, March 1953, p. 2.

36. D. Mauroc, "The Homosexual," *One*, November 1954, p. 21.

37. Lyn Pederson, "The Importance of Being Different," *One*, March 1954, pp. 4–6.

38. John Murphy, *Homosexual Liberation: A Personal View* (New York, 1971).

39. Winters, "Homosexuals Are Not People," op. cit., p. 6.

40. See Joseph Gusfield, *Protest, Reform, and Revolt: A Reader in Social Movements* (New York, 1970), p. 11. Cf. Kenneth Boulding, "Towards a Theory of Protest," reprinted in Walt Anderson, ed., *The Age of Protest* (Pacific Palisades, CA: Goodyear, 1969), p. vi.

41. Pederson, "The Importance of Being Different," op. cit., p. 4.

42. Grouped toward the end of this discussion, the concerns of all five periods are presented diagrammatically to allow easy comparison of the periods and discernment of any "evolutionary" argumentative trends.

43. Graebner, Fite, and White, *A History of the American People*, op. cit., p. 1204.

44. Martin Hoffman, *The Gay World* (New York: Basic Books, 1968), p. 93.

45. For a more complete discussion of this, see ibid., pp. 77–111; Karlen, *Sexuality and Homosexuality*, op. cit., pp. 607–18.

46. Edwin Schur, "The Case for Abolition," in Edwin M. Schur and Hugo Adam Bedau, *Victimless Crimes: Two Sides of a Controversy* (Englewood Cliffs, NJ: Prentice-Hall, 1974), p. 25.

47. "Let Us Be Proud," rpt. *Mattachine Review*, October 1957, p. 23.
48. "Editorial," *One*, February 1957, p. 5.
49. Ibid.
50. Editorial, *One*, April 1959, p. 4.
51. Ibid.
52. "Let Us Be Proud," p. 23.
53. William Lambert, Editorial, *One*, July 1961.
54. *Mattachine Review*, November 1957.
55. Hoffman, *The Gay World*, op. cit., p. 93.
56. Conger, Editorial, *One*, August 1963, p. 5.
57. Editorial, "President Johnson Speaks on Tolerance and Brotherhood," *New York Mattachine Newsletter*, Vol. 10 (May 1965), p. 2.
58. "All the Lies Fit to Print," *The Los Angeles Advocate*, January 1968, p. 8.
59. Ibid.
60. Editorials, *Eastern Mattachine Magazine*, August 1965, p. 2.
61. "Politics by the Bay," *The Los Angeles Advocate*, December 1967, p. 6.
62. Editorials, *Eastern Mattachine Magazine*, August 1965, p. 2.
63. Editorial, *One*, June 1965, p. 4,
64. Bob Stanley, "Gay Pride Week, 1970: That Was the Week That Was," *Mattachine Midwest Newsletter*, July 1970, p. 1.
65. M.J. Kuda, "MM, Gay Lib Meet Jointly," *Mattachine Midwest Newsletter*, June 1970, p, 4.
66. John Waite Bowers and Donovan J. Ochs, *The Rhetoric of Agitation and Control* (Reading, MA: Addison-Wesley, 1971), p. 7.
67. Ibid.
68. The word gay had been adopted by homosexuals as a self-referent much earlier than this, but more as a secret code than as a label of self-celebration and self-affirmation as in "Say it loud; I'm Gay and I'm proud!" See Sagarin, *The Homosexual in America*, op. cit., pp. 103–13.
69. For example, see "The Editor Comments," *Vector*, June 1971, p. 4; "Conference Stresses Unity," p. 2; "How Far We Have Come," n.p.
70. "How About Us Shorties?" *The Advocate*, January 6–19, 1971, p. 22. Reprinted by permission from *The Advocate*, copyright © 1971, Liberation Publications, Inc.
71. Saul D. Alinsky, *Rules for Radicals* (New York: Vintage Press, 1971), p. 128.
72. "Conference Stresses Unity," *New York Mattachine Newsletter*, June 1970, pp. 1–2.
73. Ibid., p. 2.
74. "The Editors Speak," *Gay*, June 1, 1970, p. 2.
75. Jim Kepner, Editorial, *One*, July/August 1972, p. 3.
76. "The Editors Speak," *Gay*, June 1, 1970, p. 2.
77. "The Homosexual: Newly Visible, Newly Understood," *Time*, October 31, 1969, pp. 56–67.
78. "The Homosexuals: A Newly Visible Minority," *Chicago Sun-Times Midwest*, December 14, 1969.
79. For example, see "Conference Stresses Unity," op. cit.
80. Gerald C. Davidson and John M. Neale, *Abnormal Psychology* (New York: John Wiley & Sons, 1974), p. 319.
81. Ibid.
82. Editorial, "A Taxing Time," *The Advocate*, April 7, 1976, p. 14.
83. Marc Williams, Editorial, *Mattachine Times*, January/February 1973, p. 36.
84. Editorial, "Off Your Knees," *The Advocate*, June 6, 1973, p. 36.
85. "A Call for Action," *The Advocate*, March 9, 1977, p. 28.

86. Editorial, *Vector*, April 1975, p. 4.
87. Williams, Editorial, op. cit., p. 4.
88. For example, see Editorial, "10 Years," *Vector*, December 1974, p. 4.
89. "The Editors Speak," *Gay*, May 7, 1973, p. 3.
90. For a detailed and thoughtful account of the problem, see John Murphy, *Homosexual Liberation: A Personal View* (New York: Praeger, 1971).
91. For a discussion of consciousness raising, particularly as applied to the gay community, see James W. Chesebro, John F. Cragan, and Patricia McCullough, "The Small Group Techniques of the Radical-Revolutionary: A Synthetic Study of Consciousness Raising," *Speech Monographs*, Vol. 40 (June 1973), pp. 136–46 (see chapter 16).
92. See Jan Carl Park, "Referendum Campaigns vs. Gay Rights: Who Wins?," paper presented to the annual convention of the Speech Communication Association, San Antonio, Texas, November 1979 (see chapter 24). See also Barry Brummett, "A Pentadic Analysis of Ideologies in Two Gay Rights Controversies," *Central States Speech Journal*, Vol. 30 (1979), pp. 250–61 (see chapter 25). Ronald Fischli, "Anita Bryant's Stand Against 'Militant Homosexuality': Religious Fundamentalism and the Democratic Process," *Central States Speech Journal,* Vol. 30 (1979), pp. 262–71 (see chapter 26).
93. Perelman and Olbrechts-Tyteca, *The New Rhetoric,* op. cit., p. 144.
94. See note 4 above.
95. "The New Morality," *Time,* November 21, 1977, p. 44.
96. "How Gay Is Gay?" *Time,* April 23, 1979, p. 72.
97. For this use of "people," see Michael C. McGee, "In Search of 'The People': A Rhetorical Alternative," *Quarterly Journal of Speech,* Vol. 61 (1975), pp. 235–49.

Chapter 20 Troy Perry: Gay Advocate

1. *The Universal Fellowship Today* (Los Angeles: Universal Fellowship Press, 1977), also Troy Perry (with Charles L. Lucas), *The Lord Is My Shepherd and He Knows I'm Gay* (Los Angeles: Nash Publishing, 1972), p. 120 ff.; the gay newspaper was the *Los Angeles Advocate,* the predecessor of the nationally distributed *The Advocate*.
2. Donna Wade, "We Are Family," *In Unity*, August/September 1979, p. 11 ff. [*In Unity* is a publication of MCC.]
3. The commercial media estimated the crowd as including from 10,000 to 75,000. ABC-TV said 250,000. The march preceding the rally, which was composed mostly of persons marching eight abreast, took approximately three hours to pass. My observation would suggest the larger figure, which was represented from the platform as being an official estimate of the Washington police.
4. Unless otherwise noted, all references to the 1969 cluster of speeches are taken from my unpublished Ph.D. dissertation, *The Rhetoric of Troy Perry: A Case Study of the Los Angeles Gay Rights Rally, November 16, 1969*, University of Southern California, 1972. All quotations from sermons and rally speeches are from transcriptions of tape recordings made on site in 1969 and 1979. Full transcriptions of the 1969 speeches are appended to the dissertation noted above.
5. This perception has been influenced significantly by the writings of Erving Goffman, particularly *Stigma: Notes on the Management of Spoiled Identity* (Englewood Cliffs, NJ: Prentice-Hall, 1963).
6. "Church Gives Perry Vote of Confidence," *The Advocate*, August 19 —September 1, 1970, p. 5.

7. November 9, 1969.
8. Sylvan Theatre speech, October 13, 1979.
9. Personal interview, June 24, 1971.
10. Perry, *The Lord Is My Shepherd*, op, cit., pp. 126 f. Used by permission.
11. Milton Dickens, *Speech: Dynamic Communication* (2d ed.; New York: Harcourt Brace Jovanovich, 1963), pp. 325–27.
12. "The Homosexual Church," *Newsweek*, October 12, 1970, p. 107.
13. John Dart, "Church for Homosexuals," Los Angeles *Times*, December 8, 1969, sec. 2, p. 1.
14. Perry, MCC service, November 23, 1969.

Chapter 21 Lesbianfeminist Rhetoric as a Social Movement

1. Vicki Nogle, "The Impact of Lesbianfeminist Rhetoric," unpublished paper presented at the Speech Communication Association convention, November 1979.
2. Leland Griffin, "A Dramatistic Theory of the Rhetoric of Movements," in William Rueckert, ed., *Critical Responses to Kenneth Burke* (Minneapolis: University of Minnesota Press, 1969), p. 462.
3. Ibid., pp. 462–63.
4. Ibid., p. 463.
5. Karla Jay and Allen Young, eds., *Out of the Closets: Voices of Gay Liberation* (New York: Pyramid, 1974), and Anne Koedt, Ellen Levine, and Anita Rapone, eds., *Radical Feminism* (New York: Quadrangle, 1973).
6. KNOW, Inc., P.O. Box 86031, Pittsburgh, PA 15221.
7. Sidney Abbott and Barbara Love, *Sappho Was a Right-On Woman: A Liberated View of Lesbianism* (New York: Stein & Day, 1972), p. 137.
8. Del Martin and Phyllis Lyon, *Lesbian/Woman* (San Francisco, CA: Glide Publications, 1972), p. 298.
9. Kristen Grimstad and Susan Rennie, eds., *The New Woman's Survival Sourcebook* (New York: Alfred A. Knopf, 1975), p. 236.
10. Jane Rule, *Lesbian Images* (New York: Pocket Books, 1976), p. 211.
11. Jeanne Córdova, "What's a Dyke to Do? And What the Dyke Is Doing," in Karla Jay and Allen Young, eds., *After You're Out* (New York: Pyramid Books, 1975), p. 16.
12. Rita Mae Brown, "Living with Other Women," in Alison M. Jaggar and Raula Rothenberg, eds., *Feminist Frameworks: Alternative Theoretical Accounts of the Relations Between Women and Men* (New York: McGraw-Hill, 1978), p. 259. Used with permission.
13. Charlotte Bunch, "Lesbians in Revolt," in Jaggar and Rothenberg, *Feminist Frameworks*, op. cit., p. 136.
14. Ibid., p. 139.
15. Córdova, "What's a Dyke to Do?" op. cit., p. 19.
16. Brown, "Living with Other Women," op. cit., pp. 257–58.
17. Radicalesbians, "The Woman-Identified-Woman," in *Notes from the Third Year: Women's Liberation* (New York: Notes from the Second Year, Inc., 1971), p. 81.
18. Ibid., pp. 81–82.
19. Ibid., p. 82.
20. Ibid.
21. Ibid.

22. Ibid.
23. Ibid.
24. Ibid., pp. 82–83.
25. Ibid., p. 83.
26. Ibid.
27. Ibid.
28. Griffin, "A Dramatistic Theory of the Rhetoric of Movements," op. cit., p. 464; see footnote 67 for original source.
29. Ibid.
30. Ibid.; see footnotes 70 and 71 for original source.
31. Radicalesbians, "The Woman-Identified-Woman," op. cit., pp. 83–84.
32. Charlotte Bunch, "Lesbian-Feminist Theory," in Ginny Vida, ed., *Our Right to Love: A Lesbian Resource Book* (Englewood Cliffs, NJ: Prentice-Hall, 1978), p. 181.
33. "The Transformation of Silence into Language and Action: The Lesbians and Literature Panel of the 1977 Annual Modern Language Association Convention" (Julia chaired this panel), in *Sinister Wisdom,* Vol. 6 (Summer 1978), p. 5.
34. Julia Stanley, in ibid., p. 4.
35. Mary Daly, in ibid., p. 9.
36. J.R. Roberts, "In America They Call Us Dykes: Notes on the Etymology and Usage of 'Dyke'," in *Sinister Wisdom*, Vol. 9 (Spring 1979), pp. 4–5. Used by permission.

Chapter 22 Gay Civil Rights and the Roots of Oppression

1. Alfred C. Kinsey, Wardell B. Pomeroy and C. E. Martin, *Sexual Behavior in the Human Male* (Philadelphia: W.B. Saunders), 1948.
2. Tom Maurer, in a speech delivered at the annual symposium of the Council on Religion and the Homosexual, October 31, 1970, San Francisco.
3. Walter Barnett, in lectures on sexuality and the law, San Francisco, Berkeley, Oakland, 1970–74.
4. *Griswold vs. Connecticut* (1965) 381 U.S. 479, 85 SCt 1678, 14 L.Ed. 2d 510.
5. *Stanley vs. Georgia* (1969) 394 U.S. 557, 49 SCt 1243, 22 L.Ed. 2d 542.
6. *Eisenstadt vs. Baird* (1972) 405 U.S. 438, 92 SCt 1029, 31 L.Ed 2d 349.
7. *SARguide for a Better Sex Life* (National Sex Forum, 1523 Franklin St., San Francisco, CA 94109), 1975.
8. Robert L. Treese, "Homosexuality: A Contemporary View of the Biblical Perspective," in Sally Gearhart and William R. Johnson, eds., *Loving Women/ Loving Men: Gay Liberation and the Church* (San Francisco: Glide Publications, 1974), pp. 28–40.
9. Del Martin and Phyllis Lyon, *Lesbian/Woman* (New York: Bantam Books), 1973, p. 3.
10. Herman Cohen, "The Climate of Communication," an address to the Western Speech Communication Association, November 25, 1975.

Chapter 23 Referendum Campaigns vs. Gay Rights

1. Randy Shilts, "The Fundamentalists," *Blueboy*, July 1979, p. 25.
2. Paul Gebhard, "Kinsey Institute Documents Gays," *It's Time: Newsletter of the National Gay Task Force*, Vol. 3, No. 7 (1977), p. 2.

3. "Cities, States Advance Gay Rights," *It's Time: Newsletter of the National Gay Task Force*, Vol. 3, No. 5 (March 1977), p. 2. *It's Time* reports "the first gay rights protection adopted in the United States was an executive order issued in Atlanta in 1971. Since that time 40 other American municipalities and Toronto, Canada, have adopted similar protections or passed gay civil rights laws. Cities, counties, and states prohibiting discrimination on the basis of sexual orientation are listed below. An asterisk appears next to Atlanta, New York City, and several other cities where the protections apply only to municipal jobs, i.e., city government" [p. 1].

Cities

*Atlanta, GA
*New York City, NY
East Lansing, MI
San Francisco, CA
Ann Arbor, MI
Washington, DC
Seattle, WA
Toronto, Ontario
Berkeley, CA
Detroit, MI
Columbus, OH (Housing/Accommodations only)
Minneapolis, MN
Alfred, NY
*Ithaca, NY
*Sunnyvale, CA
San Jose, CA (Referendum, November, 1980)
Portland, OR
*Mountain View, CA
*Cupertino, CA
Madison, WI
Yellow Springs, OH
Austin, TX
*Santa Barbara, CA
*Chapel Hill, NC
Cleveland Heights, OH
*Ottawa, Canada
*Boston, MA
*Pullman, WA
*Amherst, MA
*Los Angeles, CA
Tucson, AZ

Counties

Santa Cruz County, CA
Howard County, MD
Hennepin County, MN
Santa Clara County, CA (Referendum, November, 1980)

States

Pennsylvania (State Employment only)

4. "Referendum," *Encyclopedia Americana*, 1977 ed., p. 298.
5. *The Book of the States: 1978–1979* (Lexington, KY: Council of State Governments), Vol. 22, p. 245.
6. David Butler and Austin Ranney, *Referendums: A Comparative Study of Practice and Theory* (Washington, DC: American Enterprise Institute for Public Policy Research, 1978), back cover.
7. Howard D. Hamilton, "Direct Legislation: Some Implications of Open Housing Referenda," *The American Political Science Review*, Vol. 64 (1970), p. 125.
8. Ibid.
9. Stanley Scott and Harriet Nathan, "Public Referenda: A Critical Reappraisal," *Urban Affairs Quarterly*, Vol. 5 (1970), p. 317.
10. Laura Tallian, *Direct Democracy: An Historical Analysis of Initiative, Referendum, and Recall Process* (Los Angeles: Peoples Lobby, 1977), p. 13. For a complete history of the referendum in America, see Ellis P. Oberholtzer, *The Referendum in America* (New York: DeCapo Press, 1971).
11. Duane Lockard, *The Politics of State and Local Governments* (New York: Macmillan, 1963), p. 263.
12. Winston W. Crouch, "The Initiative and Referendum in Cities," *The American Political Science Review*, Vol. 27 (June 1943), p. 492.
13. Ibid.; see also *The Book of the States, 1978–1979*, op. cit., p. 245.
14. Lockard, *The Politics of State and Local Governments,* op. cit., p. 264.
15. Ibid.
16. Scott and Nathan, "Public Referenda," op. cit., p. 326.
17. Ibid.
18. Ibid., p. 315.
19. Butler and Ranney, *Referendums*, op. cit., p. 82.
20. Ibid., p. 84.
21. Jeanne Córdova, "Gay Rights Victories—Enemies Can Be a Blessing," *Seattle Gay News*, January 24, 1978, n.p.
22. Charles W. Kneupper, "No on Proposition 6: The San Francisco Campaign," paper presented at the Speech Communication Association convention, San Antonio, Texas, 1979, p. 1.
23. Ibid., pp. 9–10.
24. Ibid., p. 1.
25. *Referenda & Initiative: Report of the National Gay Task Force Laguna Beach Conference* (New York: NGTF, July 1978, p. 1). The report, which is available from the National Gay Task Force, 80 Fifth Avenue, New York, NY 10011, described its purpose in the following opening comments: "In July 1978, the National Gay Task Force convened a conference of the campaign managers and co-ordinators of the four gay rights ordinance referenda campaigns. The participants were the campaign directors from the efforts in Dade County; St. Paul, Minnesota; Wichita, Kansas; and Eugene, Oregon. These seasoned leaders were assembled at a Laguna Beach, California retreat for a full weekend to reflect upon and exchange their experiences and conclusions about conducting campaigns. This was done not only for the production of an educational publication useful to any city, but to help those now engaged in the Seattle and California campaigns" [p. 1].
26. Kneupper, "No on Proposition 6," op. cit.
27. *Referenda & Initiative*, op. cit.

Chapter 24 Ideologies in Two Gay Rights Controversies

1. "Battle Over Gay Rights," *Newsweek*, June 6, 1977, p. 16.

2. Wayne Wangstad, "St. Paul Voters Kill Gay Rights," St. Paul *Pioneer Press*, April 26, 1978, p. 1.

3. "City Election," St. Paul *Pioneer Press*, April 23, 1978, "Focus," p. 2; and Theodore Stanger, "Only a Few Gays Filing Bias Complaints," Miami *Herald*, May 30, 1977, p. 1A.

4. Edwin Black, in "The Second Persona," *The Quarterly Journal of Speech*, Vol. 56 (1970), p. 112, argues that an ideology is "the network of interconnected convictions that functions in a man epistemically and that shapes his identity by determining how he views the world." The concept of ideology was explored in two articles in the April 1978 issue of *The Quarterly Journal of Speech*, Vol. 61: William R. Brown, "Ideology as Communication Process," pp. 123–40, and Michael C. McGee, " 'Not Men, but Measures': The Origins and Import of an Ideological Principle," pp. 141–54. This essay intends no new theoretical explanation of ideology, but will assume the meaning of the term argued in those two essays. I take the term to mean a complex of principles, values, and assumptions that shape one's views and explanations of reality. *Any* ideology will therefore give answer to the question of what it means to be human; the two ideologies studied here are examined for their answers to subordinate issues of sex and politics.

5. Burke's pentad and its uses are discussed throughout his works, but are introduced in chapter 1, "Container and the Thing Contained," of *A Grammar of Motives* (1945; reprinted; Berkeley: University of California Press, 1962), pp. 3–20.

6. Robert Ivie, in his article "Presidential Motives for War," *The Quarterly Journal of Speech*, Vol. 60 (1974), pp. 337–45, shows that American Presidents tend to explain the origins and challenges of war to the public by fixing responsibility for war's occurrence on one or more terms of the pentad. In a different treatment of the pentad, Jeanne Y. Fischer, "A Burkean Analysis of the Rhetorical Dimensions of a Multiple Murder and Suicide," *The Quarterly Journal of Speech*, Vol. 60 (1974), pp. 175–89, probes the psyche of a murderer. Professor Fischer's article attributes the man's actions to motivations arising for him from certain terms of the pentad insofar as they represented points of symbolic ambiguity. Both these articles show how rhetoric can be understood by using the pentad as a guide to people's motivations. In another example, suppose that one were fond of fishing; where does one get that motivation to fish? Perhaps from agency: one may be fond of the hardware and tackle of fishing. Perhaps from agent: one may enjoy fancying oneself a fisherman with the aura attendant on that image. Perhaps from scene: one may like the great outdoors. For the individual or the group, the terms of the pentad suggest possible sources of motivation.

7. In Part Two of *A Grammar of Motives*, "The Philosophic Schools," Burke discusses philosophies and ideologies generated by each term of the pentad. Burke's analysis makes it clear that one need not trace the motivations given by every term of the pentad in every criticism. The present essay, for instance, ignores purpose, scene, and agency. I do not deny their usefulness, but a critic strapped for space may legitimately look at only a few terms and ratios to reveal motivations located therein.

8. Although neither term is entirely satisfactory, I shall use Anti to mean those opposed to ordinances protecting gay rights, and Pro to mean those in favor of such ordinances. I do not intend to explain all the arguments of either side in this chapter; rather, I shall address some of the more central themes. Also, this essay does not claim that people approach gay rights from *only* act or agent ideologies.

However, the most vocal arguers seem to feature either act or agent. If the reader thinks of arguments that seem to be informed by neither act nor agent, perhaps that rhetoric is best explained by some other ideology, and falls outside the scope of this essay.

9. Tom Davies, "750 Protest at Anita Bryant Performance," The Minneapolis *Tribune*, Vol. 22 (May 1977), p. 2B (continued from 1B).

10. Arthur Bell, "Anita Bryant's Ire and Brimstone," *The Village Voice*, April 4, 1977, p. 13.

11. Robert Bork, "Anti-Gay Groups Try to Ignore Human Rights, Steinem Declares," The Miami *Herald*, May 30, 1977, p. 18A.

12. St. Paul Citizens for Human Rights, "Religious Support of Human Rights in St. Paul" (single-page leaflet distributed to homes in St. Paul).

13. Brenda Ingersoll and Debra Stone, "Pro and Con Gay Rights Rallies Attract Many," Minneapolis *Star*, April 20, 1978, p. 4A.

14. Arnold Markowitz, "Gay Rights Foes Do Song, Talk Lunch Debate," The Miami *Herald*, May 30, 1977, p. 2B (continued from 1B).

15. Political ad by St. Paul Citizens for Human Rights, St. Paul *Pioneer Press*, April 21, 1978, p. 24.

16. Wangstad, "St. Paul Voters Kill Gay Rights," op. cit., p. 1.

17. St. Paul Citizens for Human Rights, "Law Works Well," St. Paul *Dispatch*, April 21, 1978, Election guide, p. 5.

18. "Picking Out Favorites in St. Paul Election," St. Paul *Dispatch*, April 19, 1978, p. 14A.

19. Dale Anderson, "The Gay Rights Proposal: No," Minneapolis *Tribune*, April 22, 1978, Opinion, p. 4.

20. St. Paul Citizens for Human Rights, "Religious Support of Human Rights in St. Paul," op. cit.

21. "Battle Over Gay Rights," op. cit., p. 26.

22. John Ekholm, "The St. Paul Vote," Minneapolis *Tribune*, April 29, 1978, p. 10A.

23. Markowitz, "Gay Rights Foes Do Song, Talk Lunch Debate," op. cit., p. 2B.

24. "Battle Over Gay Rights," op. cit., p. 16.

25. J.S. Katz, "To the Editor," Minneapolis *Star*, April 28, 1978, p. 9A.

26. Robert Ferdinand, Jr., "Decision in St. Paul," Minneapolis *Star*, April 28, 1978, p. 9A.

27. Gloria Ohland, "2500 March to Support Gay Rights," Minnesota *Daily* (University of Minnesota campus newspaper), April 20, 1978, p. 15.

28. Ibid.

29. St. Paul Citizens for Human Rights, "Religious Support of Human Rights in St. Paul," op. cit.

30. "Gay Rights in St. Paul," Minneapolis *Star*, April 21, 1978, p. 10A.

31. Anderson, "The Gay Rights Proposal: No," op. cit., Opinion, p. 4.

32. Michael Novak, "Miami and the Homosexuals," Minneapolis *Star*, June 3, 1977, p. 9A.

33. St. Paul Citizens Alert for Morality, "Gays 'Immoral,' " St. Paul *Dispatch*, April 21, 1978, Election guide, p. 5.

34. Ingersoll and Stone, "Pro and Con Gay Rights Rallies Attract Many," op. cit., pp. 1A to 4A.

35. "*Playboy* Interview: Anita Bryant," *Playboy*, May 1978, p. 76.

36. Ibid., p. 85.

37. V.L. Vauter, "Mockery," St. Paul *Dispatch*, April 17, 1978, p. 4A.

38. St. Paul Citizens Alert for Morality, "Gays 'Immoral,' " op. cit.

39. Novak, "Miami and the Homosexuals," op. cit., p. 9A.

40. George F. Will, "How Far Out of the Closet?" *Newsweek,* May 30, 1977, p. 92.
41. Associated Press release, "Anita Bryant Debates Homosexual on Rights," Minneapolis *Star*, May 28, 1977, p. 4A.
42. Paul Westman, "Gay Rights Have Nothing to Do with Human Rights," Minnesota *Daily,* May 2, 1978, p. 7.
43. Markowitz, "Gay Rights Foes Do Song, Talk Lunch Debate," op. cit., p. 1B.
44. Bell, "Anita Bryant's Ire and Brimstone," op. cit., p. 13.
45. Markowitz, "Gay Rights Foes Do Song, Talk Lunch Debate," op. cit., p. 2B.
46. St. Paul Citizens Alert for Morality, "Gays 'Immoral,' " op. cit.
47. Vauter, "Mockery," op. cit., p. 4A.
48. "*Playboy* Interview: Anita Bryant," op. cit., p. 232.
49. Wayne Wangstad, " 'Army' Recruited to Battle Gay Law," St. Paul *Pioneer Press*, April 20, 1978, p. 1.
50. Miguel Perez, "10,000 Rally for Repeal of Metro's Anti-Gay Law," Miami *Herald*, May 23, 1977, p. 18.
51. "Gay Rights Showdown in Miami," *Time*, June 13, 1977.
52. "God's Crusader," *Newsweek*, June 6, 1977, p. 21.
53. Wangstad, " 'Army' Recruited to Battle Gay Law," op. cit., p. 1.
54. "Battle Over Gay Rights," op. cit., p. 22.
55. Bell, "Anita Bryant's Ire and Brimstone," op. cit., p. 13.
56. Will, "How Far Out of the Closet?" op. cit., p. 92.
57. Novak, "Miami and the Homosexuals," op. cit., p. 9A.
58. "Battle Over Gay Rights," op. cit., p. 26.
59. "God's Crusader," op. cit., p. 21.
60. "Battle Over Gay Rights," op. cit., p. 22.
61. "*Playboy* interview: Anita Bryant," op. cit., p. 79.
62. Ibid., p. 89.
63. "Battle Over Gay Rights," op. cit., p. 17.
64. "Anti-Gay Rights Voters Hold Slight Edge: Many Undecided," St. Paul *Dispatch*, April 21, 1978, p. 1.
65. "Gay Rights Showdown in Miami," op. cit.
66. Ken Kelley, "Cruising with Anita," *Playboy*, May 1978, p. 232.
67. "*Playboy* Interview: Anita Bryant," op. cit., p. 88.
68. "Battle Over Gay Rights," op. cit., p. 22.
69. W. McPheron, "How Gays Took Over San Francisco," St. Paul *Dispatch*, April 17, 1978, p. 4A.
70. Political ad in St. Paul *Pioneer Press*, April 24, 1978, p. 13.
71. W.F. McPheron, "The Gay Rights Proposal: Yes," Minneapolis *Tribune*, April 22, 1978, Opinion, p. 4.
72. Ingersoll and Stone, "Pro and Con Gay Rights Rallies Attract Many," op. cit., p. 4A.
73. Kate McCarthy, "Anita Bryant Sick: Husband Urges Repeal of Gay Rights," Minneapolis *Star*, April 20, 1978, p. 4A.
74. Ingersoll and Stone, "Pro and Con Gay Rights Rallies Attract Many," op. cit., p. 4A.
75. Wangstad, " 'Army' Recruited to Battle Gay Law," op. cit., p. 1.
76. Westman, "Gay Rights Have Nothing to Do with Human Rights," op. cit., p. 7.
77. Brenda Ingersoll, "St. Paul Repeals Gay Rights Protection," Minneapolis *Star*, April 26, 1978, p. 1A.
78. Political ad in St. Paul *Pioneer Press*, April 24, 1978, p. 13.

79. J.W. Raymond, "The St. Paul Vote," Minneapolis *Tribune*, April 29, 1978, p. 10A.

80. "Heaven Is on Her Side, Says Anita Bryant, and There's No Sympathy Up There for Gays," *People*, June 6, 1977, p. 36.

81. Ingersoll, "St. Paul Repeals Gay Rights Protection," op. cit., p. 19A.

82. Davies, "750 Protest at Anita Bryant Performance," op. cit., p. 11A.

83. St. Paul Citizens Alert for Morality, "Gays 'Immoral,' " op. cit.

84. Markowitz, "Gay Rights Foes Do Song, Talk Lunch Debate," op. cit., p. 2B.

85. McCarthy, "Anita Bryant Sick," op. cit., p. 15.

86. McPheron, "The Gay Rights Proposal: Yes," op. cit., p. 4.

87. Edwin Black, "The Second Persona," op. cit., pp. 109–19.

Chapter 25 Religious Fundamentalism and the Democratic Process

1. Because of a threatened law suit by the similarly named Save the Children Federation, the name of Save Our Children has now been altered to Protect America's Children.

2. Press conference with Anita Bryant, Joplin, Missouri, September 24, 1977.

3. Susan Fraker and Gerald C. Lubenow, "Gay Power in San Francisco," *Newsweek*, June 6, 1977, p. 25.

4. All quoted statements by Bryant are from Anita Bryant, *The Anita Bryant Story: The Survival of Our Nation's Families and the Threat of Militant Homosexuality* (Old Tappan, NJ: Fleming H. Revell, 1977).

5. These issues are listed for approval or disapproval by the audience on a questionnaire entitled "I Want to Count Your Vote" distributed at the rallies conducted by the Revive America Crusades.

6. "NGTF Action Report," April–May 1977, p. 1.

7. Mark Allgood, "A Portrait of Anita Bryant," *Revival Fires*, Vol. 14 (November 1977), p. 8.

8. In *The Anita Bryant Story*, Bryant reported that after an initial move to cancel the show, Singer had reconsidered and "as it stands at this writing, an executive of Singer has visited with us, and the situation has yet to be resolved" [p. 71].

9. Parke G. Burgess, "The Rhetoric of Moral Conflict: Two Critical Dimensions," *Quarterly Journal of Speech*, Vol. 56 (1970), pp. 120–30.

10. W.B. Riley, "The Faith of the Fundamentalists," *Current History*, Vol. 26 (1927), p. 436.

11. Richard Hofstadter, *The Paranoid Style in American Politics* (New York: Alfred A. Knopf, 1966), p. 29.

12. Ibid.

13. Ibid., p. 31.

14. Ibid., pp. 31–32.

15. Revive America rally, Jefferson City, Missouri, November 21, 1977.

16. This is precisely the point made by Parke Burgess in the quotation cited above.

17. Edwin Black, "The Second Persona," *The Quarterly Journal of Speech*, Vol. 56 (1970), p. 112.

Contributors

BARRY BRUMMETT is an assistant professor in the Department of Communication, Purdue University, West Lafayette, Indiana. He received his B.A. from Macalester College in 1973, and his M.A. in 1975 and Ph.D. in 1978 from the University of Minnesota. His major scholarly interest is contemporary rhetorical theory, especially the "rhetoric as epistemic" school and the theories of Kenneth Burke. Professor Brummett was living in St. Paul during the Miami and the St. Paul referenda. He notes that this essay grew out of "a combination between personal outrage and an interest in Burkean theory."

JAMES W. CARLSEN is an associate professor of communications and theatre at the University of Corpus Christi, where he serves as director of the Theatre and Interpretation Program in the Center for the Arts. Professor Carlsen received his Ph.D. from the University of California at Los Angeles in 1971, his M.A. degree from Southern Illinois University in 1966, and his A.B. from San Diego State College in 1965. His most recent publication is *Literature on Stage: Readers Theatre Anthology*, published by Samuel French in 1980.

JAMES W. CHESEBRO received his Ph.D. from the University of Minnesota in 1972. He is currently an associate professor in the Department of Communication Arts and Sciences at Queens College of the City University of New York. He has been active in gay liberation since 1969. In 1970 and 1971 he functioned as the coordinator of FREE: Gay Liberation in Minnesota. In 1973 he published the first essay in the discipline of speech communication to deal with gay liberation as a communication system. In 1978 he cochaired, with Sally Miller Gearhart, the interest group that formulated and established the Caucus on Gay Male and Lesbian Concerns of the Speech Communication Association. The next year, in 1979, he served as the first contactperson of the caucus. His published books include *Public Policy Decision-Making* and *Orientations to Public Communication*. Professor Chesebro was also elected and will serve as vice president of the Eastern Communication Association in 1982, and as president in 1983. He is currently completing books entitled *Dramatism and Dramaturgy: Communication as Life and Metaphor* and *The Symbolic Construction of Social Reality: A Theory of Symbolic Determinism.* Professor Chesebro served as editor of this book.

JOHN F. CRAGAN is a professor in the Department of Communication at Illinois State University. His areas of concentration include political communication, small-group communication, and applied communication research. Professor Cragan's recent publications include *Applied Communication Research: A Dramatistic Approach*, published by Waveland Press in 1981; *Introduction to Speech Communication*, published by Waveland Press in 1981; *Communication and Small Group Discussion: A Case Study Approach*, published by West Publications in 1980; and *Public Policy Decision-Making*, published by Harper & Row in 1973. Professor Cragan received his B.S. from Northern Illinois University in 1965, his M.A. from the University of Missouri, Kansas City in 1967, and his Ph.D. from the University of Minnesota in 1972.

JAMES DARSEY is currently a Ph.D. candidate at the University of Wisconsin,

Madison, and plans to complete his dissertation by fall 1981. His primary research interests are rhetorical and communication theory, public address, and some statistical analysis. As the exchange in chapters 4 and 5 in this book indicates, James Darsey and Joseph J. Hayes interacted frequently as academic colleagues. Mr. Darsey provided Hayes' necrology for this volume.

CONNIE L. DAY received her B.A. in speech-communication from Marshall University in 1978 and her M.A. from Miami University in 1979. She is active in forensics and has received honors for outstanding forensic activities in both regional and national competition. She is currently a lecturer and debate coach at Illinois State University. Day's M.A. thesis was the basis for her essay (chapter 7) in this book.

JOSEPH A. DEVITO is professor of communication arts and sciences at Queens College, City University of New York. He received his B.A. from Hunter College, his M.A. from Temple University, and his Ph.D. from the University of Illinois. He is the author of numerous articles and books. His most recent works include *Communicology: An Introduction to the Study of Communication*, published by Harper & Row in 1978; *The Interpersonal Communication Book*, 2d edition, published by Harper & Row in 1980; and *Elements of Public Speaking*, published by Harper & Row in 1981.

LARRY G. EHRLICH received his A.B, and M.A. from the University of Kansas, Lawrence. He received his Ph.D. in 1968 from the School of Speech, Northwestern University in Evanston, Illinois. He has taught at Rockhurst College in Kansas City, Missouri, and at the University of Northern Colorado in Greeley. He is currently an assistant professor in the Department of Communication Studies at the University of Missouri at Kansas City. His undergraduate and a substantial portion of his graduate education was in traditional rhetorical studies. However, the graduate program at Northwestern introduced him to the interdisciplinary nature of communication studies, an area of interest he has pursued since 1968.

RONALD D. FISCHLI is currently completing work on his doctoral dissertation at the University of Missouri, Columbia, where he has pursued studies in the theatre arts, with a secondary emphasis in speech communication.

ELLEN M. GARFINKLE received her Ph.D. in clinical psychology from the California School of Professional Psychology in Berkeley in 1978. Dr. Garfinkle is a past member of the steering committee of the association of concern to the gay community. She is currently in private practice in Berkeley, working as a psychotherapist and psychological consultant.

SALLY MILLER GEARHART is a lesbianfeminist activist and writer who has been in the forefront of the gay and women's movements since 1969. Opening the dialogue between the church and gay people, she cochaired the Bay Area's Council on Religion and the Homosexual and coauthored *Loving Women/Loving Men: Gay Liberation and the Church*, published by Glide Publications. With the late Harvey Milk, she codirected the United Fund to defeat the Briggs Initiative and publicly debated Briggs several times prior to the defeat of his initiative. Gearhart has been acclaimed for her appearance in *Word Is Out*, a full-length documentary film on gay people that has played widely both in the United States and abroad. Her book, *A Feminist Tarot: A Guide to Intrapersonal Communication*, published by Persephone Press, has been translated into Braille, and negotiations are underway for Dutch and Italian translations. Her more recent book, *The Wanderground: Stories of the*

Hill Women, published by Persephone Press, has been declared the "new underground classic." Professor Gearhart received her A.B. degree from Sweet Briar College in drama-English in 1952, her M.A. from Bowling Green State University in speech and philosophy in 1953, and her Ph.D. from the University of Illinois in theatre and public address in 1956. Prior to her coming out as a lesbian, she taught for fifteen years in Texas and in Illinois colleges. She is now associate professor of speech and communication studies at San Francisco State University.

JOHN D. GLENN received his B.A. in 1978 and his M.A. degree in 1981, both from Temple University, Philadelphia. He is a Ph.D. candidate and a teaching assistant in the Department of Speech at Temple University. He plans to focus his dissertation on the inception of gay liberation as a rhetorical movement. His analysis of daytime television series will appear in *Inter-Media* to be published by Oxford University Press in 1982.

JOSEPH J. HAYES, a necrology by James Darsey: I never met Joseph Hayes in person, but I feel privileged to have shared some thoughts with him both in print and in private correspondence. On the basis of these exchanges, I believe I can say of Hayes that he was a man who was not afraid. As a member of the English faculty at the University of California at Fullerton, he was not afraid to help gays and lesbians organize within the Modern Language Association; he was not afraid to be among the first to publish papers in the area of gay language use; nor was he afraid to entertain critical scrutiny of his work in the truest spirit of scholarship; and, finally, if his last letters, written in late 1979, are any indication, Hayes was not afraid of the cancer that he knew would kill him. Joseph Hayes was not afraid so that those who followed would not have to be.

FRED E. JANDT received his Ph.D. from Bowling Green State University in 1970. He was formerly professor of speech communication and director of professional development and research at State University of New York College at Brockport and is currently executive director of The Human Productivity Institute, Inc., a nonprofit educational corporation, and a parttime lecturer in the department of speech and communication studies, San Francisco State College. He was one of the founders of and the 1980 contactperson for the Speech Communication Association Caucus on Gay Male and Lesbian Concerns.

RODNEY G. KARR received his Ph.D. in clinical psychology from the University of Washington in 1975. He is currently an associate staff member of the Human Sexuality Program in the Department of Psychiatry at the University of California in San Francisco. He is also associated with Operation Concern of the Pacific Medical Center in San Francisco, as well as being involved in private practice.

KENNETH L. KLENK received his B.A. in 1976 and his M.A. in 1981, both from Temple University, Philadelphia. His current focus of interest in gay studies is the "emerging gay masculinity." He has also developed a method for predicting television series ratings and is seeking employment in this area.

PATRICIA MCCULLOUGH received her Ph.D. from Ohio State University and is currently a communication consultant in private practice.

STEPHEN F. MORIN is a licensed psychologist in private practice in San Francisco, consultant in medical psychology to the Department of Health, Education and Welfare, and medical expert witness in forensic psychology for the San Francisco

Superior Court. A Ph.D. in 1971 from Ohio State University, he was previously an associate professor of psychology at California State College, San Bernardino. Morin is cofounder and past chairperson of the Association of Gay Psychologists, past chairperson of the Task Force on the Status of Lesbian and Gay Male Psychologists of the American Psychological Association, and current chairperson of the Psychological Association's Committee on Gay Concerns. He is coeditor of *Psychology and the Gay Community*.

BEN W. MORSE is currently an associate professor and coordinator of speech-communication at the University of Miami in Coral Gables, Florida. He has presented over twenty national and regional convention papers and has authored several journal articles. His published books include *Business and Professional Communication, Advanced Interpersonal Communication: A Relational Perspective*, and *Interpersonal Communications*. Professor Morse received his B.A. from William Jewell College in 1971, his M.A. from Central Missouri State University in 1972, and his Ph.D. from the University of Nebraska in 1975.

JEFFREY NELSON is an assistant professor of speech communication at Kent State University, Trumbull Campus. He received his Ph.D. in communication from the University of Michigan and has done a number of studies in the mass media area.

VICKI NOGLE is a doctoral student in speech communication at the University of Nebraska-Lincoln. Her area of focus is sociopolitical communication, especially the study of social movements. She is intrigued with how language functions both in maintaining and changing social order(s). Nogle will be the 1982 contactperson for the Caucus on Gay Male and Lesbian Concerns of the Speech Communication Association.

DOROTHY S. PAINTER completed her Ph.D. in communication at the Ohio State University in 1978 with a doctoral dissertation entitled "A Communicative Study of Human in a Lesbian Speech Community: Becoming a Member." Since the completion of her Ph.D., Professor Painter has continued ethnomethodological research concerning lesbian communication. She received her M.A. in journalism in 1975 and her B.S. in English education in 1973, both from Ohio State University. She is currently employed as an academic counselor in the College of the Arts and Sciences at Ohio State and teaches technical writing at Columbus Technical Institute.

JAN CARL PARK is currently completing his Ph.D. dissertation on the rhetoric of Anita Bryant, at Indiana University. He was the editor of *Alternative Communications*, the publication of the Caucus on Gay Male and Lesbian Concerns of the Speech Communication Association for two years. Park is currently employed by a private corporation in New York.

DAVID J. ROBINSON is currently associate professor of speech-communication at Youngstown State University in Ohio. He received his B.A. from George Redderdine College in 1957, his M.A. from the University of New Mexico in 1960, and his Ph.D. from the University of Southern California in 1972. His current research focuses on the rhetoric of minority social movements, although he finds his attention also devoted to collective bargaining issues in higher education.

PAUL SIEGEL is a doctoral student in communication studies at Northwestern University. His research interests include loneliness and social imperception, freedom of speech, and the psychology of prejudice, and he was one of six nationwide winners of the Gay Academic Union's 1979 scholarships. Siegel's previous publications include *Help for the Lonely Child*, published by E.P. Dutton in 1978, and "Homophobia: Types, Origins, Remedies," in *Christianity and Crisis*, in November 1979. Siegel is the 1981 contactperson for the Caucus on Gay Male and Lesbian Concerns of the Speech Communication Association.

STEVEN A. SIMMS received his B.S. from Illinois State University in 1979. He is currently doing research and production work at WMLA Radio, in Bloomington, Illinois. His research interests are concentrated in the areas of socialization and audience motivation through the mass media. After gaining some applied experience in the field, Simms intends to continue his formal education.